HEAR, O ISLANDS

THEOLOGY & CATECHESIS IN THE NEW MILLENNIUM

EDITED BY JOHN REDFORD

VERITAS

Published 2002 by
Veritas Publications
7/8 Lower Abbey Street
Dublin 1
Email publications@veritas.ie
Website www.veritas.ie

ISBN 1 85390 611 5

A catalogue record for this book is available from the British Library.

Cover design by Bill Bolger
Book design by Colette Dower
Printed in the Republic of Ireland by Betaprint Ltd, Dublin

Veritas books are printed on paper made from the wood pulp of managed forests. For every tree felled, at least one tree is planted, thereby renewing natural resources.

This symposium is dedicated to the
Rt Rev. Maurice Couve de Murville,
Archbishop of Birmingham 1982-2001,
the first President of the Maryvale Institute,
and to the Rt Rev. Mgr D. McHugh,
Director of the Maryvale Institute 1980-2000,
for their vision and energy in laying the foundations of Maryvale.

CONTENTS

CONTRIBUTORS

Fr John Redford, STL LSS DD, is Reader in Biblical Hermeneutics at the Maryvale Institute, and Director of the Maryale BA (Divinity) course from its beginning in 1990. He has served on national and international ecumenical and catechetical committees, and has published popular books on adult catechetics and apologetics.

Cardinal Avery Dulles, SJ, Laurence McGinley Professor of Religion and Society, Fordham University. He has published some 25 books and some 700 book reviews and articles. He has received more than 20 Honorary Doctorates and awards include one from the Cardinal Newman Society, Washington.

Dudley Plunkett, Ph.D. is Senior Academic Tutor at the Maryvale Institute where he has helped to design the Master's programme in Personal, Moral and Spiritual Development. His published works include books on education and teacher training, on the Virgin Mary and his latest is entitled *Heaven Wants to be Heard.*

Fr Richard Conrad, OP, Ph.D, STL, is currently Prior at Holy Cross, Leicester, teaches at Blackfriars, Oxford, and at Maryvale Institute where he is Director of the Master's Programme in Catholic Theology. He has Ph.D. in Chemistry. He has written many course books and one published book, *The Catholic Faith: a Dominican's Vision.*

Fr Robert Ignatius Letellier, MLitt, Ph.D., LSS, STD, writer and lecturer. He is currently supervising and teaching in a number of Maryvale degree programmes. His numerous books, articles, and reviews include a *Biblical Interpretation* monograph *Day in Mamre, Night in Sodom: Abraham and Lot in Genesis 18-19,* and the diaries of the opera composer Meyerbeer.

Andrew Beards, Ph.D. Lectures in philosophy and fundamental moral theology at Ushaw College, Durham. He also teaches in the Maryvale BA (Divinity) programme. He is author of O*bjectivity and Historical Understanding* and has written articles for academic journals including *Gregorianum* and *The Thomist.*

Fr George Woodall, MA, STD, Parish Priest and Moral Theologian, lecturing and writing coursebooks for the BA (Divinity) and MA Theology courses at Maryvale. He is also a Judge on the Matrimonial Tribunal of Nottingham diocese and has recently completed a Licenciate in Canon Law f rom Strasbourg University. He has published articles in various journals including *Medicina e Morale*, Rome.

Professor V. Alan McClelland is currently Dean of Graduate Research at Maryvale, Emeritus Professor of Educational Studies, University of Hull, and Fellow of the Royal Historical Society. His research interests are in history, religious education, theology and educational management. He has edited and contributed to a number of books, the latest being, *From Without the Flaminian Gate.*

Fr Anthony Meredith, SJ, Ph.D., lecturer at Heythrop College, London and on the parish staff at Farm Street Church. A patristic scholar, formerly he taught the history of early Christian doctrine at Campion Hall, Oxford. His books include *Theology of Tradition* and *The Cappadocians.*

Fr Aidan Nichols, OP, Ph.D., is currently Prior of Blackfriars, Cambridge, where he is an affiliated lecturer in the Divinity Faculty. Formerly he lectured at the Pontifical University of St Thomas, Rome. He has written some twenty-eight books on different aspects of historical and dogmatic theology.

Fr Thomas Norris, DD, is currently Lecturer in Dogmatic Theology at St Patrick's College, Maynooth, and lectures at the Maryvale Summer School in BA (Divinity). He is a member of the papal International Theological Commission. He has specialised in Newman studies, and written extensively on the theology of development of doctrine.

Dr Fr Gerald O'Collins, SJ, is the professor of Fundamental Theology at the Pontifical Gregorian University in Rome. An Australian, he has written prolifically in areas of fundamental theology, Christology, and specifically, the resurrection of Jesus Christ, e.g. *The Easter Jesus* and *Jesus Risen.*

Mary Shivanandan, MA, STD, is professor of theology at the John Paul II Institute for Studies on Marriage and Family and Associate Dean, 1999-2001. Dr Shivanandan has lectured in the United States and internationally, including at the Maryvale Institute. Her book, *Crossing the Threshold of Love*, is an important study of the teaching of Pope John Paul II on marriage and sexuality.

Dr Edward Hulmes is a member of the Academic Board at the Maryvale Institute and sometime Spalding Professorial Fellow in Comparative Theology, University of Durham, William Noble Lecturer at Harvard and a former Director of the Farmington Institute, Oxford. He has published papers, articles and reviews on the study of Islam, inter-faith encounter and Catholic education.

Petroc Willey, BD, Ph.D., is Deputy Director at Maryvale Institute, Director of Adult Education, Archdiocese of Birmingham, and editor of *The Sower*. Formerly he lectured in Christian Ethics at Plater College, Oxford. He has written several course-texts at Master's degree level and six volumes for *Adult Studies in the Catechism*. He has published articles in several journals.

Fr Edward Yarnold, SJ, MA, DD (Oxon.), (1926-2002), was a priest at Campion Hall and a University Research Lecturer in Theology, Oxford University, and a regular lecturer at Maryvale Summer Schools. He was a member of the Anglican-Roman Catholic International Commission for more than twenty years. His death in August 2002 was a great loss for the theological and ecumenical world.

Fr Philip Jones CSsR, STD, combines parish work with teaching. He is responsible for the Rite of Christian Initiation of Adults, Archdiocese of Birmingham. He lectures on Christology and The Trinity in the BA Applied Theology and is responsible for the Diploma in Catechetics at Maryvale Institute. He has written on both theology and catechesis in books and articles.

Rt Rev. Daniel Joseph Mullins, BA, Bishop of Menevia. His special interest as bishop has been in Catholic Education serving as Chairman both of the Committee for People in Higher Education and the Catechetics Committee, Bishops Conference of England and Wales. He is a fluent Welsh speaker, writer and broadcaster.

Caroline Farey, BA, M.Phil, MA, is currently Academic Assistant to the Director of Maryvale Institute and lectures in philosophy at Oscott

Seminary, Birmingham. Formerly she was Director for the Maryvale Courses leading to a Diploma for Parish Catechists. She has published a variety of philosophical, theological and catechetical articles in a range of journals.

Sr Kathleen M. Murphy, RSM, B.Ed, MA Ph.D., has wide experience as a classteacher, and headteacher. She has been Director both of Inservice and Continuing Professional Development, Archdiocese of Birmingham, and Initial Teacher Training at Maryvale Institute. She has lectured in England, Northern Ireland and Lithuania and has contributed articles to numerous journals.

Fr Paul Watson, STL, is Director of the Maryvale Institute and lectures regularly on several of its courses and elsewhere. Formerly he was both Parish Priest and Chaplain to a number of schools, a University and two hospitals He is on the Editorial Board of *Bible Alive* and is a regular contributor to *The Sower.*

Rt Rev. Mario Joseph Conti, Ph.L, STL, DD, KCHS, FRSE, Archbishop of Glasgow. Since he wrote the article in this book, he has been made Archbishop of Glasgow from being Bishop of Aberdeen. He has been a member of several Episcopal and Pontifical Commissions and holds secular appointments from the Scottish Executive.

COMMENDATION

It is with great pleasure that I commend this Maryvale symposium on the subject of 'Theology and Catechesis'.

The Higher Education distance learning courses at the Maryvale Institute have always linked theology with catechesis. This stems from the fact that the Institute began its life in 1980 as the Birmingham Archdiocesan Catechetical Centre. Theology at Maryvale has never been solely academic, but has been driven by the needs of priests, teachers, deacons, catechists, and indeed all members of the body of Christ, to communicate the faith more effectively.

At the commencement of the new millennium, we are living in a country where Catholic education, indeed religious education itself, is under threat. Secularism and relativism play an influential part in the public forum and the educational establishment. In this situation, there is a clear need for sound Catholic doctrine, based upon the life of prayer, which Maryvale has provided particularly for part-time distance learning. This has attracted hundreds to find Christ as the living water in the study of theology, which in Anselm's dictum is 'faith seeking understanding'. Newman's wish to have an 'educated laity' is more and more being fulfilled at Old Oscott Hill.

Fr Redford, the editor of this symposium, is to be congratulated on gathering together so many distinguished contributors on key areas of both theology and catechesis. All the contributors have had some involvement with teaching at Maryvale.

My hope is that this symposium will be not only a source of theological and catechetical reflection but also a stimulus for evangelisation in the Church today.

✠ *Vincent Nichols, Archbishop of Birmingham*
17 May 2002

FOREWORD

'Hear, O Islands' (*Audite, Insulae*) – such was the clarion call of the Servant of God in Isaiah. 'Listen to me, O coastlands, pay attention, you peoples from far away! The Lord called me before I was born, while I was in my mother's womb, he named me. He made my mouth like a sharp sword' (Isa 49:1, 2a).

This is the motto of the Maryvale Institute, and no scripture text expresses more graphically the vocation of the evangelist, the catechist, the religious educator, and the theologian. We share the mission of the Servant of God, Jesus, to 'bring Jacob back to him' (Isa 49:5), that is to gather God's people together in love and in worship. We also share the power of the Servant in our task, even if sometimes we do not feel at all that our mouth is a 'sharp sword', but rather a blunt instrument, especially in modern secular Britain. After all, the Servant himself died a shameful death on the cross, even deserted by his own followers.

But we do know that the word we speak is not our own word, but the Word of God. Again we are told in Isaiah (55:11) that this divine word 'shall not return to me empty, but it shall accomplish that which I purpose, and succeed in the thing for which I sent it'. Our obligation is to be faithful in telling out the message, in season and out of season, and to tell that word undiluted, and of course, with all our skill.

Pope John Paul II has issued the same clarion call as the prophet of old for the new millennium. He has called for a 'new evangelisation'. The short history of the Maryvale Institute is itself an example of how successful that evangelisation can be if, as the Pope invites us, we launch into the deep. Thousands of adults have deepened their faith through the various courses at Maryvale since its foundation twenty years ago.

The Hebrew word in Isaiah 49:1 is sometimes translated 'islands', sometimes 'coastlands'. It can mean either, the scholars tell us. Maryvale's main catchment area has been the islands of England, Scotland, Ireland, and Wales. But we have gone much further afield, to more distant islands and coastlands, not only for students abroad to join our distance learning courses, but to assist those responsible for catechesis and religious education themselves to spread that good news.

This symposium reflects that wide outreach of Maryvale, and our success in drawing on some of the best theological and catechetical minds nationally and internationally. This symposium also reflects the main agenda of Maryvale, to communicate the Good News, while at the same time remembering that there can be no effective evangelisation, catechesis, and religious education without sound theological and philosophical reflection, and above all without loyalty to the Magisterium of the Church, the 'pillar and ground of the truth' (I Timothy 3:15).

In providing the Foreword for this symposium, I am conscious of those who have gone before me, above all the first Director of Maryvale, Mgr Daniel McHugh, who together with the retired Archbishop of Birmingham were the pioneers of the Institute, and encouraged this present work. I wish also to record my debt to the Editor of this symposium, Father John Redford, who has worked at Maryvale since 1988, and was the founding Director of the BA (Divinity) programme, the first distance learning theological degree approved by the Vatican Congregation for Higher Education.

Finally, I would like to give my special thanks to Mary Bull, a graduate of the Maryvale BA (Divinity), who has worked tirelessly as Assistant Editor, to put together the very diverse offerings of our contributors into a readable shape. I trust that the present volume will play its small part in that New Evangelisation which is so dear to the heart of our present Pope, and which finds its literary expression in so many of the documents issued with his authority, forming the foundation texts of this symposium, especially the *General Directory for Catechesis.*

Fr Paul Watson STL, Director, Maryvale Institute

INTRODUCTION

FR JOHN REDFORD

The last thirty years of the twentieth century were characterised by a unique and steady flow of documents, from official sources in the Catholic Church, on the subjects of evangelisation and catechesis. The General Directory for Catechesis begins by mapping the progress of these documents up to 1997:

(a) 1971. First came the *General Catechetical Directory* (GCD)[1] published by Pope Paul VI. This attempted to provide the principles both of content and of praxis for catechesis. (*General Directory for Catechesis* GDC 1, p. 11).[2]

(b) 1972. *The Rite of Christian Initiation of Adults RCIA*[3] was issued. This was a modern revival of the catechumenate, and emphasised the great need for catechesis of adults, not only in the doctrines of the faith, but as part of an ecclesial and spiritual process (GDC 3, p. 12).

(c) 1975. Then came *Proclaiming the Good News* (*Evangelii Nuntiandi*)[4] of Pope Paul VI; 'This document enunciates, amongst other things, a particularly important principle, namely, that of catechesis as a work of evangelisation in the context of the mission of the Church' (GDC 4, pp. 12-13).

(d) 1977. The General Synod of Bishops on Catechesis met. In 1978 Pope John Paul produced *Handing on Catechesis* (*Catechesi Tradendae*)[5] as a parallel to the earlier encyclical *Evangelii Nuntiandi.* (GDC 5, p. 13).

(e) 1985. The Extraordinary Synod of Bishops proposed to the Pope a Universal Catechism (GDC 6, p. 14).

(f) 1992. The *Catechism of the Catholic Church* (CCC) was published as an Apostolic Constitution, a very high level of authority (GDC 6, p. 14). This was to be a sure norm of the faith. This opened up the need for the revision of the GCD. The content was provided for in the CCC. Also, there was a need for a directory leading to practical use of the CCC in catechesis, a post-CCC GCD.

Finally, then, in 1997, came *The General Directory for Catechesis* issued with the Pope's authority by the Congregation of the Clergy, the Vatican body that has worldwide responsibility for catechesis. The GDC was published in Rome at a special international Conference where the new Latin edition of the *Catechism of the Catholic Church*,[6] which was to be the normative text of that Catechism, was also presented. Heading that conference was Cardinal Joseph Ratzinger, the Prefect of the Doctrine of the Faith, together with the respective Prefects of the Congregation for the Liturgy and of the Clergy. Apart from the presence of the Holy Father himself (there was an audience later in the week) one could hardly imagine an international conference with more top brass. This emphasised the importance given to these official catechetical documents by church authority.

The one thing that is clear about any kind of catechesis is that it is a form of personal communication, usually not from the hierarchy, except on very special occasions, but more often from the local catechist, teacher, or priest. The last document a child receiving First Holy Communion will read is a document on catechesis issued from the Pope or the Vatican. The GDC is perfectly aware of this, and indeed wishes to prepare for its ideas and its inspiration to be communicated, where it matters, at local level. The GDC outlined its aims as follows:

- 'The contextualisation of catechesis in evangelisation as envisaged by *Evangelii Nuntiandi*',

- 'The appropriation of the content of the faith as presented in the *Catechism of the Catholic Church*'. (p. 15). The GDC therefore has a mediating role between the CCC and the production of local catechisms and programmes.

- The primary aim is 'that of offering reflections and principles, rather than immediate applications or practical directives. This method has been adopted principally for the reason that defects and errors in catechetical material can be avoided only if the nature and end of catechesis, as well as the truths and values which must be transmitted, are correctly understood from the outset'. (GDC, p. 16f)

Essentially the GDC is intended to be a stimulant for effective action. Furthermore, it is for those who are already active as evangelists and catechists, to make such activity better directed and more powerfully driven.

As a result, the staff and students of the Maryvale Institute, Birmingham particularly welcomed the GDC. Maryvale House, with a long Catholic history, was called *Sancta Maria in Valle* hence 'Mary's Valley', by John Henry Newman during his stay there from 1846 to 1848, after he was received into full communion with the Catholic Church and ordained a priest. By 1980, Maryvale House had been for decades an orphanage run by the Sisters of Mercy, but it became available when government policy changed to house the children in smaller dwellings. Archbishop George Patrick Dwyer then appointed Father Daniel McHugh as its Director to use Maryvale as a catechetical centre for the Archdiocese of Birmingham. Its first Director saw the vital need, during the eighties, for adult catechesis in the Catholic Church, and catechesis for teachers and catechists themselves. Successful courses for adults began immediately, in tandem with the schools education service, traditionally part of diocesan religious education. This was just after the first encyclicals from Pope Paul VI and Pope John Paul II on catechesis and evangelisation, and just before the publication of the *Catechism of the Catholic Church* and the *General Directory for Catechesis.* The Maryvale Institute's birth and early growth was particularly well timed for this catechetical interest from the highest ecclesiastical authority down.
But the new Archbishop of Birmingham, Maurice Couve de Murville, together with now Mgr. McHugh, saw the need for a more radical approach in the education of adults, in addition to the usual courses provided by catechetical institutes.

A model was seen in the highly successful Open University, which had pioneered distance-learning methodology. In England, university education had been the privilege of the wealthy or of the exceptionally clever ten percent who could pass university entrance and university scholarships. The Open University, encouraged and funded by Harold Wilson's Labour Government, attracted hundreds of thousands of mature students who could study at home while continuing in their daily employment, attending summer schools during their holiday period. The Open University has achieved full academic recognition in its own right, being high in the league of British universities in academic standards. Maryvale Institute had the inestimable benefit of the consulting services of Dr Francis Clark, who had just retired as Director of Religious Studies of the Open University.

The first distance-learning degree course was prepared at Maryvale in 1988, and was given initial validation by Maynooth Pontifical University, Ireland, receiving its first intake of some sixty students in October 1990. I have the great privilege of being the first Course Director of the BA (Divinity) honours degree in Catholic theology, and have continued in this post up to the time of the publication of this symposium. Originally, it was hoped that the prime take-up would be from Catholic teachers. As it has turned out, the number of practising teachers has been small, as they mainly opt for the Masters degree in Religious Education. But this does not mean that the BA (Divinity) has lost its catechetical orientation. On the contrary, nearly all students ranging from 18 to 80 years of age, from all professions and from the unemployed, from all countries in these islands plus further afield, such as Scandinavia and the USA, come with the specific aim of growing in their faith in order to be more effective in its communication.

A distance-learning course is for part-time students. It is also staffed in the main by part-time specialists, who write the course books, give the lectures in summer schools, and mark student essays month by month and the annual exam papers at home. Maryvale has been particularly fortunate in the continued enthusiastic support of first-class academics whether in academic post or in pastoral situations. Thus a high proportion, indeed the majority, of those contributing to this symposium are part-time or full-time members of the Maryvale faculty. Others such as Cardinal Avery Dulles, Father Aidan Nichols OP and Father Gerald O'Collins SJ, have given public lectures here. Finally, we are particularly gratified by the contributions of Bishop Daniel Mullins, on whose Committee for Catechetics I happily served, and of Archbishop Mario Conti, of Glasgow with whose former diocese of Aberdeen, the largest geographically in these islands, Maryvale has developed especially close and fruitful co-operation.

The structure of the symposium follows broadly that of the GDC itself without following its content sufficiently closely to be in any sense a commentary on it. Rather, this book is a kind of meeting point between the GDC and the continuing interests and concerns of the Maryvale Institute. On the one hand, the GDC can inform and stimulate Maryvale's continuing catechetical vocation, even push it in new directions. Particularly the GDC emphasis on evangelisation is one, which already is being considered much more acutely by Maryvale, making the contribution by Dudley Plunkett, our Chief Tutor, of particular interest. On the other hand, Maryvale can identify and further develop themes of the GDC.

The GDC, while commending many aspects of catechetical life, post-Vatican II, noted 'difficulties about the acceptance of the (Second Vatican) Council'.[7] Despite so comprehensive and profound an ecclesiology, the sense of belonging to the Church has weakened and 'a certain disaffection towards the Church is frequently noted'.[8]

By the close of the sixties, three particular phenomena noted by the GDC seemed to illustrate this growing confusion. The first was the issuing by Pope Paul VI of the encyclical *Humanae Vitae* in the summer of 1968,[9] which surprised many English Catholics by maintaining the traditional position that contraception, the deliberate prevention of conception by artificial means, was always objectively sinful. The second was the publication of Hans Küng's *Infallibility? An Enquiry*,[10] which questioned whether the infallibility of the church as such was a coherent theological concept. The third was less obvious a problem, but perhaps more subtle: the question of the whole foundation of Christian faith in the historical reality of the Gospel. Students at a well-known London catechetical college were asked, 'If the bones of Jesus of Nazareth were discovered in Jerusalem, would your faith remain the same?' The answer was clearly expected 'It would remain the same, even if the bones of Jesus were discovered there'.

Reaction to *Humanae Vitae* and Küng's *Infallibility* together challenged papal authority. The English Catholic community was known as totally loyal to the Vatican. The history of the Reformation English martyrs who had been executed for loyalty to the Pope as the successor of Peter and to the Real Presence and the Sacrificial nature of the Eucharist was strong in English Catholic minds. It was even said that Rome made the laws, and the English Catholics kept them. This loyalty to the papacy was not simply on the part of the English hierarchy, but was deep in the Catholic community itself, among the congregations. Now, with some priests and theologians openly dissenting from the Church's teaching on contraception, and an increasing number of lay Catholics unable and unwilling to play what was disparagingly called 'Vatican roulette', the use of the infertile period for intercourse within marriage (the only form of the limitation of conception open to Catholic married couples apart from abstention), the Pope himself tended to be identified as the one who prevented married couples from doing what everyone else was doing, rather than as the guardian of the true religion handed down from Peter the Apostle against the errors of Protestantism and secularism.

This was bound to have an effect on catechetics and religious education. With the growing uncertainties, teachers and catechists tended to play down the authority of the Church, and to be ambiguous about the historical authenticity of miracles and the bodily resurrection. There was a tendency for religious lessons in schools to become discussion groups without a clear pedagogical aim. These often became pupil-driven rather than teacher-driven because teachers, themselves, with the best will in the world were unsure of what to teach.

From the beginning of its commitment to catechetics, all those involved at Maryvale have been convinced that bad Catholic theology can never lead to good evangelisation and catechesis. (cf. The Deposit of Faith and the Catechism of the Catholic Church, GDC 125, p. 135; the transmission of 'genuine, satisfying, healthy and adequate food' GDC 169, p. 182). Technique can never cover up inadequate content. This point is made clearly in our leading article by Cardinal Avery Dulles, and is followed up by important contributions by Fr Aidan Nichols OP, who emphasises the need for the teaching authority for theology to be Catholic, and Fr Thomas Norris of Maynooth, our validating University, who demonstrates how the key issue in the conversion of John Henry Newman was the need for an infallible authority in order to ensure fruitful development in the life of the Church (GDC 29, p. 31).

Andrew Beards of Ushaw shares the Pope's concern, in *Fides et Ratio,* to unite faith and reason in a sound Catholic philosophy; while Fr Richard Conrad OP, a qualified scientist and theologian, Director of our Master Theology course, discusses the relationship between science and faith, seeing no conflict but rather mutual cross-fertilisation. (GDC 20, p. 23). Thirdly, in a most original contribution, Fr Robert Letellier examines carefully the influence of modern art, music and literature on contemporary culture in dialogue with catechesis and theology.

Scripture can often be a source of conflict in the catechetical world. In my own contribution, on Scripture and Catechesis, I attempt to sail through the Scylla of fundamentalism on one side and the Charybdis of dry historicism on the other (GDC, 127, p. 136). Fr Gerald O'Collins SJ puts this methodology well into practice, as he is uniquely capable of doing, in demonstrating that the bodily Resurrection is testified to by a reliable Gospel tradition of the discovery of the empty tomb and of the bodily appearances of the risen Jesus to his amazed followers. All this develops the GDC emphasis upon revelation in 'deeds and words' (GDC 38, p. 42) and the focus on the death and Resurrection of Christ as central to catechesis (GDC 65, p. 67).

We have already noted the divisive and controversial nature of the intra-Catholic discussion of morality, and in consequence its importance from the viewpoint of catechesis. Fr George Woodall expounds, most effectively, sound Catholic moral teaching in the face of relativism and secularism (GDC 30, p. 31) need for 'a more solid moral formation'), while Dr Mary Shivanandan defends the present Pope's stand against the modern 'culture of death' (GDC 23, p. 25, 'the ontological truth of the human person', GDC 85, p. 86).

Finally in this connection, Professor Edward Hulmes, a specialist on Islam, writes on the need to preserve both the ultimate truth of Christian revelation while seeing the need also to learn about other religions and ways of thought. (On 'religious research', cf. GDC 22, p. 25. On 'inculturation', cf. GDC, 109, p. 117, on 'catechesis in the context of other religions', cf. GDC 200, p. 207).

The symposium then moves to consider more directly the process of Christian initiation itself. The GDC links essentially catechesis, Christian initiation, and the sacraments of initiation (GDC 65, p. 67). Fr Edward Yarnold SJ attempts to integrate these themes in his *Theology of Christian Initiation*, relating his theological reflections in the light of the new revised *Rites of the Christian Initiation of Adults* (RCIA); while Fr Philip Jones CSsR reflects particularly on the relationship between the liturgical and catechetical process implicit in RCIA, while seeing the need for integral catechesis. (cf. GDC 167, p. 182).

The second half of the GDC enters more into the actual exercise of catechesis. Bishop Daniel Mullins writes concerning the responsibility of bishops as 'heralds of the faith' (GDC 222, p. 229), Petroc Willey discusses the essential role of parents in catechesis (GDC, 226, p. 233), while Caroline Farey, formerly Director of Parish Catechesis, notes the special role of the catechist (re: Lay Catechists, cf. GDC 230, p. 235).

Sister Kathleen Murphy writes concerning 'Prayer Formation in Primary and Secondary Schools', (GDC 259, p. 261) while Fr Paul Watson, the new Director of Maryvale, writes on the vital subject, 'Catechesis on Prayer'. (GDC 85, p. 87). Finally, Archbishop Conti writes of the need for catechesis to teach and practice devotional forms, which appeal to the popular imagination, and not simply to the cerebral (GDC 195, p. 204).

When the Bishops of the English Provinces of Westminster, Southwark and Birmingham made their *ad limina* visit to Rome in 1992, Pope John Paul II commended by name, 'for the religious education of adults'[11] two Catholic institutes of significance in their region. The first was the Catholic Missionary Society, North London. The second was the Maryvale Institute, North West Birmingham.

The papal mention of these two institutes, and in particular these two institutes together in the same paragraph of his homily, was indeed gratifying. The Catholic Missionary Society was founded in the post-Second World War period to lead missions in parishes. The missionaries were to be diocesan priests of England and Wales, with some distinction as preachers, on loan for a period of five years from their diocesan bishops. They were to be led by one of their number as Superior. Famous early names included John Carmel Heenan (later Cardinal Archbishop of Westminster) and George Patrick Dwyer (later Archbishop of Birmingham).

The Maryvale Institute has arisen out of a different need, the need for more systematic and scholastic educational methods rather than homiletic and pastoral method as with the Catholic Missionary Society.[12] But both have the same ultimate aim, to make disciples of all nations (Mt 28:19), or at least of this particular nation. May they both be ever more effective.

Notes

1. Society for the Congregation of the Clergy Ad norman decreti, 11 April 1971, 'General Catechetical Directory' in A. Flannery (ed.), *Vatican Council II: More Postconciliar Documents* (Leominster, Fowler Wright, 1982), pp. 529-605.
2. Congregation for the Clergy, *General Directory for Catechesis* (Citta del Vaticano, Libreria Editrice Vaticana, 1997).
3. 'Rite of Christian Initiation of Adults', in *The Rites of the Catholic Church*, The Roman Ritual revised by Decree of the Second Vatican Ecumenical Council and published by authority of Pope Paul VI (New York, Pueblo Publishing Company, 1976), vol. 1, p. 1-516.
4. Pope Paul VI, *Evangelii Nuntiandi*, 8 December 1975, in A. Flannery (ed.), *Vatican Council II: More Postconciliar Documents* (Leominster, Fowler Wright, 1982), pp. 711-763.
5. Pope John Paul II, *Catechesi Tradendi*, 16 October 1979, in A. Flannery (ed.), *Vatican Council II: More Postconciliar Documents* (Leominster, Fowler Wright, 1982), pp. 762-814
6. *Catechismus Catholicae Ecclesiae* (Citta del Vaticano Liberia Editrice Vaticana, 1997); English edn: *Catechism of the Catholic Church*, rev. edn (London, Chapman, 1999).
7. Synod 1985, I, 3. GDC 28, p. 29.
8. ibid.
9. Encyclical Letter on the Regulation of Births, in A. Flannery (ed.), *Vatican Council II: More Postconciliar Documents* (Leominster, Fowler Wright, 1982), pp. 397-416
10. Hans Küng, *Infallibility? An Enquiry* (London, Collins, 1971).
11. *Briefing*, 22:7 (9 April 1992), p. 5.
12. Since the preparation of this article, the Catholic Missionary Society has been given a new role. No longer will the CMS be a centre for priests working on parish missions, but rather the thrust will be to become a national agency for evangelisation. 'The new agency will be an "association" of lay people and clergy, set up by the Bishops' Conference. It is expected to begin work in the summer of 2003' *The Tablet*, 26 January 2002, p. 30. We wish the new agency every success, and look forward to its vital contribution.

THE CATECHETICAL PROCESS IN THE LIGHT OF THE GENERAL DIRECTORY FOR CATECHESIS

CARDINAL AVERY DULLES SJ

Within the memory of some of us, there was a time when even moderately educated Catholics could be counted on to know their catechism. They could give instant answers to questions such as: why did God make you? How many natures has Jesus Christ? What are the four marks of the Church, the seven sacraments, the seven deadly sins, and the six precepts of the Church? While the pedagogy of Counter Reformation catechesis may have been deficient, it did achieve some successes in communicating religious information. In these latter days many Catholic college graduates seem helpless to explain even the basic elements of the creed.

Recent Tendencies in Catechetics

Since the late 1950s a succession of revolutions has occurred in Catholic catechetics. The first move was from the scholastic to the kerygmatic, the second from the kerygmatic to the biblical, and the third from the biblical to the experiential. In this third phase attention was focused on the experience of the students, which was often seen as the source and criterion of 'relevance'. This technique was supposed to arouse the students' interest, but if this goal was in any sense achieved, it was all too often at the cost of failing to present the great deeds of God in salvation history or the meaning and coherence of the Church's credal heritage.

Summarising some tendencies in the catechetics of the 1970s, Cardinal Ratzinger notes that in a period when anthropocentrism was the order of the day, catechesis tended to revolve endlessly about problems of method, to the detriment of content. 'This,' he says, 'produced weariness precisely among the best catechists and, naturally, a corresponding weariness among the recipients of catechesis, our children. The insight that the power of the message had once again to shine forth began to gain ground.'[1]

A major remedial step was taken in 1985 with the commissioning of the *Catechism of the Catholic Church*, which was successfully completed in an initial French edition of 1992, notwithstanding severe opposition from many theologians and religious educators.[2] In 1997, the *Catechism* was followed by the *General Directory for Catechesis*, translated into English in 1998.[3] At present plans are under way for the production of new catechetical directories for various countries.

The *General Directory* does not simply go back to pre-Vatican II models. While avoiding the excesses to which Cardinal Ratzinger refers, it takes advantage of the reforms of catechesis in the past forty years. In this paper I shall present some reflections on the catechetical process in light of the *General Directory*. Instead of simply summarising what the Directory has to say, I shall draw upon my own considered views regarding the special character of religious knowledge and its transmission.[4]

A crucial point is the relationship between catechesis and evangelisation. Catechesis, as currently defined, is neither identical with nor separable from evangelisation. Unlike primary evangelisation, it is not intended to convert people who are indifferent or hostile to the faith. It is addressed to believers, and more specifically to believers who have undergone an initial conversion and seek to be more fully instructed in Christian life, worship, and doctrine. The *General Directory* clarifies this point: primary proclamation is addressed to non-believers and those living in religious indifference. Its functions are to proclaim the Gospel and to call to conversion. Catechesis, 'distinct from the primary proclamation of the Gospel,' promotes and matures initial conversion, educates the convert in the faith and incorporates him into the Christian community.'[5] In practice, the two stages overlap to some extent. The catechist may be required, at some points, to deal with objections or attitudes that come from the perspective of unbelief. Restricting the scope of this article to catechesis strictly so called, I shall assume, in what follows, that the person being catechised is a believer sincerely interested in the content of Christianity.

According to the *Directory* it is necessary 'to distinguish clearly between religious instruction and catechesis' (GDC 73, p. 73). In some state schools and non-confessional schools courses in religion must be given to Catholics and non-Catholics together, so that the teaching will have to be ecunemical or interreligious in charcter. But it is desirable, at least in Catholic Schools, for religion to be taught from a confessional point of view so that Catholic students will gain a better understanding of the teaching of Christ and the Church. Although religious instruction in such schools contributes to catechetical formation, it needs to be completed by other forms of the ministry of the word, including liturgical services (cf. GDC 74, p. 75)

Catechesis: Its Nature and Goal

The ultimate aim of catechesis, according to the *General Directory*, is communion with God as he discloses himself in his Son, Jesus Christ (cf. GDC 80, p. 81). This communion involves a certain 'feeling' for the subject matter. The recommended approach may be technically designated as knowledge by way of familiarity or 'connaturality.' Such knowledge resembles, on its own higher level, the interpersonal knowledge that friends or family members have of one another. Our knowledge of human persons is normally achieved through association and loving communion, and is mediated by signs or meaningful gestures. As the *Directory* recognises, 'Linguistic theory ... shows that symbolic thought affords an approach to the mystery of the human person which would otherwise remain inaccessible' (GDC 20, p.23). The same is true, *a fortiori*, when knowledge of divine persons is in question.

The whole process of catechesis begins, progresses, and ends in faith. Christian faith, as we know, has two aspects: subjective adherence on the part of the believer (*fides qua creditur*) and a divinely given content that is believed (*fides quae creditur*). The two aspects of faith are mutually interdependent (GDC 92, p. 99), since the quality of the adherence is shaped by the content, and since the content is not fully accessible without the willing adherence of the subject who believes.

The Triadic Structure of Religious Knowledge

This bipolar account of faith is still too general for our purposes. Because God lies beyond all possibilities of description or definition, the content of faith cannot be fully objectified. It must be mediated in the first instance by symbols – that is to say, by signs that evoke a richness of meaning not accessible to discursive thought. More precisely, Christian faith goes out to the meaning of the signs given by God in salvation history. These signs are a form of divine discourse, since God speaks to his people by means of them. Faith, then, is a form of knowledge through signs (GDC 108, p. 116). By presenting the gestures and words of God as remembered by the Church and interpreted in the light of faith, catechesis can lead to a discovery of the mystery contained latently in these signs (*ibid.*). The Church therefore employs 'a pedagogy of signs where words and deeds, teaching and experience are interlinked' (GDC 143, p. 159). The special character of this pedagogy invites further examination.

The structure of religious knowledge, I conclude, is triadic. The inquiring believer constitutes the subjective pole, the signs constitute the objective pole, and the meaning or content of faith arises from the encounter of both. This triadic pattern may be illustrated by the action of reading a text. The subject is the reader, the polar object is the text itself, and the resultant meaning is achieved through the encounter of the subject and object. The meaning is intended by the author, but it does not exist formally in the text; rather, it is evoked in those who have the skills needed to read the signs making up the text.

In the case of Christian revelation, the primary signs are the persons and facts of salvation history, which cohere in a pattern and are centred on the Paschal event of the death and Resurrection of Jesus. These signs, taken in unison, disclose their meaning when interpreted with the help of grace, which bestows what theologians call the light or the eyes of faith.

Symbols are particularly important for the pedagogy of faith because they have special power to transform those who submit to them, permitting them to make sense of statements that might otherwise appear to be incredible, meaningless, or absurd. Symbols open us up to new horizons; they also elicit loyalty and commitment, as is obvious in the uses made of flags and insignia. Without inner transformation, communion with the transcendent, and loyal commitment, faith would wither away.

Religious instruction has not always given sufficient scope to the pedagogy of signs, as it has just been described. Three deviant tendencies may be noted.

The first aberration, rationalism, overlooks the pedagogy of signs. Some rationalists make the mistake of supposing that the content of faith can be clearly and exhaustively spelled out in doctrinal propositions, the truth of which can be demonstrated by syllogistic logic. A more moderate form of rationalism, which may be called supernaturalist, recognises the need of grace for the assent of faith, but still depicts Christianity in an almost Cartesian fashion, as a system of propositional truths. Catholic apologetics between the Counter Reformation and Vatican II sometimes veered in the direction of supernaturalist rationalism.

Positivists err by supposing that the content of faith is reducible to historical facts. They are constantly digging into the sources to find out what actually occurred at this or that moment in the past. But their reconstruction is often limited by their use of an historical method that tends to exclude the supernatural. In their preoccupation with factual details, they often neglect the meaning of the events and the role of the community of faith as a carrier of that meaning.

The third deviation, subjectivism, focuses on the inner feelings of the believer. It depicts faith as a mystical encounter with an ineffable Transcendence, which is often left unnamed. While their sense of mystery is laudable, subjectivists err by slighting the truth-content perceived by the rationalists and the facts of salvation history emphasised by the positivists. In this way they minimise what is specific to Christian revelation and Christian faith.

The triadic approach I am recommending incorporates what is valid in each of these three approaches, while overcoming their respective limitations. By giving due attention to the factual, doctrinal, and mystical components, this approach sets all the elements in balance and brings them into a higher synthesis.

The Ecclesial Character of Catechesis

For Christian faith to exist at all, the believer must have reliable access to the person of Jesus Christ, his saving action on our behalf, and his saving doctrine. Today, at a distance of some 2000 years, such access cannot be had except in a mediated way. The revelation of God is transmitted through a chain of witnesses, who are divinely assisted bearers of the faith. The primary believer, in the case of Christianity, is the Church, the community of faith to which the revelation of Christ was delivered. The Christian Scriptures were composed in the Church and were subsequently recognised by the Church as inspired and trustworthy guides to the data of salvation history and their right interpretation.

Holy Scripture is much more than a historical document or a compendium of doctrine. As a highly interpreted account of the words and deeds of God, it makes extensive use of stories, parables, symbols, metaphors, and paradoxes in order to mediate effectively the deep mystery that God wishes to disclose. As an inspired record stemming from the foundational era, Scripture pertains to the immutable deposit on which the Church continues to build. The Church, in the Catholic understanding, has authority from Christ himself and is gifted by the Holy Spirit with the charisms necessary to certify the contents of the biblical canon and apostolic tradition and to judge the acceptability of interpretations of the Word of God. Each individual believer participates to some degree in the faith of the Church. Without the authority of the Church to protect it, the revelation would be progressively overlaid with human opinions and would ultimately become inaccessible.

The whole process of catechesis, therefore, must be social and ecclesial (GDC 30, p. 31; GDC 78, p. 80). The catechist ought to be, in principle, a duly accredited representative of the Church. The student or catechumen is presumed to be seeking to appropriate the faith of the Church as such, not the particular opinions of a given catechist, interesting though these may be. The catechist should surely be well versed in the doctrine of the Church, but personal spiritual qualifications are also required. Growth in religious knowledge takes place through a kind of apprenticeship in which neophytes are guided by mature believers, who have gained the necessary skills for discerning the meaning of the signs and symbols in the deposit of faith. This apprenticeship replicates to some degree the process of discipleship whereby Jesus brought his closest followers to share his vision and his mission. Unless the catechist has some familiarity with Christ through prayer and worship, the process will go awry.

The nurturing of faith, like any major commitment, demands a congenial environment. Faith normally requires for its proper development a community of believers who support one another in their religious convictions and aspirations. The greater the gulf between authentic Christian attitudes and the prevailing ethos of the secular culture, the more crucial it becomes for believers to maintain close association with one another. Sociologically speaking, they may constitute a subculture, not totally unlike a ghetto. As a divinely constituted community of faith, the Church supports the faith of its members through all the means of grace at its disposal.

Christianity is indivisibly a body of doctrine, a system of worship, a code of conduct for the community of believers. Catechesis, in fostering integral Christian formation, attends to all these aspects. 'In virtue of its own internal dynamic, the faith demands to be known, celebrated, lived, and translated into prayer' (GDC 84, p. 84). The faith is 'lived out by the Christian community and proclaimed in mission' (*ibid.*). Catechesis therefore includes four dimensions: knowledge of the faith, formation in worship, life in community, and preparation for mission. These goals must be pursued concurrently. Unless all four are being cultivated, the others will be impaired.

The Doctrinal Component

Christianity, as the joint meaning of all the Christian symbols, can never be fully objectified in doctrines. The content of faith always remains to some extent tacit. We know more than we can tell. But doctrines must be taken seriously inasmuch as they express aspects of the revealed mystery and articulate truths intimately connected with revelation.

The dogmas of the Church proclaim, interpret, and defend the treasure of revealed truth. Some of them are intended to present the joint meaning of a whole constellation of symbols. For example, when we say, 'I believe in the Holy Spirit, the Lord and giver of life,' we briefly summarise a multitude of more particular insights imbedded in the community's memory of events narrated in Scripture, from the animation of Adam at his creation (Gen 2:7) to that of the Church at Pentecost (Acts 2:1-4). The baptismal creeds of the early Church recapitulated, in very condensed form, what the catechumens had been taught in the course of instruction preceding their reception into the Church. The creed consists of a number of articles, and the term 'article,' derived from the Latin word for 'joint,' implies that their meaning is a joint one. They cannot without violence be severed from one another.

Many doctrinal assertions were formulated to ward off heretical misreading of elements in the deposit of faith and thereby to protect the community's internal unity and its authentic continuity with the apostolic witness. The definitions of the essentials of Trinitarian and Christological faith by the early councils were formulated predominantly as condemnations of errors, as were many subsequent definitions. Some dogmas, however, have been proclaimed in order to celebrate the Church's achievement of full clarity concerning truths that were from the beginning implicit in the deposit of faith and had become evident through long centuries of worship, meditation, and theological discussion. This celebratory quality is evident in the modern Marian dogmas of the Immaculate Conception and the Assumption.

Not all dogmas or articles of faith are on the same level of importance. Vatican II, in its *Decree on Ecumenism,* taught 'in Catholic doctrine there exists an order or "hierarchy" of truths, since they vary in their connection with the foundation of the Christian faith' (UR 11). Thus it is proper in catechetics to call attention to certain 'fundamental articles' or 'more outstanding elements of the Christian message' (GDC 120, p. 129) that should be explicitly known by all adult believers. These truths, stated in the early creeds and commemorated in the Church's liturgy, are at the root of many more specific doctrines. It would, however, be a mistake to imagine that the believer's assent could be limited to these 'fundamental' truths. The entire system of Christian doctrine constitutes an organic whole, in which all the parts cohere and lend credibility and intelligibility to one another (GDC 114, p. 121). Uninstructed believers assent globally to the teaching of the Church, and through that global assent adhere tacitly to many dogmas of which they are not specifically aware. Religious instruction, which expounds the contents and implications of faith, contributes to a fuller appreciation and a more confident adherence. By reflecting on the Church's doctrinal heritage, believers can achieve an authentic wisdom that fulfils to a notable degree the native drive of the human spirit for truth and understanding.

Dialectic of Authority and Experience

In the transmission of revelation, the principal aim will be to grasp in faith what God has revealed. Revelation is handed down through the sacred channels of Scripture and tradition. To enable the Church to identify the inspired Scriptures and interpret them rightly in the light of tradition, Christ equipped it with an authoritative magisterium. Different pronouncements of the Magisterium carry different degrees of authority, ranging from defined dogmas to officially approved opinions. Catechesis must take account of the varying weight of magisterial pronouncements and recognise that the hierarchical teachers do not always invoke the full authority of their office. Only rarely do they call for definitive assent to their teaching. Strictly dogmatic pronouncements are binding in faith in the sense that anyone who deliberately refuses to accept them can no longer be considered as living in the Catholic communion.

Human experience is a very complex reality, unfolding on different levels. In some respects Christian faith is contrary to experience, since it embraces mysterious truths that Jesus and the biblical writers often conveyed by way of paradox. The mysteries of the Trinity, the Incarnation, the Cross and Resurrection, and the Eucharist are of such a nature that they challenge the axioms of common sense and overrule the impressions that arise from ordinary experience. We believe them in spite of evidence to the contrary.

Experience can, however, lead to faith and confirm it. People are drawn to faith by the 'nostalgia for God' that is implanted in the human heart. The radiance of God shining on the faith of Jesus Christ and reflected in the saints has an experiential impact. Believers have access to deeper experiences in faith that solidify their Christian commitment. By devoutly receiving the sacraments, by meditating on the truths of faith, and by consistently following the law of the Cross, they experience that Christ's yoke is easy and his burden light. The martyrs, for example, are able to rejoice in the midst of suffering that would be too great to be borne in the absence of faith.

Experience, therefore, should not be discounted, but because of its ambiguity it should be treated with caution. Persons lacking in powers of discernment are often misled by their feelings. Some use their experience as an excuse indulging their momentary desires and for rejecting all discipline. Others, driven by subjective impulses, wander off into strange cults or join fanatical sects. Catechesis is necessary because the feelings of Christians need to be educated by instruction in the faith.

In order for the catechetical process to work, it is important for the persons undergoing it to be actively engaged. They must sincerely aspire to gain the familiarity with God that is the goal of catechesis. As they struggle to find answers to the great problems of truth and meaning that have always concerned thoughtful men and women, they must be encouraged to formulate their real questions. Only in this way can the Christian message be seen to cast light upon the enigmas of the human condition, including the riddles of suffering and death.

Essential though authority is, it must be distinguished from authoritarianism. Efforts to impose the acceptance of answers that initially seem meaningless or absurd are self-destructive. Such tactics lead to one of three results. Sometimes they destroy interest in the subject matter and breed indifference. Sometimes they produce anger and resentment, even apostasy. And sometimes the student, shielded from seeing the plausibility of non-Christian interpretations, is led to become narrow-minded and fanatical. Mature believers recognise that faith, while it can claim to be supported by powerful reasons, cannot be logically demonstrated from self-evident truths. It is a free and grace-given submission to God's testimony, relayed by qualified witnesses.

While questions should be welcomed, they should be proposed with appropriate modesty. A defiant attitude toward authority can prevent the faith from taking root. Anyone seeking instruction from the Church must be animated by fundamental trust and be disposed to accept rather than reject her teaching. If we sit with folded arms, demanding cogent proofs for everything attested by the Bible and the Church, we shall never arrive at faith.

Worship and Communal Life

The initial approach to faith in the pre-baptismal catechesis of adults must be conducted with loving reverence toward the God who is being sought. The attitude of prayer directs our tacit powers of apprehension to the divine and focuses our attention on the authentic mystery that we are seeking to explore. As we relate ourselves to the hidden God, the signs that point to him are illuminated, so that we can interpret them better. The law of prayer, as the saying goes, establishes the law of belief, and conversely, the law of belief guides and inspires prayer.

Pre-baptismal catechesis reaches its climax in the handing on of the creed (*traditio symboli*), to which the candidate responds by a rendition of the creed (*redditio symboli*), which takes the form of a threefold confession of faith in the Father, the Son, and the Holy Spirit. This confession is accompanied by the triple immersion of baptism. Confession of faith and liturgical worship thus converge in a single ceremony.

In post-baptismal catechesis (which presumes that a responsible act of Christian faith has been made) the baptised receive mystagogical instruction in the sacraments of initiation – baptism, confirmation, and Eucharist. This instruction is designed to 'help the newly baptised to interiorise these sacraments and incorporate themselves into the community' (GDC 89, p. 93). In the liturgy the faithful are nourished at the two tables of word and sacrament. The word of God 'is celebrated in the sacred liturgy, where it is constantly proclaimed, heard, interiorised, and explained' (GDC 95, p. 103). Baptism, as an immersion in Christ's saving death and Resurrection, is a first incorporation into Christ's body. Confirmation, as the completion of baptism, marks the achievement of a certain maturity of faith and qualifies its recipient to give public witness as a believer. Participation in the Eucharist, the culminating sacrament of initiation, is a plenary insertion into the mystery of Christ's Paschal sacrifice and into the unity of his Mystical Body.

In the Catholic tradition liturgy has always been recognised as a school in which a living sense of the faith takes root. Those who have learned to pray in the worshiping community will possess an instinctive feeling for the true significance of the Christian symbols, enabling them to appreciate the language of doctrine, whereas others who approach the doctrines from a detached academic perspective may find them empty or inassimilable. Many Catholic dogmas simply express in abstract and definitional language what the Church came to understand through centuries of prayer and worship.

Together with doctrinal and liturgical formation, moral education is an indispensable ingredient of catechesis (GDC 85, p. 86). Christian moral formation is intimately linked with the faith and worship patterned on Jesus. In his preaching he never ceased to insist on purity of heart, justice toward the poor, and charity toward all. Throughout the New Testament, the conduct of Jesus is proposed as a basis for Christian morality. He is exemplary in his humility and obedience in accepting death on a cross, his patience in suffering, his forgiveness of enemies, and his compassion toward the sinners he was sent to redeem. In accepting Jesus as our teacher and model we begin to live in him according to the spirit of the beatitudes. Christian belief, worship, and Christian morality therefore interlock.

Participation in Mission

A final task of catechesis is to initiate new and younger Catholics into the mission of the Church. Authentic faith can never be sterile. The word within has a dynamism that irresistibly calls for expression, transforming believers into committed disciples. Recognising this intrinsic connection, the *Directory* calls upon catechists to motivate and 'equip the disciples of Jesus to be present as Christians in society through their professional, cultural, and social lives' (GDC 86, p. 89).

The Church is not a mere shelter where people take refuge from the world. It exists for the sake of the whole world as a catalyst and harbinger of the promised Kingdom of God. By spreading faith, justice, peace, and love the Church carries out its divine commission.

Pope Paul VI memorably said that the deepest vocation and the true identity of the Church consist in evangelisation – that is to say, in preaching, teaching, and transforming every human life and institution according to the gospel of Christ.[6] John Paul II speaks repeatedly of a new evangelisation – new in ardour, in methods, and in language.

Properly catechised Christians should see themselves as agents in this process. They can never be satisfied to be passive consumers of the benefits that the Church offers. They are called to participate in the total apostolate of the Church according to their own particular gifts and condition. In appropriate ways they must seek to bring Christ into the home, the work place, and the public square.

Catechesis, then, is a self-perpetuating process. Those who are formed by it take part in the formation of others. As mature disciples they can help to make disciples of those with whom they come into contact. In a variety of ways they evangelise; they catechise.

Notes

1. Joseph Ratzinger, 'On the Prehistory of the Catechism' in Joseph Cardinal Ratzinger and Christoph Schönborn, *Introduction to the Catechism of the Catholic Church* (San Francisco, Ignatius, 1994), pp. 11-15, at 14.
2. *Catechism of the Catholic Church* (Vatican City: Libreria Editrice Vaticana, 1994). The Latin *editio typica* appeared in 1997, with some corrections.
3. Congregation for the Clergy, *General Directory for Catechesis* (Washington DC, United States Catholic Conference, 1998).
4. My views on religious epistemology may be found in various books, notably *Models of Revelation* (new edn, Maryknoll, NY, Orbis, 1992). In this article I reproduce some ideas from my lecture, *The Communication of Faith and Its Content* (Washington DC, National Catholic Educational Association, 1985).
5. *General Directory for Catechesis*, §61, pp. 55-56. The quotation in this passage is from the Apostolic Exhortation *Catechesi tradendae*, §19. Numbers in parentheses in my text will refer to numbered paragraphs of the *General Directory*.
6. Paul VI, Apostolic Exhortation *Evangelii nuntiandi*, §14 and passim.

THE NEW EVANGELISATION OF PEOPLE AND CULTURES

DUDLEY PLUNKETT

Old preacher: Have you been born again?
New woman: No, I am exercising my right to choose.

At the beginning of what is regarded as 'the oldest extant Christian document'[1] St Paul commends the Thessalonians 'because when we first brought the Good News to you, it came to you not only as words, but as power, and as the Holy Spirit, and as utter conviction.' (1 Thess 1:5). The three expressions used here to characterise the impact of the gospel together convey a sense of the full Pentecostal force of the living Word in the young Church. There has been a rebirth in the Spirit that has swept away doubts and sin and imparted new life and faith. St Paul judges that his evangelising work has been effective, and he is thanking God for this. Nearly two thousand years later Pope John Paul too makes a judgement, which is recalled in the *General Directory for Catechesis* (GDC), when he refers to situations in which 'entire groups of the baptised have lost a living sense of the faith, or even no longer consider themselves members of the Church, and live a life far removed from Christ and his gospel.'[2] So serious is the general situation for the contemporary Church, the Pope has called for a 'new evangelisation', and he sees this as the unifying mission of the whole Church at the turn of the Millennium.[3]

In this article I want to examine the nature of the new evangelisation, its justification, its essential character, and its practical expression. To do this I must relate it to evangelisation as usually understood, and I need to outline some of the wider implications of a new evangelisation, and especially the notions of inculturation and evangelisation of culture.

The Three Aspects of Evangelisation

At its very simplest, evangelisation is telling the good news of God's salvation through Jesus Christ. According to the GDC, in considering God's providential plan, there are basically three aspects: the revelation of God, the offer of salvation, and the definitive call.[4] It will be helpful to review them briefly. The revelation is not only from God, but is precisely 'of' God. As Pope Paul VI wrote in *Evangelii Nuntiandi* (EN), 'There is no true evangelisation if the name, the teaching, the life, the promises, the kingdom and the mystery of Jesus of Nazareth, the Son of God are not proclaimed.'[5] Therefore all evangelisation refers in the first place to Jesus, and to a personal encounter with him.[6] The 1998 Synod of Bishops for the Americas *Instrumentum Laboris* took this very theme as its title: 'The encounter with the living Jesus'. Second, there is the message concerning what Jesus has done. He has redeemed us and given us the promise of eternal life if we accept him as Lord. This message is contained in Revelation, that is in scripture and the tradition of the Church which predates scripture and has constantly interacted with it.[7] And, thirdly, as Pope John Paul loves to express it, we are all called to make a 'pilgrimage to the house of the Father',[8] whether we are non-believers, lapsed believers or consider ourselves to be faithful Christians. For all, the spiritual path is one of ongoing and continuous conversion and purification.

The telling of the Good News is in itself a significant activity of the Christian community which needs pondering, if only because it is so often less successful in practice than intended. Whether we refer to preaching activities, or to the liturgy and life of the Church, or to other more or less planned and deliberate efforts to make contact with unbelievers, the means chosen frequently encounter obstacles of a psychological or cultural nature. These are matters that need to be explored in any treatment of the theme of the new evangelisation.

New Evangelisation

In his constant appeals for a more evangelising Church, Pope John Paul is simply echoing the words of Christ, who commissioned his disciples to go out into the whole world to proclaim the good news. In recent World Mission Day Messages, the Pope has reiterated this call. In 1997 he said: 'I hope with all my heart that on the threshold of the new Millennium the whole Church will experience a new impulse of missionary commitment.'[9] A year later he spoke, in a complementary fashion, of the modern secular world's great need of God 'modern man, when he rejects God, is less man, full of fear and tension, closed in on himself, dissatisfied and selfish' ... and of how 'in the more developed societies there is a preoccupying sterility, which is both spiritual and demographic.' The work of providence can thus be seen to be preparing people for the 'evangelical message', not just in these negative ways but through the immense spread of gospel values shown in the awareness of human rights, the longing for peace, for the disappearance of the barriers between classes, races, cultures, and 'the rejection of political international authoritarianism and the consolidation of democracy and an aspiration to a more balanced justice.'[10] But for the Pope, the resolution of this tension between God's command and man's need can only be a spiritual one: 'there must be unceasing prayer to nourish the desire to carry Christ to all men and women.'[11]

But the new evangelisation is not simply a further effort of evangelisation nor a response to the failure of past efforts. The GDC also distinguishes the traditional mission *ad gentes* from the 'new' evangelisation.[12] The phrase 'new evangelisation' has been used by Pope John Paul to call the Church to what he understands to be a new mission: 'I sense that the moment has come to commit all of the Church's energies to a new evangelisation and to the *mission ad gentes*'.[13] Since 1983 he has sought to guide the Church towards this effort to recapture the hearts and minds of people who were either once Christian believers themselves or who at least belong to nations and cultures with a strong Christian core to their values and customs.[14] The need for a new evangelisation has been especially recognised among the least catechised in once mainly Catholic countries, particularly in Latin America where it is being said that four hundred members are lost to the Church every hour, mainly to Pentecostals and the sects.[15] *Ecclesia in America*, the papal exhortation following the Synod of Bishops for the Americas emphasised that this phase of evangelisation was to be 'new in its ardour, methods and expression'.[16] We can recognise that such a threefold renewal means the overcoming of a certain inertia, a diversification of approaches and a language and style more appropriate to current needs, but what this is to mean in practice still needs to be more fully worked out.

Within the overall mission of the Church, to 'proclaim the Good News to all creation' (Mk 16:15), the new evangelisation is thus particularly addressed to those whose families or cultures once belonged to the household of the faith. While this mission is an obligation for all

Christians, it is not something that they can undertake in their own strength. The 'principal agent' of this work is the Holy Spirit: 'it is he who in the depths of consciences causes the word of salvation to be accepted and understood.'[17] The entire work of the spreading and developing of faith in God and his redemptive plan for humanity is energised and guided by the Holy Spirit, from the mission *ad gentes* and new evangelisation to the catechesis of Christians both within and outside the Church, the eventual illumination of the Jews and the reconciliation of all humanity. When the Pope speaks of God preparing a springtime of the Church [18] he does not set dates on it, but with frequent allusions he clearly intuits a great work of divine Providence for the Third Millennium.

The New Advent

The new evangelisation is a significant part of this springtime, but it will not happen until Christians accept their part in preparing it. God patiently awaits people's response, just as he awaited the response of Mary at the Annunciation. Indeed, Mary's 'Yes' to the coming of the Redeemer is a model for Christians' 'Yes' to his Second Coming. Since the beginning of his pontificate Pope John Paul has spoken of the new Advent, identifying it especially with the arrival of the Third Millennium. Over recent years he has developed the idea that there is a time being prepared by God, through the Holy Spirit, when God's kingdom will more visibly be restored. The new Advent is closely linked to the Marian presence in the contemporary Church. Not only is there a Marian dimension contrasting with the Petrine order in the Church, but also there is a specific God-willed role for Mary in the economy of salvation.[19]

In calling the Blessed Virgin the 'Star of Evangelisation' guiding the whole Church to the Lord,[20] the Pope associates her with the new Advent of faith. This is a theme to which he frequently refers, as when more recently in the exhortation following the Synod of Bishops for the Americas in 1999 he evoked the role of the Blessed Virgin in a most graphic manner:

> In America, the *mestiza* face of the Virgin of Guadalupe was from the start a symbol of the inculturation of the gospel, of which she has been the lodestar and the guide. Through her powerful intercession, the gospel will penetrate the hearts of the men and women of America and permeate their cultures, transforming them from within.[21]

While the Virgin of Guadalupe is particularly associated with the evangelisation of America,[22] the evangelising role of Mary has been marked in Europe by her numerous visitations over the past century and a half. At the rue du Bac, La Salette, Lourdes, Fatima, Medjugorje, and other places, the message has always been to prepare, through prayer, penance and living the values of the gospel, for a new triumph of God's love in the world.

The tone of urgency pervading these heavenly messages is evident too in Pope John Paul's repeated calls to mission. The work of rebuilding Jerusalem, the scriptural metaphor for the Kingdom, is in a state of inertia. However much there are signs, and even prophecies, that a new Pentecost is imminent, it is not yet even the time of the Church's resurrection, though we can detect new life coursing through it, an unlimited hope encompassing a vast missionary horizon. If, in some mysterious manner, the Church must undergo the pattern of life of its Lord, then it might be said that we are in the time of Gethsemane, with the disciples failing to recognise the real situation while they persist in sleeping. God, in Jesus, seeks to awaken them, but they are unable to respond.

The world is still crucifying its Saviour. Persecuting him in every way, it fails to see that the crown he wears is a true one, one that masks his majesty because of the lack of faith of his nearest brethren. They desert him, wishing to save their own skins, and perhaps because they are disillusioned or seduced by the world's scepticism and complicity in refusing the evidence offered to them. What, after all, is truth? Only a remnant stay by his side, finding their strength in his strength, their courage sustained by his, their humble living out of the crucifixion mirroring his own. The seed of evangelisation is sown by those who so closely follow Christ that they are already doing his work. His life is itself a proclamation, and by living it they too become proclaimers of Christ in the Kerygma that prepares the way for the conversion of others.[23] And so, throughout human history, we have the image of Mary, the 'purest realisation of faith',[24] standing by the Cross as the greatest human witness there ever can be of Christ's true majesty.

Evangelisation can never be a matter of mere words, and the principles given in the GDC certainly need more concrete formulation and practical development. It is as well to know that we are only at the very beginning of the new evangelisation. This means that contemporary preachers of the gospel can only follow Christ and those disciples who accompanied him. Prayer, humility, faithfulness, courage, perseverance, are the stones that mark the way. However, it would not be responsible if today's evangelisers did not use every insight and talent they have to discern this way, how to live it, how to proclaim it, how to build the Kingdom of Christ on earth in our time as well as in eternity.

The Evangelisation of Culture

In many of his speeches and in many Church documents influenced by Pope John Paul the new evangelisation is seen as evangelising not just of people but also of cultures. Already, in *Evangelii Nuntiandi*, Pope Paul had said:

> The split between the Gospel and culture is without a doubt the drama of our time, just as it was of other times. Therefore every effort must be made to ensure a full evangelisation of culture, or more correctly of cultures. They have to be regenerated by an encounter with the gospel. But this encounter will not take place if the Gospel is not proclaimed.[25]

The concept of the evangelisation of culture has since frequently featured in Magisterial documents, without perhaps gaining enough recognition and understanding. Pope John Paul says:

> ... the gospel penetrates the very life of cultures, becomes incarnate in them, overcoming those cultural elements that are incompatible with the faith and Christian living and raising their values to the mystery of salvation which comes from Christ.[26]

It is an awesome idea. If a whole culture has developed around atheism, materialism, consumerism, moral relativism and a rejection of the value of life and the civilisation of love, an individual has little chance of detaching himself from it without a massive re-education; the new woman must indeed be born again if she is to relinquish her claimed 'right to choose'. Therefore, a necessary dimension of evangelisation must be the confronting of secular culture as a whole way of life and understanding.

Like every person, all cultures need to be evangelised. Persons and cultures are dynamic. They are growing, searching and experimenting. And therefore they need direction and guidance. To evangelise a culture is to enable it to become open to the Holy Spirit and to the truth of the gospel. As far as the culture to be evangelised is concerned, two kinds of problem are posed. The aspects of that culture which conflict with the gospel, for example, the presence of anti-life values, or racial and ethnic prejudices, permissive sexual norms, traditional non-Christian marital customs or anti-Christian beliefs, all present barriers to the evangelist and obstacles to faith for members of that culture. On the other hand, there is the issue of who the evangelists themselves are, with their prejudices, customs, concepts, moral weaknesses, and the cultural image that they carry, or that the Church to which they belong carries in the eyes of others. Moreover, there is no doubt that a properly conceived ecumenism forms part of an evangelisation of cultures.

It follows that we cannot be evangelists until we are ourselves evangelised. We cannot be an evangelising Church before we are an evangelised Church. In fact the first culture to be evangelised is that of the Church itself. Pope Paul called for this is in *Evangelii Nuntiandi,*[27] and the scope of this self-evangelisation has been broadened by Pope John Paul in Tertio Millennio Adveniente (TMA), where in a striking way he proposes an examination of conscience by the Church and a repentance for past failures, errors and injustices.[28] The wide support in the Church for this identification of failures and the search for a renewed commitment to conversion is evidenced in the *Instrumentum Laboris* for the 1999 European Synod of Bishops.[29] However, it is not simply a question of cancelling out wrongdoings, but of developing a new approach that is supple enough to relate to its contemporary social environment rather than presenting rigidities to those people and cultures that encounter it. The importance of this work, which needs much broader support in the Church, is to remove obstacles that prevent people today from taking the Catholic faith seriously, from coming near to examine it, from thinking it might have something to offer them. A further need is for Christians to have a strong faith, to show to their contemporaries that it is still possible to hold this faith and to derive benefit from it in contemporary society. The concomitant hope and love of the gospel are desperately needed by today's world: hope to give meaning, love to give purpose to living. However, these can only be offered where they are already practised, and it is this task of the evangelisation of the Church that is an indispensable prerequisite for the evangelisation of non-Christian, or anti-Christian cultures.

An evangelisation strategy must therefore involve, first, self-evangelisation to purify the gospel message being carried, then inculturation to ensure that this message is expressed in a way that can best be received by those to whom it is being directed and, finally, the targeting of the message for the particular culture, to cope, for example, with its human problems, its rationalism, its moral relativism, its false spiritualism or its nihilistic values. While this huge task is partly, and primarily, a spiritual one, it is also a theological and broadly intellectual undertaking, since it demands psycho-sociological understanding and creative pedagogy across the whole culture, including its institutions, laws, social customs and values. This unique combination of spiritual, theological and social-scientific insights empowers the evangeliser to offer a genuinely prophetic message.

The inculturation of the gospel, the making accessible of Christ's message within different cultures, and therefore by different means and in different terms, has existed from the beginning. It is the story of Pentecost. However, the degree of cultural diversification as well as the contrary movements towards cultural homogenisation or cultural globalisation that have characterised the modern world are such that it is scarcely any longer possible to evangelise by traditional means. The discernment of the evangelical wealth and poverty of cultures has been a constant theme of Pope John Paul's encyclicals and other teachings, as is recognised by the GDC:

> In this work of inculturation … the Christian community must discern, on the one hand, which riches to take up as compatible with the faith; on the other, it must seek to purify and transform those criteria, modes of thought and lifestyles which are contrary to the kingdom of God.[30]

The evangelisation of culture takes us to another stage of the process. It refers to an undertaking that has often been named but never adequately defined, let alone planned. The GDC hardly refers to the evangelising of culture, beyond some basic ideas in paragraph 51 and a later reference to 'evangelised culture',[31] and thus reflects little of its complexity. For example, it mentions the media,[32] but not the Internet, which has become a massive element of contemporary communication. The more recent document of the Pontifical Council for Culture *Towards a Pastoral Approach to Culture* (TPAC) goes further in indicating what is needed as 'revitalising a de-christianised world whose only Christian references are of a cultural nature'.[33] This prompts another paraphrasing of Nicodemus: how can a culture be born again? The 'Towards' of TPAC's title reveals the uncertainties of the first steps being taken in this field. The gospel is a sign of contradiction for a world without God, but the way in which that gospel needs to be proclaimed must include all the media of social communication both as instrument and object of the new evangelisation, from the mass media, family life and schooling to liturgy, academia, the arts, science, politics and social welfare, or every facet of modern life taken not only singly but together as a system of values and mores, that is, a culture. Many of these sectors of human life are addressed schematically in the 'Concrete Proposals' section of TPAC, leaving room for major further analysis and development. Where, for example, in this perspective, do we situate new age beliefs, religious sects, political correctness, feminism, and other aspects of post-modern culture that are scarcely even adumbrated in the GDC?

Unfortunately, there is often a gap between the broad principles that are contained in strategic documents about evangelisation from Vatican dicasteries, on the one hand, and the specific actions of particular evangelising groups and communities, which can be highly pragmatic. This gap needs to be filled by thoughtful analysis and planning that can inspire a pastoral formation and outline a whole methodology for the new evangelisation, including the evangelisation of culture. Perhaps the example of liberation theology in Latin America illustrates this need most graphically. A false diagnosis, which placed political needs before spiritual and human ones, ensured that the Church lost many people to Evangelical and Pentecostal groups who understood better the felt needs of the poor for basic living resources, care, spirituality and healing. The liberation theologians could not evangelise the culture of the people, however much they sought to do so through base communities and group meditation on the Word of God, because they were caught up in an agenda that did not itself come from the gospel of the beatitudes.

To conclude this introductory treatment of the topic of the evangelisation of culture some of its main features and key issues they raise for discussion can be identified.

1. It suggests modes of engagement with contemporary culture, such as speaking, writing, and broadcasting. These will rarely be the results of individual efforts, but rather of groups and institutions, such as parish communities, colleges, church bodies, associations and networks. There is a whole field of formation activities in basic evangelisation, apologetics, catechesis and in communication media needed to support initiatives that such organisations might develop.

2. It suggests the need for enough independence of view to be able to stand against secularism. When the Pope contrasts the culture of death

and the civilisation of love he aptly captures the prevailing antinomy that distinguishes true Christianity from secular material untruth. As Towards a Pastoral Approach to Culture (TPAC) puts it,

> The challenge for a pastoral approach to culture is to help people discover transcendence ... A coherent culture is based on the transcendence and superiority of spirit over matter ....[34]

3. Pope John Paul proposes a particular role for philosophy in coming to terms with contemporary culture in relation to the faith:

> Philosophy moreover is the mirror which reflects the culture of a people. A philosophy, which responds to the challenge of theology's demands and evolves in harmony with faith, is part of that 'evangelisation of culture' which Paul VI proposed as one of the fundamental goals of evangelisation. I have unstintingly recalled the pressing need for a new evangelisation; and I appeal now to philosophers to explore more comprehensively the dimensions of the true, the good and the beautiful to which the word of God gives access. This task becomes all the more urgent if we consider the challenges which the new millennium seems to entail, and which affect in a particular way regions and cultures which have a long-standing Christian tradition. This attention to philosophy too should be seen as a fundamental and original contribution in service of the new evangelisation.[35]

What this suggests in practice, apart from the vital formation role it offers Catholic institutions of learning, is the importance of well-ordered teaching, indeed of a new apologetics that can engage with the values, the thinking and the self-justifications of contemporary cultures.

4. It involves living out its tenets, enough to give witness or example. As both Pope Paul and John Paul have said, the world no longer wants words, it wants deeds and example.[36] It is always striking how people respond to the genuinely holy person, as has been exemplified on several occasions recently when such people have received acclaim from secular societies when they died. Their lives speak, just as Jesus' did, but that is not the end of the matter. These great efforts have to be followed up.

5. It will always involve proclaiming Jesus as the way, the truth and the life. We best follow up the work of Jesus by proclaiming him boldly. The kind of discussion of Christianity that occurs in contemporary media is usually so anodyne that it puts people to sleep more than it wakes them up. Even many Christians would rather speak of ideas, or of Christianity, or of human problems, than acknowledge their commitment to the person of Christ. But contemporary society must be more resolutely challenged by a full proclamation of the living Christ.

6. It will inevitably involve counter-cultural ways of dealing with contemporary issues, such as poverty, hunger, discrimination, and respect for human life. Where human and social problems are under discussion, the Christian response has to be other than the secular. This is because the Christian does not take the problem to himself, but rather entrusts it to God. This does not prevent hard work being undertaken, but always in reliance upon the Holy Spirit. Never has this sentiment been so apt as at the present time when rationalism and science are so confident in their autonomy, the state of mind often referred to by Pope John Paul as the 'culture of death' and which TPAC defines as 'a counterculture which reveals the sinister contradiction between the affirmation of a will to live and an obstinate rejection of God, the source of all life.'[37]

7. There is a reflexive aspect to the evangelising of culture in the sense that it should also refer to the way the Church recognises and purifies its own culture. It is, for example, evident that conflict in the Church and Christian disunity are in themselves major barriers to evangelisation. Theological pluralism can also be an obstacle for neophytes. The implication is that the Church must strive to apply to its own values and mores the same stringent principles that it would wish to invite others to assume, whether in the media, educational institutions, or the field of medical ethics.

8. One of the most challenging aspects of the new evangelisation, however, is its interactive aspect. We cannot sustain the view of evangelisation as a one-way process. It is an encounter with a person, initially the person of Christ, but then with each other person involved in the evangelising encounter, each being for the other, another Christ. This is not just a theological concept or metaphor. It surfaces in the

difficulties of communication arising from language and culture. Such problems can only truly be resolved by cooperation, exchange, and love, and these must be experienced reciprocally for there to be real fruit. Which evangeliser is not himself – or herself evangelised? In the new evangelisation, which intending evangeliser does not find repentance, humility, love, sympathy, and purification in the encounter? When Christ is proclaimed he is encountered:

> By putting Christ back as the keystone of existence and restoring the place of reason enlightened by faith, a pastoral approach to culture could strengthen Christian identity by a clear and enthusiastic invitation to holiness.[38]

While we cannot envisage evangelisation, or the 'new' evangelisation, as simply remedying a deficit, we do speak of the 'loss' of faith. But these words can mislead us. No one loses their faith like an umbrella on a bus. The loss is a process. And that process has to be reversed if faith is to be restored. Indeed, the process is often so profound, so immersed in the passing events of life, so inaccessible to the conscious mind, that its reversal is invariably more a matter of grace and healing than it is a response to some deliberate human intervention. Once again, the evangeliser is led to humility and trust in God. And when we think in terms of the general apostasy that afflicts most of the older Christian countries, it is nothing less than 'pentecostal' grace that can find and restore all the dysfunctional trails that have led people away from God.

The New Pentecost

There is a way in which all these seemingly disparate elements can be unified. Hope for a new Pentecost is both a gleam in the eye of the evangelist and an evident reality in our world. It is perhaps surprising that the GDC, in spite of the importance it gives to the activity of the Holy Spirit,[39] does not take up this theme, so beloved of Pope John Paul. There are many harbingers of this springtime for those who want to see them. The Pope constantly speaks of the new communities as a hope for the Church. He sees them as a work of the Spirit, and 'a new Pentecost',[40] both bringing their members to Christ and bringing Christ to others in the world through their efforts to witness to the gospel and to undertake works of direct evangelisation among youth, often in student circles, or amongst particular professions. The capillary action to which the Church is subject through these and other 'pentecostal' influences ensure the dissemination of their evangelising action. The renewal of scriptural prayer and community spirituality, of liturgy, of lifestyle, of sacred art, of Eucharistic and Marian devotion, of shrines and pilgrimages, do not mean a going back to the past in a conservative movement, but a representing to the world of holiness of life. It would be surprising indeed if such obviously Spirit-led developments did not excite interest and draw new adherents. This is the point at which the new evangelisation needs to be succeeded by catechesis that focuses upon the fuller scriptural and doctrinal message of the faith.

Notes

1. *New Jerome Biblical Commentary*, 773:11.
2. *Redemptoris Missio*, 33.
3. *Tertio Millennio Adveniente*, 21.
4. GDC, 37.
5. *Evangelii Nuntiandi*, 22.
6. GDC, 53.
7. GDC, 44.
8. TMA, 49.
9. *World Mission Day Message*, 1997.
10. *World Mission Day Message*, 1998.
11. *World Mission Day Message*, 1999.
12. GDC, 58.
13. RM, 3.
14. Martin and Williamson, 1995.
15. A statistic quoted at the New Evangelisation of America Conference, Dallas, Texas, December 1998.
16. *Ecclesia in America*, 66.
17. EN, 75.
18. RM, 1 and 86.
19. 'Lumen Gentium', 55.
20. TMA, 59.
21. *Ecclesia in America*, 70.
22. The New Evangelisation of America Conference, attended by many Latin American bishops and by representatives of organisations involved in the new evangelisation, was held under the patronage of Our Lady of Guadalupe.
23. GDC, 56.
24. GDC, 55, quoting the *Catechism of the Catholic Church*.
25. EN, 20.
26. *Pastores dabo vobis*, 55.
27. EN, 15.
28. TMA, 34-36.
29. Synod of Bishops, Second Special Assembly for Europe, *Instrumentum Laboris*, 1999.

30. GDC, 109.
31. GDC, 203.
32. GDC, 160.
33. TPAC, 1.
34. TPAC, 9.
35. *Fides et Ratio*, 103.
36. EN, 41; TMA, 37.
37. TPAC, 8.
38. TPAC, 23.
39. GDC, 43 and 55.
40. *Address to Seminar on Movements and New Communities* OR: 28, 14 July 1999.

Bibliography

Brown, R. E., Fitzmyer, J. A., Murphy, R.E. (eds), *The New Jerome Biblical Commentary*, London, Chapman, 1993.

Cleary, E. and Steward-Gambino, H. (eds), *Conflict and Competition: the Latin American Church in a Changing Environment*, Boulder, Lynne Rienner Publishers, 1992.

Congregation for the Clergy, *General Directory for Catechesis.* London: Catholic Truth Society, 1997.

John Paul II, *Redemptoris Missio*, London, Catholic Truth Society, 1991.
Tertio Millennio Adveniente. London: Catholic Truth Society, 1997
Pastores dabo vobis. AAS 84, 1992.
Address to Movements and New Communities. OR: 28, 14 July 1999.
Fides et Ratio. London: Catholic Truth Society, 1998.
Ecclesia in America, the papal exhortation following the Synod of Bishops for the Americas. Vatican website, 1999.
World Mission Day Messages, Vatican website, 1999.

'Lumen Gentium', in Flannery, A. (ed.), *Vatican Council II: The Conciliar and Post-Conciliar Documents*, New York: Costello, 1988.

Martin, D., *Tongues of Fire: The Explosion of Protestantism in Latin America*, Oxford, Blackwell, 1990.

Martin, R. and Williamson, P. (eds), *Pope John Paul II and the New Evangelisation.* San Francisco: Ignatius, 1995.

Paul VI, *Evangelii Nuntiandi*, London, Catholic Truth Society, 1975.

Pontifical Council for Culture, *Towards a Pastoral Approach to Culture.* OR:23, 9 June 1999.

Synod of Bishops for the Americas, *Instrumentum Laboris*, Vatican website, 1998.

Synod of Bishops, Second Special Assembly for Europe, *Instrumentum Laboris*, Vatican website, 1999.

SCIENCE AND FAITH

FR RICHARD CONRAD OP

Introduction

The subtitle of a recent newspaper article began: 'Scientists proved that God does not exist.'[1] Apart from mentioning how science had shown that the world was not made in six days, the article dealt with the difficulties of certain philosophers and poets! But the subtitle's possibility implies that for many people 'Science' is the supreme court, and – for some – has disproved religious beliefs. We Christian teachers may feel we are fighting a rearguard action: we explain that the creation in six days was not *really* part of our faith; generally, we try to show that Science 'leaves a space' within which the essential truths of faith can survive.

If we give the impression we are defending an ever-smaller fortress of doctrine against the onslaught of science, we seem to give a tentative 'Yes' to the question, 'Can we still be Christians in a scientific world?' We should not let our agenda be set by that question; we need to be 'pro-active'. Rather than show that science *may* leave room for Faith, let us say that science properly flourishes in a Christian milieu, for *the Christian Faith validates and welcomes science.* Another recent article argued, 'Catholic theology tells us that the natural world is good, orderly, rational, contingent and open to the human mind, and these beliefs are essential for science. This enables us to understand why it was that science, as we know it now did not develop into a self-sustaining enterprise in any of the great civilisations of antiquity. Science achieved its first viable birth in Western Europe during the High Middle Ages, when for the first time there was a society dominated by Christian beliefs, and the social structure that allowed the free discussion of novel ideas.'[2] I shall argue that the time is ripe to emphasise that the Church is by nature *a critical friend of science.*

When that point is made, there remain certain areas where tensions are *perceived* between faith and science. I shall outline some of those, and offer ideas that may be useful in discussing them.

The Church as the Critical *Friend* of Science

In 1941, Albert the Great (1200–1280) was declared patron saint of natural scientists. In the thirteenth century he and his pupil Thomas Aquinas (*c.* 1225-74) defended the value of the newly-recovered treatises on the natural world written by the pre-Christian philosopher Aristotle. Aristotle's project of discovering the 'forms' (the recurring structures) found in the world was probably more at home in a Christian context than in the ancient Greek world. That world thought in terms of recurring cycles; but for Christians and Jews history is linear and actions have permanent consequences, and the world's beauty reflects the wisdom of the creative Artist who has given *us* the power to know the world. However, some thirteenth-century people accepted Aristotle uncritically and began to doubt certain Christian doctrines; others, in a 'fundamentalist' way, wanted to restrict the study of these texts. Albert and Thomas urged a *critical acceptance* of Aristotle: new insights about the world and human nature will help us glimpse God's beauty and the wisdom of how He leads us to our goal in Him.[3] But we must think carefully about what Aristotle said; Albert insisted on the importance of testing *experimentally* what we are told about the world, and took every chance to do so.

The approach of St Albert and St Thomas is typically Catholic. The Church encourages science as she encourages art and music. Suspicion and fundamentalism are not typically Catholic.[4] This may seem disproved by Galileo's case. The correct interpretation of that case is much disputed. In the early seventeenth century Copernicus' hypothesis was freely discussed; the Inquisition's anxiety was that it be presented as an *hypothesis,* not a certainty. What *may* have happened is that Galileo (1564-1642) offended Pope Urban VIII, who had supported discussion, by making fun of the Pope's own argument for the geocentric universe, and the Pope pressured the Inquisition to find some pretext for punishing Galileo.[5] What went on behind the scenes naturally could not be known, and this miscarriage of justice could give the impression that the Church was suspicious of new scientific hypotheses. Nevertheless, Catholics made important contributions to science before *and after* Galileo.[6]

Fundamentalism did not typify the early Church. A wooden reading of some Biblical texts implies the flat earth floats on water beneath an upturned bowl. No first-century Jews or Christians thought that; they accepted the current scientific picture of a spherical earth.[7] Nor did fundamentalism typify the Catholic reaction to the Theory of Evolution. J.H. Newman wrote: 'it is as strange that monkeys should be so like men with no *historical* connection between them, as the notion that there should be no history by which fossil bones got into rocks,' and, 'I see nothing in the theory of evolution inconsistent with an Almighty Creator and Protector.'[8] Newman was not afraid of scientific discovery: '... if anything seems to be proved by an astronomer ... in contradiction to the dogmas of faith, that point will eventually turn out, first *not* to be proved, or secondly, not *contradictory*, or thirdly, not contradictory to anything *really revealed*, but to something that has been confused with *revelation*.'[9] Newman's desire for a good school of science in the proposed Catholic University[10] is matched by the Church's support for science through such means as the Pontifical Academy of Sciences.

The Church's support for science needs to be reaffirmed. It is *timely*, since 'post-Christian Britain' has not seen Christian faith replaced by 'hard scientific logic'. For some, science's all-sufficiency has become a new *faith* to preach; others (perhaps feeling spiritually under-nourished by technology) have taken refuge in the occult, even magic; a few people have revived paganism, and worship the natural forces which Genesis 1 taught us were created by the only God to serve us, and which modern technology has shown we *can* harness. Besides resisting the enthronement of Science, the Church must again warn people against dabbling in the occult and against the irrational worship of nature, and must *ally* herself with the prudent scientific use of reason and the respectful harnessing of natural forces. *She* does nourish people spiritually, with Scriptures and Sacraments that promote the worship of God with mind as well as heart, and encourage practical charity.[11]

It follows that our presentation of the Christian world-view should include the following points:

- God, as a wise Artist, has made a world of order and beauty.
- God has given us the ability to understand the world and the responsibility of using it wisely.
- The Church has typically promoted scientific investigation and discovery.

- We should not accept scientific hypotheses uncritically.
- But we should be in sympathy with a rational, scientific enjoyment of the world.

Creation, Miracles, Suffering and the Last Day

Once it was known that the Universe is expanding, two rival hypotheses emerged: the 'Big Bang Theory' supposed that the Universe began in a state of extreme density and heat, from which it has expanded; the 'Steady State Theory' supposed that it is infinite in size and age, and expands without changing its overall appearance because new matter is created to fill the gaps. The Steady State Theory was popular among scientists because it was *neater*, until evidence proved its rival.[12]

It can seem that the Big Bang Theory points to a Creator who set the Universe up. Stephen Hawking's *A Brief History of Time* was therefore taken to 'relieve God of a job'; because it suggests that the first moment of time has no special status. Since space and time are interrelated, Hawking proposes seeing the whole Universe, spread out in space *and in time*, as a single entity, whose overall pattern is described and determined by equations – determined, because the Universe has to be exactly of *this* kind if it is to be viable. There is no need for a God to decide how to set the Universe up, because its condition at the time we label zero is as much determined as at any other.

In fact, the vindication of the Big Bang Theory was not needed to support our faith in a Creator! – as St Thomas showed in the thirteenth century. Aristotle was found to teach that the Universe never had a beginning in time – a kind of 'Steady State Theory'. Did that imply no act of creation? Thomas pointed out that God's 'characteristic job' is to *give existence*. The very being of things points to God who exists without cause (for His Existence is totally other in kind than ours) – all things must be held in being by His love moment by moment. If He so wish, God – who totally transcends time as well as space – can hold in existence a universe infinite in age; and if He so wish He can hold in existence a universe finite in age.[13]

Hawking seems to *agree* that God's real job is to give existence; *equations* cannot cause a universe to *be*. Even if there can only be one 'grand theory', he says:

> It is just a set of rules and equations. What is it that breathes fire into the equations and makes a universe for them to describe? The usual approach of science of constructing a mathematical model

> cannot answer the questions of why there should be a universe for the model to describe.[14]

Herbert McCabe sees God as 'whatever answers our question, how come everything?', and goes on to point out, 'When we have concluded that God created the world, there still remains the scientific question to ask about what kind of world it is and was and how, if ever, it began.'[15]

We must consider the theory that the Universe is 'the ultimate free lunch' because it 'adds up to nothing.'[16] A vacuum is not strictly empty, but – briefly – two equal-and-opposite particles can pop into existence so long as they 'add up to nothing'. Perhaps the Universe began when something like that happened, and for some reason the two particles did not recombine? This model may well not be valid, for the only vacuum we can meaningfully speak of is a vacuum *within* an already existing universe. More importantly, if the Universe does 'add up to nothing' this does not imply that no things exist (!), so that God is not needed to cause them; it merely implies that *a mathematical formula abstracted* from the things that do exist adds up to zero, neatly.

God holds *all* things in being, including the causal relationships ('laws of nature'[17]) science uncovers. Since He is *so intimately* present in things, we sinners can forget His presence; therefore – especially if He is to reveal His purpose – He must do *striking* things that speak to us rather as gestures do. These are, first, Jesus' life, Death and Resurrection, which we glimpse in the Sacraments and Scriptures; but also *miracles.* Miracles are not a case of a God 'interfering' who is normally aloof; they are the God who is always present doing special things, or ordinary things but without the usual created causes. If it seems unscientific to believe in miracles, consider Chesterton's words:

> Somehow or other an extraordinary idea has arisen that the disbelievers in miracles consider them coldly and fairly, while believers in miracles accept them only in connection with some dogma. The fact is quite the other way. The believers in miracles accept them (rightly or wrongly) because they have evidence for them. The disbelievers in miracles deny them (rightly or wrongly) because they have a doctrine against them.'[18]

Consider, too, the Church's reluctance to admit claimed miracles until after searching investigation.

One difficulty mentioned in the first article referred to is nature's 'heartlessness'. Suffering as a result of natural disasters is disturbing. Science can help us begin to see our way through this problem, for it shows us how finely balanced an eco-system must be within which life can evolve, and what the place of pain is in animals' ability to learn and react. Suffering is 'parasitic' upon the particular kind of delicacy and beauty that marks the Earth; the basic reality is the world's goodness.[19]

If the Universe is finite, science predicts it will stop expanding and eventually contract to a 'fireball'. That seems contrary to our hope for the resurrection of the dead, after which those who are saved and know God will enjoy a common glory patterned on the risen Christ's. But that transformation of the Universe has nothing to do with the 'Big Crunch' and is naturally something science cannot predict; it must involve God 'breaking in' to achieve something no physical or human power can achieve.

To sum up this section:

- Discussions can be sparked off by quotations like those from Hawking, McCabe and Chesterton.
- God makes the Universe *to be.* Science describes the causal interconnections *within* it.
- It is *un*scientific to refuse to believe in miracles.
- The world is very good; there could not be evil and suffering if there were not so much good.
- Our Christian hope takes us beyond anything science could grasp, into the heart of God.

Human Nature

Both faith, and certain sciences, ask, 'What is the human being?' For some thinkers, it is an extremely complex material structure – and no more. Evolution fully explains our presence, our bodily structure, and our social behaviour. Consciousness is 'an epiphenomenon of biochemistry' – that is, once you have an animal of such complexity, the behaviour we call conscious, and the experience we call consciousness, emerge as an aspect of the chemical reactions that go on within us. Freedom is an illusion in that character and behaviour are determined by genetic inheritance and/or environment. There is no need to invoke an immortal soul in order to explain anything. That, if true, would make Christian hope impossible, for it would mean that at death we completely perish, and no souls survive to pass through Purgatory and come to the vision of God. It would mean that anyone who died could not be raised, since no element would survive to ensure that the person who died and the person raised are the same being. There would be no eternal reward for loving God – not that we could freely love God, since religious behaviour would be programmed into some of us.

This view is *not* well answered by saying that the human being is really *two* entities: a body which is an extremely complex machine; and an immortal soul, the real person, free and *self-conscious*, which 'inhabits' the body until released at death. This alternative view does not account for the importance of the resurrection *of the body*; it fails to explain why much character *is* determined by genetic inheritance and environment; and it leaves people bewildered by the 'discovery' that some animals are conscious.

In fact, the materialist view of human nature is not something science has proved, but a philosophical presupposition; and the dualist view is not authentic Catholic teaching, but a philosophical tradition the Church has opposed. Truly open research into human nature, and a Catholic understanding of human nature, are not at all in conflict.

St Thomas Aquinas was aware of the higher animals' ability to organise and interpret sense-data, and their emotions. For him, human nature is not defined by consciousness, but by the unique conjunction of *animality* and *the ability to reason.*

In an 'organic interplay' between intellect and sensation, we draw concepts from experience, and transcend the here-and-now to know *what* a cat, or cabbage, is, so that we can reason validly about past or future, present or distant things. And since we can *know what is good* we have the faculty of will, the ability to pursue the good in a higher way than the other animals, which, by instinct,[20] pursue the sense-perceived good.[21]

Many earlier thinkers had tended towards a dualist view of human nature. Thomas saw the human being as a 'single if uniquely complex organism'. For Aristotle, the soul of a plant or animal was 'the form of its body', that is, its whole 'pattern of life' present in the here-and-now. A cat could not be just a complex arrangement of atoms, for cats really exist as whole beings. At the same time, what a cat can do depends very much on how the elements are arranged within it. St Thomas refined[22] this: for human beings, too, the soul is 'the form of the body'; but, by contrast with the other animals, the *human* 'form of life' transcends the here-and-now by the way it can grasp truth and goodness. What you can do reveals what you are: if human thought is not limited to the material environment, the human soul too is not limited in the way other souls are. They perish at death; the human soul does not, and retains the use of reason and will so that (if saved) it can know and love God, though it is partly frustrated until it can again form its body. So the human soul is both the form of the body and 'a spiritual substance' with two faculties (intellect and will) whose functioning is not in itself the act of a bodily organ.

Human life is therefore of a higher kind than the other animals': whenever a human being comes into existence, by a special creative act God produces something a biological process by itself could not, something that lives in but transcends the world of coming-to-be and passing-away – the human soul is directly created by God.[23] But the human being is conceived within, and naturally lives within, this material world, as part of the human community. Hence to a large extent our intellect and will must work with – even rely on – sensation and emotion, whose functioning is the act of bodily organs. That is why much human behaviour is partly determined by inheritance and environment, since we do not always need to 'step back from' our inherited emotional make-up (further formed by experience), and people do not always do so when they should.[24] Likewise reason's functioning is influenced or impeded by fear, desire, drink, sleep, injury to the brain, and so on; while some people's specially keen imagination (due, we would now say, to extra connections in the brain) makes them more intelligent, for human thinking relies very much on manipulating things like images.

Human language reflects human unity-in-complexity, being a means of communication in which sounds remembered in the brain convey meanings the intellect holds. It can be used for reasoning and for emotional effect. Since it employs so much that we share with the other animals, it need not disturb us if some chimpanzees have learned some use of language from human beings. Our kind of language is not *natural* to them, nor can they use it in the creative, 'open-ended' way that we can. This Thomist view allows for the inheritance of patterns of behaviour and accommodates the new discoveries in neurophysiology; it even seems to me to be more in tune with actual science than the materialist view. A materialist view is *reductionist*: it sees everything in terms of its component parts, whether protons and electrons, or at least molecules like DNA.[25] Modern science's successful *analysis* of things needs to be complemented by a *synthetic* approach that sees how the parts find their place in whole beings, which rely on, yet in some ways transcend them. Many sciences do study whole beings as such. Cell biology employs physics and chemistry in its investigation of cell processes, but examines the complex life of whole cells; when it deals with the cells of multicellular organisms – where cells' development and behaviour depend on their context – it points beyond itself to the biology of organisms, which studies the life-patterns of whole living things. Human psychology is aware of mechanisms by which drugs influence the psyche, but treats human beings as wholes that have characteristic patterns of consciousness. The language of such sciences, and the behaviour of their practitioners, do not suggest that everything may be reduced to physics.[26]

The immortality of the human soul can be defended on the grounds that physicality cannot explain our ability to transcend physicality. But it seems to me that the modern understanding of matter implies many levels of transcendence, of which human transcendence – our openness to truth and goodness, and therefore to God – is the culmination. Quantum mechanics (still subject to intense philosophical debate) does not allow us to think of subatomic particles as 'billiard balls' bouncing off each other deterministically. The arrangements they take up depend to some extent on their environment. Complex molecules like DNA also need a complex environment if they are to function. The proper behaviour of cells depends on their interactions with other cells in the same organism, rather as each organ can only carry out its function as part of the whole – even if kept artificially for a time during an operation, an eye could not function as an organ of sight outside the animal. Even below the level of the human psyche, there seem to be many levels of functioning that rely on their components but also represent something new and essentially higher.

Discussions in class might cover the following interrelated areas:

- Outline the reductionist/materialist view of the human being – how does it fall short?
- Does the reductionist view even account for the behaviour of pets and apes?
- Outline the dualist view of the human being – how does it fall short?
- Evoke a sense of wonder at the complexity of even simple living things, then at human life.
- What can we conclude from language, culture, thought, technology, and hopes for immortality?
- Does an account of the human being that sees it as a complex whole, something bodily and spiritual at the same time, make most sense of our experience and of our Christian hope?

Evolution and Human Origins

The Theory of Evolution holds that new species evolve from existing ones. Evidence for it includes the immense overlap between the DNA of different species, and the fossil record of new species emerging and old ones dying out. Classical Darwinism holds that new species emerge because some small changes (mutations) are beneficial and so favoured by 'natural selection'; hence they accumulate. Small changes are indeed sometimes observed *within* species, which otherwise seem remarkably stable. But this mechanism does not seem to everyone to account for the emergence of *new* species[27] or at least of radically new features. The fossil record does not show us 'missing links'; and all living things fall neatly into discrete species. It is often pointed out that a half-evolved eye could not be advantageous![28] As sometimes presented, classical Darwinism may not take sufficient account of the two-way interaction of organism and environment.

Before rejecting evolution, note that we are only beginning to discover how it might work. Much of an organism's DNA is not expressed; perhaps mutations can occur there 'safely' until a new gene is ready to be brought into play. Apart from cases like our sex chromosomes, genes occur in pairs; a significant mutation to a functioning gene might multiply in a population, but not be expressed until widespread enough for the birth of individuals in whom both genes of the pair possess it. If, as can happen, this mutation has a profound effect on bodily structure, owing to the way the organism develops, a new species would emerge 'ready-made', with enough members for breeding to start.[29]

For some, chance mutations and natural selection sufficiently explain evolution. For others, the chances of simple life emerging, and of advanced life evolving, are so minute as to demand the intervention of divine providence.[30] In fact, chance and providence are not mutually exclusive, for chance events, though not determined by causes within the world, still need to be held in being by God. Therefore, even if evolution is adequately explained in terms of chance mutations (together with natural selection), and even if the ingredients of life could have come together by a not implausible chance, we can ask how these processes may reflect God's wisdom. God's primary purpose is to give us His own self in friendship so that we come to share His happiness. Why then is the universe so large and so old? Perhaps because in that way human life could evolve by the chances inherently allowed for in matter – chances that of course were also guided by providence – and by the structured interactions proper to the material universe. Then the *whole* universe would be a suitable home for us, and besides reflecting God's beauty in itself, could reach fulfilment as a whole by 'giving birth to God's children' (Rom 8:19-23) in the final resurrection.

While having no problem with the theory of evolution, the Church insists that the human soul cannot be produced by biological evolution, any more than by the biological process of reproduction.[31] We should not envisage God arbitrarily creating souls to send into certain potential human beings so that they became human. When a human child is conceived, God's creative power is at work in intimate connection with the biological process, so that a single, but more-than-biological, being is conceived. The same would be the case if the first humans were conceived by pre-human parents.

Genesis 2 does not by itself require us to believe that the original human beings were precisely two in number. St Paul's contrast between Adam and Christ in Romans 5 seems to imply that the human race fell in an historical Adam, and the Council of Trent's Decree on Original Sin (1546) takes Adam's historicity for granted. That prejudices us in favour of the descent of our race from a single couple.[32] However, some theologians hold that St Paul was concerned to emphasise Christ's power, not reveal Adam's historicity, and that Trent was concerned to define the reality of Original Sin and Christ's power to heal it, not address the question of Adam's historicity. Hence, they suggest, we may be descended from an original, small group. Our descent from them was meant to be the basis for the life of grace; because the peace of that group with God and within itself was destroyed by the sin of all or some of its members, human descent could not fulfil that role, and grace must be restored by rebirth in Christ. The Church has not adopted this view; neither has she seen fit to condemn it.[33] (Note that the discovery of 'Mitochondrial Eve' does *not* prove that we are all descended from one woman. Mitochondrial DNA is passed down the female line, and all human beings now alive have inherited it from one woman; but since the mitochondrial DNA of any woman who has no daughters that survive to reproduce dies out, there may have been other strains of human mitochondrial DNA in the past, as far as science can tell.[34])

It is not a valid use of the Theory of Evolution to hold that human cultures evolve into higher and better forms, or that 'master races' evolve within the human family – on the contrary, all human languages are of roughly equal complexity, and there is very little genetic diversity among different human groupings; we very clearly form a single 'family'.

This area is likely to spark off animated discussion, especially as the Press tends to report many new discoveries relating to human origins.

- What is the evidence for the theory of evolution?
- What difficulties does it raise?

- How might evolution help us see the beauty and harmony of God's creation? – or would natural selection by itself make the world seem harsh?
- Is human dignity demeaned by the theory that we are descended from apes or does that descent make us 'priests of the world'?
- Does the theory of evolution lend support to attitudes like racism?

So, Does the Scientific World Point to God?

One frequent argument for God's existence is the 'argument from design', famously expounded by William Paley: '... marks of contrivance in nature abound every where about us; therefore there must have been a contriver: proofs of design and intention are to be seen on all hands; therefore there must have been some one to have designed and intended.'[35] A stone lying on the ground would not surprise us; a watch would imply deliberate manufacture – how much more the complexities of living things! Richard Dawkins' *The Blind Watchmaker* (1988) argues that the Darwinian Theory of Evolution explains these complexities, eliminating the need to invoke conscious design; in any case a Creator would have to be even more complex, so what explains him?[36] Not all proofs of God's existence start, like Paley's, from the physical world, for example Newman's argument from conscience.[37] Thomas Aquinas' famous Five Ways[38] do; can they be subverted in the way Dawkins subverts Paley's proof? The Fifth Way starts from the importance of *purpose* in explaining animal behaviour: animals cannot rationally plan for the future, so a Creator must have instilled purposeful patterns of behaviour in them. A Dawkins would say that *apparent* purpose evolved because beneficial patterns of behaviour deriving from mutations improved survival rates; he might also say that conscience evolved. Do such scientific explanations stop the world pointing to God? The lines of our answer may already be clear.

It would be difficult (if not impossible!) to prove that the emergence of life, and the stages of its evolution, are too improbable to be explained without divine intervention; in any case, that line of argument might leave us with a 'God' who relates to the world simply by poking it now and then, when it can't manage its own affairs. Such a 'God of the gaps' is susceptible to Dawkins' question, 'What explains God?' But if God makes all things to be, including their causal relationships, the questions that point to God, and the questions that lead scientists to uncover causal relationships, are asked at different levels, and their respective answers can be complete at their own level without being in competition with each other. So we do not answer Dawkins by picking holes in his account of evolution. (If we do argue that he is wrong to reject the sudden emergence of new species, we promote a variant scientific account of how evolution actually happens.) We need to show that Dawkins has ignored an important perspective, a valid question complementary to his valid interest in how things work; we need to show how the beauty and the very being of things point to the God who, as the whole world's *Ground of Being*, is at work too intimately and pervasively for 'intervention' to be a good label, and who is too transcendent for the question 'What explains God?' to be meaningful. We need to show that *The Blind Watchmaker* rules out the kind of 'God' we do not believe in, and that belief in the true God encourages us to see the natural world in all its details even more clearly.

St Thomas' Fourth Way invites us to see the degrees of goodness and beauty around us pointing to their transcendent Source. Those to whom such concepts seem insubstantial are asked by the Third Way to wonder at the very *being* of things.[39] The proof's first step demonstrates the 'precariousness' of many beings: dogs and dandelions can cease to exist; they depend on things which 'have a firmer hold on existence' (for Thomas, that was the sun as source of energy; for us, it might be electrons and protons, which do not decay). This readies us for the main step,[40] which asks us to see *all* beings as 'precarious': even the most permanent of them *need to be made to be* – not in the sense that they have to be made from something else, but in the sense that they have to be made to exist instead of nothing at all. Unlike '2 + 2 = 4', the statements 'This electron exists' and 'St Michael exists' – even 'The universe exists' – do not *have* to be true. A visitor from Mars who read about aardvarks and leprechauns would know *what* they are, but would not know *whether* they are without looking or being told: things' natures do not cause them to exist. Once we become able to wonder at the very *being* of all things, then all things point to the God from whom they must receive being as a gift. This implies how *different* God is: in Him there is not even a distinction between what He is and whether He is, let alone any of the other kinds of complexity that make creatures point beyond themselves. Despite God's transcendence, He wills us, once in heaven, to know Him as He is; then we shall see that 'God exists' does have to be true – God needs no explanation, His Being needs no cause.

If the Theory of Evolution can explain the natural world's complexities without need for special divine *intervention*, the very existence of the whole world and of the process of evolution can only be explained by

God's creative love. Once we have seen this, the world's orderliness, as much as any events that astound us by their improbability or miraculous nature, manifests God's wisdom, which does not replace the causes scientists look for, but gives them their existence and effectiveness. In the light of God's creative love and wisdom, believers need not fear analysis of how things work, as if it were *gaps* that point us to God; and people like Dawkins need not fear to see things as planned and created by God in their wholeness, as if delight in a tiger's *existence* would devalue discussion of its evolution and physiology. In particular, a Dawkins need not be afraid of the human being's spiritual dimension. By creating us, God does not sever our connections with the world science investigates, but gives us animals the ability to do what mere animals cannot – to contain in our minds the world that contains us! Our practice of science is one sign of the higher level of being God gives us.

It is worth detailing ways in which the scientific perspective should be complemented:

- The 'design' of living things does after all reflect God's 'artistry', for He holds in being a world in which complexity can and does evolve by mutation and natural selection.
- Purposeful behaviour – fully explicable at the scientific level in terms of evolution – also manifests God's care, His purpose to hold in being a world in which animals can evolve so as to flourish.
- Dawkins' desire to see how plants and animals work at lower and lower levels,[41] by itself, leads him to see their bodies as being for the sake of their DNA.[25] But God as Creator primarily intends their life and flourishing as whole beings, of which their evolution and reproduction are part. Sharing that perspective, we can also say that DNA is for the sake of whole plants and animals.
- Thus God's creative delight in living things prompts us to delight both in their intricate structures and causal relationships, and in their whole beauty, goodness and being – which reflect God's.
- Seeing the human soul as the *form*, not just the 'inhabitant', of the body, we glimpse our unique unity-in-complexity, and how richly we are in God's image. Instead of choosing between biological, psychological, intellectual and theological accounts of humanity, we can give each its due place.
- We can also recognise the environmental, embryological and social factors involved in human evolution, and see them as incorporated within the special creativity by which God makes us in His image. We can trace the evolution of the unique complexity of the human brain,

and of the unique combination of features that supports our linguistic, social life – and see them as 'calling out for' and as supporting the creation of the spiritual soul. Thus we need not reject our spiritual dimension; nor need we see our creation as fitting awkwardly into, or 'cutting across' the process of evolution. God's ways are typically gentle; His higher gifts affirm His lower ones even as they ennoble them by placing them in a higher context.

- For example, 'feelings of conscience' are to some extent due to evolutionary and psychological forces – but they also subserve conscience as the *forming of rational moral judgements*, which we are able and inclined to do because we are made in God's image and for God.
- Though we do not need to suppose some mythical drive to higher forms of being is inherent in matter, we can see evolution as leading, in God's plan, towards the human beings intended to enjoy His friendship. Then evolution becomes our historical context and the material universe our home, from which we are to be brought to birth into the future and the eternal home that is God.

To answer Dawkins by urging this *enlarged perspective* does not imply we leave rationality to the natural scientists and take refuge in an anti-intellectual form of mysticism. A world-view that sees God as the Source of all things' being and beauty validates natural science, and puts it into an even more intellectually satisfying context. The same world-view urges the true mysticism of thanksgiving, of sharing God's love and care for the world, for ourselves and for each other, and of journeying into God – all of which is taught us and given us in the Holy Eucharist.

The Church as Critical Friend of Science – the Ethics of Science

Although he did not want science and religion to be rigidly compartmentalised, Newman knew that the scientist must be given proper freedom: 'Unless he is at liberty to investigate on the basis, and according to the peculiarities, of his science, he cannot investigate at all.'[42] The Church does not presume to criticise the findings of science as such; she *is* entitled to point out that hypotheses are not certainties, and to give warning when false philosophical ideas masquerade as science.

The Church is not alone in being concerned about *the ethical use of technology*. This *is* where she can exercise a key critical role. For neither scientists, nor governments, nor public opinion, automatically follow correct principles when evaluating the use of technology. Treatments for infertility may be welcomed without proper reflection on what they involve; the genetic modification of foods has evoked a 'gut reaction' of fear. The Church does not disapprove of the artificial just because it is artificial, rather, she asks whether any action is humanising or dehumanising: does it cherish human dignity and life, or diminish and destroy them? Does it speak against human life and proper relationships? If so, it damages the individual or society that perpetrates it. 'Bioengineering is a good if it seeks to cure, but an evil if it violates the personality of man to the point of eugenicism and the construction of human beings to use them as an organ factory.'[43]

Areas for discussion can easily be found in the media. Here are some, with some pertinent points:

1. Genetic modification of foods: What are the risks to the environment, which is our home? (Prudence is an important virtue; in Catholic moral theology, 'prudence' does not mean excessive caution, but moral wisdom – which can take justified risks.) Is the genetic modification designed to help feed the hungry, or to increase multinationals' profits?[44]
2. Eugenics: Is it not a misuse of the theory of evolution to seek to breed 'better' human beings? Does not the special dignity of human beings demand that we do what our special talents permit, and help those who are weak to live lives as full as possible, rather than be concerned to eradicate the weaker specimens? On the other hand:
3. Gene therapy: Should we not seek to eradicate diseases, not by the abortion of diseased babies, but by making up defects in their (or older people's) DNA? But should we ever obtain healthy strands of DNA from aborted babies rather than, say, modified bacteria?
4. Embryo experimentation: Does not the modern understanding of reproduction imply that the fertilised ovum is already a distinct individual of the human species? May we then ever treat it as a means rather than as an end?

There is a danger that the Church will seem to be always trying to catch up with developments in technology, unable to pronounce on them before they are being widely used. We need to make it clear that such developments demand careful reflection, and that the Church has a vibrant tradition of moral reflection that deserves to be heard in public debate.

Science in Catholic Schools and Universities

We noted Newman's concern that science have its place in a Catholic University. In British Universities the Catholic Chaplaincy can be a forum for that respectful dialogue between different disciplines which shows that the scientific route to truth is not the only one,[45] but rather it and the philosophical and theological routes can enrich each other.[46] By promoting the good teaching of science at every level, and serious research, the Church can show she is a friend of science.

It is not necessary for the science teacher to point out at every turn how science supports faith; that would be wearisome. Besides being prepared to discuss the religious questions raised by science, however, she must help students recognise the part played by authority, fashion, a desire for theories to be neat, and philosophical presuppositions, in the actual conduct of science – that will help them not accept uncritically whatever any scientist says. If the school or university is also a worshipping community, and the science teacher is seen to pray, it is made clear that a scientist can be a Christian, and all the better a scientist as a result.

Finally, let us propagate the spirit of St Albert the Great, who saw the intricacies of even the smallest creatures as glorifying God. He and St Thomas Aquinas did not make naïve leaps from scientific facts to theological truths; rather, they let knowledge of the natural world keep their philosophical feet on the ground, so that their philosophy and their understanding of humanity helped them expound the beauty of the salvation communicated through Jesus Christ, who shows us more richly our nature and destiny.[47]

Notes

1. A.N. Wilson, 'Gone but not forgotten', *The Guardian Saturday Review* 5 June 1999.
2. Peter Hodgson, 'If we think of science as a tree, religion is to be found among the roots, not among the fruits' (Faith and Science series.) *The Catholic Herald* 28 May 1999. cf. JAKI, *The Savior of Science*, in the bibliography.
3. Pope John Paul II, Encyclical Letter *Fides et Ratio* of 14 September 1998 (henceforth FR), paragraphs 19, 43-45.
4. cf. FR 17 on no enmity between faith and reason.
5. This interpretation is based on J.M. Jauch, *The Trial of Galileo Galilei*, a lecture delivered at CERN, Geneva, on 20 February 1964. CERN 64-36 (13 July 1964).
6. As argued by Peter Hodgson, 'The secular myth about science.' (Faith and Science series) *The Catholic Herald*, 19 September 1999.
7. Dante's *Divine Comedy* witnesses to the Mediaeval belief in a spherical earth.
8. J. Newman, *Philosophical Notebook*, E. Sillem (ed.) (Louvain: Nauwelaerts Publishing House, 1969), vol. 2, p. 158 (entry for 9 December 1863). And:

Letter to Rev. David Brown, 1874, in *Letters and Diaries* (Oxford, OUP), vol. 27, p. 43. For the references to Newman I am indebted to the lecture 'Newman and Science' delivered by Peter Hodgson at the Newman Conference at Oriel College, July 1998 – papers to be published.

9. J.H. Newman, *The Idea of a University* (London, Longmans, Green & Co., 1947), p. 342.
10. F. McGrath, *Newman's University, Ideal and Reality* (London, Longmans, Green, 1971), pp. 330, 369 & 435.
11. See *General Directory for Catechesis* (henceforth GDC) 20 on a rationalism 'which integrates (our) affective dimension'; 193 on spurious forms of religion.
12. For a semi-popular account: Steven Weinberg, *The First Three Minutes: A Modern View of the Origin of the Universe* (Fontana/Collins, 1977). Refinements have since been proposed.
13. For Thomas' nuanced discussion of the world's beginning, see *Summa Theologiae, Prima Pars*, 46, 2. For God sustaining things in being, see, for example, *Prima Pars*, 8, 1.
14. Stephen Hawking, *A Brief History of Time* (London, Bantam Press, 1988), p. 174.
15. Herbert, McCabe, 'Creation' Essay 1 in *God Matters* (London, Geoffrey Chapman, 1987), republished by Mowbray, 2000, in Contemporary Christian Insights series, pp. 6, 8.
16. Discussed by Paul Davies, *God and the New Physics* (London, J.M. Dent & Sons, 1983), pp. 31-32, 214-217.
17. 'Laws' may be a misleading term. It suggests too much 'rigidity' in the world, and gives the wrong impression it can run itself while God stands aside. The 'laws of nature' we formulate are patterns we abstract from a world intelligible but more complex than we can fully grasp.
18. G.K. Chesterton, *Orthodoxy* (London, John Lane, The Bodley Head, 1909), pp. 276-7.
19. For a further discussion of this issue, see for example McCabe, 'Evil', Essay 3 in *God Matters* (cf. note 15).
20. Do not think of instinct in so wooden a way that you cannot see how animals can *learn.*
21. For key texts see: T.S. Hibbs, *Aquinas on Human Nature* (Indianapolis: Hackett Publishing Co., 1999). Also Thomas Aquinas, *Summa Theologiae, Prima Pars*, Qu. 75 – 89 – Qu. 78 covers the faculties we share with the other animals; article 4 makes it clear that all complex animals organise and interpret sense-data. cf. F.C. Copleston, *Aquinas* (Harmondsworth, Penguin Books, 1955), Ch. 4. Also: R.A. O'Donnell, *Hooked on Philosophy, Thomas Aquinas Made Easy* (New York, Alba House, 1995), Chs 4 and 5.
22. I say, 'refined' because Aristotle left it unclear how to connect the human intellect with the 'rest' of the human soul. In *Prima Pars* 76, 2, Thomas argues, against certain Aristotelians, that there is an intellectual power in each human being, not just one for the whole race.
23. *Prima Pars* Qu. 90; *The Catechism of the Catholic Church* 366.
24. I am to some extent translating Thomas into modern idiom. He took for granted that the heavenly bodies influence matter on earth, and so have effects

on our senses and emotions, effects many people do not resist. See *Prima Pars* 115, 4. In our world-view, genetics has a similar role.

25. In Richard Dawkins, *The Blind Watchmaker* (London, Longmans, 1986; Penguin, 1988) (henceforth BW), p. 192, we read: 'An individual body is a large vehicle or 'survival machine' built by a gene cooperative, for the preservation of copies of each member of that cooperative.' cf. p. 111.
26. John Polkinghorne, *Science and Christian Belief*(London, SPCK, 1994), Ch. 4, combats reductionism.
27. It *might* do so if two populations of a species are isolated from each other for a long time; certainly *varieties within species* are observed to arise in that way.
28. BW, Ch. 4, argues that, at each stage, a more fully evolved eye (or other feature) could be an advantage. Dawkins may still be playing down the need for radical innovations at certain points during evolution.
29. J.H. Schwartz, *Sudden Origins: Fossils, Genes and the Emergence of Species* (New York, John Wiley and Sons, 1999). (The historical part of this book is marred by the author's assumption that Christianity has typically opposed a scientific approach to the world.)
30. BW, chapter 6, discusses the 'luck' involved in life emerging by chance – quite helpfully, if you pass over the mistakes about God's complexity and the possibility of a statue waving purely by chance. The book as a whole argues that subsequent evolution does not require implausible luck.
31. Pope Pius XII, *Humani Generis*, Encyclical Letter of 12 August 1950, Part III.
32. *ibid.* Some commentators note a reticence in the Pope's words, implying that at some time it might appear how our descent from a small group *can* be reconciled with the doctrine of original sin.
33. Perhaps the chief exposition of this view is Karl Rahner, 'The Sin of Adam' *Theological Investigations,* vol. 11 (London, DLT, 1974), pp. 247-262. See also: E. Yarnold, *The Theology of Original Sin.* (Theology Today Series, 28) (Cork, Mercier Press, 1971). And: three articles in *Communio* XVIII, 4 (Winter 1991).
34. Covered by Richard Leakey, *The Origin of Humankind* (London, Phoenix, 1994). Roger Lewin, *The Origin of Modern Humans* (New York, Scientific American Library, 1993/98). These also discuss the evidence for a sudden emergence of the complex of features that characterise true humanity.
35. From his Sermon 31. See also *Natural Theology – or Evidences of the Existence and Attributes of the Deity Collected from the Appearances of Nature.* Published 1802.
36. For the latter point, see BW pages 141 & 316.
37. J.H. Newman, *Grammar of Assent* (London, Burns, Oates, 1870). Ch. V, 1.
38. *Summa Theologiae, Prima Pars,* Question 2, article 3.
39. FR 83, 90 & 97 urge the retention/recovery of a philosophy of being; 88 mentions the danger of the refusal to acknowledge that concept.
40. Commentators often struggle with the first step, and neglect the second. I have tried to 'unpack' the second by use of ideas found nearby in the *Summa.* See Isaiah 40:12-31 for a poetic presentation of the perspective on God that Thomas was to present academically.
41. BW, page 13.

42. J.H. Newman, *The Idea of a University* (London: Longmans, Green & Co., 1947), p. 349. cf. GDC 243(a).
43. From a recently reported interview with Bishop Elio Sgreccia, Vice-President of the Pontifical Academy for Life. cf. 'We are increasingly encouraged that the advantages of genetic engineering of plants and animals are greater than the risks. The risks should be carefully followed through openness, analysis and controls, but without a sense of alarm.'
44. It was reported in *The Times* on 5 October 1999 and *The Independent* on 6 Octoebr 1999 that Monsanto had agreed not to exploit 'terminator technology' that would produce infertile crops and force farmers to buy new seed each year.
45. cf. FR 88 on the false idea that only experimental sciences have access to truth.
46. See GDC 211-2 on the need for catechesis to penetrate areas such as scientific research.
47. GDC, 116.

Select Bibliography

Many significant writers in this area are not Catholic, such as Barbour, McGrath, Polkinghorne and Torrance. On some issues, therefore, they may lose touch with the Catholic tradition: for example, Polkinghorne sees creation as an act of *self-limitation* on the part of God!

Works accessible to secondary-school students:

Catechism of the Catholic Church 282-314, 337-344 & 362-366 (on creation and human nature).

Priests and People Vol. 13 No. 10 (October 1999) – special issue on 'Science – a Help to Faith?'

Hodgson, Peter, Faith and Science series in *The Catholic Herald*, 1999.

Holloway, Edward, *The Path from Science to Jesus Christ*, Shaftesbury, Faith Pamphlets.

Jones, David A. *Can Catholics Believe in Evolution?* London, CTS, 1991.

Nesbitt, Roger, *Evolution and the Existence of God*, Shaftesbury, Faith Pamphlets.

Nesbitt, Roger, *Evolution and Original Sin*, Shaftesbury, Faith Pamphlets.

Nesbitt, Roger, *The Path from Science to God*, Shaftesbury, Faith Pamphlets.

Polkinghorne, John. *Quarks, Chaos and Christianity – Questions to Science and Religion*, London, Triangle, 1994.

Scally, John, *A Brave New World?* Dublin, Veritas, 1998. (On ethical issues raised by science.)

Works accessible to teachers and university students:

Barbour, Ian G., *Religion and Science: Historical and Contemporary Issues*, London: SCM, 1998.

Jaki, Stanley L., *Cosmos and Creator*, Edinburgh, Scottish Academic Press, 1980.

Jaki, Stanley L., *God and the Cosmologists*, Edinburgh, Scottish Academic Press, 1989.

Jaki, Stanley L., *The Savior of Science*, Edinburgh, Scottish Academic Press, 1990.

McGrath, Alister E., *The Foundations of Dialogue in Science and Religion*, Oxford, Blackwell, 1998.

McGrath, Alister E., *Science and Religion – An Introduction*, Oxford, Blackwell, 1999.

O'Hear, Anthony, *Beyond Evolution: Human Nature and the Limits of Evolutionary Explanation*, Oxford, Clarendon Press, 1997. (Heavy.)

O'Rourke, K.D. & Boyle, P., *Medical Ethics: Sources of Catholic Teachings*, 2nd edn, Washington, DC, Georgetown University Press, 1993. (On issues raised by biotechnology.)

Polkinghorne, John, *Belief in God in an Age of Science*, The Terry Lectures. Newhaven and London, Yale University Press, 1998.

Polkinghorne, John, *Science and Christian Belief*, London, SPCK, 1994.

Polkinghorne, John, *Scientists as Theologians – A Comparison of the Writings of Ian Barbour, Arthur Peacocke and John Polkinghorne*, London, SPCK, 1996.

Southgate, C., Deane-Drummond, C., Murray, P.D., Negus, M.R., Osborn, L., Poole, M., Stewart, J. & Watts, F., *God, Humanity and the Cosmos: a Textbook in Science and Religion*, Edinburgh, T & T Clark, 1999.

Torrance, T. F., *Space, Time and Incarnation*, new edn. Edinburgh, T & T Clark, 1997.

Torrance, T. F., *Space, Time and Resurrection*, new edn, Edinburgh, T & T Clark, 1998. (These two discuss key doctrines in the light of modern science.)

Visual and Audio Aids

A panorama of creation and salvation. God's Master Plan in Christ: Shaftesbury, Faith Pamphlets, 1998

The Origins of the World:

1. Is there a God?
2. Human Beings, body and soul, Shaftesbury, Faith Pamphlets, 2000

THE ARTS IN A SECULAR POST-ROMANTIC AGE

FR ROBERT IGNATIUS LETELLIER

Linguistic theory, for example, shows that symbolic thought affords an approach to the mystery of the human person which would otherwise remain inaccessible. A rationalism which does not dichotomise man but which integrates his affective dimension, unifies him and gives fuller meaning to his life, is thus indispensable.
(*The General Directory for Catechesis*, No. 20)

I turn to you, artists of the world, to help consolidate a more constructive partnership between art and the Church. ... Let us rediscover the depth of the spiritual and religious dimension of great art from the past. ... Artists of the world, may your different paths lead to that infinite ocean of beauty where wonder becomes awe, exhilaration, unspeakable joy.

I appeal especially to you, Christian artists. I wish to remind each of you that, beyond functional considerations, the close alliance that has always existed between the Gospel and art means that you are invited to use your creative intuition to enter into the heart of the mystery of the incarnate God, and, at the same time, into the mystery of man.
(Pope John Paul II, *Easter Letter to Artists*, 1999)

The Power of the Word at the Turn of Time: Some Millennial Perspectives on Poetry and Transformation in the Twentieth Century

To reflect on the arts generally, even in a specific period, or from a specific point of view, is a very challenging task, the dimensions of which are potentially limitless. To try and understand the arts in our times, a 'secular post-Romantic age', in a context of theology and catechesis, provides a more delimited brief, but again, where does one begin to enter this vast ocean of manifold reflection on human experience? The General Introduction of GDC refers to 'linguistic theory', and by implication the whole realm of language and symbolism. And since it is Jesus who is our Word, and words about him are our true *métier*, perhaps our consideration of the arts should take its cue from this, and focus particularly on the mystery of words, and that special concentrated use of words in which we distil our deepest reflections.

What role has poetry played in this 'secular post-Romantic age', in revealing ideas and notions we can call 'spiritual'? Has poetry, literature in general, been a force for reflection, or even change? Has it had anything to say about Jesus, and the advent of his Kingdom?

The twentieth century has been a tumultuous age for humankind. The great conflict of 1914–18 saw the demise of an old world order. Four great empires, and the centuries of culture and stability they signified, were destroyed. New nations emerged which took on a mantle of personal responsibility for which they were often ill prepared. Age-old structures were swept away, and with them many of the values that had characterised the self-expression of the European nations for hundreds of years. The unresolved political situations, exacerbated by the catastrophic economic conditions of the depression years, saw the emergence and temporary triumph of violent and atheistic world views, particularly Communism and Fascism/National Socialism, which intensified the traumatisation of culture and its questioned Christian values. The opulence and even decadence of the late and Neo-Romantic movements, were to be replaced by the nightmares of Expressionism,[1] or the disturbing challenges of Modernism – from the analytical cubist distortion of Picasso,[2] to the action abstractions of Jackson Pollock[3] from the atonalism[4] of Schoenberg and Berg's Viennese School, to the aleatory music of John Cage.[5]

The challenge and apparent chaos of so much modern art reflects the fear and anguish of an age in which the relationship between man and God has been perceived to have been weakened, if not to have disappeared altogether.[6]

In fact since the Enlightenment there has been a fading of the image of God. The new scientific view of the world and the progressive view of history, not to mention the universal sorrows and sufferings of this century, have resulted in people having difficulty in accepting that God is interested in the individual. If this is so, then good or bad deeds do not interest God in this vast universe. If God has nothing to do with us, then the concept of sin disappears, and there is no Son of God who redeems the world and our wretched human condition. There is little reason to be concerned with atonement, sacrifice or the forgiveness of sin. It is a characteristic of the modern Europe that people are weary of the Church. Saying, 'yes' to Jesus and 'no' to the Church has become typical of entire generations, and the whole problem is to do with faith. The human side of Jesus touches us, but professing him as God's only begotten Son seems alienating to the modern mentality. Separating Jesus and the Christ is, at the same time, separating Jesus and the Church. Since the Enlightenment, there has been a drive to find the 'historical' Jesus, behind the 'myth' of the Gospel. The spiritual meaning of the sacraments, of the Church, of the Word itself, fall apart.[7] What remain are impoverished symbols of community and rituals that simply hold communities together and stimulate them to take some kind of action in the world. But the Christian doctrine of redemption is no longer properly understood, and this has had a radical consequence for art, and the focus of its expression.[8]

But if the 'religious' dimension of art has been weakened in our age, the mysterious power of language, of the word, has not. If the whole notion of the unconscious was opened to us by Freud,[9] and the universality of archetypes and symbols was revealed by Jung,[10] we must look in our own days to Noam Chomsky for a radically new view of the nature and analysis of language. He changed attitudes to language. He transformed the status and relevance of theoretical linguistics, and made a remarkable connection between the possibilities of language as a biologically determined and transmitted structure, a criticism of extreme behaviourist psychology, and the responsibility of men of knowledge to challenge the authoritarian state in any of its agencies. It was Chomsky's conviction that human beings are different from animals and machines, and that these differences should be respected in science and government. His convictions, born of his radical Jewish background, underlie and unify his politics, his linguistics and his philosophy.[11]

The whole modern phenomenon of sociolinguistics, further, has emerged from this perception of the interconnection between language and society. Specific points of connection have been discovered in this process, and this in turn is related to the theories that throw light on how language and social structures interact.[12] The use of language in literature is central to this.

The 'Word' and Poetic Experience

Art is fundamental to human self-expression, a vital aspect of the religious impulse in all humanity to search for and reflect on the experiences and meaning of life. Art accompanies all human activities, from the simplest pastimes, to the most dramatic and thought-provoking reflections. It can be commandeered for political purposes, or as erotic stimulation. But in its most fundamental expression in our everyday speech, the words can become a lyrical bridge, and can have effects that carry over into our lives. The mystery of the word is a great one, a holy one, associated with the purest ideals of Apollo, and the instinctive frenzies of Dionysius.[13] But it is in confronting death, perhaps, that we experience the strongest sense of the necessity of poetry to our complete human self-expression, and we reserve our greatest gratitude to the poets, the purveyors of words in their purest and most concentrated form, for having unlocked the power and magic inherent in the ordinary. Perhaps this is because, as no other, the poet is one who makes things 'capable of eternity', as Rainer Maria Rilke observed.[14] Poetry is a vital part of art, of literature and of religion, and as we stand on the threshold of a new millennium, and, dare one hope, a new and better age, the mystery of the word in our lives, and its meaning in making sense of past, present and future, is worth thinking about for a few moments.

The Religious Mystery of the 'Word'

In the Prologue to the Gospel of John, it is the *logos* or 'divine word' which is the self-communicating holy presence that existed with God, and was uniquely manifested in Jesus Christ. This Johannine concept is strongly parallel to the concept of wisdom in Hellenistic Jewish thought, where wisdom and the word were intimately associated (Wisdom of Solomon, 9:1-2). Wisdom or Word was God's creative presence through which the world came into being. John's Gospel affirms that this divine presence was fully and uniquely present in Jesus Christ, a redemptive presence that was necessary because the world had rejected the original creative presence of God. The Word was in Jesus, not simply as verbal communication, but entered fully into human life. The incarnation of the word brought life to human beings, to whom it was otherwise unavailable (Jn 1:1-18).

In the Hebrew Bible the word of God is both creative (Gen 1; Is 55:10-11) and commanding (Amos 3:1). This background contributed to the general usage of the term *logos* in the New Testament, where the 'word' often signifies the Christian message (2 Cor 2:17; cf. 1 Cor 1:18). This in turn links it with the Greek field of meaning, where *logos* implied both spoken word and pervading principle. Stoic philosophy, using the latter meaning, saw the *logos* as the ordering principle of the universe; the wise person aims to live in harmony with it.[15]

The Word as (Non-) Communication Between God and Man

The challenge and puzzle of the word of God, as divine revelation, as communication, and as organising universal principle, has also preoccupied the twentieth century. Take for example Arnold Schoenberg's opera *Moses und Aaron.* The first acts were completed in 1932, but were not produced until June 1957 in Zürich. The story centres on Moses as he leads the Children of Israel in the wilderness to the foot of Mount Sinai, the giving of the Ten Commandments (Exodus 19) and the episode of the Golden Calf (Exodus 32). The theme explored is a profoundly mystical one, the nature of communication between God and man. The work explores the distortion suffered by the pure truth (received by Moses from God in the form of the divine words which make up the Law of the Lord) when it undergoes the inevitable exposition (by Aaron) in terms comprehensible to man. Moses receives the Word of God, but he lacks the power of communication, which is the special gift of his brother Aaron. While Moses is delayed on the mountain, Aaron encourages the People of Israel to erect the Golden Calf as a tangible object, approximating the notion of the divine, for a simple people to worship. The ensuing orgy is interrupted by Moses, who, in horror, shatters the tablets of commandments, and yearns to be released from his divine mission as transmitter of God's Law. His closing statement, 'O Word, thou word that I lack' is a searching observation about communication, with very strong theological, as well as artistic, concerns. The whole thematic nexus is compounded by the radical language of the composer's chosen musical mode of atonalism, and conveys great emotional power which did much to vindicate Schoenberg's musical reputation.

Another great Jewish artist has confronted the challenge of the word as Law, as meaning-bearing agent in the midst of life's incomprehensibility and emptiness. Franz Kafka (1883-1924) had a love-hate relationship with Judaism characteristic of his assimilated contemporaries in Austria-Hungary.[16] Although his work seems to have a blank, uncanny lack of any frame of reference, some pieces, such as his fragment 'Before the Law' (later incorporated into *The Trial*) explicitly, as his other stories and novels do implicitly, present a haunted, absurd, Job-like demand for justice. Elsewhere in *The Trial*, Joseph K., searching for the 'law books' studied by his mysterious accusers (and later executioners), can find only clumsy pornography. To the extent that Kafka's dark parables refer to the Bible, the tone is consistently hostile. 'In the Penal Colony' speaks of the old and new 'Commandment', sacred but unintelligible 'scripts', an impossible commandment to 'BE JUST'. In his eerily reasonable prose, he complained always about the failure of the world to resemble that of the Bible, yet he was never free to leave the subject alone, and used his own words to explore and reflect on the intangibility of the Word as the organising principle of a just existence.[17]

The pull between the perception of the word as something holy, something associated with the divine, the creative and redemptive self-communication, remains even in an unbelieving age. A number of other twentieth-century atheistic writers, such as Jean-Paul Sartre (1905-80), Albert Camus (1913-60) and the practioners of 'the Theatre of the Absurd' (e.g. Luigi Pirandello, Eugene Ionescu, Samuel Beckett), can be seen as conducting a life-long argument with the biblical version of the world, shaking their fists at what had become for them an empty heaven. The medium of this rage is nonetheless the word in all its mysterious power of communication. The 'nausea' experienced by Sartre's autobiographical hero, Antoine Roquetin (1938), is a kind of metaphysical malaise caused by the fact that 'everything in existence is born without reason, prolongs itself out of weakness, and dies by accident'.[18] Although Roquetin, like Proust, seeks relief in art from a universe perceived without God, he defines himself by the very notion he rejects: the idea of creation. The 'word' once again becomes a salvific vector, a signifier of value and meaning.

Samuel Beckett's play *Waiting for Godot* (1955) is impregnated by nostalgia, a futile hankering for the apparently lost world of the Bible. Although Beckett defined Godot as whatever one hopes for, he is clearly an image of a biblical God perceived to be nonexistent, and who is also tragically incompetent. Like Kafka, Beckett plays endless variations on the theme of being condemned to hope. But while for Kafka hope is almost a crazy commandment, a cruel illusion, for Beckett it is an incurable sadness from which all humanity suffers.[19] Only the medium of the word can help to provide a context of meaning for such objectifying reflection.

The Word as Political-Liturgical Vector

The mystery of the word is intimately bound up with a heightened perception of life, and the successful communication of this perception. What good or use is poetry anyway? This perennial question has been answered in many different ways, and one of the most vital twentieth-century responses was provided by W.H. Auden in his poem 'In Memory of W.B. Yeats', written between the Irish poet's death in January 1939 and the Nazi invasion of Poland which led to the outbreak of World War II. The last lines of this valediction are an invocation, almost a prayer, to the dead poet, asking for the continuation of poetry itself, and its constant work of transformation:

> *In Memory of W.B. Yeats*
>
> Follow, poet, follow right
> To the bottom of the night,
> With your unconstraining voice
> Still persuade us to rejoice;
>
> With the farming of a verse
> Make a vineyard of the curse,
> Sing of human unsuccess
> In a rapture of distress;
>
> In the deserts of the heart
> Let the healing fountain start,
> In the prison of his days,
> Teach the free man how to praise.
>
> W.H. Auden

The emphatically rhymed and confidently metrical lines celebrate poetry as a force for life, a pledge of heroic effort, and a contribution to the enlargement of the spirit.[20]

Even as Auden was writing these lines, it was poets and musicians who were shaking the system in other totalitarian parts of the world, not by penning propaganda, but by sticking to the concentrated discipline of lyric writing.

The example of Oslip Mandelshtam (1891-1938) in the repressive years of the Stalinist purge is a case in point. His persecution by the Soviet authorities for evident lack of ideological and literary conformism appears to have begun with his arrest in the early 1930s. The circumstances of his death are unclear, but apparently he died in Eastern Siberia on his way to a gulag or concentration camp. In spite of his several exiles and constant threat of death, he understood the rights of lyric poetry as an equivalent of fundamental rights and freedoms denied by the state. Poetry for him indeed had prophetic and liturgical function. The age of revolution and the ensuing upheaval and tyranny, which provoked in him an awestruck fascination, then a mixture of pity and terror, and finally a desperate urge to escape from the spiritual darkness of his confined environment to the promised land of ancient Greece and the cultural values of Europe, constitute an enshrinement of liberty in the medium of words.[21]

A different kind of poetic reaction, and yet in parallel with Mandelshtam's, is that of Boris Pasternak (1890-1960). In spite of two epic poems in praise of the revolutionary movement, in 1934, with the mounting pressure exerted by the Communist Party to ensure the ideological conformity of Russian writers, and their acceptance of the principles of 'Socialist Realism', he stopped writing poetry for nine years. Once in 1946 when the Party launched a new attack on deviationist writers, he fell silent this time until Stalin's death in 1953. Since 1946 he had worked on his novel *Doctor Zhivargo*, which was banned in the Soviet Union and could be published only abroad in Milan (1957). As a consequence he was awarded the Nobel Prize in 1958, but under severe political pressure and scurrilous attack from the Soviet authorities, was forced to decline. His novel, impregnated with religious imagery and philosophical reflection, although in no sense an overt attack on the Soviet regime, is profoundly at variance with its official ideology in its repudiation of the philosophical inadequacies of Marxism and of the inhumanity of the Revolution, in its Christian interpretation of the problems of life and death, and in the prime emphasis it lays on spiritual integrity of the individual and the value of human compassion. The poems which form an appendix to *Doctor Zhivargo* are his supreme lyric achievement and reveal him as a great Christian poet. Once again the word had been used to convey a positive message, an affirmation of life and love, above and in spite of the oppression of an atheistic ideology.[22]

The Word as Atheistic Prophecy

After World War II and its revelation of the Holocaust, a new darkness came over the century, entering consciousness like another instance of the universal fall of mankind, only not this time some new myth of creation and redemption, but an actual part of history, the unimaginable horror at the back of the human psyche, come out into the open, the fable of Hell brought out on to the surface of this green earth.

For some the world could never be the same again. For Primo Levi (1919-87), the Italian-Jewish writer, God ceased to exist after Auschwitz, and the inevitable consequence for him was the breakdown of the word as transmitter of meaning, as metaphor for God and his self-communication to the world. His knowledge of chemistry and insight into humanity draws on his experience of growing up with fascism, and its clinical notions of purity, as well as his time with the anti-fascist resistance. *If This Is a Man* (1947) and *The Truce* (1963) explore the horror of what followed his capture and experience of the death camps. The narrative's increasing awareness of evil and its fulfilment echoes Dante's descent into hell. Levi's testimony became more urgent where some historians began to deny that so vast and rigorously documented mass slaughter could have taken place at all.[23] This he said was to 'kill the dead twice'. The nightmare of guilt and terror never left him. This breakdown in the ancient covenant between God and his creation can only spell meaninglessness, with the inevitable consequence of lifelessness: Levi was eventually to take his own life in April 1987.

For others the word continues to carry life and hope, albeit without the transcendent divine spark. Spiritual richness is there, but it is now without the presence of the Word himself. Carlo Levi's novel *Cristo si e fermato a Eboli* (1945) which inaugurated the post-war trend to social realism and documentary novel, depicted the Southern Italian way of life in all its hopelessness, material poverty and generous qualities of soul. Now in his work on Sicily *Le parole sono pietre* (1955), words have become stones.

An even stronger sense of a nihilism nonetheless obsessed with Christianity is to be found in the work of Nikos Kazantzakis (1885-1957) (as in *Christ Recrucified* (1954), *The Last Temptation of Christ* (1960) and *Report to Greco* (1965)). Christ is still God, but the author embraces the human, doubting part of the Messiah as he too chooses life, but in a dream sequence. That this life should involve sex was the grounds for shock, but in exploring the alternatives to a hideous martyrdom the author tries to render the ultimate sacrifice as all the more selfless and saving of the human condition.[24]

All of Pier Paolo Pasolini's work was motivated by his belief that the writer has a significant contribution to make towards the reform of social and political structures. The kind of words used by the writer are must reject the dogmatism of traditional literary style (which is nothing other than the linguistic superstructure of the ruling classes) and must try to reproduce, with almost philological accuracy, the language of the common people. He was interested in popular poetry which he edited (*Canzoniere italiano* (1955), and used a linguistic realism which still has the power to shock the reader. His poems and novels oscillate between autobiographical confessions and the bitter sorrowful contemplation of life at its lowest level (*Ragazzi di vita* (1955), *Una vita violenta* (1959), *Il sogno d'una cosa* (1962)). The word is once again an agent of insight and compassion.[25]

The Word as Medium of Change

For others the Holocaust has provided an opportunity for a more positive and ironically life-affirming view of the world. The Australian novelist, Thomas Keneally, is always concerned with the moral dilemmas and a compassion for the poor and dispossessed. His best-known work, *Schindler's Ark* (1982), describes the story of Oskar Schindler's work of saving his Jewish workers from the death camps. The novel examines moral ambiguities in the face of ultimate horror: not only did it win the Booker Prize in 1982, but was filmed in 1994, and has become a vital text in a world which must never forget these terrible events.

The haunting influence of World War II is indeed obvious in the film industry. In the 1940s and 1950s, Hollywood celebrated self-sacrifice for the greater good in films such as *They Were Expendable, The Sands of Iowa Gima* and *Bridge over the River Kwai.* In the 1960s and 1970s came the larger-scale sweep of history with *The Longest Day, The Guns of Navarone* and *The Battle of the Bulge.* Then as the miasma of Vietman infected the American consciousness, doubts appeared. The Japanese pilots in *Tora! Tora! Tora!* (1970) were depicted as human beings, not merely a caricatured enemy. In *Apocalypse Now* (1979), Francis Ford Cappola used Vietnam in an attempt to destroy any possibility of a decent, justifiable war. Stephen Spielberg's *Empire of the Sun* (1984) even dares to enter into a searching, sympathetic analysis of the enemy Japanese mentality, through the experiences of an idealistic child protagonist. Now at the end of the century we are on a private rather than a public quest. Spielberg's *Schindler's List* (1994) and *Saving Private Ryan* (1999) dramatise the truth and goodness of individual compassion in the midst of universal terror. A culture that notices and troubles to save one man is a triumphant culture.

But for many artists the Holocaust remained a nightmarish backdrop, as in the important poems by Sylvia Plath (1932-63), like 'Daddy' and

'Lady Lazarus' published in her 1965 collection *Ariel*. These and others of her poems show the power of the poetic word to influence things, even in a political sense. The resurgence and defiance in her work, despite her personal problems and historical perceptions, are expressed in a combination of artistic achievement and the personal liberation this signifies.[26] The effect of these words was to generate an important current in what was first called women's liberation, then feminism, and finally gender politics. Plath's work had the 'kinetic' effect described by James Joyce in his novel *The Portrait of the Artist as a Young Man* (1915) to depict the power of art, especially the word, to have a carry-over effect in life.

But what effect, one could ask, has the compassionate, but atheist, vision of Pablo Neruda or Bertold Brecht had in helping the poor and the oppressed? There is no answer, but there is a certainty that something real and positive did occur. Likewise, there is no doubt that the soldier poetry of World War I (by Wilfred Owen, Rupert Brooke, Siegfried Sassoon) went on to affect attitudes towards mass-slaughter and loyalty to nationalist mythologies; that Eastern European poets who refused to conform to the Communist ideologies kept alive the spirit of resistance that finally triumphed in 1989. Poets like Allen Ginsberg, and the Beats in general, changed the atmosphere of American culture,[27] helped the anti-Vietnam war movement and accelerated the sexual revolution, and women poets, in the wake of Plath's achievements, affected the social and political climate. Poets of ethnic minorities (like the Scot Hugh MacDiarmid) have also successfully made their words into part of an extended work of solidarity and empowerment.[28] The work of all these poets did make something positive happen; because no true and lyrically charged use of words is unconcerned with the world it contemplates, answers for, and sometimes answers to.

The Word as Reflective Transformation

The mystery of the word as reflecting the transforming power of something divine is essential to all poetry, indeed to all literature, and reflects the life-giving and affirming qualities of God's plan for the world. At the beginning of this brief pre-millennial survey, the power and mystery of the word and its communication and communicability were considered in terms of Schoenberg's opera *Moses und Aaron*. Here the power, and even forcefulness, of the word is conveyed, but often in perplexity, and in the medium of the alienating atonalism of the setting. It is interesting that one of the pieces of music which has achieved so much by way of its overwhelming appeal and eloquence in the closing years of the century is one that captures the mystery and mystique of the word, in the context of the troubled years of human experience in this century. Using the techniques of the minimalist school of music with its obsessive ostinatos, returning to the clear textures and haunting modalities and melismatas of ancient folk and religious music, Henryk Górecki's *Symphony of Sorrowful Songs* (1989) seeks to address the almost unendurable burden of grief and disillusionment born of the collective experiences of the past sixty years.[29]

Górecki was born near and educated in Katowice, close to the town which has become the symbol of sorrow for our age, Oswiecim, or Auschwitz. The central of the three movements of this symphony is a simple setting of a prayer inscribed on the wall of a basement cell in the Gestapo headquarters in Zakopane, by a prisoner, Helena Wanda Blazusiakowna, and dated 26 September 1944.

> No, Mother, do not weep,
> Most chaste Queen of Heaven.
> Support me always.
> Ave Maria.

This simple invocation to the Virgin in the hours of terrible need captures the essence of the poetic impulse, its mode, its sorrow and its universal statement. The song of abandonment and despair is also a prayer, a statement of faith, hope and love. This elegy is the central panel of a triptych, the first being a setting of the fifteenth-century 'Lamentation of the Holy Cross Monastery', words of the Virgin at the deposition, when the dead body of the Son of God is laid in her arms. The third movement is a folk song in the dialect of the Opole region, and is also a lament, the grieving song of a mother for her lost son whom she presumes is murdered. The elegy becomes a lullaby for the lost one, passed over into a new realm of existence.

The composer has chosen a medieval prayer, a modern war poem and a folk song, all in the archetypal mode of the *pietà*, or situation of mourning, and the music in the style of the threnody, or song of sorrow. By taking poems both old and new, and a grieving fundamental to all human experience, Górecki has produced a work which has, more than any other piece of contemporary 'classical' music, captured something of the essence of the agony, the pain, the loss and yet enduring optimism of everyman and every nation at the end of this century of wrenching revolution, cataclysm, and fear.

But the word/Word springs ever green, and man's irrepressible spirit, drawing wisdom from the collective experience of the ages, and the hope, born of faith, looks forward in optimism to new beginnings and the promise of enduring life which is enshrined in the mystery of the word and its almost sacramental use in lyric utterance.

Some Christian Words as Dynamic of Reflection

The overtly Christian concern of the word as a source of transforming reflection has found particularly rich expression in various English-language contributions to different literary genres over the past 50 years. W.H. Auden's turn to a Christian range of reference has already been mentioned, while T.S. Eliot's literary responses to the Bible are reflected in such poems as the 'Journey of the Magi' (1927), 'Ash Wednesday' (1930) and his confrontation with time in relation to eternity in the magisterial *Four Quartets* (1935-42).

The Oxford scholar C.S. Lewis (1898-1963), who initially applied his immense intellect to the history of English poetry, and then to the defence of Christianity, was a reluctant convert, but responded to a deep inner conviction that Christianity outshines all religions. This was born of insights gained from his sufferings in the First World War, and from his own experience of the sorrow caused by the sickness and premature death of his wife.[30] He explored the psychology of believing, the nature of temptation, the meaning of grief.[31] His early science fiction novels (beginning with *Out of the Silent Planet*, 1938) already revealed a strong Christian flavour; *Perelandra, or Voyage to Venus* (1940) is a Miltonic retelling of the Eden story, with a new Eve tempted by a new Satan. *That Hideous Strength* (1945) foreshadows the explosion of the atomic bomb, and raises ethical questions that have become common concern since.

But it was his response to what he perceived to be a dearth of good children's literature that resulted in a series of stories that can be read as a Christian apology. The seven Narnia books, of which *The Lion, the Witch and the Wardrobe* (1950) is the most famous, become increasingly Christianised (with Aslan the lion a messianic figure), until by *The Voyage of the Dawn Treader*, the allegory is made all but explicit ('In your world you must know me by another name').

The message of J.R.R. Tolkien (1892-1973) is not so obvious. As a scholar, and deeply influenced by Celtic and Teutonic mythology, and Anglo-Saxon literature, his novels *The Hobbit* (1937) and the trilogy *The Lord of the Rings* (1954-55) made him the most influential and best-selling of all fantasy writers.[32] This vast modern fairy story is resonant with biblical theme, motif and language: the quest at the heart of the work, to find and destroy a ring which confers infinite power, and hence leads to cosmic corruption, is redemptive in its models and messages. Its wide appeal is partly explained by the emphasis it gives to the little people, the endangered elves, 'the first born' who use magic as a power for good; it is they who carry the burden of experience and the message, rather than the conventional virtuous knight in shining armour. The essence of Tolkien's view is a discovery, through the Hobbits, of the little land of the shire, the variousness and majesty of the world which is fighting to keep alive against 'the darkness that threatens to obliterate the natural separateness of living things'.

Much of this appeal lies in its simple reaction to a world of industrialisation and impersonal social organisations. Although Tolkien professed to hate allegory, and denied that his creations have much in common with the real world, his sweeping vision emerged as a powerful influence, especially with the 'hippie' generation. His emphasis on the small person and the pure values of the natural realm, have played a prophetic role in affecting and shaping modern perception of this planet, its ecology and its destiny.[33]

A similar emphasis on the little man, and the reality of God's love, even in tawdry and extraordinary circumstances, is the special contribution of Graham Greene (1904-1991) whose novels encode a strong spiritual message. He converted to Catholicism in 1926, and his religious beliefs play an important part in his fiction, a seedy, exotic world of tainted anti-heroes. His skilful adaptations and variations on the thriller, the detective story and the travelogue, brought him a combination of critical and popular acclaim.

Greene used his wide range of geographical location and variations of tone to explore moral dilemmas (personal, religious and political) in an attempt to distinguish 'good-or-evil' from 'right-or-wrong'. In his turbulent landscapes (like Mexico, Cuba and Argentina), his trapped Anglo-Saxon characters, confronted by betrayal, are caught up in agonising problems, and try to confront them while maintaining their integrity. Whether in Brighton or in West Africa, they are in life and death situations, and realise the full potential of the troubled but searching conscience facing impossible decisions, confronting what must be the author's central concept of 'the appalling strangeness of the mercy of God'. 'Make me believe in the mercy of God' (*The Heart of the Matter*, 1948) could be another way of putting it. Pinkie, the ex-Catholic criminal protagonist of *Brighton Rock* (1938), is, in spite of his moral confusion, in contact with the 'possibility' of grace because of his Catholic upbringing: he has access to the means of distinguishing between good and evil. *The Power and the Glory* (1940), which opposes Catholic and Marxist doctrines as a means of judging individual human actions, introduces a compromised 'whiskey priest' as the hero, a man who ironically seems closest to God because of his sin; his violence and decay as a priest produce his resurrection as a man, and his modern crucifixion story pledges the inevitability of the Church's triumph.

Greene, in the middle of the twentieth century, grappled with the problem of providing a solution to the questions of the nature of morality. Treating his 'heroes' in terms of Greek tragedy or Catholic doctrine, his work suggests the view that grace is the necessary condition for true and meaningful life, and without it even virtues are contemptible.[34] Even though his novels can be read as just 'entertainment' (as he himself styled many of them), they are at the same time a medium of transformation, providing one of the most profound (and ironically hopeful) examinations of morality in modern fiction.[35]

The idea of a transforming moral power inherent in the word, and with the capacity to change life or perception of the world, is also evident in one of the great artistic phenomena of the last years of the century. James Cameron's film *Titanic* (1998), which was made at the cost of millions, and has netted an unprecedented popularity around the world, used history (the sinking of the legendary liner on 14 April 1912 off Newfoundland, with loss of 1,523 lives), literature (the chronicle, the frame story, the screenplay), music (the haunting score of James Horner) and the film (that most successful of twentieth-century genres) to recreate a myth for our times.[36] The story of an actual event becomes the moral medium of a parable for the closing century. The famous ship can be seen as a symbol of creation and human achievement. The sophisticated triumph of the technology it represented, makes it a symbol of modern progress and achievement; the range and diversity of its passengers becomes a cross-section of the people of the world, of all human society in the mythical confrontation with the mystery and challenges of life. The arrogant indifference of the travellers and their ignorance of the impending disaster, have archetypal implications, with the ship in all its brilliance, babble and diversity, a type of the Tower of Babel, and the sinking analogous to the Flood. The ship of dreams, what could have been the ark of human endeavour and righteousness, has become the *Narrenschiff*, the ship of fools, full of the bonfires of human vanity. The cataclysm tears away the veneer of civilisation and presents every individual on board with the stark choices for life or death, both literally and metaphysically. Humankind is so powerful, and yet so vulnerable, even helpless. What does life mean? What do we do with the world and the opportunities given to us? The self-sacrifice of the boy Jack who gives up his chance of survival willingly so that his friend may live, is full of the nuances of redemptive love, and lives out the Gospel injunction of Jesus' words 'a man can have no greater love than to lay down his life for his friends' (Jn 15:13).

So much has been achieved over the past hundred years, and yet so many have died needlessly and tragically because of our corporately selfish and unregenerate heart. The focus of this parable can indeed speak of transformation to those who have ears to listen and hearts to reflect.

The Word as Vector of Hope

But at the end of the twentieth century, which has seen unparalleled technological development and the worst degradation and sorrow of collective human experience, it is appropriate to focus briefly on a point of bright light in this cultural meditation on our times.

The rise of pop music has been one of the sociological phenomena of the past 50 years, and, one could reasonably argue, perhaps even *the* voice of authentic self-expression in an age when the young have felt alienated and distant from their Occidental heritage, the positivist, imperial and essentially Christian birthright of the West. Elvis Presley, the 'King', is one of the most potent icons of the age,[37] while John Lennon[38] and Bob Dylan[39] established themselves as philosopher-teachers through the medium of song.

But the group that captures something very special, a note of joy and genuine optimism, is not from the brigade of guitar heroes who mouthed a youthful dissent from the world and values of their forefathers, nor from the Blues, nor from the Beatles, nor from any other American-derived genre that has inspired generations of post-War pop aspirants, right down to the boy bands *de nos jours*. It is the Swedish group ABBA who won the 1974 European Song Contest, and who, from then until 1981, enjoyed an outstanding run of eighteen consecutive UK top-ten hits (265 weeks in the charts) before breaking up in 1982.[40] They were sneered at as trite and unfashionable in the 1980s, but since 1992 have staged an amazing comeback, with bands like Erasure and Björn Again reviving their music, and the new musical *Mamma Mia!* (London, 1999), which is built around 27 of their songs, corroborating Abba's position as a worldwide phenomenon. A new generation, bored with the self-conscious movements such as glam, disco and punk, and numbed by the pretensions and humourlessness of underground, techno and rap, have rediscovered the joy of pure pop in the recycling and representation of what had been dismissed as 'yesterday's kitsch'.

Abba represent a paradox, because, while apparently plumbing the depths of burlesque and parody in their glitzy clothes and petit-bourgeois, pedestrian image, they wrote brilliant pop tunes, relentlessly catchy and up tempo, with singable melodies that epitomise the European folkloristic tradition. What is of unique interest though, is their use of the word in their songs. These words have been dismissed as 'nursery-rhyme lyrics', but in fact their songs have an extraordinary ability to carry a narrative, and in fact establish themselves as little 'psychodramas' in which the perfect pop is counterpointed by a most surprising seriousness, sometimes even a Scandinavian bleakness that can elicit a mood of considerable reflection. The songwriters Benny Anderson and Björn Alvaeus sounded a note of unease and realism, as the vocalists Agnetha Faltskog and Anni-Frid Lyngstad sang of the personal problems and dilemmas of life for ordinary people in the late twentieth century: friendship found and lost ('Where is the spring and the summer?'), emotional struggle, betrayal and disillusionment ('Knowing me, knowing you', 'Angel eyes'), cash problems ('Money, money, money'), the desolation of urbanisation and grind of daily work ('Another town, another train'), nostalgia, the challenge of aging and the precious gift of liberty ('Fernando'), the hope finding some meaning in love ('I do, I do, I do', 'Take a chance on me', 'Bang-a-boomerang is love'). The need for hope in the human condition comes through again and again. The lyrics are often full of pain. Take the song 'Chiquitita':

> Chiquitita, tell me what's wrong,
> You're enchained by your own sorrow.
> In your eyes,
> There is no hope for tomorrow.

But there is always a vital uplift:

> Chiquitita, you and I cry,
> But the sun is still in the sky,
> And shining above you.

The surprising notion of hearing a message, essentially Christian in ethos, being sung in the exhilarating context of resurgent pop, is a paradox not fully appreciated, but one that no doubt subconsciously influences new perceptions of Abba's extraordinary appropriation of words and music. They tell us frankly that

> People need hope,
> People need loving,
> People need trust from a fellow man.
> People need love to make a good living,
> People need faith in a helping hand.

But not only do they touch on the theological mysteries of faith, hope and love (cf. 1 Cor 13:13), they proclaim a view startling in positing a brotherhood of man based on kindness, forgiveness and compassion (cf. 1 Jn 3:14-18).

> Treat him well he is your brother,
> You might need his help one day.
> We depend on one another.
> Love him, that's the only way.

That a form of popular music should promote a tacitly evangelical view of life, is indeed a source of joy and hope, a corroboration of a redignified humanity which is heir to a divine calling. The mystery of the incarnate God is also the mystery of man, and as the Pope has pointed out, creative intuition is a way into the heart of this enigmatic wonder.

Conclusion

At the end of a century that has seen the nuclear mushroom clouds over Japan, and the genocidal smoke from the gas ovens in Europe, seen the dustbowls and the melting icecaps, the acid rain and the eroding ozone layer, all the destructive and desolating truths can be acknowledged. And yet the glory of creation, and the fundamental nobility of the human ideal can still be held to, and can still be proposed, in the mystery of the Word/word.

The poet Joseph Brodsky has observed that human beings are put on earth to create civilisation. And if one is able to accept this definition as the *raison d'être* of humankind made in the image and likeness of God, then we will admit that in a century when inhumanity has exercised such terrifying sway, poets and musicians as purveyors of the word have been true to that purpose, and have proved central to its transforming potential.

'The gifts he gave were that some would be apostles, some prophets ... for building up the body of Christ, until all of us come to the unity of the faith and of the knowledge of the Son of God ...' (Eph 4:11-12). Poets, whether they know it or not, are profoundly caught up in this mystery, and their force for purveying in words the power of spiritual values, for helping us to integrate our affective dimension, bringing us closer to the wonder of God's love, and so giving fuller meaning to our lives, is indeed Apollonian, truly a divine gift.

Perhaps we should draw together some of these ideas with another word from W.H. Auden, one of whose special gifts was to express deep thoughts in the bright, fresh, easy words of contemporary language:

> Our apparatniks will continue making
> the usual squalid mess called History;
> all that we can pray for is that artists,
> chefs and saints may still appear to blithe it.[41]

And then there is Abba, who with their wonderful melodic uplift and thoughtful lyrics, capture something of the rapture that art can bring to our lives, as a very special pledge of hope in our divine destiny, beyond *hac lacrimarum valle*:

> Thank you for the music
> the songs I'm singing;
> Thanks for all the joy they're bringing.
> Who can live without it,
> I ask in all honesty?
> What would life be?
> Without a song and a dance what are we?
> So I say:
> Thank you for the music,
> For giving it to me.

Finally let the power of the word return to its deepest meaning:

> Not from a monstrance silver-wrought
> But from the tree of human pain
> Redeem our sterile misery,
> Christ of Revolution and of Poetry,
> That man's long journey through the night
> May not have been in vain.[42]

Notes

1. The disturbing painting *The Scream* by Edvard Munch (1863-1944), a forerunner of Expressionism, is regarded as a proleptic vision of the horror of so much human experience in the twentieth century.
2. 'No man has changed more radically the nature of art. Like Giotto, Michelangelo, and Bernini, he stands at the beginning of a new epoch'. See Peter and Linda Murray, *A Dictionary of Art and Artists* (Harmondsworth: Penguin, 1959; rev. 1965, 1968; rpt. 1975), p. 323.
3. Jackson Pollock (1912-56), the chief American exponent of 'action painting', made studies for his apparently unpremeditated works done on continuous lengths of canvas tacked to the floor, and later cut up with selective care. He abandoned the use of brushes in 1947, pouring the paint straight on to the canvas.
4. 'Atonalism' implies keylessness, later (from about 1923) systematised into the *twelve-note technique* devised by Arnold Schoenberg, and of great influence internationally. Abstract art and atonal music are expressions of an untethered, discontinuous and ambivalent twentieth-century universe.
5. John Cage (1912-92), the American composer, was especially noted for his 'music' which seemed to involve the abdication of the composer, e.g. his *Imaginary Landscape* for twelve radio sets, first performed in 1951, requiring 24 performers. 'Aleatory' applies to the tendency of some composers to leave elements in their compositions in an indeterminate state, in which random chance genuinely plays a part in performance.
6. For a recent exploration, and stimulating interpretation, of the meaning of art as an expression of the challenges and puzzles of life during this century, see Peter Conrad's *Modern Times, Modern Places: Life and Art in the 20th Century* (London: Thames & Hudson, 1998). Conrad invites us to review how the creative arts in the modern age have foreseen and charted the abandonment of a sense of permanent certainties, enshrined within centuries of tradition, to the relativism and subjectivity of our times. The same subject is addressed with concern by Pope John Paul II in his encyclical *Ratio et Fides*; he notes that this abandonment must ultimately lead to confusion and despair.
7. This is a topic too vast to broach directly within the confines of this limited exercise. A sustained analysis of the 'desacralisation' of mankind's perception of himself, of his world, and of his faith, is provided by the very bold and simulating ideas of Theodore Roszak in *Where the Wasteland Ends: Politics and Transcendence in Post Industrial Society* (London: Faber and Faber, 1973). Speaking of the place of the Virgin in Christian life, he observes: 'But with the advance of Protestantism, this residual, popular mythology was seared away at the roots; it too was identified as idolatry. Myth, like sacramental symbolism, fell away under the iconoclastic ban. Nothing was to remain as a support for faith but the remote scriptural narrative, a cold, increasingly literal commitment to historical fact which would finally produce the higher criticism, the quest for 'the historical Jesus,' and programs (like that of Rudolf Bultmann) for the total 'demythologisation' of Christianity ... It is only after Protestant iconoclasm has at last rooted sacramental perception out of our

culture that we arrive for the first time in history, at a condition of true idolatry. All knowledge becomes a single-visioned knowledge of mere objects, an *objective* knowledge from which we feel certainty, mastery, security, affluence flow' (pp. 133, 135). 'It is only within the past few generations – thanks to the inspiration of Romantic art and the daring of psychoanalysis – that myth has been salvaged from the positivist slagheap. It now begins to enjoy its proper dignity as a depth dimension of the human mind' (p. 133).

8. This thesis is developed at length by Joseph Cardinal Ratzinger, *A New Song for the Lord* (New York: Crossroads, 1996). For a perspective on the cultural turmoil of the radical 1960s and its impact on today's world, see Henrik Roelof Rookmaaker's *Modern Art and the Death of a Culture* (1970: London Inter-Varsity Press, 1994). His analysis looks at modern art in a broad historical, social, and philosophical context, revealing the despair and nihilism that pervade our era. He shows the role that Christian artists can play in proclaiming truth through their work.
9. See Sigmund Freud, *Introductory Lectures on Psychoanalysis* (2 vols. Harmondsworth: Pelican Books, 1973) for a succinct account of his groundbreaking ideas. These lectures were delivered during the First World War at the University of Vienna, and present the full range of his theories and observations.
10. A compact presentation of Jung's legacy to the world is contained in *Man and His Symbols: Conceived and Edited by Carl Jung* (London: Picador, 1964). Jung explains his theory of the significance of symbolism in dreams and art, and the importance of its comprehension to the full understanding of the unconscious human mind.
11. Chomsky is one of the leading intellectual figures of modern times. His contribution to the study of language has influenced many other disciplines, including history, philosophy and psychology. His belief in the innate structuring principles, which he sees only humans possessing, led him to search for the universal in language. See John Lyons, *Chomsky* (Glasgow: Fontana/Collins, 1970; rev. 1977) for a classic introduction to Chomsky's ideas. Neil Smith, *Chomsky – Ideas and Ideals* (Cambridge: Cambridge University Press, 1999) analyses Chomsky's key contributions to the study of both language and the mind, and explores the controversy surrounding his work.
12. Ronald Wardhaugh, *An Introduction to Sociolinguistics* (Oxford: Basil Blackwell, 1986) provides a comprehensive survey of the central topics of this wide-ranging interdisciplinary subject.
13. For an account of these gods, their spiritual and cultural significance, and their place in the ancient pantheon, see Carl Kerényi, *The Gods of the Greeks* (Harmondsworth: Penguin Books, 1951), pp. 115-32 (Apollo) and pp. 220-41 (Dionysius).
14. Rilke (1875-1926) wrote lyrical, mystical poems, like the *Duino Elegies* (1922) and the *Sonnets to Orpheus* (1923) which are regarded as amongst the finest religious verse of the twentieth century.
15. A coherent account of the whole notion of the *Word of God* is provided by John Muddiman in Bruce M. Metzger and Michael D. Coogan (eds.), *The Oxford*

Companion to the Bible (New York/Oxford: Oxford University Press, 1993), pp. 818-19.

16. Kafka's visionary, metaphorical and psychological fiction expresses, indeed perfectly captures, the anxiety and alienation of twentieth-century Western society. See, for example, Thomas Bertram Lonsdale Webster's *The Terror of Art: Kafka and Modern Literature* (1960).
17. David Lyle Jeffrey's account of 'Literature and the Bible' (*The Oxford Companion to the Bible*, op. cit., pp. 438-60) provides a detailed and stimulating survey of secular literary responses to the Scriptures. The above discussion of aspects of Kafka's work is indebted to him.
18. *La Nausée*, like all Sartre's novels, expounds his philosophy of Existentialism.
19. Originally written in French as *En attendant Godot*, the English version (1955) made a great impact, and from this time Beckett became widely known as a playwright associated with the Theatre of the Absurd whose use of the stage and dramatic narrative and symbolism was revolutionary for drama, especially in England.
20. In his early poetry, Auden explored the means of preserving through poetry the 'private spheres' amidst a 'public chaos', as he saw life in the 1930s. His response was a left-wing, near-Marxist one, although after his *New Year Letter* of 1941 his poetry became more Christian in tone.
21. With Akhmatohva and Gumilev, he founded the Acemist school of poetry; its interest in the reality of things, rather than their symbols and ciphers, extends to Mandelshtam's idea of words. In his mouth, they became entities in themselves, and he could ask: What's meaning but vanity? A word is a sound one of the handmaids of the seraphim. This sense of their being or essence, organised in restrained and formal stanzas, makes them so essential and underlies his classically restrained, terse, resonant verse.
22. The hero's appended poems show the author's continued faith in Christian imagery and complete identification with his central character.
23. This interpretation of history, for example, is officially adopted by the French right-wing National Front founded by Jean-Marie Le Pen in 1972.
24. Although Kazantzakis was at odds with Orthodoxy, he was possessed of a profound spirituality, which is imbued with the mysticism of the Far East (as in his play *Buddha*), and finds echoes in the Orthodox liturgy itself. The Church's view of the Holy Spirit as the giver of life, filling all things, was very much his own as well.
25. Pasolini (1922-75) was equally famous as an actor, scriptwriter and producer in the film industry. His socialist politics strongly influenced his approach to films, but some, like *The Gospel According to St Matthew* (1964), convey a powerful compassion for humanity in its simplicity, plain style and use of amateur actors.
26. *Ariel* (1965) connects the themes of female subjectivity, suffering and negativity to the Holocaust and questions of racial identity. Plath's life and work present a consistent and unique challenge to the way we think about women's identity: she constantly forces her reader to examine the links she establishes between the woman writer, madness and history. See Julia Wagner-Martin, *Sylvia Plath: A Literary Life* (London: Macmillan, 1998)

27. Allen Ginsberg (1926-1997) is regarded as the leader of the 1950s 'beat generation'. Ginsberg saw drugs and sex as a liberation, and had much influence on the hippy culture of the 1960s. His poem *Howl* (1956) includes the claim that his friends were the 'best minds' of the 1950s, among them Jack Kerouac (1922-69). His most popular work is the semi-autobiographical novel *On the Road* (1957), an episodic account of the ramblings across America of a young writer and his friend.
28. Hugh MacDiarmid (1892-1978), poet and critic, produced in his masterpiece *A Drunk Man Looks at the Thistle* (1926) an allegory of awakening Scottish consciousness that influenced many writers.
29. Henryk Górecki (1933-) lives in obscurity on the Silesian border. He shot to international fame in 1992 when his third symphony sold more than 600,000 copies worldwide, making him the world's most successful living composer.
30. See Lewis's autobiography, *Surprised by Joy* (1955) for a discussion of his convictions.
31. *The Problem of Pain* (1940) and *The Screwtape Letters* (1942) are the best known of Lewis's religious works.
32. For a critical survey of contemporary responses to his work, see N.D. Isaacs and R.A. Zimbardo (eds.), *Tolkien and the Critics* (1968).
33. A wide-ranging discussion of the typical concerns of the ecological-political studies that have emerged in the last decades is represented by Gregg Easterbrooks, *A Moment on the Earth: The Coming of Age of Environmental Optimism* (Harmondsworth: Penguin Books, 1995).
34. This is the opinion of Angus Ross in his discussion of Graham Greene in *British and Commonwealth Literature* (Harmondsworth: Penguin Books, 1971), p. 225.
35. For a selection of thoughtful opinion about Greene's fiction, see R.O. Evans (ed.), *Graham Greene: Some Critical Considerations* (University of Kentucky Press, 1963). This work contains a useful bibliography.
36. A full review of the film, its creation and its historical background is provided by the souvenir issue of the *Sunday Times, Titanic: The most Famous Tragedy at Sea of All Time, the Most Successful Film the World has Ever Seen* (ed. Andy Bull; February, 1998).
37. Elvis Aaron Presley (1935-77) became one of the most popular and controversial rock singers during the 1950-60s, universally recognised as a great popular singer and interpreter of ballads.
38. John Winston Lennon (1940-80) was a rock guitarist, singer and songwriter, a member of the Beatles, the most popular rock group ever. Their success was largely based on the successful songwriting partnership of Lennon with Paul McCartney.
39. Bob Dylan (1941-) became the most prominent 'protest' folksinger of the 1960s. His lyrics, which are highly regarded by some critics, were influenced by Woody Guthrie, and in their turn, had their effect on other folk artists like Joan Baez.
40. It is a measure of Abba's worldwide influence and success that in 30 countries (from Korea to Poland, from the Czech Republic to Argentina, Portugal and

Taiwan), *Abba Gold*, the compilation of their greatest hits which appeared in 1992, has achieved platinum sales. An insight into the story of this remarkable group is provided by Agnetha Faltskog who published her autobiography, *As I Am: ABBA Before and Beyond* in 1996.

41. 'Moon Landing (August 1969)'.
42. This is the last stanza of the poem 'Ecce Homo' by David Gascoyne (1916-) (Peter Levi (ed.), *The Penguin Book of English Christian Verse* (Harmondsworth: Penguin Books, 1984), p. 357).

PHILOSOPHY AND EVANGELISATION: THE VISION OF *FIDES ET RATIO*

ANDREW BEARDS

The response of the secular media in Britain to the publication of Pope John Paul II's encyclical on faith and reason, or philosophy, *Fides et Ratio*, in 1998 was truly remarkable. In national newspapers such as *The Daily Telegraph*, *The Times*, *The Guardian*, and *The Independent*, one could read lengthy articles analysing the encyclical on pages that were also adorned with pictures of St Augustine, St Thomas Aquinas, St Edith Stein and Cardinal Newman – saints and scholars whose images are normally found in books tucked away in theological libraries, not in national dailies. The appraisals of the Pope's encyclical were, for the most part, very positive; with some disagreeing with his Catholic world vision but agreeing with some of the philosophical points he made. This reaction on the part of Britain's press invites not a little reflection as a phenomenon, which in itself is indicative of subtle changes in our society's attitudes to the questions of religion and of a 'philosophy of life'. For one thing the reaction demonstrated how far a traditionally Protestant or Anglican country like Britain has come in its reactions to the Catholic Church in the course of this century: from anti-Catholic bias, to an attentive listening to the words of the Vicar of Christ, which was at least respectful, and at best enthusiastic. Further, it directs our attention to the way people in our society and culture could well understand the importance of what the Holy Father was saying. And what was he saying? He was writing on a matter which in another period of our cultural history might have just been passed over by those outside the world of theologians as something to do with 'ivory tower' academics: the relationship between philosophy and faith. The perception that John Paul II was not writing a dusty academic treatise was, of course, enhanced by the way the themes were treated by the Pope in the encyclical. Ever a priest who senses how his audience can be stirred and challenged, Pope John Paul speaks to the world in this encyclical in a way that meets us in the West, at least, just where we are at this crucial moment in cultural history, and at once he is able (also as one trained. in professional philosophy) to banish the myth that philosophy is only something for ivory tower academics (a myth fostered in no small measure by some of those academics themselves), and show us that we are all 'philosophers' by nature. That is, we are all called to love wisdom (*sophia*) and truth and goodness, and to seek these values. The understanding was also there in the media evaluations of the encyclical that the Pope speaks to us and calls us to live up to our true selves at a time when many in the West are beginning to appreciate that our culture is in crisis precisely because we have abandoned basic, fundamental values and have allowed ourselves to drift towards an abyss: an abyss of relativism and hedonism. The alternatives for our society and ourselves are stark, the Holy Father tells us. Are we simply to drift with the crowd after pleasure seeking materialism, and like Pilate in the Gospels brush aside any question of ultimate value or truth with the cynical question, 'Truth, What is that?', or are we to turn again and realise that we cannot live either individually or socially as mere drifters?

The newspaper commentators who wrote on the encyclical *Fides et Ratio* could appreciate that the problems in our society, such as broken homes and the drug addiction of the young are symptoms of something far deeper. They are not problems that can be resolved over night by social engineering, although, of course, society has to attempt to develop effective schemes which help to reduce such problems. Rather, they are indications of a 'sickness of the soul', a disorientation in our society regarding the meaning and purpose of human life. The Pope had raised the age old human questions of the meaning of existence, questions which every culture, religion and philosophy has drawn attention to, and he had raised these questions with regard to the contemporary chaos of the Western world, in such a way as to touch a nerve, to issue a challenge that could not be avoided by thoughtful men and women.

The encyclical itself and these reactions to it, then, demonstrate that philosophy has a vital role to play in evangelisation. In the rest of this chapter I will attempt, following the indications given in *Fides et Ratio*, to examine a little further how this is the case, and to highlight areas where,

I am sure, the reader will to some extent already be aware that questions concerning philosophy, or 'a view of the world', affect reception and/or resistance to the preaching of Catholic faith.

This turn to philosophy, or openness to it, manifesting itself in our culture follows a very ancient pattern in cultural history. Fourth-century B.C. Athens, the birthplace of western philosophy was, like the western world today a place of social and cultural tension and change: old assumptions and attitudes were being called into question, people were being driven to ask about the fundamentals of life amidst turmoil. Into this arena of social change came relativists (including cultural relativists), sceptics, atheists and others who thought it best to avoid profound questions of truth, and simply educate the youth of the elite in political 'spindoctoring'. Philosophers like Socrates, Plato and Aristotle, on the other hand, stressed the great vocation of human persons to know the truth and the real good and to follow these. They also demonstrated some continuity with the religious traditions of the past insofar as they believed, in one way or another, in a Divinity that was at the basis of the Cosmos. So too, in the West today we find that three decades after the social revolution of the sixties assumptions which were once taken for granted as the basis of social life have been gradually whittled away. What are the basics of life? What is life about? The Christian heritage of the West once provided basic assumptions upon which to build a society. Now that is not so much the case, and as the whittling away process goes on one increasingly realises, as the words of the song have it 'You don't know what you've got till its gone': one realises that the Judeao-Christian roots of our culture ran so deep that in uprooting them we are faced with a cultural chasm. It is as if years after many in our culture had ceased to hold an active Christian faith, they continued to 'draw money' from the Judeao-Christian bank account, and now have become aware that funds are exceedingly low. On a more hopeful note, however, (and this does not escape the Pope's notice in the encyclical), other cultural assumptions that had become established in the minds of western peoples, assumptions at odds with Christianity are now being fast eroded and abandoned. Thus Marxist materialist atheism has collapsed as a political force in the West. Further, what the Holy Father calls *Scientism*, is also on the wane. By 'scientism', or 'positivism' is meant the view that science, as opposed to religion, will answer all the great questions of life and will by the transformation of the world, remove the need for religion. In many different ways people have been losing faith in this anti-Christian creed. 'The revelation in areas such as nuclear or biomedical engineering that science is simply a human tool and is wielded by frail and sinful human beings for good or ill, has certainly done much to tarnish the myth of the 'man in the white coat' as the earth's saviour. Beyond this there is the increasing realisation that science does not answer the great questions of the meaning of life nor does it explain why there exists anything at all. The Holy Father then, notes both the positive and negative aspects of the scene for the prospects of evangelising the West with the Christian philosophy of life. He writes of the, so-called, 'post-modern' situation (*Fides et Ratio* 91), pointing out that, indeed, 'postmodernity' is a very vague phrase, yet it indicates both the challenges and the opportunities for evangelisation offered by the collapse of previously held cultural assumptions.

As we noted above, in the encyclical Pope John Paul wants to bring home to his readers that philosophy is not something distant and academic, but that we are indeed, all philosophers: we all have some kind of 'philosophy of life'. Such philosophies of life are no doubt constructed from all kinds of family, social and religious backgrounds. Yet we are all capable to some degree of reflecting upon our own philosophy of life, and really the tradition of 'academic philosophy' is simply a history of the way human beings have engaged in sustained reflection in this way.

Our faith, in fact, demands such self-reflection and self-examination. It is such self-examination that makes possible conversion to the faith, when someone asks, 'Am I right in holding what I hold, or is the truth, or a 'fuller' truth, elsewhere?' Within the life of faith one is asked to engage in self-reflection, be it the examination of conscience before Confession, or the reflection upon one's spiritual life and calling, or reflection upon one's progress in understanding and deepening one's knowledge of Catholic faith. Of course when we think of our Catholic faith as itself a particular 'philosophy of life' we must at once affirm that it is no human philosophy: it is a pure gift of God. God's revelation is pure gift to us, and in comparison all human philosophical thinking is seen to amount to very little indeed.

That being the case we all have some sense, however, that Divinely revealed Catholic faith is something that makes sense of life; it is not believing things that are simply absurd or useless (like there are five invisible apples under my desk now). Rather it is belief that we can in some way appreciate what makes sense of our life. In other words it is reasonable to believe, although faith tells us of realities such as the Trinity and the Incarnation) that we could not work out as being true simply by our own reflections. This awareness of faith as gift of God given from beyond us, and as something that is reasonable, is developed in a more explicit way in the Church's own teaching on the relationship between faith and reason, philosophy and theology. Examples of that teaching are the doctrines of Vatican I (1869-70) and the Holy Father's *Fides et Ratio* itself.

This Catholic teaching on the relationship between faith and reason, philosophy and theology, steers a middle course between the heresy known as Pelagianism, on the one hand, and some of the more extreme forms of fundamentalism and anti-intellectualism from the Reformation period, on the other. Pelagianism (a fourth century British-born heresy) underestimates the way original sin, historical sin and personal sin wound our minds and hearts to such an extent that bias and evil habits weaken our own endeavours to use our minds to get to know objective truth and value. At the other extreme, some forms of Protestant reformation thinking (but not all) over emphasise the wounded nature of our minds through sin and find no room for the products of philosophy (which have often been produced or influenced by pagans) in Christian thought. A twentieth-century representative of this kind of thinking (who in other areas was a great theologian, praised highly by Pius XII) was the Protestant Karl Barth. According to Barth belief cannot reason with unbelief – there is no bridgehead between the world of the believer and that of the unbeliever provided by philosophy.

On the Catholic view reason and its product philosophy, are indeed wounded and affected by sin; but reason is certainly not wounded fatally. After all in 'reason' and in the philosophical and religious expressions of mankind we see that Divine spark in man, that ability to ask questions and to seek the true and the good that is placed in man by God. Indeed, it is the human capacities evident in these expressions, human intellect and will, that make man like to God. As one can see from the whole Catholic tradition up to and including the document *Gaudium et Spes* of Vatican II and the latest Papal encyclical, philosophy, the work of human reason unenlightened by revelation, is valued as an element that enters into the theological reflection of the Church and as a way to dialogue with non-believers. Such dialogue has a very long history. In *Acts of the Apostles* 17, St Paul attempts to preach the Gospel by first meeting Greek philosophers at the Areopagus on their own philosophical terms. Such dialogue continued with the Church Fathers, St Clement, Justin Martyr, and St Augustine. In the Middle Ages St Thomas Aquinas produced a set of works for theology students called the *Summa Theologica*; but he also produced a work entitled the *Summa Contra Gentiles* or the 'Work for, or addressed to the Gentiles or pagans'. In that work he does not presuppose Christian faith but rather uses the arguments and approaches of the philosophical dialogue, which was underway in the Middle Ages, with Muslim and Jewish philosophers.

Theologians use ideas which arise from secular philosophy (increasingly even the Protestant traditions found they could not resist this process as time went on), and philosophy is a medium for evangelisation because it can make a case for the truths of faith in terms of reasoning that those outside the Church can appreciate. So, the Church does not teach that non-Catholics who do not go to Mass on Sunday are guilty of mortal sin, (although it does argue simply in terms of human reason that keeping Sunday 'holy' or special is good for the family and society). However, the Church does teach that abortion or exploitation of the poor are grave offences even when committed by non-Christians, since in terms of human reasonableness and responsibility alone one can demonstrate that these are violations of basic human good. When the Church enters the debate in such areas she does so with an assurance that such rights are inviolable which comes both from Revelation and from reason, but insofar as she engages non-Christians in debate she involves herself in debate at the level of philosophical ethics.

It is sometimes argued that the Church erred by going to the other extreme, that as simple, primitive Christianity was left behind the Church sold out to Greek philosophy by turning the preaching of the Gospel into a Greek philosophical system. On this view, the great Councils of the Church, which had to define Catholic faith regarding the nature of the Trinity and Christ Our Lord, became trapped in human philosophy. Another example would be the doctrine of the substantial change of bread and wine into the Body, Blood, Soul and Divinity of Our Lord. Transubstantiation, as we refer to this, was, on this view a corruption of faith by Aristotelian philosophy, which dominated the Church until the seventeenth century. But as the Holy Father indicates in *Fides et Ratio* (Chapter IV), and as many Catholic theologians and historians have argued this theory of 'hellenisation' is quite wide of the historical mark. Rather the dialogue between faith and philosophy was always one of 'critical tension'. St Paul dialogued with the Greek philosophers as we have noted, but he also affirms that the Christian doctrines of a God who becomes man and dies on the cross is 'folly to the Greeks'. This dialogue in tension or 'dialectic', as some call it, meant that Greek and Roman thought were bent and buckled by the new doctrines of Christianity concerning God, Salvation and human morality. The new wine could not be poured into the old wineskins, but pieces of the sundered old wineskins could certainly be used as Christian faith and preaching developed. This is true for Aristotle's influence. The Fathers looked upon Aristotle with some suspicion and even when his thought entered in a new way into the medieval Christian West it did so in the context of 'critical dialogue'. St Thomas Aquinas who used Aristotle's thought in many ways went beyond it and altered it, and, in fact, in the case of transubstantiation St Thomas' thought actually goes against some fundamental tenets of Aristotle's philosophy concerning how one thing can be said to change into another state. In 1277 the Archbishop of Paris condemned 219 Aristotelian propositions which appeared to go against the Christian doctrine of God and His utter freedom in creating. It is interesting to observe in this regard that modern scholars of the history of science, like Stanley Jaki and A.C. Crombie, show that this Church condemnation played a vital role in the rise of modern science. For the largely beneficial influence of Aristotle's thought on scientific development was offset by the way his thought tended to emphasise 'arm-chair' philosophising in areas where only scientific experimental method could answer questions. The Church rejection of those elements at once stimulated scientific experimentation in order to discover how God had actually created the Universe; for given that God was free to do as he wisely willed, one could not, *pace*, Aristotle, work out in advance how He *must* have done so.

Pope John Paul II in *Fides et Ratio*, then, encourages all Catholics to deepen their understanding of the rich tradition of Catholic philosophy as part of a renewal in evangelisation. But what is philosophy?

I have already given some indications above regarding an answer to this question. For as we have seen the Holy Father wants to stress, in the encyclical, that we are all philosophers: that the desire for truth and value and beauty is what is most human about us. The sustained and explicit reflection on things like truth, value, the ultimate meaning of life and the universe, are what philosophy is concerned with. If one goes into a philosophy department in a modern university one will observe that the subjects taught include some of the following: logic, epistemology, metaphysics, history of philosophy, philosophy of science, philosophy of Art (or aesthetics), ethics. Logic is certainly an important area and has some importance for evangelisation and apologetics. Advanced logic as studied in universities enters into the realm of mathematical symbolism and, indeed, may appear to be a rather abstruse subject with little relevance to everyday life (it is interesting to observe, for what it is worth, that this symbolic logic developed by philosophers like Venn, Bole, B. Russell, C.S. Peirce and others led to the development of the electronic computer). However, a study of what is called 'informal logic' can be useful in helping one reflect on good and bad ways of arguing. One may have had the experience of, perhaps, seeing some pro-abortionist on television arguing in a way that one could see in some way did not 'stand up'. A study of logic can help to improve one's 'seeing' of what does and what does not stand to reason in these cases.

Even a 'little logic' can go a long way in helping one to see some of the rather foolish doctrines that have become established in the 'politically correct' creeds of western societies; doctrines that resist Catholic evangelisation. So one has the dogma of 'lazy relativism': every view or position is as good or true as every other one. As we noted above, relativism, even cultural relativism is not new; the ancient Greeks knew it. A little logic shows such a doctrine to be nonsense, for it is a self-destructive or self-defeating position. Why? Because if I say that every position is equally true I am at once excluding as false the position that holds 'not every position is equally true', but then I claimed I was, in fact, excluding no position as false!

The fact that, as I said, the ancient Greeks knew this relativism, and many of them demonstrated its folly, shows the importance of the history of philosophy for an adult Catholic faith and apologetic. Theology has been influenced by different philosophical ideas throughout the ages, so it is important to understand the history of philosophy in the process of deepening one's knowledge of the faith. However, simply studying that history can dramatically tarnish the lustre of many of the 'politically correct' anti-Christian myths of the present by demonstrating that what is put forward as exciting and 'new' is not so. A great apologist and evangeliser for the faith in the twentieth century, whose works are ever worthy of attention, was the convert G.K. Chesterton. If ever there was an 'instinctive philosopher' or 'instinctive logician' (he was not an academic philosopher) who wielded the logical axe against the anti-Catholic myths of the twentieth century, but always with great wit and warmth, it was Chesterton. Chesterton had the knack of reducing to one witty phrase a whole mass of philosophical and theological debate. Two examples may be useful here. Regarding the importance of philosophy and reason in developing an adult Catholic faith for evangelisation, (which Pope John Paul insists upon), Chesterton's remark that 'the only alternative to thought-out thought is unthought-out thought' comes to mind. That is, in order to evangelise effectively we need to become aware of the assumptions and presuppositions of the thinking of the culture around us. Often, as I have pointed out, such thinking is 'politically correct' and shallow even to the point of being illogical. Further, a study of the history of philosophy and culture can help us to see where many of these unthought-out anti-Christian assumptions have come from: it can make us aware of our cultural context and give us some critical distance from it so that we do not simply drift along with it (and away from our faith) because 'that's what everybody does'. If we do not take up the challenge of thinking through the thought and assumptions of our time, we run the risk of being passively carried along by the myths of the crowd, myths, which may lead us to drift away from our faith. Another philosophical gem from Chesterton has to do with defending the right and responsibility of the Catholic to believe in dogmas. Of course for the 'cool cultural elite' of the twentieth century 'dogma' or 'dogmatic' are dirty words. But Chesterton's retort is: 'There are only two types of people: those who believe in dogmas and know they do and those who believe in dogmas and don't know that they do'. The point is a profound philosophical one: many of our beliefs are taken on trust, and that trust is at the basis of the development of society and the sciences and humanities. For example, when I believe eminent scientists about the age of the earth or in something I have not discovered myself. If each person were to do away with belief and start again, each person would have to go back to the stage of pre-Cro-Magnon man. This is a point also insisted upon by Newman and the Catholic philosopher-theologian Bernard Lonergan.

In reading the encyclical *Fides et Ratio,* one will encounter repeatedly the Pope's insistence on the importance of the areas in philosophy of epistemology, or 'theory of knowledge', and metaphysics, or 'philosophical knowledge of reality'. These areas are, according to the Holy Father, vitally important for theology and for an effective preaching of the faith. The dangers in this area, he claims, are of 'subjectivism' in the area of theory of knowledge, (such that one will end up denying the possibility of knowing objective truth), and, with regard to metaphysics, that of denying that there can be such philosophical knowledge of the world. I will now look at each of these areas in turn, reflecting upon their importance for Catholic faith and the preaching of that faith, and I will suggest a philosophical approach which, I believe, supports the positions Pope John Paul takes on these issues.

In *Fides et Ratio* the Holy Father points in the direction of a way to do philosophy, or argue for a philosophical position. He claims (*Fides et Ratio* 4), that one may discern a kind of 'implicit philosophy', implicit within the reasonable and responsible operations of human persons. Further, he points out (*Fides et Ratio* 83) that modern philosophical approaches which begin with the human person and human consciousness, may provide a valuable and enriching starting point as long as a study of subjectivity opens out into objectivity: into an analysis of the way human persons can come to objective truth, and reflection upon metaphysical truths, that is, truths concerning the reality of the world and the human person arrived at through philosophical investigation.

I believe the philosophical work of the Jesuit philosopher-theologian Bernard Lonergan (1904-84) provides a singularly fruitful way of pursuing the kind of philosophical approach the Holy Father is indicating in the encyclical. On a personal note, I would say that during thirteen years studying and teaching in secular, even somewhat anti-religious philosophical environments I found no other contemporary Catholic thinker whose work translates so effectively into the secular, non-religious philosophical world as does Lonergan's.

In the area of epistemology, or theory of knowledge, Lonergan's work (which emerges from influences such as Aquinas, Newman and modern English-speaking and continental thought) supports Pope John Paul's contention that a proper study of subjectivity brings one to acknowledge the objectivity of human knowing, and the human capacity to know truth. Defending that capacity is a vital aspect of evangelisation, for the Catholic claim is that we are made for truth and recognise the truth of God's revelation through grace, when we receive it. On Lonergan's view far from objectivity and subjectivity being in opposition the truth is that, as he puts it, 'Objectivity is the fruit of authentic subjectivity'. If I want to understand a friend's moods and attitudes I should want to be objective in doing so, rather than being rash or biased. Objectivity does involve being 'dispassionate' in one sense, in trying to look at things clearly, but it may also involve burning passion: the great scientist is passionate for the truth. Developing elements put forward in St Thomas Aquinas's work on human knowing, Lonergan develops what he terms a 'Cognitional structure' account of knowing which emerges on three levels of our consciousness. There is a level of 'Experience' on which we see, hear, taste, smell and feel; a level of 'Understanding' on which we ask questions about our experience, try to come to insight, develop concepts, ideas, theories, hypotheses; and a level of 'Judgement' on which we ask questions about our insights, concepts and theories and attempt to judge whether they are true or false (whether or not they correspond with objective reality). In a way, on this view, each one of us is an internalised courtroom: we listen to theories' pro and con that are put forward to explain the data and we attempt to reach a verdict, or judgement. A further aspect to Lonergan's approach which should be emphasised here is that he employs the kind of 'self-destructs' or 'self-supports' arguments we mentioned above. Just as Aquinas points out that the man who claims as true 'there is no truth' is involved in a self-destructive argument, Lonergan argues that if one attempts to argue that Cognitional structure and its three levels is not the case, one will find that one is using the very activities outlined in Cognitional structure in order to do so.

This kind of argument is also used by Lonergan and others to develop a metaphysics or philosophical approach to knowledge of reality, and the argument is pursued in such a way as to bear out the Holy Father's point that there are implicit principles in the thinking and moral choosing of human persons. The approach is, in fact, to make these principles explicit. Metaphysics is an area of philosophy that treats such matters as the ultimate nature of reality, of God, of the nature of the human person (does that person have a spiritual element a soul?), and is very important for faith. The Christian view of the Universe holds that it is created by a good and loving God, so that the children of God would return to Him, through free, engraced, acts of love. It is as true today as it was in the first centuries of Christianity that one cannot preach this world-view as reality without engaging in dialogue and debate in the area of metaphysics, in the area of human thought which reflects upon the ultimate nature of the world and of the human person.

Metaphysics has been in and out of vogue in philosophy in various traditions at various times. Thirty years ago Anglo-American philosophy as a result of both its positivist ('only science is objective'), and linguistic analysis ('only ordinary language is meaningful') phases was largely hostile to metaphysics, while continental philosophy (phenomenology, existentialism, personalism) appeared fairly fertile ground. This situation is, in a number of ways now reversed; although I do not think religious people and even theologians are sufficiently aware of this. While post-modern deconstruction is all the rage in continental thought (one should be careful of over-generalisation, however), and there is a consequent denial of the mind's capacity to attain objectivity, reality and therefore the realities posited in the metaphysics of Aristotle or St Thomas, in Anglo-American thought there is an upsurge in metaphysical thinking. This is evident if one looks through the last few years of such key Anglo-Saxon philosophical journals as *Mind* or *Philosophy*, and if one turns to the work of leading philosophers in this field including David Lewis, D. Widgeons, Alex Oliver, and D. Armstrong.

Let us now return to the question of an approach to metaphysics that makes that which is latent and implicit in the mind explicit. One such principle that we bring to knowledge of reality is, as the Holy Father says the principle of 'non-contradiction', the principle that something cannot be both false and true of reality. This is a principle with which we have worked, of which we have been aware since early childhood: we know that there cannot both be and not be milk in the fridge. Scientists also work with this principle, and presuppose it: note, they do not attempt to prove it, for it is not something you can check by looking down a microscope. Another implicit principle used by all of us that may be rendered explicit is one formulated by Lonergan: 'Reality (Being) is that which is to be known by intelligence and reason'. That is, it is to be known through the operations of the understanding and judging levels of Cognitional structure. The principle says, in other words, 'reality is intelligible'. This does not mean that we are limited in what we know or may come to know, but it does mean that in order to be, something must be inherently intelligible or knowable. The way to validate this claim, indeed the way to move this from being an implicit principle with which we all operate to an explicit principle, is, again, to attempt to argue against it. For to use intelligence and reason to argue against the principle that 'whatever is to be known by intelligence and reason' is self-defeating. Notice how this principle of intelligibility is presupposed by all scientific work. Scientific theories about the world come and go, no doubt science has progressed and some broadly held theories about the Universe will not be revised. But it remains that science is inherently revisable. If that is the case what is even more basic than any given scientific theory is the intelligence and reason we use to revise and improve science. The argument that we can know that, in very broad terms, the universe, reality, is intelligible then leads on to arguments for the existence of God. For the universe could not be if there were not sufficient reason for its existence. Again to argue against sufficient reason is just to mount the same self-defeating argument against intelligibility: if there is not sufficient reason for something then it is not the case, and in arguing against that, one will be arguing in terms of sufficient reason.

Such an approach to metaphysics is also helpful in reflecting upon such key areas as human spirituality and freedom, and upon notions such as 'substance' and 'accidents', important for reflection upon, among other matters, the Blessed Sacrament. However, space does not permit such further reflection here.

I believe in the profound importance the message *Fides et Ratio* has for all Catholics involved in the work of evangelisation (that is all of us!) on the threshold of the third millennium. The Catholic philosophical heritage is a veritable gold mine, which for a number of reasons remained somewhat neglected in the years after Vatican II. We now see that in the new period of evangelisation emerging in the West there is a growing awareness of the need to mine that precious seam in order to retrieve its profound insights and ways of thought for a renewed apologetic. Such an apologetic invites others to see, and to share in, the wonderful cogency and beauty, which the gift of Catholic faith brings to human life.

Further Reading

His Holiness Pope John Paul II, *Fides et Ratio.*

His Holiness Pope John Paul II, *Veritatis Splendor.*

The Catechism of the Catholic Church, 286, 1951.

Second Vatican Council (A. Flannery, editor), *Gaudium et Spes,* 19-21.

Beards, Andrew, 'Self-refutation and Self-knowledge', *Gregorianum,* 76 (1995), 555-573.

— 'Christianity, Interculturality and Salvation', *The Thomist,* forthcoming.

Jaki, Stanley L., *God and the Cosmologists,* Edinburgh, Scottish Academic Press, 1989.

Kreeft, Peter, *A Short Summa,* San Francisco, Ignatius Press, 1993.

Meynell, Hugo A., *Redirecting Philosophy,* Toronto, University of Toronto Press, 1998.

Schmitz, Kenneth L., *At the Centre of the Human Drama,* Washington, Catholic University of America Press, 1993.

Tekippe, Terry J., 'What is Lonergan up to?' in *Insight: A Primer,* Collegeville, Liturgical Press, 1996.

MORAL THEOLOGY POST VATICAN II

FR GEORGE WOODALL

Introduction

The catechetical work of the Church includes transmitting moral teaching, since accepting Jesus Christ, the fullness of God's self-revelation, is not just a matter of faith content, but entails a life-long radical conversion of heart, transforming the way we live.[1] Self-giving faith in Christ, immersion in Christ through baptism, presupposes and demands that self-centredness and sin be replaced by love of God and neighbour. Participating in the sacrificial death of the Lord to rise in Him to eternal life implies this total self-gift; the Christian moral life is inseparably part of discipleship.

Morality concerns not only Christians, but also all people. An earlier moral theology sought to present its message in terms accessible to all, but texts devised to assist confessors in the pastoral care of penitents often focused on duty and law, with only incidental references to Christ or to the Bible. A renewal of Scripture study and of Christology inspired a renewal of moral theology.

Vatican II and the Renewal of Moral Theology

Moral theological renewal was urged as part of a general appeal for Scripture to be made the 'very soul' of theology.[2] It was to be rooted more firmly in sacred Scripture and in the mystery of Christ, and was to highlight the 'exalted vocation of the faithful in Christ' to help them to 'bring forth fruit in charity for the life of the world'.[3] It was in *Gaudium et spes* that the Council's dual focus on Christ and on openness to non-

Christians and non-believers emerged most completely. The first part of that document both examined moral concerns common to all (the significance of the human person, of his role in society and of his action in the world) and emphasised that the only adequate answer to them was to be found in the light of the Gospel of Christ.[4]

The clarion call of the renewal of moral theology in the aftermath of the Council was that it should be personalistic. This concept was not precisely defined, but it seemed to mean that moral theology should not be so legalistic, that the human nature under-pinning natural moral law should not be seen as impersonal or primarily biological, that conscience should assume greater responsibility than mere obedience to authoritative decrees, and that moral theology should become person-centred rather than act-centred.[5]

'Humanae vitae' and the Crisis in Moral Theology

The renewal of moral theology did not occur in a vacuum. The pastoral crisis arising from Paul VI's teaching on responsible parenthood quickly transferred to a crisis of moral theological doctrine in general. This encompassed the features of personalism just noted, but it extended into a systematic questioning of Magisterial competence to teach on moral matters.[6] The inter-action between the pastoral crisis and the challenges of personalism provoked a major critique of the evaluation of moral acts. Versions of what has come to be called proportionalism queried the traditional moral theological understanding of intrinsically immoral acts, of objective morality, of specific teachings of the Magisterium. The crisis in moral theology was fed by subsequent teachings especially over sexual questions such as premarital sex and homosexual acts, and bioethical issues such as euthanasia, abortion, assisted procreation, etc.[7] Moral theological renewal soon turned into a battle ground, revealing wide-ranging and deep fissures between rival groups of theologians. The debate increasingly lacked precision of thought; acerbic exchanges of assertions and slogans hampered the authentic renewal of moral theology and did a serious pastoral disservice to the faithful.[8]

The key aspects of moral theological renewal remain valid. It will be important to evaluate them and to assess their significance for authentic catechesis.

Scripture and the Renewal of Moral Theology

The *General Directory of Catechesis* calls for Sacred Scripture with Tradition to 'permeate' catechesis 'with Biblical and evangelical thought, spirit and attitudes'.[9] This coheres with Vatican II's instructions on the renewal of moral theology. How to achieve authentic renewal on that basis is perhaps not as straightforward as it first appeared.

It is not enough to pepper texts with Biblical citations. As the word of God written in the words of men, Scriptural texts need to be understood according to their human authors' intentions, their literary genre, their historical and cultural context (*Sitz-im-Leben*).[10] This task of exegesis is a precise one, demanding care and expertise; it is not to be reduced to the personal impressions of teachers, catechists or others, whose skills lie elsewhere. Valuable exegetical work has been done for moral theology by a painstaking analysis of the moral content of the diverse books of the New Testament.[11] An investigation of the context of commandment, the historical and cultural settings for various redactions of the Decalogue in general and the treatment of particular precepts in the varied genres and authors of the Old and New Testaments provides a model for Biblical moral theology.[12]

A Biblically renewed moral theology needs to go beyond exegesis. Nor will a pious reading of relevant texts suffice. Renewal was to foster a 'scientific presentation of moral theology'.[13] Some texts on morals seem to have little to do with today's affairs, such as those dealing with whether or not Christians might eat meat, which might have come from temples of idols without incurring the risk of idolatry or apostasy (cf. 1 Cor 8, 10; Rom 14; Acts, 15). A proper hermeneutic is required to identify the meaning of the sacred text itself, points of contact with today (e.g. ways to respect the conscience of the weak or un-informed) and so an application of the text.[14] Other texts which may seem more directly applicable need to be carefully assessed too.

Beyond distinctions of poetry, law, etc., moral writing is often classified as paraenetic (exhortative) or normative. The first urges us to do what we already know to be right or good, but which we tend to overlook, by giving motives for action (e.g., not to misuse the body sexually because the body is the temple of the Holy Spirit, we are members of Christ's Body (1 Cor 6:12-20). The second seeks to work out the norm which ought to operate for a given situation, (e.g. the extent to which Jesus' teaching on divorce and remarriage applies in the Greek world (1 Cor 7:10-16), to settle its content and its binding force.[15]

These principles seem fine in the abstract. Post-Conciliar moral theology has seen excesses in their interpretation and application. Where divergence between the Biblical author's horizon and contemporary context has been exaggerated, it has sometimes seemed as if the Bible has nothing to say beyond giving a general perspective. More usually, a Scriptural text is said not to support a moral norm today as morally binding without exceptions. The intention of the author has been said to be other than the preoccupations of modern readers.[16] Finally, some have claimed that nearly all moral teaching in the Bible has an essentially paraenetic function, designed to stimulate us to do better, but not to establish norms binding on us today.[17]

To illustrate this problem for moral theology and for moral catechesis, consider the example of the Biblical condemnation of homosexual acts as evil.[18] Rules of Jewish hospitality in Genesis and of ritual purity in Leviticus, the impact of idolatry in Romans, and the need to amend behaviour at odds with the life of the baptised in 1 Corinthians and 1 Timothy may be the main focus of these texts. Reference to homosexuality is 'almost parenthetic, ... not the main concern'.[19] Other preoccupations of the Biblical authors in texts cited, the lack of coverage of all homosexual acts, the paraenetic character of the New Testament texts, lead some moralists to raise seemingly rhetorical questions about the application of such texts to prohibiting all such acts today.[20] Yet, the Bible never mentions such acts without strong moral condemnation. The fact of other concerns, even primary, in a text does not invalidate the truth of what is secondary, especially as its truth would have been clear and not in need of analysis.[21]

This issue demonstrates how complex the Biblical renewal of moral theology is. Similar approaches to a range of moral questions could mislead us into thinking that the Bible is unreliable in what it teaches on morals, can only provide generic exhortations to do good. Hence Pope John Paul II's proper concern for the truth-content of Biblical morality:

> In the moral catechesis of the Apostles, besides exhortation and directions connected to specific historical and cultural situations, we find an ethical teaching with precise rules of behaviour.[22]

A Biblically renewed moral theology can and should bring out the vocational dimension of morality for the Christian as a disciple of the Lord. It can motivate him (paraenesis) to live by radical Gospel values, challenging a view that morality is only about obeying abstract rules. The Sermon on the Mount, for all its paraenesis, also makes normative moral demands. Avoiding murder will not suffice, but violating a brother's dignity and basic rights (the root of what leads to murder – not calling him 'fool' or 'renegade') are enjoined as Gospel demands (Mt 5:21-26). The warning that a vague norm of agapaic love risks an excessive distinction between formal disposition and concrete action, with almost any concrete behaviour thus being legitimised, is timely.[23] A careful hermeneutic, seeking a true fusion of Biblical and modern perspectives to uncover the full moral demand on us now, neither renders the word of God vacuous nor exposes it to the danger of manipulation, even subconscious, by a dilution of its import for our discipleship today.

Natural Moral Law

An area of intense debate in post-Conciliar moral theology has been that of natural moral law. Positivist extrinsicism perhaps is inclined to declarations of right and wrong rather than to facilitating an understanding of moral responsibility. Theology sought a Christocentric focus even for natural law.[24] The *Humanae vitae* dispute provoked a major problem as the encyclical and Magisterial teaching on sexual and medical ethics before and after were accused of embracing a biologistic or physicalist concept of human nature, not a personalist one. Rooting human morality in what man had in common with animals rather than what was specific to his dignity as a rational and spiritual being was another criticism.[25] An alleged derivation of moral obligation from biological facts (an 'ought' from an 'is') implied fallacious argumentation.[26] How has Catholic moral theology responded?

On the one hand, there are expressions, which, taken in isolation and out of context, could give the impression of biologism to a superficial reader. *Humanae vitae* refers to 'biological processes' and 'biological laws which are part of the human person' (n. 10), God-given 'natural laws and rhythms' (n. 11), 'direct interruption of the generative processes' (n. 14) and 'natural rhythms immanent in the generative processes' (n. 16).[27] This would seem to lend support to those who seek a broader, more personalistic approach. Yet, this whole section follows a clear statement that this moral problem, like all others, 'must be considered *beyond partial perspectives* – whether of the biological or psychological, demographic or sociological orders – in the light of an *integral vision of man and of his vocation*, not only ... natural and earthly, but also ... supernatural and eternal (n. 7).[28] An incisive, rich résumé of what marital love is (n. 9) is followed by a broad range of factors involved in responsible parenthood (n. 10). This integrated, unitary anthropology, summarised in *Gaudium et spes* (n. 14) as man being 'one in body and soul' (*corpore et anima unus*) is reflected in his being characterised by the intra-personal dimension just noted, an inter-personal (social) dimension towards others and a transcendental dimension towards God.[29]

On the other hand, criticism of alleged biologism based on higher human capacities stresses autonomous decision-making and tends towards relativism, to a rejection of specific moral absolutes. Thus, we are urged to become 'creator(s) of an original version of human sexuality', to 'invent the unedited truth of our liberated humanity'.[30] On this view moral norms would be what man 'in an autonomous manner lays down for himself', having their source 'exclusively in human reason'.[31] Yet, reason is not an absolute, but is bound by God and by truth, so that 'the autonomy of reason cannot mean that reason itself creates values and moral norms'.[32] Personalism as responsibility and freedom needs qualification.

Another aspect of the critical reaction against 'biologism' is precisely a lack of proper attention to the corporeal dimension of the person; a dualism of a contrary kind can emerge. Versions of natural law seeking to embrace historicity, cultural diversity, comparative sociology, 'whole-ness' may impress initially, but often lack precise analysis as to how such factors and our bodily dimension ought to operate normatively.[33] Either the bodily aspect is ignored or it can even be treated as if it were a field of action in which the 'person' (reason, freedom, spirit) is to act; the body is effectively objectified.[34] This mentality lies behind the slogan: 'I have the right to do what I want with my own body', often asserted to claim a 'right' to destroy another, distinct human being. The significance of the debate can be grasped not only by thinking of its relevance for abortion, but by reflecting upon sexual conduct in which persons use others for their own gratification and discard them or upon the exploitation of those not protected at work or unjustly paid and denied access to basic needs. The debate over natural moral law and the underlying concept of human nature has led to some clarification. 'Natural law is that law of human conduct which arises from the *full reality of human nature as ordered to its ultimate end*.'[35] It concerns the true and complete good of the human person, insofar as it can be grasped without specific divine revelation, that good being multi-dimensional and integrated. Our true good comprises *basic human goods*.[36] It cannot be deliberately neglected, much less directly attacked, without sin. Nor may any basic good directly be attacked for the supposed promotion of another; the *integral* fulfilment of the person is not just, not advanced by such action, but is directly compromised. Such behaviour would be intrinsically morally wrong; it would damage our true good, our *integral* human fulfilment.[37]

Recognising the moral good, including duties in regard to the basic human goods, does not imply violating the naturalistic fallacy. Aquinas did not canonise biology; *recta ratio* identified moral duty. The '*inclinationes naturales*' are discussed within a comparison between practical and speculative reasoning, not the derivation of the former from the latter.[38] A direct apprehension of the moral claim avoids the fallacy.[39] This philosophical clarification has enabled moral theology to renew its understanding of natural law.

Alert to this asperous debate, the Magisterium has refined its presentation of natural law teaching. Although only a careless reading of *Humanae vitae* could suggest biologism, that misinterpretation and the damaging pastoral confusion subsequent to the encyclical have caused the Magisterium to specify explicitly what its means by nature and natural law.

> ... The true meaning of natural law ... refers to man's proper and primordial nature, ... the person himself *corpore et anima unus*, in the unity of all his spiritual and biological inclinations and of all the other specific characteristics necessary for the pursuit of his end ... This law cannot be thought of as simply a set of norms on the biological level ... Only in reference to the human person in his 'unified totality' ... can the specifically human meaning of the body be grasped.[40]

The renewal of natural moral law has encompassed the theological dimension. Thomas Aquinas considered it in a theological context in the *Summa theologiae*, both in the *exitus-reditus* scheme of the whole work and more specifically in the treatise on law between the eternal law of God and the new law of grace. As what can be known by right reason in principle, it remains open to God and his revelation in Christ, yet it facilitates dialogue with non-believers and can be a preparation for the Gospel. Its correct discernment in a fallen world is aided by grace and our capacity to fulfil it likewise depends upon grace.

The Moral Act and Virtuous Living

A further dimension of the personalist renewal of moral theology sought to emphasise persons rather than acts. A reaction against a de-personalised dissection of human acts may explain this. Following the *Humanae vitae* debates, this appeared as the claim that the person should himself decide what ought to be done on the basis of the 'totality' of ends, object and circumstances.[41] Analogous to an alleged 'biologism' of natural law was the charge of a 'physicalist' analysis of the moral act. An object described in terms of *what is done* appears mechanistic, de-humanised, and inadequate to the complexities of moral action, apart from the person who acts. An act presented in its sheer physicality is inherently ambiguous for the moralist, capable of varying evaluations according to the agent's intention and to its circumstances. The concept of *finis operis* can seem odd in that an 'act', it would seem, cannot have an end as such, while the *finis operantis* acquires greater weight by being what the agent purposes.[42] Finally, an act-centred morality implies a disjointed moral life in contrast to the life-long pursuit of Christian beatitude.[43] This last point is entirely valid, but how are act, intention and integrated moral existence inter-related?

Plausible as these arguments are, their elaboration was perhaps in origin the result of an attempt to provide pastoral guidance to many people surprised and even shocked that Paul VI did not permit contraception, at least through the anovulant pill. Could the norm taught be seen to apply as an ideal or on most occasions, but admit of exceptions in particularly pressing circumstances for an proportionate reason?[44] The issue raises a general question; can *any* moral norm apply universally?[45] No moral theologian actually says that *no* norms apply universally, but where such validity is accorded only to 'transcendental norms of moral goodness', the question recurs as that of the universal validity of certain 'categorial norms of moral rightness'. A denial of 'specific moral absolutes' and a proportionalist analysis of the moral act have thrown into question not only the doctrine on responsible parenthood, but a range of Magisterial teachings on morals and indeed the very competence of the Magisterium to teach on morals in any way beyond paraenesis.

One development in the complex renewal of moral theology since Vatican II is the more precise specification of the moral object of the human act as more than merely physical. The same physical gesture is capable of varying interpretations: putting money into the SVP box at church can be a virtuous act of charity, an act of hypocrisy or a preliminary to robbery.[46] Claims that physical actions constitute the object of the act as opposed to the agent's personal intention are misleading. Precisely because the moral object (*finis operis*) is what a person *deliberately chooses* to do, it is a critical element in the evaluation of the act. 'By the object of a given moral act one cannot mean a process or event of the purely physical order. ... Rather, the object is the proximate end of a deliberate decision'.[47] The agent's intention (*finis operantis*) is also critical for evaluating the morality of an act, but a morally good intention does not justify morally wrong (deliberately chosen) means. What we deliberately choose to do determines the morality of the act just as does the reason why we do it; if either is morally wrong or 'disordered', the act is morally vitiated.[48] An action 'incapable of being ordered to the good', *intrinsically morally disordered*, cannot be justified by any good intention.[49] This sort of act has been especially in view in moral theological debate.

The seemingly impressive claim to consider not just the object (wrongly seen as physicalist), but also the act's end and circumstances as a 'total' reality and to permit a merely 'premoral evil' at times for a 'proportionate reason' is weak when viewed more closely. Of key significance is the act's relationship to the true end of life; judging that is a moral and not merely a premoral evaluation. Intrinsically evil acts 'are contrary to the true goal of human life and can never serve as an end to it'.[50] Further, it is often not possible to know all the consequences of an act, to assess proximate and remote effects accurately, to judge objectively when under personal pressure, above all to 'weigh' qualitatively different (incommensurate) goods, etc. Too often overlooked is the impact of the moral act upon the person performing it, the inevitable self-determination of the person as just, vicious, etc., according to what he deliberately chooses to do.[51]

Post-Conciliar moral theology has not successfully emerged from an 'act-centred' to a 'person-centred' approach in some respects. Such terms can be mere slogans whose vagueness masks a growing subjectivism and relativism, as objective norms are attenuated and adapted through proportionalism. Fundamental option theory attempted to provide an integration of the moral life, but that too is ridden with ambiguity, especially in versions where a positive Christ-centred option is alleged to be compatible with intrinsically immoral acts. If this contradiction is avoided, the act of faith itself can be seen as a true fundamental option, the originary, directing and integrating factor in Christian moral life, but reinforced, weakened or reversed through our deliberate acts.[52] Channelling this through a major vocational, life option is important.[53]

A more effective implementation of Vatican II's call to highlight the faithful's vocation in Christ has been through attempts to examine the role of virtue. The deliberate pursuit of the moral good as such for its own sake and the integrating role of the virtues in the moral life of the individual combat an atomistic act-centred limitation. Proponents have tried to recover the Thomistic virtue-structure of moral theology, embracing objective moral norms, specific moral absolutes, etc.[54] This has permitted the recognition that the person realises himself through deliberate moral acts. Morality is not just about what he does, but who he becomes; yet who he becomes depends inexorably on what he deliberately chooses to do.

The Authority of the Magisterium to Teach on Moral Matters

The crisis in post-Conciliar moral theology has been felt very powerfully in the dissent from Magisterial teaching on moral matters both in the lives of the faithful and in the writings of many moralists. Here, too, perhaps an earlier reliance on obedience to declared norms provoked a reaction. Querying the Magisterium's competence to teach authoritatively on moral matters unless they directly concerned salvation, at the 'transcendental' level, undermined acceptance of norms of conduct.

The authority and vocation of the Bishops of the Catholic Church in union with the Pope to teach in the name of Christ with the assistance of the Holy Spirit is here presupposed.[55] The function of the Magisterium in moral matters is above all to associate the light of the Gospel of Christ with the moral problems of the day.[56] No exception can be taken to the claim that its *originary* function is the positive one of stimulating believers to adhere to the Gospel and of guiding them to find positive ways of bringing its message to bear in society. This would imply a *subsidiary* function of indicating negatively what is to be avoided as incompatible with that.[57] While this will often involve exhortation, moral Magisterium must include normative teaching even in respect of norms of conduct. Even so, its role is not to replace, but to enlighten, conscience; 'The Church puts herself always and only at the service of conscience'.[58]

Whether in integrating valid insights of human reason or in challenging contemporary culture (including members of the Church) on the basis of Christ's Gospel, the Magisterium's proper authority is not in technology or science as such, nor does it lie in offering opinions about current developments; it lies precisely in the *moral dimension* of such realities.[59] While particular Magisterial teachings on moral matters are more likely to be understood and followed if the rationale behind them is clear and while there is a duty for the Magisterium to render its teachings as transparent as possible, it is primarily the Magisterium's role to give authoritative moral doctrine rather than the explanations and analysis which are more precisely the task of theology.

What is the degree of authority involved and what ought our response to be to such teaching? Non-infallible teaching is the most common. This means that there is not the absolute guarantee that there could not be an error in a specific teaching, but this does not imply that there is likely to be error. Rather, the assistance of the Holy Spirit, even here, indicates a *praesumptio veritatis.* Where infallibility is operative, the assistance of the Holy Spirit is such as to preclude any possibility of error, which does not prevent later development of the doctrine in a manner consonant with, and never contrary to, it.

An *obsequium religiosum* of the mind and will is due to authoritative teaching, while assent is due to doctrine infallibly proposed. Anyone who 'disagrees' with a doctrine he knows has been infallibly taught knows (in his conscience) that his opinion is necessarily false; it cannot justify acting contrary to the teaching. Where the teaching is authoritative, but not necessarily infallibly proposed, an *obsequium religiosum* means 'following' (*sequi* = to follow) the teaching for a *religious* motive, i.e. because it has been given in the name of Christ and with His authority to enlighten conscience.

The virtue of prudence demands that we seek the truth and implement it. An emotional reaction against a specific teaching or a culturally conditioned inclination to reject it is inadequate. An *obsequium* implies a readiness to seek to understand the teaching given, a willingness to seek advice from those not opposed to it, who understand it, an attempt to form conscience on the basis of it and to live accordingly. It involves not ignoring the teaching, not treating it as merely one opinion on a par with our own or with anyone else's, even a theologian's.[60] If we have an objective doubt (not merely a subjective one), we cannot be acting prudently if we 'prefer' our 'own opinion or the opinion of theologians to the certain teaching of the Magisterium'.[61] In relation to *non-infallibly proposed teaching*, the point is that, in doubt, we ought to follow the best guide to truth available, but our doubt is not a surer guide to truth than what the Magisterium has taught (it is certain that the teaching has been given), nor can the opinions of theologians contradicting that teaching be a surer guide to us in our doubt that what the Magisterium teaches because of the authority with which it teaches. This does leave open the possibility of acting contrary not to Magisterial teaching in general, but to a specific moral teaching, where a person is honestly convinced (i.e. is not in doubt), not through obduracy or pride but sincerely *both* that the Magisterium is wrong in this particular instance (only) *and* that God *requires* that he act contrary to that teaching. Our duty to live by the truth requires that we follow that teaching. As B. Ashley puts it:

> This obligation arises not from arguments given by the Church – these arguments may sometimes seem less probable to us than contrary arguments – but from the authority the Church has from the Holy Spirit which is superior to that of any merely human expert.[62]

Vatican II itself provided important indications of the degree of *obsequium* required: according to the level of Magisterium (the Pope would be higher than an individual bishop), the frequency with which a specific teaching is given, the manner in which it is expressed (e.g., never to be done as intrinsically wrong, an exhortation to find ways positively to foster a virtue, etc.).[63]

One feature of this has been the attempt to explore the implications of *Lumen gentium's* reference to the infallibility of the ordinary universal Magisterium. A tentative application to *Humanae vitae's* doctrine on responsible parenthood was followed by an express claim, with the aim of helping people pastorally not to be misled.[64] It is argued that this applies to any teaching condemning what is intrinsically evil.[65] Pope John Paul II explicitly invoking his role as the successor of St Peter, his communion with the Bishops of the Church and the constant teaching of the Magisterium on the intrinsic immorality of the direct killing of innocent human beings, of direct, procured abortion and of direct euthanasia states that these doctrines are taught by the universal ordinary Magisterium.[66] The very least that can be said of *Humane vitae* is that it is at the highest level of non-infallibly proposed teaching and so demands the highest degree of *obsequium.*

Post-Conciliar moral theology has been very divided on this matter, but an earlier reaction against in the wake of *Humanae vitae* has given way to a more careful and positive analysis of the role of the Magisterium.

The Renewal of Moral Theology: Sexuality

While sexuality has remained an area of deep debate, there have been some notable developments in its presentation in moral theology. First of all, the primacy of procreation has given way to Paul VI's doctrine of the inseparability of the essential meanings of the conjugal act, the unitive and procreative.[67] This development of doctrine incorporates the role of love, an achievement of moral theological trends since 1930. Secondly, an integral anthropology has figured prominently in Papal catecheses on sexuality. The body, not a thing which we have but part of the persons we are, facilitates inter-personal communion and promotes the communion of persons which marriage is to foster (the Pope speaks of the 'nuptial meaning of the body'). The deep personal and inter-personal realities of conjugal love and of procreation, seen within the transcendental relationship with God, form the context for assessing matters of conjugal morality. This anthropological truth has replaced a vague 'personalism', a major achievement owing much to the theology of the present Pope.[68] Thirdly, the vocational dimension has emerged. Vatican II's doctrine of the universal call to holiness, the holiness of the marital vocation and the celibate vocation too feature in this analysis rooted in the Council.[69]

Moral theology has encountered new challenges as homosexual persons seek to justify homosexual intercourse and to live as 'couples', as people *de facto* increasingly cease to marry or remain faithful. In a culture of merely asserted 'rights', moral theology roots authentic rights in truth, anthropological and moral. Persons have rights as created in God's image and likeness, as called to the glory of heaven, not because of their homosexuality or their cohabitation.

One area of study has been that of the moral difference between upright natural family planning and contraception; the latter entails, for some, a contra-life will, for others an inauthentic love neither truly uniting the spouses nor being fruitful.[70]

The implications of these developments for catechesis are considerable. In today's pervasive hedonistic and erotic culture moral catechesis must avoid the relativism that will damage the young and others. The anthropological and moral truths articulated by the Magisterium provide the only satisfactory basis for catechesis. Chastity, not a repressive mechanism, but a positive way to relate to one another properly as sexual beings according to our state in life or vocation is an indispensable virtue to foster with God's help.[71] Certain objective truths need to be pursued as part of this growth; that we neither degrade others, or ourselves, never treat our own bodies or those of others as things we possess, but only as part of who we are as persons. The life-long commitments of marriage and family life or of celibate existence need to be revitalised also in catechesis.

The Renewal of Moral Theology: Bioethics.

In bioethics moral relativism aligned to consequentialism often predominates in our culture. An essentially technical approach that sidesteps the moral question prevails: what people want to do, if the technical means become available, they implement without posing the ethical question proper.[72] The range of issues in medical ethics or bioethics is too vast to permit detailed comment, but Catholic moral theology since the Council has made an irreplaceable contribution to their proper evaluation.

Key points, which have emerged, include the following. The principle of totality inherited from our forebears stated that it was at times permissible to remove or damage the part for the sake of the whole.[73] On this basis, surgery, vaccines, medicines in general may be used where necessary or useful to cure a pathology, limit its advance or reduce suffering. Pius XII's insistence that the principle be restricted to the one individual, to preclude abusive manipulation of some for the 'good' of society as a whole (as in the case of Mengele's Nazi eugenics), would seem to deny the application of the principle to organ or tissue donations from live donors.[74] To call this 'physicalist' and not 'personalist' is misguided. To propose that transplants work on the basis of a principle of charity, excluding the exploitation of the sick and the poor by pecuniary inducements, is good. However, it does not justify a 'personalist' reading of the principle of totality, which fails to maintain the safeguards Pius XII rightly urged. Moral theological debate on live transplants has led to the articulation of a principle of functional integrity, according to which organs or tissues may be donated, provided the donor whose anatomical integrity is affected can never-the-less function effectively (e.g. with one healthy kidney) without serious impairment.[75] This seems to be what John Paul II teaches.[76] It is not 'physicalism', but the authentic personalism of an integrated anthropology that justifies interventions on an individual person by the principle of totality and also transplants from living donors by the principle of functional integrity.

Secondly, intense political debate and moral theological disputes have attended analyses of abortion, experimentation upon the human embryo, etc. To specify human life as a relative, but not absolute, value (salvation is absolute and justifies sacrificing human life in martyrdom) has some validity. The danger of a proportionalist 'weighing' of a life against other values or other lives (e.g. mother/ child) is real. More precisely, bodily life is 'a fundamental good; here below it is the condition for all the other goods'.[77] John Paul II repeatedly refers to it as life 'in its earthly phase'.[78] By reason of its origin in creation and of its destiny in eternal life, he rightly refuses to treat it as a 'good' or 'value' capable of being balanced against others, which are incommensurable with it. Directly and deliberately to attack innocent human life is intrinsically immoral.

Thirdly, scientific and technological developments have presented new challenges to moral theology. An ethical and not merely a technical approach is needed to confront issues at the beginning of life. Factors arguing that the human zygote is not 'personal' (e.g. twinning, implantation, differentiation of cells, absence of the brain cortex, delayed animation) have been used to attempt to justify abortion, destructive experimentation upon the human embryo and now harvesting of embryos for cells for therapeutic cloning. Delayed animation, predicated on long superseded biological presuppositions, lacks plausibility other than as a pretext for performing such procedures. The unique genetic code, the rapid, self-propelled, coordinated process of increasing complexification of the embryo indicate the growth of a new individual from fertilisation in a continuum. With twinning a further individual begins by a kind of asexual reproduction, but no point in the continuum otherwise sees a new being begin to be.[79] Delayed animation, now implausible, can neither be verified nor falsified scientifically, but the possibility that the zygote and embryo could be fully 'personal' is enough to ground the moral obligation not deliberately and directly to destroy or expose to unnecessary risk this innocent human being. The classical moral theological principle of tutiorism, an expression and requirement of prudence, applies in regard to human life.[80] This has led to a development of moral doctrine; the human being is 'to be respected and treated *as a person* from the moment of conception' and his fundamental human rights, firstly the right to life, are to be respected.[81]

Fourthly, although tensions in moral theology continue, the greater recognition of the need for an integrated anthropology and of specific moral absolutes has permitted a more careful treatment of issues. It has facilitated moral theological renewal in a way that has permitted a proper integration of valid insights and acquisitions of inherited moral theology. The principle of double effect with its nuanced, inter-related criteria helps to distinguish the immoral direct perpetration of wrong from an indirect action with foreseen, evil side-effects can sometimes be accepted.[82] It can apply to the administration of drugs, surgery, indirect sterilisation, removing a patient from a ventilator, which has been demonstrated to be futile, etc. As with the object of the human act in general, the distinction between direct and indirect intention or between what is deliberately chosen and what is accepted, as an inevitable side effect is crucial; we are responsible for what we deliberately choose to do.[83]

Areas of bioethics where further moral theological reflection is still needed include the determination of death in a prospective donor of a vital organ, the need for clear informed consent for treatment, especially for experimentation, the elaboration of more precise norms for non-germline, genetic therapy, etc. The conditions for material cooperation in another's evil in the context of living wills, requirements by law or regulation for form-completion and referral for immoral services such as abortion, contraception and sterilisation need constantly to be reviewed. What moral theology has achieved is a clarification of the principles, which ought to apply, and of the anthropological basis upon which reflection ought to occur.

The Renewal of Moral Theology and Justice

The renewal of moral theology in the area of justice has been somewhat erratic. Important philosophical work has been done relating concepts of justice to approaches to reason more broadly.[84] Theologies of liberation, attempting to apply the Gospel more directly to societies, especially in the Third World, at times lacked sufficient critical force in respect of social and political theories employed. Elements in earlier treatises on justice, such as contracts and prices, received scant attention. Yet, there has been some effort to look at justice in the light of the Gospel, the relationship between justice and mercy, justice and agapaic love. Perhaps more substantial have been attempts to consider justice and human life, to re-examine just war doctrine in a nuclear context and with specific attention to the obligations not directly and deliberately to attack innocent human life nor in many cases to act in a way that may have the foreseen side-effect of causing death.[85] The assessment of the injustice, towards spouses, those born, others conceived by in vitro fertilisation has been valuable.[86]

Perhaps the intensity of the moral theological controversies in sexuality and bioethics explains in part why justice has been treated more sporadically. The Church's social teaching has received inadequate attention, even though it has been stated to be part of moral theology.[87] A useful survey of social teaching, itself needing critical reading, has been produced.[88] Recent work on social teaching is more promising.[89] Grisez's recent work is an important exception. Carefully distinguishing rights from justice, natural from acquired rights, etc., he analyses justice as moral rectitude and fairness in dealing with others, argues that the common good and basic human goods are co-relative.[90] His assessment of our duties to sub-personal beings and resources, as well as the extent of our responsibilities to civil laws, the State, etc., is nuanced and valuable. It seems that the major impetus to moral theology in this field has been the Magisterial documents themselves. The bulk of Papal moral teaching in the twentieth century has been not in the realm of sexuality or medicine, but in that of social justice. John Paul II's integral anthropology has had its effect here too. From *Redemptor hominis* onwards there has been a theological underpinning of human rights stronger than anything before. John XXIII's advance upon secular human rights texts by his recognition both of correlative duties and of the social and international dimension of human rights has been taken much further. The Christocentric thrust of Vatican II and its openness to all of goodwill have remained central. Paul VI's radical insistence that peace is a product of development has been pursued in terms of social and cultural development, participation and solidarity.[91] The hierarchy of values – who man is rather than what he has is what counts – has become a key principle of social teaching.[92]

An example of John Paul's penetrating analysis, prior to the collapse of European communism in 1989, reflects his intimate acquaintance with Marxism-Leninism and his appreciation of capitalism. He gives a powerful critique of both from the standpoint of the Gospel. The Marxist view that work is the key to the social question is agreed, but to see work as good for man, facilitating his development as man counters its allegedly self-alienating character.[93] To insist on the priority of the subjective over the objective dimension of work, on the priority of labour over capital, on the right to collaborate not *against* others (classes or groups) but only *for* justice, and on the vocation to use our talents and the resources of the universe in the service of others is to elaborate a theology of work and of development for our age critical of both socialism and capitalism.[94] Insistence on the conditional nature of the right to private property, compared to the inalienable right of universal destination of the goods of the earth does likewise.[95]

A final point to note is the purpose of government to promote not the particular 'good' of parties, but the common good of all, the authentic human good of persons and of communities. Mere consent or public opinion is not enough; only respect by all of the basic rights of all assures true development and the common good; democracy is valid provided it serves this good of the person.

These key principles of the Church's social teaching need further investigation in moral theology, but they ought to form a specific part of moral catechesis.[96]

The Renewal of Moral Theology and the Theological Virtues

The theological virtues of faith, hope and charity are often treated in dogmatic theology. Efforts to consider the integration of *fides qua* and *fides quae*, to reflect carefully upon the eschatological tension in the virtue of hope and to give content to the virtue of love, in a way that integrates both Decalogue and Beatitudes, continue. There is a need to give more attention in moral theology to the specifically religious aspects of our moral responsibilities and to relate them to the rest of our lives. Properly conceived, moral virtues can be theological, where they are inspired and imbued by God's grace and evince a collaborative response from us. Important contributions have been made to this task in recent years.[97] It needs to be pursued both to prevent a fragmentation of moral theology and consequently of moral catechesis and to ensure that moral theology is truly theological.

Conclusion

It is apparent that the controversies in moral theology, which have bedevilled catechesis in the last generation, have not been overcome. Progress in moral theology has been very patchy and inconsistent. Nevertheless, it seems to be much healthier now than it was twenty years ago. A Scriptural-based moral theology, in the setting of Christian vocation and discipleship, needs to avoid the superficial and ultimately abusive approach to the Bible, which would empty it of its objective moral demands and promote relativism. A nuanced reading is required, but one in harmony with Tradition as authentically interpreted by the Magisterium in the service of conscience and truth. Further work on the virtue approach to moral theology needs to be undertaken. A Christian, integrated anthropology and an analysis of the moral act, which highlights what we deliberately choose to do as crucial, are helping to provide foundations for an approach to moral issues in all spheres which is able to respond positively and critically to modern presuppositions and problems. This will permit the Gospel to provide objective moral standards for our world and to enable us to fulfil the exalted vocation of the faithful in Christ.

Notes

1. Vatican II, Dogmatic Constitution on Divine Revelation, *Dei verbum*, 4, 8.
2. *ibid.*, 24.
3. Vatican II, Decree on Priestly Training, *Optatam totius*, 16.
4. Vatican II, Pastoral Constitution on the Church in the Modern World, *Gaudium et spes.*, 10, 22.
5. B. Haring, *La loi du Christ: Théologie morale à l'intention des pretres et des laics; I, Théologie morale générale* (Tournai, Desclée, 1956), pp. 13-16; ID: *Free and Faithful in Christ: Moral Theology for Priests and Laity*, I, *General Moral Theology* (Slough, St Paul's, 1978), 7ff. ; S. Pinckaers, *The Sources of Christian Ethics* (Edinburgh, T. & T. Clark, 1995), pp. 302-05.
6. C.E. Curran, 'Utilitarianism and Contemporary Moral Theology: Situating the Debates' in C.E. Curran and R.A. McCormick (ed.), *Readings in Moral Theology*, I, *Moral Norms and Catholic Tradition* (New York, Ramsey, Toronto, Paulist, 1979), pp. 341-62 at pp. 353-54; Final Document of the Congress of Italian Moral Theologians (1973) in A. Di Marino, 'Morality and Magisterium' in C.E. Curran and R.A. McCormick (ed.), *Readings in Moral Theology*, III, *The Magisterium and Morality* (New York, Ramsey, Paulist, 1983), pp. 91-112 at pp. 91-96, especially pp. 92-93: note that Di Marino remarks that 'This whole discussion took place in the aftermath of *Humanae vitae*', p. 91.
7. Sacred Congregation for the Doctrine of the Faith, Declaration on Certain Questions of Sexual Ethics, *Persona humana* (London, CTS, 1975), 5-8; ID., Declaration on Euthanasia, *Jura et bona* (1980); ID., Instruction on the Respect for Human Life in its Origins and on the Dignity of Human Procreation, *Donum vitae* (1987), II, 1-6.
8. C. B. Daly, 'The Church's Magisterium in the face of the moral crisis of our time' in L. Gormally (ed.), *Issues for a Catholic Bioethic: Proceedings of the International Conference to celebrate the Twentieth Anniversary of the Linacre Centre, 28-31 July, 1997* (London, The Linacre Centre, 1999), pp. 23-33 at pp. 29-30; B. Ashley, *Living the Truth in Love: A Biblical Introduction to Moral Theology* (New York, Alba House, 1996), pp. 124, 131.
9. Congregation for the Clergy, *General Directory of Catechesis* (London, CTS, 1997), 127.
10. *Dei verbum*, 12.
11. R. Schnackenburg, *The Moral Teaching of the New Testament* (London, Burns and Oates, 1965); W. Schrage, *The Ethics of the New Testament* (Edinburgh, T. & T. Clark, 1988).
12. E. Hamel, *Les dix paroles: perspectives bibliques* (Bruxelles, Paris, Desclée; Montréal Béllarmin, 1969).
13. *Optatam totius*, 16.
14. E. Hamel, 'La scientificità in teologia morale' in K. Demmer and B. Schuller, *Fede cristiana e agire morale* (Assisi, Cittadella, 1980), pp. 11-31.
15. *ibid.*, 13.
16. A. Kosnik et al., *Human Sexuality: New Directions in American Catholic Thought* (New York, Paramus, Toronto, Paulist, 1977), pp. 29-32: 'Looking at the

plurality of the statements and attitudes on human sexuality in the Bible, the inconsistencies among them and the historical circumstances that gave rise to them, critical biblical scholarship finds it impossible on the basis of the empirical data to approve or reject categorically any particular sexual act outside of its contextual circumstances and intention.' cf. P.S. Keane, *Sexual Morality: A Catholic Perspective* (New York, Ramsey, Toronto, 1977), pp. 15-17.

17. B. Schuller, *Wholly Human: Essays on the Theory and Language of Morality* (Dublin, Gill and MacMillan; Washington, D.C., Georgetown University Press, 1986), pp. 16-32.
18. The texts concerned are Gen 19:1-11; Lev 18:22; Rom 1:18-27; 1 Cor 6:9-10 and 1 Tim 1:9-10. cf. Congregation for the Doctrine of the Faith, *Letter to the Bishops of the Catholic Church on the Pastoral Care of Homosexual Persons,* (London, CTS, 1986), 5, for comment alert to exegetical and hermeneutical factors.
19. Kosnik *et al., op. cit.*, p. 195.
20. Keane, *op. cit.*, 81; Kosnik *et al., op. cit.*, p. 195.
21. cf. M. Gilbert, 'La Bible et l'homosexualité', *Nouvelle revue théologique,* 109 (1987), pp. 78-95.
22. John Paul II, Encyclical letter, *Veritatis splendor*, p. 26.
23. Hamel, 'La scientificità in teologia morale', *loc. cit.*, pp. 26-28. See also John Paul II, *Veritatis splendor*, 8, 14-15.
24. J. Fuchs, *Natural Law: A Theological Investigation* (Dublin, Gill and Son, 1965).
25. cf. Keane, *op. cit.*, pp. 43-46; Kosnik *et al., op. cit.*, pp. 118-19, pp. 123-24; A. Guindon, *The Sexual Creators: An Ethical Proposal for Concerned Christians* (Lanham, New York, London, University Press of America, 1986), pp. 3-9; D. Mieth, Geburtenregelung: *Ein Konflikt in der katholischen Kirche* (Mainz, Matthias-Grunewald, 1990), pp. 147-48.
26. The point at issue is that raised by D. Hume and expressly articulated by G.E. Moore that we may not validly deduce an 'ought' from an 'is', the naturalistic fallacy; cf. A. MacIntyre, *After Virtue: A Study in Moral Theory,* 2nd edn (London, Duckworth, 1985), pp. 57-59, 83-84, 148. MacIntyre qualifies the asserted fallacy, at least for functional concepts.
27. Similarly, *Persona humana* uses terms like 'sexual faculty' and its 'finality' (7-9), not evocative of personalism.
28. My emphases. cf. D. Tettamanzi, *Un'enciclica profetica: La 'Humanae vitae' vent'anni dopo* (Ancora, Milano, 1988), pp. 19, 37-42.
29. John Paul II, Apostolic Exhortation, *Familiaris comsortio,* 11). The expression 'incarnate spirit' seems unfortunate, although it is clear that 'one in body and spirit' is intended. An incarnate spirit is a pre-existing spirit become flesh; true of God the Son becoming man, but not properly of man as such.
30. Guindon, *op. cit.*, pp. 12, 14.
31. John Paul II, *Veritatis splendor*, 36.
32. *ibid.*, 40.
33. Haring, *Free and Faithful in Christ*, I (Slough, St Paul Publications, 1978), pp. 314-33.
34. cf., John Paul II, *Veritatis splendor*, 48.

35. K-H. Peschke, *Christian Ethics: Moral Theology in the Light of Vatican II*, I, *General Moral Theology*, 3rd edn (Alcester, Goodliffe Neale, 1997), p. 105; my emphasis.
36. G. Grisez, *The Way of the Lord Jesus*, I *Christian Moral Principles* (Chicago, Franciscan Herald Press, 1983), pp. 121-25. See his remarks on the implied dualism of those who attack 'biologism', urging that 'biological' fecundity be humanised, pp. 198.
37. *ibid.*, pp. 185-92.
38. T. Aquinas, *Summa theologiae*, I-II, q. 94, a. 2.
39. J. Finnis, *Natural Law and Natural Rights* (Oxford, Clarendon, 1980), pp. 33-36.
40. John Paul II, *Veritatis splendor*, 50.
41. Paul VI, *Humanae vitae*, 14, notes the 'so-called principle of totality'. cf. J. Fuchs, 'The Absoluteness of Moral Terms' in Curran and McCormick, *Readings in Moral Theology*, I, pp. 94-137 at 120-21, where such a principle is articulated.
42. Peschke, *op cit.*, I, 251ff; L. Janssens, 'Ontic Evil and Moral Evil' in C.E. Curran and R.A. McCormick (ed.), *Readings in Moral Theology, I,* pp. 40-93 at 41-44.
43. R. Cessario, *The Moral Virtues and Theological Ethics* (London, Notre Dame, University of Notre Dame Press, 1991), pp. 3-4; K. Demmer, *Die Lebensentscheidung: Ihre moraltheologischen Grundlagen* (Munchen, Paderborn, Wien, Schoningh, 1974), pp. 6-7, 22.
44. cf. Fuchs, *art. cit.* ; Janssens, *art. cit.* and P. Knauer, 'The Hermeneutic Function of the Principle of Double Effect' in Curran and McCormick *Readings in Moral Theology.*, I (New York, Paulist Press, 1979), pp. 1-39; B. Hoose, *Proportionalism: The American Debate and its European Roots* (Washington, Georgetown University Press, 1987).
45. The role of conscience and the question of intrinsic moral disorder are treated elsewhere in this volume. cf. the article by Teresa Iglesias.
46. G.J. Woodall, *Adult Studies in the Catholic Catechism*, IV, *Introduction to Morality* (Birmingham, Maryvale Institute, revised edition, 1998), pp. 48-49.
47. John Paul II, *Veritatis splendor*, 78.
48. *Catechism of the Catholic Church*, 1751ff. cf. T. Aquinas, *Summa theologiae*, I-II, q. 18 a. 5; q. 19 a. 6 ad 1: '*Bonum causatur ex integra causa; malum, autem, ex singularibus defectibus*'.
49. John Paul II, *Veritatis splendor*, 78.
50. B. Ashley, *Living the Truth in Love…*, p. 136.
51. B. Kiely, 'The Impracticality of Proportionalism', *Gregorianum* 66 (1985), pp. 655-86., *passim.*
52. John Paul II, *Veritatis splendor*, 66.
53. Demmer, *Die Lebensentscheidung*, *passim.*
54. Good examples are Cessario, *op. cit.* and Ashley *op. cit.*
55. cf. F.A. Sullivan, *Magisterium: Teaching Authority in the Catholic Church* (Dublin, Gill and MacMillan; Washington, DC, Georgetown University Press, 1983). The chapter on morals is the weakest in the book and not reliable.

Sullivan is not a moral theologian, but an ecclesiologist. He relied uncritically upon moralists of a proportionalist stamp, very vocal at the time.

56. Vatican II, *Gaudium et spes*, 33, 43.
57. K. Demmer, 'La competenza normativa del magistero ecclesiastico in morale' in K. Demmer and B. Schuller (ed.), *Fede cristiana e agire morale*, pp. 144-70 at 158-67.
58. John Paul II, *Veritatis splendor*, 64.
59. ID, Encyclical letter, *Centesimus annus*, (1991), 3.
60. Vatican II, Decree on Religious Liberty, *Dignitatis humanae*, 14.
61. ID., 'Allocution to second international Congres of Moral Theology', 12 November, 1988, *L'osservatore Romano*, Italian weekly edition, 17 November, 1988, pp. 14-15.
62. Ashley, *op. cit.*, p. 69.
63. Vatican II, Dogmatic Constitution on the Church, *Lumen gentium*, 25.
64. J.C. Ford and G. Grisez, 'Contraception and the Infallibility of the Ordinary Magisterium', *Theological Studies*, 39 (1978), pp. 258-312; G. Grisez, J. Boyle, J. Finnis and W.E. May, 'Every marital act ought to be open to new life: Toward a clearer understanding', *The Thomist* 52 (1988), pp. 365-426.
65. G. Grisez, *The Way of the Lord Jesus* (Chicago, Franciscan Herald Press, 1983), I, p. 847.
66. John Paul II, Encyclical letter, *Evangelium vitae*, 57, 62 and 65.
67. cf. G.J. Woodall, *The Principle of the Indissoluble Link between the Dimensions of Unity and of Fruitfulness in Conjugal Love: A Hermeneutical Investigation of its Theological Basis and of its Normative Significance* – excerpt (Rome, Gregorian University Press, 1996).
68. John Paul II, *The Theology of the Body: Human Love in the Divine Plan* (Boston, Daughters of St Paul, 1997), pp. 60-66.
69. *ibid.*, pp. 276-78.
70. G. Grisez, *The Way of the Lord Jesus*, II, *Living a Christian Life* (Quincy, Illinois, Franciscan Press, 1993), pp. 506-10; I. Fucek, *La sessualità al servizio dell'amore: Antropologia e criteri teologici* (Roma, Dehoniane, 1993), pp. 92-98.
71. Cessario, *op. cit.*, pp. 64-65, 76-80.
72. D. Tettamanzi, *Bioetica: nuove sfide per l'uomo* (Casale, Piemme, 1987), pp. 31-33.
73. H. Noldin and A. Schmitt, *Summa theologiae moralis iuxta codicem iuris canonici; II, De praeceptis Dei et Ecclesiae*, 27th edition (Leipzig, Ratisbon, Rome New York, Pustet, 1941), 328.
74. Pius XII, Allocution to Urology Congress, 8th October, 1953, *Acta apostolicae sedis*, 45 (1953), 674; B. Haring, *Medical Ethics* (Slough, St Paul's, 1974), pp. 62-63.
75. B.M. Ashley and K. O'Rourke, *Health-Care Ethics: A Theological Analysis*, 2nd edition (St Louis, Miss., Catholic Health Association of the U.S.A., 1982), pp. 309-11.
76. John Paul II, Allocution to the First International Congress of the Society for Organ Sharing, 21 June, 1991, in *L'osservatore romano*, Italian edition, 24 June, 1991, quoted in Grisez, *The Way of the Lord Jesus*, II, footnote 146, p. 543; ID., *Catechism of the Catholic Church*, n. 2296 calls a 'disabling mutilation', immoral.

77. Sacred Congregation for the Doctrine of the Faith, Declaration on Procured Abortion, *De abortu procurato*, 1974, 9.
78. John Paul II, Encyclical letter, *Evangelium vitae*, 30, 38, 47, 58.
79. AA. VV. 'Identity and status of the human embryo' in *Medicina e morale*, supplement to no. 4, 1989, 2.
80. *ibid.*, n. 6.
81. Congregation for the Doctrine of the Faith, Instruction on Respect for Human Life in its Origins and on the Dignity of Procreation, *Donum vitae*, I, I; John Paul II, *Evangelium vitae*, 60.
82. Grisez, *The Way of the Lord Jesus*, I, 299-300; Ashley, *Living the Truth in Love*, pp. 141-43.
83. John Paul II, *Veritatis splendor*, 78.
84. A. MacIntyre, *Whose Justice, Which Rationality?* (London, Duckworth, 1988).
85. G. Grisez, *The Way of the Lord Jesus* (Quincy, Illionois, Franciscan Press, 1993), II, pp. 482-87.
86. T. Iglesias, *In vitro Fertilisation and Justice: Moral, Social and Legal Issues related to Human in vitro Fertilisation* (London, The Linacre Centre, 1990).
87. John Paul II, Encyclical letter, *Centesimus annus*, 55.
88. D. Dorr, *Option for the Poor: A Hundred Years of Vatican Social Teaching* (Dublin, Gill and MacMillan; New York, Orbis, 1993); this book is not confined to the option for the poor.
89. R. Charles, *An Introduction to Catholic Social Teaching* (Oxford, Family Publications; San Francisco, Ignatius, 1999). cf. the more substantial work of this author, ID., *Christian Social Witness and Teaching from Genesis to Centesimus annus*, 2 vols., (Leominster, Gracewing, 1998).
90. G. Grisez, *The Way of the Lord Jesus*, II, pp. 320-34.
91. Paul VI, Encyclical letter, *Populorum progressio*, 76-77; John Paul II, Encyclical letter, *Sollicitudo rei socialis*, 38-40.
92. Vatican II, *Gaudium et spes*, 35; Paul VI, *Populorum progressio*, 19; John Paul II, *Centesimus annus*, 36.
93. ID., Encyclical letter, *Laborem exercens*, 6, 25.
94. ID., *Laborem exercens*, 6, 8-9, 12-14.
95. ID., *Centesimus annus*, 30-34, 43.
96. *General Directory of Catechesis*, 30, 133.
97. cf. Cessario, *op. cit.*, and Ashley, *Living the Truth in Love* (New York, Alba House, 1996).

Further Reading

AA. VV., 'Identity and status of the human embryo' in *Medicina e morale*, supplement to No. 4 (1989).

Ashley, B., *Living the Truth in Love: A Biblical Introduction to Moral Theology* (New York, Alba House, 1996).

Ashley, B. and O'Rourke, *Ethics of Health-Care: An Introductory Textbook* 2nd Edition,(Georgetown University Press, Washington, DC 1994).

Cessario, R., *The Moral Virtues and Theological Ethics* (London, Notre Dame, Notre Dame University Press, 1991).

Charles, R., *An Introduction to Catholic Social Teaching* (Oxford, Family Publications, San Francisco, Ignatius, 1998).
Finnis, J., *Natural Law and Natural Rights* (Oxford, Clarendon, 1980)
Grisez, G., *The Way of the Lord Jesus*, I, *Catholic Moral Principles* (Chicago, Franciscan Herald Press, 1983).
— *The Way of the Lord Jesus*, II, *Living a Christian Life* (Quincy, Illinois, Franciscan Press, 1993).
— *The Way of the Lord Jesus*, III, *Difficult Moral Questions* (Quincy, Illinois, Franciscan Press, 1993).
Kiely, B., 'The Impracticality of Proportionalism' in *Gregorianum 66* (1985), 655-86.
MacIntyre, A., *After Virtue: A Study in Moral Theory*, 2nd edition (London, Duckworth, 1985).
— *Whose Justice, Which Rationality?* (London, Duckworth, 1989).
Pinckaers, S., *The Sources of Christian Ethics,* 3rd Edition (Edinburgh, T. & T. Clark, 1995).
Schrage, W., *The Ethics of the New Testament* (Edinburgh, T. & T. Clark, 1988).
Smith, J.E., *Humanae vitae: A Generation Later* (Washington, D. C., Catholic University of America Press, 1991).
Smith, J.E. (Ed), *Why Humanae vitae was Right: A Reader* (Ignatius Press, San Fransisco, 1993).

RELIGIOUS INSTRUCTION IN SCHOOLS: A THEOLOGY OF CATHOLIC EDUCATION

V.A. McCLELLAND

To attempt to encapsulate in brief form the aim, thrust and motivation of religious education and catechesis in a Catholic school is not a simple task. The essence of what it embraces, however, can be summed up in the words of praise of the psalmist:

> How many are your works, O Lord!
> In wisdom you have made them all,
> The earth is full of your riches.
> There is the sea, vast and wide
> With its moving swarms past counting
> Living things great and small.[1]

The psalmist exults in the operation of Divine Providence in which, as Ronald Knox expressed it, the human family has to believe if it is going to make sense of life at all.[2] The nearest definition of a theology of Catholic education that can be devised is that of the 'making sense' of life! The image of the sea, in this regard, is particularly potent. Man ventures upon the vastness of the waters, sometimes the swell is calm, sometimes turbulent, sometimes subject to sudden squalls. His vision must be directed to the point where the golden sun, too bright for human eyes, tips the horizon and seems to still the impatient flood. In the laborious journey to the desired goal, man is comforted and directed by increasingly familiar sights upon the way, by rocks and promontories, by barks and beacons. This reassuring image, when applied to daily life, recognises amid such manifestations along the journey towards our omega point, the supports and strengths provided by family, by friends, by relationships, by schools, by work, by society, by history and tradition and, above all, by the faith community in which man discovers his true self and in which he sets his sights towards holiness.

In section 73 of the *General Directory for Catechesis*,[3] religious instruction in schools and the process of catechesis are seen as complementary activities. This is of crucial importance in the contest with those systems of education that seem to set one against the other. Over forty years ago, Christopher Dawson pointed out prophetically that the modern world was especially ill-equipped to cope with three crucial constituents of the Christian faith – namely, the future and a future life, the human soul and the abiding presence of God. Catechesis is concerned with the obligations these constituents of faith signify for human beings living in individual and specialised environments. Dawson complained that religious education was often regarded as 'a kind of extra, insecurely tacked on to the general educational structure, not unlike a Gothic church in a modern housing estate'.[4] Such an attitude is discernible today in some State schools with their overtly secular orientation but it can also be found in some denominational schools.

The fundamental malaise at the heart of the Catholic educational system was referred to by the headmaster of Ampleforth College in an address he gave to the Catholic Grant Maintained Schools Conference in 1996. He criticised, in particular, the reaction of some Catholic religious educators in the face of 'the steeply rising rates of divorce, the abandonment of marriage, the campaign for an active homosexual lifestyle to be regarded as of equal legitimacy to heterosexual [and] the discovery of serious moral failures within the Church'.[5] They seemed to wish to adopt a spirit of accommodation to the secular liberal agenda. In some instances this had led to 'the abandonment of doctrinal teaching on the grounds that human language and thought is incapable of transmitting certainties about the infinite God'. But, he reminded his audience, 'the Catholic faith holds that God is revealed in the historic person of Jesus Christ and in His Word', and that 'religious truth can be contained and is contained in the tradition of the Church ....'[6] There could hardly be a stronger argument than that contained in these two points for the complementarity of the teaching of religious knowledge inspired by sound catechetical objectives.

Ecclesiastical tradition, moral realism, Christian hope, spiritual fulfilment, all achieve meaningful relationship within the doctrine of the communion of saints, a doctrine which, it seems, it is no longer fashionable to locate in centre stage in the religious education programme of some Catholic schools. This lack of emphasis is a curious aberration because, when the Second Vatican Council used the term 'family' in relation to Catholic education, it kept before it the view that all human beings in the evocative expression of Kenneth Woodward, '[are] radically connected over space, through time and even beyond death'.[7] It is today somewhat fashionable to argue man belongs to a new dispensation and that, as Knox had described it in his own day, he can draw a line across the page of history, apart from making a nod of apology for perceived or imagined misdemeanours by his predecessors or ancestors. If educators allow themselves to be inveigled by such a specious way of thinking and subscribe to the view that actions and philosophies can be seen as 'wholly or essentially discontinuous' with the past or, indeed, if they are ready to boast of the merit of rejecting unwanted 'historical baggage', then as Knox tells us 'we shall not even have the gloomy satisfaction of profiting by experience'.[8]

It is important that Catholic schools have the communion of saints at the very heart of their religious teaching and experience, their catechesis and their daily living. It is a doctrine that must permeate concepts of family, community, wholeness and integration. Only in this way can a challenge be presented to a society that delimits and narrows its world in all sorts of ways but especially by its espousal of materialism, individualism and utilitarianism. James Hitchcock in his book, *Recovery of the Sacred* – the title itself is significant – cautions that 'strong and vital communities are likely to be precisely those which have a significant common past of which the community is keenly aware'. While his book acknowledges 'a community that seeks to live primarily on its past will petrify,' it argues that a community 'which loses contact with its past or comes to repudiate much of its past, is likely to disintegrate'.[9] Essentially, to be a Catholic means to be bonded 'with millions of other people not only throughout the world, but also through time'. Those who have gone on before us in faith and virtue 'are still living members of the Body of Christ and, in some unimaginable way, we are all connected'.[10] The Catholic school, if it is anything, is vitally concerned with the concept of the organic connection of the whole human family of God's creation, a concept illustrated more generally by the psalmist in the quotation used at the head of this contribution. It is only within that concept, *in Christo*, that human lives, influenced as they are by the determinants of biology, psychology and emotional or social need, are clearly elevated to the spiritual plane. The decline of a sense of tradition in the Church and in her schools, leads to a flawed grasp of coherence in the present. The horizons of the young are inevitably determined by the nature of their personal experiences. The Catholic school must be in a position to broaden and deepen those experiences in the ambience of the Church's teaching within a true concept of the communion of saints.

Recently, in an address entitled 'Time and Trinity in the Christian Tradition',[11] Professor Jaroslav Pelikan of Yale University, drew attention to the *Confessions* of St Augustine for their significance of a true understanding of tradition. Augustine argued 'perhaps it would be exact to say there are three times, a present of things past, a present of things present, a present of things to come'. This description posits a blend in the human consciousness of memory, immediate awareness and expectation. Children in Catholic schools are not simply being prepared to cope with the world into which they are immersed but to possess the vision and desire necessary to change the world in the light of Christ's teaching, to become an essential part of the Church's evangelising mission.

Catholics believe there *is* objective truth and there *is* objective religious truth: such subscription must hold central place in the formation and education of children. They maintain 'Christian holiness is a synthesis of truth, truth in thought, in word, in action. It is inspired by a divine, objective ideal; it depends on trustworthiness, upon man's power of knowing, judging, believing and choosing, according to a common rational standard'.[12] Indeed, a Catholic education must always take into account, as Dieter Velten expressed it, that there cannot be 'a sharp distinction between faith and education', because 'there is no absolute distinction between the various areas of life and aspects of reality'.[13] Mary Warnock finds it less important to form judgments about education itself than about the life to which it is leading. In her *Schools of Thought*, she argues that teachers have to think 'about what one hopes for children when their education is over'.[14] The fundamental realisation is that if teachers lack understanding and vision of the wider outreach of education, they cannot articulate a coherent view of the immediate task confronting them.[15] To achieve the latter position it is important to emphasise the point underpinning sections 73 and 74 of the *General Directory for Catechesis*.[16] Not only must religious education in schools be a rigorous scholarly enterprise but also it must lead to interdisciplinary dialogue, thus manifesting the ideal of wholeness and integrative awareness at the heart of the Church's concept of Catholic education. The cultural context of religious education thus finds its true place in a way of life and an intellectual consciousness that posits a true dimension of 'evangelic preparation' for life and work. In a secular sense, also, the cultivation of sound individual faith and values constitutes a key to effective citizenship.

One of the problems encountered in recent times by Catholic schools in England and Wales has been that related to their role in relation to a multi-cultural, multi-racial and multi-faith society and the challenges posed to a particular faith community when substantial numbers of non-Catholics are admitted onto the rolls of Catholic schools, partly as a result of demographic trends, partly because the ethos of a faith school attracts parents, partly because of the particular need to serve a local community and partly because of academic success. There is interesting fruit for reflection in this regard in a document issued by the Sacred Congregation for Catholic Education in 1977.[17] Here the Catholic school sees its missionary role, making Jesus known in the world and among all peoples, to be at a premium. The school achieves its missionary imperative by being open to the world from the strength of its own faith commitment, a commitment that permeates its daily living. The school must not lose sight of its fundamental mission in the compact it makes with all the people participating in its work or those who are becoming part of its family and community. Provided parents are well aware of the ethos of a Catholic school and are instructed in regard to the witness it gives in its daily life to a faith commitment, there can be no objection to others participating in what it has to offer. In such circumstances, the Catholic school has a duty to discover the key that will unlock the hidden door of love and right living for all the children in its care. It must learn 'to grow and give life to others' as well as 'receive life from them'.[18] There is an image presented by W. Baush in *The Christian Parish* which is helpful in this regard. Slightly adapted, it conveys the message that whenever a Catholic school is established 'though dismal slums surround it', hell is opposed by a rumour of good news, 'by an irrational confirmation of the plenitude we feel is our birthright'.[19] It is not without significance that nineteenth-century Catholic bishops in England and Wales often erected a Catholic school before a church in a new parochial area.

The key document of the Second Vatican Council on the subject of education, *Gravissimum Educationis*, defines the special mission of the Catholic school as being 'to develop in the school community an atmosphere animated by a spirit of liberty and charity based on the Gospel' and thus, so to orientate 'the whole of human culture to the message of salvation, that the knowledge which the pupils acquire of the world, of life, and of men is illumined by faith'.[20] This teaching is not new. It reinforces the encyclical letter, *Divini Illius Magistri* of Pius XI, written some thirty-five years before. But there are implications in it for both religious education and catechesis. The Catholic school is charged with the forging of a special form of bond-community in three particular ways: in its recognition of the importance of the soul, in its attempt to synthesise religious and moral teaching in the spirit of Christ, and in its honest and open acceptance of the teachings of the *magisterium* with all that is implied in that process in terms of individual and community.

The quality of life lived in daily relationship within a Catholic school community should be clearly manifest. Donald Nicholl in his popular book on *Holiness* (1981)[21] pointed out a family is influenced in its stability by its becoming a *schola caritatis* or school of love, punctuated in its daily life by a number of signposts and rituals which add appropriate degrees of support and correction and indicate the duty of each member to attend to the common welfare of all. If the Catholic school is to be truly a family, serious attention has to be given to the rituals that emphasise community need and punctuate the school day. At the heart of this process lies not only a belief in the integrated man but also in the concept of responsibility, a sense of caring and commitment and the consciousness of obligation. The harmonised diversity associated with the organic unity of man is thus emphasised, while at the same time the school functions as a safe haven and a family refuge for children who are suffering the effects of a broken home, physical or mental maltreatment, or handicap in all its varied manifestations. The school community, therefore, has a compensatory role to play at a time when the tight bond between home, parish and school has been heavily eroded.

The teacher is, of necessity, social worker and spiritual guide as well as inspiritor of the intellect. He or she must be convinced of the need to bind together children, parents and teachers in the fulfilment of a community life, a process involving both compassion and co-operation. Thus we have a new emphasis placed upon the need for appropriate teacher-education and formation. Dudley Plunkett has written that Christianity itself 'is about constantly transcending the idols we all have' and that it is a religion that ought to enable us 'to overcome fragmentation, conflict, sectarianism, ideologies and all kinds of divisions'.[22] Amen to that!

Notes

1. Psalm 103, vv. 24-25.
2. Ronald Knox, *Occasional Sermons* (London, Burns & Oates, 1960), p. 332
3. pp. 73-74, published by CTS, 1997.
4. Christina Scott, *A Historian and His World* (London, Sheed & Ward, 1984), p. 178.
5. Dom Leo Chamberlain, OSB: 'The Faith, Society and Catholic Schooling Today'. Speech delivered to the Catholic Grant Maintained Schools Conference, 14 November 1996.
6. *ibid.*
7. Kenneth L. Woodward: *Making Saints* (Chatto & Windus, 1991), pp. 402-403.
8. Ronald Knox: *God and the Atom* (London, Sheed & Ward, 1946), p. 12.
9. James Hitchcock: *Recovery of the Sacred* (New York, Seabury Press, 1974), pp. 89-90.
10. Woodward, *op cit*, pp. 402-403.
11. Reported in *The Catholic Times,* 30 August, 1998.
12. M. O'Leary: *The Catholic Church and Education* (London, Burns & Oates, 1943), p. 18.
13. Dieter Velten: '*Christian Thinking in Education*' in *Spectrum,* 261, 1994, p. 63.
14. Mary Warnock, *Schools of Thought* (London, Faber, 1977), p. 173.
15. I have argued this in *'Quality and Initial Teacher Education'* in V.A. McClelland & V. Varma (eds): *The Needs of Teachers* (London, Cassell, 1996), pp. 1-9.
16. pp. 74-75.
17. S.C.C., *Malgré les declarations,* 24 June 1977, reproduced in A. Flannery (ed): *Vatican Council II* (Leominister, Fowler Wright, 1982), pp. 606 seq.
18. J. Vanier, *Community and Growth* (Darton, Longman & Todd, 1989), pp. 6-7.
19. W. Bausch, *The Christian Parish,* 1980. The original was concerned with the Catholic parish per se.
20. *Gravissimum Educationis,* 28 October 1965, Flannery: *op cit,* vol. I, 1975, pp. 732-733.
21. p. 121.
22. Dudley Plunkett, *Deciding Educational Values: End of the Phoney War?* Occasional Paper. No. 7, Farmington Trust, 1987, p. 3.

Bibliography

Congregation for Catholic Education, *The Religious Dimension in a Catholic School*, (1988).

Philip Fogarty SJ, *Why Don't they Believe Us? Handing on the Faith in a Changing Society*, (Columba Press, Dublin, 1993) esp. chapter 6 onwards.

Edward Hulmes: *Commitment and Neutrality in Religious Education* (Geoffrey Chapman, London, 1979).

V. Alan McClelland (ed.): *Christian Education in a Pluralist Society* (Routledge, London & New York, 1988) esp. chapters 1, 2 and 5.

T. McLaughlin et al (eds), *The Contemporary Catholic School: Context, Identity and Diversity* (Falmer Press, London & Washington, 1996) esp. chapters 7-10 (inc).

Pope John Paul II, *'Apostolic Exhortation: Catechesi Tradendae'* in A. Flannery (ed.): *Vatican Council II. The Conciliar and Post-Conciliar Documents*, vol. II, section 121, (Northpost, NY, Costello Publishing Co., 1979).

GOD ONE AND THREE

FR ANTHONY MEREDITH SJ

On being asked by the Pharisees on one occasion what was the centre of his message and of religion, Jesus replied by citing a verse from Deuteronomy 6:

> Thou shalt love the Lord thy God with thy whole heart, with thy whole soul and with thy whole mind. This is the first and the greatest of the commandments. The second is like it. Thou shalt love thy neighbour as thyself. (Matth 22, 37-39)

The human person is by nature a worshipping being, who is to find his purpose and fulfilment in adoring God as well as caring for the welfare of his fellow human beings. The important and difficult relationship between these two ideas of love of God and love of neighbour clearly presented a challenge to Saint Augustine and he deals with it in several of his writings, notably *On Christian Teaching* in 397 and slightly later in *On the Trinity.*[1]

It is very important to note at this point that the idea of worship of God should not be separated from that of the individual Christian's fulfilment and ultimate happiness. The worship of God is not foreign to our individual nature, but perfects it and gives it meaning. It begins in this life and reaches its perfection in the life to come. This thought finds one of its most satisfying expressions in the final chapter of St Augustine's *City of God.* (xxii, 30), where he writes:

> There we shall be at rest and we will see, we shall see and we shall love, we shall love and we shall praise. Behold that shall be at the end which has no end.

In that short paragraph he joins together the two ideas of self-realisation and the praise of God. We are only able to escape the trap of self-interest in religion, if it is insisted that the supreme act of worship is to be turned upward in praise of God.

The Natural Knowledge of God

1. 'Who is this God I am made to worship and how may I find out about him?' There are two basic ways in which God reveals his nature and will to us: through reason and through special revelation.

Even without the aid of any supernatural revelation the philosophers of Greece, above all Plato and Aristotle, arrived at the conclusion that both ethical values and a right understanding of the world, if they were to be something more than private preferences, must be based on a knowledge of some supreme, immutable value of reality, existing in and of itself. Plato, whose initial concern was ethical, called the ultimate values, ideas. In his dialogues he called them either absolute goodness (in the *Republic*) or perfect beauty (in the *Symposium*) though the ideas were not to be identified with the gods of Greece. His ideas belong to the realms of philosophy rather than to that of religion, strictly so called.

Hardly surprisingly such a perception on Plato's part was thought to justify the inference that he was really affirming by them the existence of God. St Augustine, in a well-known passage in the tenth book of the *Confessions,* does indeed identify God with absolute beauty, when he writes, 'O thou beauty so ancient and so new, too late have I loved thee'. The impersonal absolute of the *Symposium* of Plato has been at a stroke transformed into a personal deity.

Aristotle, likewise, came to the conclusion in the twelfth book of his *Metaphysics* that the motion of the world demanded the existence of an unmoved mover, and this conclusion was supported by St Thomas Aquinas in his *Summa Theologica,* when he says; 'And this, all men call God.[2]

The bible itself on occasions witnesses to the truth of the religious perceptions of the human race, even outside the Judaeo Christian tradition. Isaiah in a superb passage in chapter 45 writes; 'Thus says the Lord to his anointed, to Cyrus, whose right hand I have grasped' and seems to admit thereby the religious relevance of Ahura Mazda. More importantly in the Acts of the Apostles (17, 16-34) St Paul argues on the Areopagus from the religious perceptions of the Greeks, citing one of their poets, Aratus, and identifies the Unknown God with the object of his own preaching; 'What you ignorantly worship, him preach we unto you'. In other words for him eternal reason and natural religion do not exist on a totally different plane or level from that of special revelation. (cf. GDC 36)

This in itself is hardly surprising. God is the author of both orders of nature and of grace, reason and faith and it is a form of treachery to him to separate the two from each other, as some have done and argue that natural theology is either the work of the devil or quite useless in the human heart's and mind's search for ultimate meaning of which the recent papal encyclical *Fides et Ratio* spoke.

Such an affirmation of the divinely inspired nature of natural theology is reinforced by St Paul both in his sermon in the synagogue at Lystra (cf. Acts 14, 14-17) and in his Letter to the Romans (1, 18-23) where he censures the godless wickedness of men on the grounds that 'all that may be known of God lies plain before their eyes ... His invisible attributes, that is his everlasting power and deity have been visible ever since the world began'.[3] Finally, in 1870, Vatican I insisted against the prevailing tide of fideism and irrationalism that by reason alone God's existence could be proved (cl. DS 3004; 3026).

2. It must be readily admitted that despite the authority given to natural theology by both the bible and the church, for various reasons, even within the church, it has been either outright dismissed or regulated to a very minor role. The reasons for this demotion are complex but two above all require mention. They amount in effect a) on the one hand to the distrust of reason as being either totally inadequate or a demonic, ungodly force and b) on the other to an exaltation of reason above all as it operates in the field of natural science being the supreme arbiter above all else. This amounts in practice to an affirmation that; 'What in principle cannot be discovered by experiment cannot be affirmed or denied'.[4]

(a) The first of these positions, at least, lies in the belief that reason has been corrupted to such an extent above all by the effects in every human being of original sin, that it is unable to be relied upon in the religious area of life. This is at root the position of the Reformers, primarily Luther, who saw in reason, above all in matters of faith, an enemy rather than an ally. Basing themselves partly on some passages in St Paul, but especially on the opening chapters of the First Letter to the Corinthians and at Colossians 2,8, partly on disgust of scholastic philosophy and partly, as we have seen, on a strong doctrine of the fall, stronger even than that of St Augustine, many Reformers came to reject the competence of fallen human reason to engage in natural theology and find God in that way.

This cleavage between faith and reason is a mark of many Christian writers and can be traced back as far as Tertullian[5] in the end of the second century. Even now this strand of antirationalism can be found in the works of great theologians like Karl Barth (1886-1968). For him any attempt to arrive at a knowledge of God without revelation ends up in distortion and idolatry. For him the god of natural theology is an idol, the construction of men's depraved intelligences. Human reason has no power to attain to the knowledge of God. Influenced above all by S. Kierkegaard, he held that the revelation of the Word of God as communicated in the Bible stands against human philosophies. Clearly such an outlook almost automatically rules out Natural Theology.

(b) The second of these positions, though approaching the subject from the opposite angle, has the same final result in that it succeeds in detaching faith from reason as a result of the emancipation of science and philosophy from faith and theology. This process began with the gradual emancipation of natural science and philosophy from the control of theology and the Church and was particularly evident in the growth of universities. As a result science and philosophy have not only become free, they have succeeded in marginalising faith and with faith God. God is no longer regarded in the way St Thomas had regarded him as the condition of the possibility of motion, order and beauty in the universe. If science can explain everything, why appeal beyond it to a transcendent cause? As a result, even those who admit the existence of some sort of supreme being, tend to restrict his powers of intervention to a minimum.

The combination of these two factors produced, above all in the period of the Enlightenment, a marked tendency to 'keep God in his place'. This meant in effect for those who believed in God a lapse into either fideism (a rejection of reason and appeal to faith alone) or into deism, (an acceptance of God, but only of a God who set the mechanism of the world in motion and then left it to itself, without being either willing or able to interfere with its mechanism). This deism, which influenced writers as powerful as Newton and Locke in England, had the effect of turning the universe into a closed system, in which miracles were effectively outlawed. What on the face of it appears to be a miracle may turn out on inspection to be the natural result of a previously unknown law of the universe. The iron laws of a mechanistic universe may perhaps admit the need of a God to set things in motion in the first place, but nothing more. Deism, therefore, needs to be carefully distinguished from theism, which does permit some interference by God into the world that he himself created (GDC 20).

The weakness of this form of natural theology practised in the eighteenth century was that it relied heavily on 'gaps' in the system, for which God's existence was invoked. In other words it appealed to our present ignorance of the causes of things in order to assert the existence of a god. This is particularly clear in the famous case of 'Paley's watch', in which the universe's complex structure was likened to a watch discovered on the shore, whose workings demanded an explanation in the shape of a designer.

Unfortunately for this general approach it laid itself open to the difficulty that what might NOW appear to be an insoluble problem could well in the future with the progress of science turn out to be no problem at all. And this is indeed what has happened. God has been pushed back and back by the discoveries in science, which offer so adequate an explanation of the world that no other hypothesis in the shape of the 'God of the gaps' is required. So successful have been the discoveries and theories of men like Charles Darwin and Sigmund Freud, that in the words of Matthew Arnold in his poem *Dover Beach* written in 1867 'The sea of faith ... is forever retreating', and exists now only, if at all, on the fringes of our experience. The end result therefore of the emancipation of science from faith and theology has been the relegation of religion to the realm of private conviction, unsupported by reason and argument.

This is tantamount to atheism, which GDC 22 (p. 25) regards as 'one of the most serious problems of our time'. The result of this assertion is the refusal on the part of many to allow anything to interrupt the pursuit of their own satisfaction, irrespective of the demands of any objective moral code.

3. The apparent strength of deist/atheist position should not produce a paralysis in the minds of theists. Part of our grounds for trusting in reason is that if God is the creator of the world, then it would be strange if he left in his work no trace of his existence and nature. The weakness of the traditional defence of theism does indeed lie in the attempt to argue to the existence of God who is conceived of primarily as explaining the order and structure of the physical universe. Order and motion in the world may turn out, as we have seen, to be either illusory or explicable on other

grounds. The argument proceeds from the way the world is to existence of a hidden cause.

However, one of the arguments of St Thomas proceeds by a different root, the way of contingency. Instead of asking the question, 'Why are things as they are?', he asks the very different question; 'Why is there anything at all?'. In doing so Aquinas appeals by implication to the 'principle of sufficient reason'.[6] In doing so he goes beyond the normal arguments from design and motion, asking instead a metaphysical question.

This is a momentous step. We are able to think of the world of our normal existence as not existing at all. It is radically unable to account for its own existence. Its very frailty and openness to corruption suggests this to us. We are entitled, therefore, to ask whence does it derive the fact of its existence, and to this question the only satisfactory answer is in the existence of a being about whom such a question cannot be properly asked. St Thomas ends his third proof as follows; 'One is therefore forced to suppose something which must be, and owes this to no other thing than itself; indeed it is itself the cause that other things must be' (*Summa Theologica* part 1; question 2,3). It is an appeal to the philosophy of being or ontology, which has been much stressed by the present Holy Father in his recent encyclical *Fides et Ratio*, above all in section 97.

But this natural revelation of God, vital though it is, is supplemented and greatly enriched by the supernatural revelation of God to us above all in the Bible. But what precisely is it that revelation 'adds' to reason, the super natural to the natural? The most important difference between the supreme value of Plato and the unmoved mover of Aristotle and the God of the Bible is that the former is above all entirely concerned with nature and morality, the latter with history. God in the Bible reveals himself primarily as the God of the people of Israel, for whom he acts and with whom he enters into a covenant. He is a religious figure who demands worship, reveals his will on particular occasions to particular figures and demands obedience. None of these facts is true of either the idea of the Good or of the Unmoved mover.

4. To this distinctive perception of Judaism Christianity has added the two great and distinctive doctrines of the Trinity and Incarnation. Neither of these two great truths is found explicitly in the New Testament, though it is possible to infer them from the data there offered. As now expressed in the creedal formulae of the church they owe their existence to the activities of the first four ecumenical councils of the church, held, at the

wish of the emperor, at Nicaea (325), Constantinople (381), Ephesus (431) and Chalcedon (451). For all their abstract language, partly provoked by heresy in the church, partly derived from Greek philosophy, they lie at the very heart of the Christian message (GDC 30). These essential truths of faith serve to distinguish the Christian faith from all other faiths whether monotheistic or pluralist.

However, in the general atmosphere of religious tolerance, which alas too easily collapses into religious indifference, the temptation to marginalise them in the interests of a wider ecumenism is great. This temptation is all the more marked because from the nature of the mystery they disclose they are hard to understand, if indeed they can be adequately understood at all. It is far easier to agree with the great philosophers of Greece, Plato and Aristotle and with the great monotheistic faiths of Judaism and Islam in asserting the existence of one ultimate principle, than to assert the threeness of the one. It is very important, therefore, for the Christian to believe that the doctrine of the Trinity far from being an impossible conundrum reserved for the theologian to understand, is instead the very heart and stuff of the Christian gospel.

Despite the very obvious discrepancies that exist between Greece and Jerusalem and between the natural and supernatural revelations of God, between a god who appears to be an impersonal absolute 'ground of being'; and the personal God of Abraham, Isaac and Jacob and the Father of Our Lord Jesus Christ, it is still true that in their differing ways they all acknowledge the need to assert the existence of a transcendent being. This being does not 'belong' to the universe of time and space and yet in some way is the ground of the existence and essence of this world. It is particularly important to insist on the existence of this transcendent being, as he is the source and end of all finite created life. Without his existence it is hard to discover a ground for morality or to make sense of the whole idea of worship. If there is no such reality, then it is hard to justify the existence of any form of organised religion, as all their differing ways express the demand for worship which is embedded in human nature.

Revelation as the Communication of the Life of Christ

At this distance of time it is hard to realise that churchmen fought passionately about what to us appears as seemingly abstract issues. In so far as religion impinges on the consciousness of western secular man it takes the form of secondary issues like feminism, animal rights, and ecumenism. The first five centuries of the history of the Church hardly concerned themselves with such practical issues. Partly under the influence of the questing and defining spirit of Plato they explored more precisely the implications of the religious truths, which they derived from the bible and the tradition of the Church.

Important, however, though the truth content of revelation is, it is not to be thought of as simply an offering of the mind. We are always in danger of identifying revelation quite closely with particular verbal formulae. It is important therefore to stress, as does GDC 24, that catechesis involves' (1) a new and vital experience of God as merciful Father, (2) a more profound rediscovery of Jesus Christ, not only in his divinity, but also in his humanity, (3) a sense of co-responsibility on the part of all for the mission of the Church in the world; (4) a raising of the consciousness with regard to the social obligations of the faith.' We should also note that the lives and histories of individual, saintly Christians embody doctrines and opinions, and it is through their witness that the truths of faith become real for the whole world.

At the heart of the promise of Jesus and of the message of the gospel is the hope of eternal life (cf. John 17, 3), which in its turn is related to the knowledge of the Father and the Son, though avoiding the trap of treating this knowledge in a purely cerebral fashion. In a well known passage the great second century bishop and theologian, Irenaeus in book 4 of his treatise *Against Heresies*, expressed this important truth as follows, when he writes: 'The glory of God is man alive; and the life of man is the vision of God'. He is not here advocating simply liveliness, which need have nothing particularly religious about it, but rather an awareness, even now, of the wonder and majesty of God. The danger arises when a cleft develops between the questioning intellect and ordinary life and the two find it only too convenient to dwell in separate compartments.

The aim of any good teacher, preacher and catechist, therefore should be to help people to see the connexion between life and truth, above all religious truth. The motto should be; 'Only connect'. In this way life will be freed from total dependence upon purely material self-understanding, while the teaching of the church will be enriched and made relevant by reference to life. So will the fateful divorce between the two be to some extent avoided.

One of the distinctive features of the New Testament is its Trinitarian dimension. This emerges clearly for the first time at the moment of Christ's baptism, when Jesus is pointed out by the dove (the Holy Spirit) and the voice of the Father is heard. This truth becomes particularly clear in the Farewell Discourses of the fourth gospel and also in a passage in the letter to the Galatians, (esp. 4,1-7) where the power both to become sons of God and so to call God, Father, is attributed to the presence and action of the Holy Spirit. Again the so-called 'grace' at the end of the Second Letter to the Corinthians brings all three persons together.

It should not, therefore, be necessary to speak, as some have done, of the 'Forgotten Trinity'. Even if we put on one side the sacramental dimension of the church, it is helpful to recall the insight of St Augustine in this matter. In his work *On the Trinity* (book 10), he explores the Trinitarian dimensions of human consciousness. He begins from the axiom that there ought to be a trace of the Trinity in the human spirit, precisely because human beings are made in the image and likeness of God (cf. Genesis 1, 26) and God being Trinity, this threefoldness should be reflected in the human soul. This enables him to 'discover' the spiritual trinity in each of us of memory, understanding and will, without, however, suggesting that there is an exact equivalence between the Father and memory, the Son and understanding, and the Holy Spirit and will.

The Trinity and the Liturgy

1. *Baptism.*

The initiation of the Christian into the life of Christ, his rebirth through water and the Holy Spirit,and his going down into the tomb with Christ and subsequent rising with him, take place through the sacrament of baptism. The form of words in which the sacrament is conferred go back to words of Jesus at the end of Matthew's gospel (28, 29). In the *Teaching of the Twelve Apostles,* known as the *Didache* (section 7), a document which gives instructions on Christian life and practice and which arguably is as old as the four gospels we read the following: 'As touching baptism, thus baptise ye .... Baptise in the name of the Father and of the Son and of the Holy Spirit'. Exactly the same form of words is to be found in Justin (*First Apology* 61) and slightly later in the *Apostolic Tradition* of Hippolytus.

This constant tradition became in its turn the basis from which later writers argued to the divinity of the third person of the Trinity. So we find St Basil in about 375 in his *On the Holy Spirit* arguing on several occasions from the wording of the baptismal formula in St Matthew to the equality of the Spirit with the Father and the Son, in other words from equality of honour to equality of nature. The following short passage from that work, (section 24) runs as follows: 'When the Lord established the baptism of salvation, did he not clearly command his disciples to baptise all nations 'in the name of the Father and of the Son and of the Holy Spirit'? He did not disdain his fellowship with the Holy Spirit, but these men say we should not rank him with the Father and the Son. But how could the Father, Son and Spirit be united in a different or more suitable way?' In this passage and in others elsewhere we see the Trinitarian formula of baptism being used as a proof text. It is a good example of what came to be called the 'Lex orandi'. In other words the law of liturgical prayer comes to help determine the way we ought to believe. This fact by itself helps to reinforce the general principle that there is and ought to be a close and clear connexion between liturgy, practice and belief.

2. *The Mass.*

The whole structure of the Mass is directed to the Father, through the Son in the Holy Spirit. Every celebration opens with the sign of the cross in the threefold name and the final blessing repeats the opening formula. The same is true of the opening prayer, which concludes with the doxology, while the Sunday creed is an affirmation of the three persons of the Trinity. Even the Gloria, which is primarily addressed to the Father and the Son ends with the words: 'with the Holy Spirit'.

However, as was suggested above, it is the whole movement of the central Eucharistic prayer, which insists on the Trinitarian dimension of the central act of Christian worship. This is particularly clear in the third Eucharistic prayer, which opens with the words, 'Father you are holy indeed, and all creation rightly gives you praise. All life, all holiness comes from you through your Son, Jesus Christ, our Lord, by the working of the Holy Ghost'. Again the elements are transformed into the body and blood of Christ by the double action of the epiclesis, the prayer for the illapse of the Holy Spirit on the gifts and by the words of Institution, 'This is my body… and … This is my blood'. The final doxology before the Lord's Prayer highlights the Trinitarian dimension of the whole. The second Eucharistic prayer, modelled on the third century canon of Hippolytus makes the same point with hardly less clarity.

3. The other sacraments, above all penance or the sacrament of reconciliation and the anointing of the sick are both administered in the name of the Trinity and so too is the exchange of rings at marriage.

4. This means that the Christian is brought into the very life of the Trinity through the sacramental life of the church. It is therefore of vital

importance, as GDC 29 and 30 make clear, that the incorporation into Christ and the Church through the Christian sacraments of initiation should be accompanied by adequate catechesis. The reasons for this are both negative and positive, negative in order to evade the suggestion that the sacraments work by a sort of magical efficacy, positive to indicate that there is no gap between sacraments and the intelligent understanding and appreciation of what is being done.

This method has been the aim of several important treatments of the sacraments. Origen, the first great creative theologian of the early church, after the New Testament strove to reconcile the existence of an ecclesiastical external institution with the existence of an invisible church of holy people, who did not always fit neatly into the external structure.[7] Later, Cyril of Jerusalem (died 386 AD) in the fourth century and even more strikingly by the eccentric anonymous figure toward the middle of the sixth century, known as Dionysius the Areopagite, whose *Ecclesiastical Hierarchy* endeavours to link together the sacramental system with a highly philosophic approach, which owes much to the writings of a late Platonist philosopher, Proclus (413-485) showed that Sacrament and catechesis, rite and understanding must go together.

Notes

All references to GDC are to the *General Directory for Catechesis* (Catholic Truth Society 1997)

1. On the dual command see St Augustine *On Christian Teaching* 1, XXVI, 27 and *On the Trinity* 8, VII, 10.
2. St Augustine, *Confessions* 10, XXVII, 38; for the quinque viae of St Thomas Aquinas cf. *Summa Theologica i. 2.*
3. The argument to the existence of a supreme orderer from the order of the universe is Stoic rather than Aristotelian or Platonic in origin. It occurs as early as the third century BC in Cleanthes' *Hymn to Zeus* and in chapter 53 of the *Enchiridion* of the Stoic slave, Epictetus, in both of which 'god' is thought of as the immanent principle of order in the world rather than as its transcendent cause.
4. This whole approach is dangerously close to the two basic principles on which Logical Positivism reposes, namely that only those types of proposition are to be taken as meaningful which are either logical definitions and to that extent tautologous or can at least in principle be verified empirically.
5. For the anti-rational approach of Tertullian there is a passage in his *Apology* section 46, written at the close of the second century; 'But then what have the philosopher and the Christian in common, the disciple of Greece and the disciple of heaven '. His famous remark, often misquoted, '*credo quia ineptum*' 'I believe because it is strange' comes in his treatise *On the Flesh of Christ* section 5.
6. G W. Leibnitz (1646-1716) was the first to enunciate the principle as follows: 'sufficient reason, in virtue of which we hold no fact can be genuine or existent and no proposition true unless there is sufficient reason why it should be so and not otherwise'. (*Monadalogy* 31/32)
7. An excellent account of the whole problem of the relationship between external structures and the sacraments of the church and their internal meaning above all in Origen may be found in K. Rahner, *Theological Investigations* 15, number 8 'The Penitential System of Origen'.

A REVELATION TO TRANSMIT: THE MAGISTERIAL PROJECT

FR AIDAN NICHOLS OP

A Catechism can never replace catechesis – the living voice of the teacher. And yet a Catechism is not merely a manual. It is an instrument of sanctification. This it could not be, of course, unless its content were an expression of divine revelation – a saving revelation that aims to bring men to their supernatural goal, through grace to Glory. The connexion of the two Catechisms and Glory – is made via a number of conceptual junctions. So we must consider in turn (1) the presuppositions of the revelation idea; (2) that idea as realised, above all in its centre-point, Jesus Christ, who is the Revealer; (3) the transmission of revelation in Tradition; (4) Tradition's milieu, the Mass; (5) its single most important monument, Holy Scripture; (6) its other media of expression; (7) the need for an organ of interpretation of all of this, the meeting of this need in the sacred teaching office, and the rôle of that office in articulating the development of doctrine and the establishing of doctrine's right proportions – not least through the present *Catechism of the Catholic Church.*

Presuppositions of the Revelation Idea

In a largely secular society, the very idea of revelation-dependent thinking and acting easily becomes inaccessible. In the contemporary Church found in the countries of the North Atlantic civilisation, the historic homelands of secularism, the notion of revelation eludes the grasp of Christians themselves, unless a serious doctrinal effort is made to affirm and explore it.

Revelation has two foundational presuppositions. First, the world around us is endowed with a capacity to be 'iconic': to image or echo its divine Creator. That ability of the created order – whether as a whole or under some aspect or in some particular instance – to point to its divine source is the basis for 'natural revelation', the disclosure of God in created being that underlies the world religions in different ways, as well as in myth and literature, dream motifs and art. Over and above this, it belongs to the Creator to be able to enhance the iconic potential of things in such a fashion as to serve his saving design for the repair and consummation of the creation – to act as vehicles for the 'second gift' of salvation which is to make good, and take beyond itself, the 'first' gift of created being itself.

But then secondly, man – the human animal – must be able to interpret aright the revelatory force of things (no 'disclosure' can be successful until it finds its recipient). In the case of post-lapsarian humanity (lapsarian: a believer in the doctrine of the fall of man from innocence), with its darkened and error-prone (though still truth-directed) intellect and its distorted and weak (though still goodness-seeking) will, that interpretative work needs the help of divine grace even with regard to natural revelation. But in the case of supernatural revelation, it follows from the nature of the case – from the kind of divine activity involved – that the human person could not scan aright its epiphanies in the experience of prophets and apostles, nor grasp correctly the lessons those epiphanies contain, unless our natural human powers of knowing and willing, thinking and loving, were supernaturally energised, were raised into a new order of activity that corresponds to the purpose of God in his saving self-disclosure.

What makes revelation possible from the side of *God*? Here also there are two principal presuppositions we must mention. First, as the philosophy of religion can tell us – at least when providentially steadied in its intellectual gaze and thus sharpened in its argumentative focus – there must be in God a communicative freedom analogous to, though infinitely exceeding, that ability to disclose our purposes and so the direction of our personalities which characterises the (microscopic) spiritual beings we ourselves are. As the creative archetype of those gifts in us (we are made, so the Genesis writer tells us, to his image and likeness), the Divinity may reasonably be lauded for a liberty of self-communication of which our *métier* as linguistic and social beings, living by language and friendship, is the dim reflection. But secondly – and here only the biblical kerygma, as found by reference to the apostolic rule of faith can serve our turn, revelation from the side of God is only possible if God in fact *desires* us as his conversation partners, desires, indeed, to share his life with us. It is the faith of the Church that the God who is from all eternity a living act of self-communication (Father to Son in the Holy Spirit) has elected to-share with human beings the knowledge and love he has of himself in his own triune life, with a view to not only healing our corruption but bringing us to Glory.

Revelation is, then, a wonderful conspiracy of created potential with the divine will. By light, Light. The Swiss dogmatician Hans Urs von Balthasar, with aid from a younger Dutch colleague, puts it like this:

> The fact that Being in its totality can be present and reveal itself in individual beings: that – in Augustinian terms – the individual being is illuminated by an absolute light and can be read and interpreted in that light: and that the very uniqueness of the individual being causes the indivisible uniqueness of Being in its totality to shine forth with peculiar clarity – all this ... provides the basis for God's revelation in the individual form and figure of Jesus Christ and for man's transcendental ability to apprehend it.
>
> Insofar as the reality which thus presents itself erects no barriers against the absolute Ground, the absolute Ground not only has infinite possibilities of manifesting itself to sensory awareness but it becomes free to present and authenticate itself in a manner that is absolute and definitive.[1]

The light of revelation is, we can say, at once a 'Thaboric' light, shining upon our senses through epiphanies in the incarnate order – as, paradigmatically, in the features and the vestments of the transfigured Jesus on the mountain and also a 'noetic' light that from *within* (for, after all, our Creator is, as Augustine realised, more interior to us than we are to ourselves) enlightens our understanding and inflames our will.

Our present difficulty in grasping imaginatively (never mind conceptually!) what 'revelation' may be derives from the institutionalised intellectual pride of the post-Renaissance Western cultural tradition. Much of the intellectual and cultural leadership of early modern and modern Europe withdrew the mind from penetration by the light of revelation, a light whose transcendence requires, uncomfortably, the intellect's submission. That sin of intellectual pride – taken with full seriousness by the spiritual masters (it is a plausible explanation of the angelic Fall) – became embodied in educational and civil institutions, and pervasively 'around', finally, in the mental air we breathe. It has been, in the twentieth century, a major part of the vocation of Christian poets so to discipline our sense for the effulgence of creation – the lesser light – that our intellectual eye may be re-sensitivised to the epiphanies of supernatural revelation – the 'Greater Light' as the chorus calls it in T. S. Eliot's *The Rock.*

> O Light Invisible, we praise Thee!
> Too bright for mortal vision.
> O Greater Light, we praise Thee for the less;
> The eastern light our spires touch at morning,
> The light that slants upon our western doors at evening,
> The twilight over stagnant pools at batflight,
> Moon light and star light, owl and moth light,
> Glow-worm glowlight on a grassblade.
> O Light Invisible, we worship Thee![2]

Revelation's Realisation in its Midpoint, Jesus Christ

Eliot's range of examples of the lesser light of creation reminds us that, indefinitely 'open' as the powers of our soul may be, we are nonetheless earthlings – for whom the light of day and its extinction at night are crucial to our biorhythm, who need the roof, walls and domesticity of homesteads, and share an environment with other species. It was, accordingly, altogether appropriate that the supreme epiphany to serve as revelation's vehicle took the form of the Word's incarnation, when he who is, as the Creed proclaims, 'Light from Light', was seen as a babe at his human mother's breast. The Incarnation, celebrated liturgically in the Church of the Byzantine rite under the superlatively fitting title, then, of the *Theophany* – the epiphany of God in his own person, unfolds its own purpose in the subsequent events of Jesus' childhood, Baptism, public ministry, and – above all – in his suffering, death, and Resurrection and its aftermath, the coming of his Pentecostal Spirit, the Spirit of divine-human fullness. For it is here that we see the scope of revelation – both in the current English and the original Greek sense of that word 'scope', Here, in the Christ of the Nativity and the ensuing scenes of the incarnate life up to the Cross, the rising from the Tomb, and that mystery of presence in absence which is Pentecost, we see both revelation's amplitude (its 'scope' in the English meaning) and its goal (its Greek sense).

As the definitive revelation both of the divine and of the human, and therefore of their interrelationship, and in the new light he throws by his words and actions on the earlier history of revelation in the 'Elder

Covenant' with Israel, and on the created order itself, the incarnate Word makes available to the world the greatest truth the world has ever known or can know. This is the 'greatest' truth because it possesses more far-reaching implications than any other, and because it is more wonderful, more inexhaustibly than any other the appropriate object of that admiration or wonder which Aristotle identified as philosophy's true point of departure. Here is revealed what St Thomas calls so simply the *iter ad Deum*, the 'way to God'.

Letting the 'islands hear' the truth of divine Revelation – in the words of the lovely Isaianic text that appears on the device of Maryvale and in the title of this symposium – is inseparable from letting the islands *see* that same truth, embodied as it is in a Person, at once human and divine. So indeed the same prophetic oracle about the Servant of God implies:

> I will give you as a light to the nations. That my salvation may reach to the ends of the earth (Isa 49, 6).

From Revelation to Tradition

From revelation to Tradition is no great step, since Tradition in the high theological meaning of the word, dignified by an initial capital, is revelation as registered by the corporate mind of the apostolic Church. The revelation in Christ, which is also the revelation (natural and supernatural) that came to its climax as Christ, would not have been a *successful* supreme disclosure of the way and will of the triune God in his saving outreach to us unless it was suitably received into the minds of its first and most crucial destinees, the apostolic founders of the Church. The question of whether the media of revelation in its transmission are to be thought of as written alone (*the sola Scriptura* principle of the sixteenth century Reformers) or as both oral and written (as Catholicism and Orthodoxy hold) is altogether subsidiary to the primary question of Tradition as the aboriginal inhering of revelation in the corporate consciousness of the apostolic witnesses. That is why the best modern Catholic theology treats Scripture as a monument of Tradition, one locus where the apostolic mind comes to expression, and not as an alternative to Tradition. To say that something belongs to Tradition in the high theological sense – to *Holy* Tradition – is not as yet to make any comment on its written or non-written form.

It is because Holy Tradition inheres in the Church's 'deep' – that is, not always explicitly conscious – mind as herself the apostolic Church, the Church built on Peter and the Eleven, that the *primary* virtues she must practice in its regard are fidelity and good stewardship, not theological creativity and pastoral ingenuity (these come later).

The gift of revelation to the Church constitutes Tradition. The salvation which is revelation's content is not only what God has done and does for her but also what he has been and is for her. So the revelatory gift includes its Giver – the triune Lord in Jesus Christ. For this reason, the Church has always possessed Tradition's plenitude.

Still, as the Russian Orthodox thinker Sergei Bulgakov put it:

> The life of the Church, whilst being mysterious and hidden, is not for all that a-logical and a-dogmatic. On the contrary, the Church has a *logos*, a doctrine and a message.[3]

The Son of God did not come to her as Word without truths to convey, nor did the Spirit of truth come to her as Paraclete, to complement the mission of the Word, without bringing to the apostolic mind all that Jesus had taught the Twelve, and leading them into 'all the truth' (Jn 16:13). Thanks to the twofold economy of the divine Word whose cutting power is sharper than a double-edged sword (Hebrews 4, 12) and the divine Spirit, subtle in his wisdom (Wisdom 7:22), Tradition, though it be the comprehensive vision that fills the Church's mind, is also doctrinal substance. Speaking of the classical Christian understanding of the patristic 'golden age', the Scottish divine Thomas Torrance wrote:

> Faith was not regarded in Nicene theology as some form of non-cognitive or non-conceptual relation to God, but was held to involve acts of recognition, apprehension and conception, of a very basic intuitive kind, in the responsible assent of the mind to truth inherent in God's self-revelation to mankind. Faith arises in us under the creative impact of the self-witness and self-interpretation of God in his Word, and in response to the claims of his divine reality upon us which we cannot reasonably or in good conscience resist. It takes the form of listening obedience to the address and call of God's Word, and the specific beliefs that are called forth from us like this entail at their heart a conceptual or epistemic consent … to divine truth and become interiorly locked into it.[4]

Tradition, as what is received in the corporate faith of the apostolic community, is delivered to the *understanding* heart.

Among the truths with which it tingles those concerning the saving acts of the God-man will be crucial. Just as revelation's midpoint is Jesus

Christ, in the acts that embodied epiphanically his unique being and consciousness as the God-man, so Tradition's centre is the apostolic witness to the meaning of his atoning work and saving teaching.

The Mass as the Milieu of Tradition

The Church entertains the Holy Tradition given to her in the milieu of the Mass. That is where, *par excellence*, the Church reads the Old and New Testaments in the unity of the canon as the biblical Word addressed to her as Spouse of Christ in the here and now of the assembly of her faithful. As the homilies of the patristic period, and their continuators, indicate, she finds in those Scriptures the narrative of the triune God's self-revelation with its climax in Christ the Head and its consequences in the life of his Church-body (here the typological reading of the Bible suggested by its inner structure but mandated by the use of Scripture in the ancient liturgies is key).

But it is not only the Fore-Mass, the Mass of the Catechumens, the Liturgy of the Word, that is Tradition's milieu, the setting where the apostolic registering of revelation is at its most palpable. In the Eucharistic oblation itself, the Church, by the power of the Spirit, re-actualises the mystery of the Lord's saving work on the Cross, in the Burial, and at the Easter tomb. In the Eucharistic Prayer, as that portion of the *Canon Missae* called the *anamnêsis* shows, the Church does not – cannot – separate the remembering of her Saviour, his identity and work, from the daily rediscovery of who she herself is as the Bride made immaculate on the Cross and so the mediatrix of his Sacrifice. This- the Eucharistic action – is the purest form of encountering Holy Tradition as divine revelation committed so utterly to the Church's keeping as to be one with her spiritual intelligence – even though the unity of the two (the Word of God, the mind of the Church) is a 'Chalcedonian' union without confusion, brought about and sustained by grace alone. All doctrinal understanding in the Church is linked to the liturgical re-actualisation of Scripture and the celebration of the mysteries of Christ's life which are also, by Dominical gift, her own. 'All that was visible in the life of our Redeemer' has passed over into his (sacramental) mysteries.[5] In the words of the abbé Jean Corbon;

> The passionate love of the Father for human beings (Jn 3, 16) reaches its climax in the passion of his Son and is henceforth poured out by his Spirit in the divine compassion at the heart of the world, that is, in the Church. And the mystery of tradition is

> this joint mission of the Word and the Spirit throughout the economy of salvation; now, in the last times, all the torrents of love that pour from the Spirit of Jesus flow together in the great river of life that is the liturgy.[6]

Scripture as Tradition's Primary Monument

Given this essay's theological option to treat Tradition as embracing *both* what the Council of Trent called 'all traditions concerning faith and morals' *and* the Scriptures ('all the books of both Old and New Testaments'), then Scripture must have pride of place as Tradition's single most signal expression. Once we regard Tradition in the singular (not discussed in the Tridentine decree and mentioned only once, seemingly, in the Council chamber) as the impress of revelation on the corporate subjectivity of the apostolic community thanks to the economies of Word and Spirit, then it must of course englobe Scripture. The Gospel was traditioned before ever any apostle or 'apostolic man' set pen to parchment. Revelation – and therefore Tradition – will always be larger than any single expression of itself, larger even than the Bible.

Nonetheless, as the rise of nineteenth and twentieth century theological subjectivism demonstrate, it is imperative that revelation, through Tradition, enters object form – for the safeguarding, precisely, of that ecclesial subjectivity which actually is authentic, authoritative, because it was apostolically received.

If the experience of individuals or groups within the Church is not to be falsely elevated to the status of theological norm – whether after the fashion of German Romanticism in the nineteenth century, or driven by agendas drawn from social, economic, racial or sexual politics in its successor, it must stand over against the minds of groups or individuals in all its hard and clear difference from human projection.

This is why Tradition – revelation in transmission – becomes text as Holy Scripture. Thanks to the charism of inspiration received by the hagiographs, the sacred authors, and its consequence, inerrancy in all that concerns (even factually, in matters of history or natural science, where pertinent) saving truth, and the locating, when the canon is constructed, of the limits of the literature that bears these hallmarks, the Church can point to this body of texts in all their objectivity by way of negatively, admonition, and, more positively, education of those who would construe what, by reception of revelation, is in her mind. The Church gazes into the mirror of the Word of God and sees there not her *face* but her *faith* as Bride of the Word.

Tradition's Other Media of Expression

The Tridentine Fathers were aware from the débâcle of the Protestant revolt that Scripture by itself cannot suffice to render the full Gospel proclaimed by the Church's preaching, celebrated in her sacraments, lived out in her ethos. Either because not all of articulable Tradition has passed into the biblical text or because the full meaning of that text is not recoverable by scanning of its content alone (the bishops at Trent did not wish, seemingly, to adjudicate these alternatives) the Church cannot rely on the Bible only. If the content of Tradition were not to suffer a truncation that diminished the Gospel, Tradition must be recognised as having twofold form. There are not simply the Holy Scriptures; there are also the divinely originated oral traditions necessary for the complementing or elucidation (here again was the question the *Tridentinum* left open) of the Bible's plenary sense. In this crisis over the 'sources of revelation', resolved by Trent's insistence on parity of esteem, with Scripture, of traditions continuously maintained in the Church *de fide et moribus* coming 'from the mouth of Christ or inspired by the Holy Spirit,[7] we have in fact an example of how guardianship of Tradition (with its capital 'T') supernaturally works. As a modern Irish interpreter of John Henry Newman's thinking on this subject has commented:

> For Newman, tradition represented the enduring unconscious instinct of the Church drawing from the infinitely subtle resources of the early Christian apostolic memory, revealing itself anew in every generation at the instigation of heresy.[8]

Well and good, but as so often, a dogmatic determination ends a doctrinal crisis by setting a theological task. For the question at once arises, where are these divinely originated oral traditions needed for Scripture's fullness (or at any rate the successful perception of its fullness) to be found? They are found, we can say, in a host of other monuments. These can be verbal, as with the baptismal Creeds – augmentations in the light of the rule of faith of those summaries of the apostolic preaching of which we get a glimpse in the Book of Acts. Verbal likewise are the texts of the Church Fathers who play a rôle in the transmission of Tradition second only to the apostles themselves. In the way in which the Fathers registered the Tradition that had found its objective medium in Scripture – in the way they received the biblical revelation – they acted under God as makers of the Christian religion in its final form, summarising and clarifying the rule of faith, establishing the *grandes lignes* of the historic liturgies, and, not least, determining that crucial canon of Scripture. The 'score' of the Church's liturgies was also of course in part verbal, but with the Liturgy – considered now not as the milieu of Tradition in the singular but as a monument of the traditions in the plural – we also broach the visual medium, for the Liturgy is enacted in gestures, and supremely in the sacramental signs.

Visual too is the witness to Tradition of the Church's art, where, at their most evangelically ambitious, iconographers attempt a rendering of the whole Gospel in visual form, an artistic counterpart of the written Gospels and indeed of the message of the Bible as a whole, which comes to its head in the kerygma. Divine revelation, as Catholic Christianity understands it, is not only audial but visual, not only verbal but ocular – which is why iconography is so outstanding a witness to Tradition, to the fullness of the revealed truth proposed in Scripture, and the *Catechism of the Catholic Church*, if modestly, an illustrated text. The inseparable character of these media – the preached words of the Word and the sensible signs of his actions – is also attested in the lives of the saints, formed as these were by the apostolic preaching to be, in the pattern of their lives, its visual expression, and thus the living seals on the revelation to which the *Catechism* would grant access.

Here we must note a complication. We have said that Tradition is revelation in transmission, as apprehended by the corporate mind of the apostolic Church – a Church with a worshipping life and a life of discipleship, crucially conditioning factors in the appropriation of Tradition as these must be, which is why *Dei Verbum*, the Dogmatic Constitution on the Divine Revelation of the Second Vatican Council, can say that

> what was handed on by the apostles includes everything which contributes to the holiness of life, and the increase in faith of the People of God and so the Church, in her teaching, life, and worship, perpetuates and hands on to all generations all that she herself is all that she believes.[9]

That tradition (and here I deliberately use a lower case 't') does not, however, consist exclusively of the divinely originated oral traditions, (along with Scripture, Tradition's primary monument). For there is also such a thing in the Church as unwritten traditions, in matters, especially, of worship and discipline, *originating from the apostles themselves* as endowed with a unique authority – imparticipable, unlike the other functions of their ministry, by the subsequent episcopate – to determine what divine revelation had left open in the life of the Church as a believing, worshipping, acting and praying people.[10] One thinks here, for instance, of the putting in place of the orders of bishop, presbyter, deacon as the local 'applications' of the apostolic office, and the setting aside of the need for circumcision and the rest of the ritual Torah as a condition for the entry of Gentiles into the covenant life of the Church. One could add: the establishing of the main hours of Christian prayer (later to be the divine Office), such liturgical gestures as the Sign of the Cross, and doubtless much in the concrete form of the sacraments, as well as the continence (not yet celibacy) of bishops if not presbyters. What is common in the contents of such a list is being *apostolically given* – but this, evidently, is not the same thing as divinely originated oral tradition which was, rather, *apostolically received.* The 'apostolic tradition', then, consists of Tradition, plus the traditions the apostles left behind.

That complication should alert us to a difficulty. Wealth – in the Church's inheritance as in personal property – always means complexity.

The Need for a Magisterium and its Task

It might be thought that the ability to contextualise Scripture in so rich a garden of theological delights would render facile the interpretation of Scripture as Tradition's objective correlate. For various reasons this is not so. Firstly, richness is all very well, but there is such a thing as an *embarras de richesse.* Christians unsympathetic to biblicism as excessively narrow, and to theological liberalism as dispiritingly thin are often attracted – as with High Anglicans – to the kind of 'multi-media' portrait of Tradition I have painted. But if at the same time (as with such Anglicans) they are hostile to, or lack the experience of, a sacred teaching office, they soon find that faced with the bewildering variety of Tradition's monuments from numerous points in space and time they are as much launched on a sea of private judgment as any primitive Lutheran or, for that matter, sophisticated Latitudinarian. In the Councils and the *ex cathedra* definitions of the Popes the Creeds are extended by reference to further aspects or entailments of themselves, just as the same Creeds came into existence as expansions of the brief dogmatic nuclei of the New Testament's own kerygmatic affirmations (such as, 'Jesus is Lord' (I Corinthians 12, 3). Episcopate and papacy (assisted, evidently, by theologians who are – or should be -learned in the lore of Tradition's multi-faceted expression) interpret those multifarious monuments by virtue of the 'charism of truth' the apostolic ministry exercises in fulfilment of the promise of its Lord. We come thereby to be explicitly aware of 'new' (to us) doctrines, fresh articulations of the tacit content of the 'given' of Tradition, faith's 'deposit'. Such dogmas are dramatic (generally) examples of doctrine hard won, honed (usually) in intellectual strife. But all the time, in the ordinary preaching of the Church's pastors (the Pope for the universal Church, the bishop for the local church), the same process is continuing more gently and therefore (normally) less remarkably – unless, that is, as with such issues as the simultaneously procreative and unitive character of sexuality, what is taught enters into sharp collision with the *Zeitgeist.*

Secondly, it is not just a matter of discovering what Tradition has to say (the content of doctrine), but how Tradition says it (doctrine's overall shape or proportions). For someone may be aware of all the Christian truths discreetly in such fashion that either they entertain them atomistically or do so by a false majorisation of one or another doctrine, thus distorting the face of revelation as a whole. For with faces, to change one feature is to change everything. Here is where the task accepted by the magisterium from the sixteenth century onwards of overseeing the presentation of Christian truth through commissioning, promulgating or at least authorising and confirming *catechisms*, is such a vital one. We need to see the shape of the faith in its entirety, or else we shall not see the wood for the trees. So seeing is not to solve an intellectual puzzle, but to move forward on that journey of transfiguration of mind and heart and all our powers, which we call growth in holiness. We cannot profit by the gifts of God unless we are taught which they are and how they are related as well as how they are obtained. We must be equipped for the journey to Glory.

It is in the prosecution of this hugely important mission in Christian education that the *Catechism of the Catholic Church* will play so essential a part in the opening century of this millennium.

Notes

1. H.U. von Balthasar, *Theo-drama. Theological Dramatic Theory.* II. *The Dramatis Personae. Man in God* (Et San Francisco, Ignatius, 1990), p. 22, with an internal citation of H.J. Verweyen, *Ontologische Voraussetzungen des Glaubensaktes. Zum Problem einer transzendental-philosophisches Begrundung der Fundamentaltheologie* (Düsseldorf, Patmos, 1969), p. 184.
2. T. S. Eliot, *'Choruses from The Rock',* X, in *idem., Collected Poems,* 1909-1962 (London, Faber, 1974), pp. 183-184.
3. S. Boulgakoff, *L'Orthodoxie* (Paris, Félix Alcan, 1952), p. 12·.
4. T.F. Torrance, *The Trinitarian Faith, The Evangelical Theology of the Ancient Catholic Church* (Edinburgh, T& T Clark, 1988), pp. 20-21.
5. Leo the Great, *Sermons* 74, 2.
6. J. Corbon, *The Wellspring of Worship* (New York, Paulist Press, 1988), p. 184.
7. H. Denzinger, *Kompendium der Glaubensbekenntnisse und kirchlichen Lehrentscheidungen,* 27th edn, ed. P. Hünermann (Freiburg, Herder, 1991), 1501.
8. P. Roe CSSp, *'A Hermenentical Study of the Relationship between the Theology of Tradition and Inculturation: Using as Horizon the Thought of John Henry Newman and Hans Georg Gadamer',* D.D. thesis (Pontifical Faculty of Theology, Maynooth, 1998), p. 49.
9. *Dei Verbum,* 8.
10. cf. A. Nichols, O.P., *Epiphany. A Theological Introduction to Catholicism* (Collegeville, Minn, Liturgical Press, 1996), p. 51.

Select Bibliography

J.G. Boeglin, *La question de la Tradition dans la théologie catholique contemporaine* (Paris, Editions du Cerf, 1998).

Y. M-J. Congar, *Tradition and Traditions* (London, Burns and Oates, 1966).

A. Nichols O.P., *Epiphany. A Theological Introduction to Catholicism* Collegeville, Minn., Liturgical Press, 1996), ch. 2.

From Newman to Congar. The Idea of Doctrinal Development from the Victorians to the Second Vatican Council (Edinburgh, T. and T. Clark, 1990).

The Service of Glory. The Catechism of the Catholic Church on Worship, Ethics, Spirituality (Edinburgh, T. and T. Clark, 1997).

The Shape of Catholic Theology. An Introduction to its Sources, Principles and History (Edinburgh, T. and T. Clark, 1991).

The Splendour of Doctrine, The Catechism of the Catholic Church on Christian Believing (Edinburgh, 1995).

'CATHOLIC FULLNESS' THE BIRTHRIGHT OF CATHOLICS: THE WISDOM OF CARDINAL NEWMAN

FR THOMAS NORRIS

What stands out in a special way in the life of John Henry Newman is his witness to the search for truth and the cumulative impact of the discovery of various truths along the way upon that search. It is his love for the truth, regardless of the personal implications for the re-ordering of one's life, that makes the figure of Newman both attractive and inspirational today. He was always prepared to count the cost and to pay it in full. That is why a distinguished Anglican scholar could write by way of estimate of Newman's search, 'Never was a mind so unceasingly in motion. But the motion was always growth, and never revolution.'[1] That search in fact made him travel a journey eulogised by Pope Paul VI as 'the most toilsome, but also the greatest, the most meaningful, the most conclusive, that human thought ever travelled during the last century, indeed one might say during the modern era.'[2]

The task this essay sets itself is to understand Newman's insight into what the *General Directory for Catechesis* calls 'the source and the '*sources*' of the message of catechesis'.[3] To do so it is absolutely necessary to trace first the broad contours of the journey of discovery by which Newman gradually but relentlessly assembled the elements of the Catholic Faith, what he called memorably on one occasion, 'Catholic fullness'.[4] In the second main section of the essay I will attempt to draw out the imperatives for catechesis implicit in his discovery and understanding of the faith.

It may be safely claimed that it was the very gradualness of his itinerary into the fullness of faith that gave him such a vivid grasp or 'real apprehension' of the elements of the Faith which the Church is duty bound to transmit to all ages and all nations. And so we turn to study how somebody who disliked, even detested, for a great part of his young life the phenomenon of Roman Catholicism came in the end to embrace that very faith and to defend it and communicate it with a vigour and a depth that remain striking.

The Greatest Journey

The beginning of Newman's odyssey was his experience of God at the age of fifteen. 'When I was fifteen (in the autumn of 1816) a great change of thought took place in me. I fell under the influence of a definite Creed, and received into my intellect impressions of dogma which, through God's mercy, have never been effaced or obscured'.[5] This experience was destined to have a lasting effect on him. There were two immediate impacts. First of all, his religion was going to be dogmatic, that is, founded on the perception that Christianity is revealed truth. 'I know no other religion, I cannot enter into the idea of any other sort of religion. As well can there be filial love without the fact of a father, as devotion without the fact of a Supreme Being'.[6] Henceforth 'Christianity is faith, faith implies a doctrine, a doctrine implies propositions'.[7]

The second impact was the radical choice of God as the ideal of his life, or rather of God as enfleshed and revealed in Christ and communicated to us in word, sacrament and the Holy Spirit. This impact led him to make the choice of God as the ideal of his life. Apart from a few wobbles during his twenties, he was now set on a way of obedience to the God whom he vividly apprehended in his conscience and who lived in his spirit by grace and faith. His early and lasting motto was, 'Holiness before peace'. Life is for holiness, and holiness is an adventure, indeed the only real adventure and the genuine yardstick of a successful existence! As C.S. Dessain perceptively comments, 'True Christianity is the Presence of Persons – to know Christ and through Him, the Father. Obedience, not a frame of mind, is the test'.[8]

In the second phase of his life, which commenced with his taking of Holy Orders in 1824, Newman set before his congregations in Oxford the religion of the Scriptures as this was put forward by the Evangelicals who were his particular religious mentors at this time. There was a distinctly Calvinist tone to much of what he said and wrote in the 1820s, simply because he had been under the influence of authors of a Calvinist mindset such as Thomas Scott and Walter Mayers.

The Church of the Fathers

His encounter with the Fathers, however, was the beginning of a new and *third* phase in his life. This encounter had an almost accidental start: he was asked to write a volume on the First Ecumenical Council for a projected history of the early Councils. In his research of Nicaea he *encountered* the Fathers of the great School of Alexandria: Clement, Origen and Athanasius. Their teaching came like music to his inmost ear, as if in response to ideas and intuitions he had long held. They, and the other Fathers of both the East and the West, became his 'paradise of delight'.[9] And in a particular way they opened up to Newman the vision of a Church that was to become both model and inspiration for the young Oxford leader. With the start of the Oxford Movement in 1833 he set about the gigantic task of bringing out the principles of Athanasius and Augustine, of Basil and Ambrose into the Anglican Church. He saw the Church threatened from within and from without by the rising tide of religious liberalism. This liberalism reduced doctrine to opinion, played down the significance of sacrament, and subjected the episcopate to government in what Newman called Erastianism. The Anglican Church thereby lost her sovereignty and with it too the freedom to move and to be as plain spoken in her message as the times required.

Newman quickly realised that the Church of the Fathers was founded on three central principles. These were the sacramental principle, the dogmatic principle, and the hierarchical principle. In the sacramental principle he recognised the fact that the life of the Redeemer comes in appointed channels bearing his tokens, channels that unlock the treasure-house of grace. The dogmatic principle is the fact that the truths of the Creed are revealed, being original derivations from revelation, which is the initial and essential idea of Christianity. Or as he puts it in the *Essay on the Development of Christian Doctrine*, 'The dogmatic principle is to Christianity what conscience is to the individual'.[10]

Finally, in the hierarchical principle he saw the truth that the bishops of the Church were the successors to the apostles and as such the guarantee of the apostolic credentials of the Christian community. The Church was a visible, as well as an invisible, reality set up by the Lord and not simply reducible to the actual number of its members. When the Oxford Movement began in 1833, however, he wanted a second reformation for the existing Anglican Church so that it might emulate the Church of the Fathers and be its worthy modern successor.

With his colleagues in the Oxford Movement he was deeply convinced of the value of their project and confident of a happy outcome to their endeavours. They felt they had found the happy medium between Protestantism and that Romanism whose principal faults lay in the decrees of the Council of Trent, as well as in its unbiblical devotion to Mary and its unhistorical claims for the Bishop of Rome. As additions to the original deposit of truth, these were importations and corruptions, not developments and authentic growths. They amounted to a serious departure from the standards of apostolic truth and the principles of the Church of the Fathers.

The discovery of the Church's Catholicity

A new and alarming phase of discovery, however, was now about to open in his itinerary. In the Summer of 1839, he made two discoveries that were to pulverise his theory of the *Via Media.* Both discoveries involved the Fathers. First, he read the history of the Monophysite controversy that beleaguered the whole Church for most of the fifth century. In his reading he came face-to-face with the bishop of Rome, Leo the Great, whose interventions in the council of Chalcedon were decisive and vital. Leo's majestic person and authority suggested a presence in Rome that was as unique as it was necessary for the well-being of the whole Church at a crucial junction in the history of the Church.

A month later, an article in *The Dublin Review* jolted him even more. This time it was a comment of St Augustine in his controversy with the Donatists, '*Securus judicat orbis terrarum*' ('The whole Church has no chance of Being wrong').[11] Here he saw a simpler rule than that of antiquity for the settling of disputes in the Church. 'St Augustine', he wrote in the *Apologia*, 'was one of the prime oracles of antiquity; here then antiquity was deciding against itself'[12], that is in favour of the further principle of catholicity. Avery Dulles comments very perceptively on the significance of this discovery for the leader of the Oxford Movement, 'The *existing* church, and not simply the prior church, was the oracle of truth'.[13] Newman had suddenly encountered the authoritativeness of the living existing Church. The principle of catholicity was beckoning with fresh force.

From this time forth Newman sees the Fathers not only as witnesses to the apostolic faith but also as provokers of its creative elaboration. 'It was in the Fathers – existing and acting concretely in history as Catholic persons – that Newman met the real force of Catholic reality. ... They were imbued with the life-giving power of God who in Christ has taken up human weakness, redeemed it and perfected it. He found in the Fathers the Christ of the apostles as the life-giving Spirit active in the history of mankind and leading it to conformity with his spiritual and perfect form'.[14] In that way the Catholicity of the Church stole upon him and stole over him. He began to look at Rome with less fierceness and animosity! And this disturbed him greatly.

The development of doctrine

Rome, however, still had the stains of additions to apostolic truth upon her countenance. Could they be justified by any means? At the end of a further three years a fresh and original idea struck him, the idea of the possible development of doctrine. He thought of an unfolding of divine revelation in the time of the church, in a manner analogous to its unfolding in the Old Covenant and in the New. If the Word of God in revelation had been since his conversion as a juvenile the first principle of his religion, he now began to think more concretely of the Word of God's manifold presence and activity in the life of the Church. A first fruit of that thinking was his sermon on 'The Theory of Developments in Religious Doctrine' in 1843, which was the concluding sermon of the *Oxford University Sermons.* The following year he began a full study of the subject. An *Essay on the Development of Doctrine*, perhaps his most seminal and challenging theological work, outlines a view of developments in doctrine throughout the history of the church.

A growing consensus of scholars see in the *Essay* not only an answer to an 'objection against Catholicism'[15], in the form of the obvious presence of doctrines that were not there in explicit form from the beginning, but also and perhaps more importantly a fresh vision of the reality of Christ present in, but not absorbed by, the vicissitudes of history. Christ who is the fullness of divine revelation is always larger than what may be said of him, being the fullness of divinity in the human condition of time and history (Col 2:9). 'The development of doctrine, then, involves uniquely the unfolding presence and deepening incarnation of Christ in history through the faithful remembering and reliving of what has been received (*anamnesis* : I Cor 11:23; 15:3f) and the faithful giving of it to humankind whom Christ came to gather into the kingdom of his Father (*diakonia*)'.[16] Far from corrupting the revelation has been once and for all entrusted to the saints (Jude 3), development is the sign of its life and one of the constitutive principles of the whole church system, a point that he makes in the later editions of the work.

Now there is an extraordinary parallel between this insight into revelation and that proposed in *Dei Verbum* where one reads 'the Tradition that comes from the Apostles makes progress in the Church, with the help of the Holy Spirit. There is a growth in insight into the realities and the words that are being passed on'.[17] Newman sees a Christological focus as the indispensable key to the whole Church system. Jesus Christ is the Lord of his Church and the Lord of history making a new history, yes the history of God with us. Since he has made 'the new covenant in his Blood' (I Cor 11:25; Lk 22:20), he has crossed a threshold that will never be reversed. He goes before us, reminding us indeed of the revelation given to the apostles (see Gal 1:11-2; II Cor 11:7,10) but calling us to him and after him in the adventure of making, with his help, a new history.

In this perspective one can see that the choice of Christ and his Word as the ideal of our lives is both the first principle of living in the Church and the precondition for its authentic development. Does not Vatican II's masterpiece, *Lumen Gentium*, begin with the words, 'Since Christ is the light of the world. ... '? And a Christian who does not prefer Christ to everything else under the sun sheds little of the reflected glory of Christ on the Church, but instead sullies and stains and burdens the holy *Catholica*. The christocentricity of Newman, a christocentricity opening upwards to the Trinity and outwards into history, means that each Church must be converted to the Lordship of Jesus Christ and its practical demands. It is this same choice of Christ that is also the indispensable precondition for an effective ecumenism between the Churches, a fact which Newman stressed and Vatican II highlighted in its *Decree on Ecumenism*.[18]

'The Most Meaningful Journey'

The fruits of this enormous faith-odyssey for Newman were quite enormous, particularly so for the content and method of catechesis. He had assembled systematically the elements of the Catholic Faith. That faith, it is true, had its origins in the persons and events of the biblical age, but its dynamism did not reside in dead documents nor empty rituals nor in formularies repeated by officers with the duty of merely keeping good order in a religious polity. On the contrary, the power of the faith was in the present. He who had promised to be with his own until the end of time, and who therefore saw the end from the beginning, had naturally decreed the means to reach that goal. Those means included Scripture, Tradition, the Apostolic Succession of Pope and Bishop, together with superintendence of the Holy Spirit and a subtle but powerful *'sensus fidei'* on the part of sincere believers.

What he had discovered while studying the Fathers, namely, that the Christianity of the early Church was dogmatic, sacramental and hierarchical, he now saw alive and well in 1845. Thus he could write the following year, 'I believed that our Lord had instituted a Teaching, Sacramental, organised Body called the Church, and that the Roman Communion was as an historical fact its present representative and continuation. … I have at various times since my reception had to insist on this'.[19] In the evening of his life, in the famous Preface to the Third Edition of the *Via Media*, he could formulate the form of the Faith as follows, 'Christianity, then, is at once a philosophy, a political power, and a religious rite: as a religion, it is Holy; as a philosophy, it is Apostolic; as a political power, it is imperial, that is, One and Catholic'.[20] If one allows for the linguistic freedom that Newman adopts in the course of his reflections, one has no difficulty in seeing the harmony between the patristic prototype of the Church and the contemporary expression. It was the perception of that harmony that made him a Catholic.

A special fruit of his odyssey was the discovery of a magisterium that when certain conditions are fulfilled is infallible. What is interesting here is that he *always* saw in the claim to magisterium, as the infallible organ of truth, a 'main tenet' and 'fundamental dogma' of Roman Catholicism.[21] As an Anglican he believed this to be the root cause of all deviations in the whole Roman system, and as a Catholic he defended vigorously the claim itself.[22]

While an Anglican he clung to Antiquity as his guide and norm. He then saw the Romans as depending upon infallibility. What the Church has, however, is indefectibility in the essentials of the faith. For the Anglican Newman this was sufficient and a replacement for infallibility. His position had much in common with the view of Hans Küng for whom the Church has indefectibility, which he defines as a 'fundamental remaining of the Church in the truth, which is not annulled by individual errors'.[23]

In presenting Newman's conversion to the infallibility of the Church one would do well to heed the advice of Avery Dulles, 'One must consider not only the date but also the exact circumstances of each writing and its intended audience. Newman was frequently writing as a controversialist or as a spiritual director. Sometimes he was writing against the Catholic Church, sometimes against liberals and Protestants, who denounced infallibility altogether, sometimes against extreme ultramontanists who recognised no safeguards'.[24]

Newman's positive argument for infallibility resembles that of Karl Rahner.[25] Both utilised antecedent probabilities.[26] Since revelation comes to us as the Word of God, and therefore as divinely true and free from all error, that is, as infallible, it is obvious that God would have intended it to remain in this state. Given this state of affairs, it would be antecedently likely that the Giver of Revelation will have made provision for its protection against error and dilution. Only such an ingredient within revelation itself could be strong enough to 'make a stand against the wild living intellect of man'.[27] This allows Newman to define infallibility as 'an extraordinary divine protection when the Church speaks *ex cathedra.* Infallibility prevents her from falling into error'.[28]

Very significantly Newman argues for the infallibility of the Church without investigating in the first instance the organs or agents of that infallibility apart from the obvious connection of the gift with the apostolic ministry of the pope and the bishops. However, this question was to become acute not long after his entry into the Catholic Church. The context was, as is well known, the calling by Pope Pius IX of the First Vatican Council. Newman's attitudes in the years leading up to the Council, during the Council (1869-70), and subsequently are now a matter of history.[29]

Suffice it to say that, on the analogy of the early christological and trinitarian Councils of the Church, when one Council defined one portion of the truth only to require a second Council to put the defined portion 'in proper perspective through further definitions and declarations'[30], so too with the teaching of Vatican I: a later Council would one day pick up where the teaching of Vatican I ran out. In that way Newman anticipated the teaching of Vatican II where in *Lumen Gentium*, chapter three, the teaching on the infallibility of the College of Bishops together with the Pope rounds off and refines the teaching of the previous Council.[31]

'The New Catechism and Newman'[32]

In Newman's vision of faith[33] there is a wonderful unity between the many truths composing the one and only encompassing 'mystery of our religion' (I Tim 3:16). We have noticed this already in the *Essay on Development.* 'One thing alone has to be impressed on us by Scripture, the Catholic idea, and in it they (doctrines) are all included. To object, then, to the number of propositions upon which an anathema is placed, is altogether to mistake their use: for their multiplication is not intended to enforce many things, but to express one'.[34] For Newman, then, 'doctrines are a witness to the vitality of revelation, its inexhaustible riches, and assist in the realisation of these riches. They represent a folding out of the one great idea that is Christ, and must always be made to fold in to their mysterious source'.[35] That explains his insistence on 'that true religious zeal which leads theologians to keep the sacred Ark of the Covenant in every letter of its dogma, as a tremendous deposit for which they are responsible'.[36]

Newman underlines the reality of the deposit of faith, a reality which he saw already in the Pastoral Epistles. It is enough to give one quote to show the thrust of his thinking, '*Those things which thou hast heard from me through many witnesses*,' says St Paul to Timothy, '*commit these same to faithful men, who shall be able to teach others also.*' This body of truth was in consequence called the *depositum*, as being substantive teaching, not a mere accidental deduction from Scripture. Thus St Paul says to his disciple and successor Timothy, *Keep the deposit* (I Tim 6:20), *Hold fast the form of sound words, Guard the noble deposit* (II Tim 1:14). ... What is 'the deposit'? 'That which has been entrusted to you, not which thou hast discovered; what thou hast received, not what thou hast thought out; a matter not of cleverness, but of teaching; not of private handling, but of public tradition'.[37] Here one finds the foundation for Newman's thinking on the objectivity and the coherence of the content of faith, his conviction that Christianity is eminently an objective religion. And here one finds also the justification for a systematically doctrinal catechetic, not as an optional extra as it were, but as the only valid statement of the Faith!

In this emphasis, however, he is out of step with much of the theory of catechetics in the anglophone world and beyond. In this world many of the practitioners seem to be convinced that such a catechetics is unnecessary if not well nigh impossible. But not so the *Catechism of the Catholic Church*. Newman's very language anticipates the words with which Pope John Paul II opens the Apostolic Constitution, itself called *Fidei depositum*, 'Guarding the deposit of faith is the mission which the Lord entrusted to his Church, and which she fulfils in every age'.[38] Newman's mind, then, a mind whose extraordinary odyssey we have looked at in order to appreciate his profound personal appropriation of the Faith, emphasises the integrity and objectivity of the Faith, the apostolic deposit. In fact, in his *Theological Papers on Faith and Certainty* he writes that 'an accurate knowledge of the catechism is a *motivum credibilitatis*'.[39]

It would be a major error, however, to conclude that Newman placed exclusive or even primary emphasis on the objective pole in the transmission of the faith, and so, by implication, in the catechetical enterprise. Nothing could be further from the truth! Faith for him is famously *a matter both of the head and of the heart.* He disliked intensely the idea that 'belief belongs to the mere intellect, not also to the heart'.[40] The very goal of the whole of catechesis is to facilitate above all a person-to-person rapport with Jesus Christ. Failure to achieve such a personal and experiential encounter with the Saviour of humankind could not but have the direst consequences for the faith of Christians. 'This is why we see such multitudes in France and Italy giving up religion altogether: they have not impressed upon their *hearts* the life of our Lord and Saviour as given us in the Evangelists. They believe merely with the intellect, not with the heart'.[41] It is little wonder that when he became cardinal he should choose as his motto the words, *Cor ad cor loquitur.*

This subjective or experiential dimension of revelation and faith gains a quick and warm welcome from the majority of catechists in the Anglophone world. However, they often emphasise this dimension at the partial or even total expense of the doctrinal and objective dimension of the Faith. It is this attitude, too, which more than anything else underlines their misgivings about the CCC.[42] As for Newman, he did not come down on the one side or the other. Nor did he sit on the fence as it were. Insisting on both for the integrity of the catechetical enterprise, he actually reinforced the tension between the objective truth of the Church's doctrines and the need for the believer to achieve a personal possession of them. This is the key to a characteristic that runs from beginning to end of all he wrote and did, the characteristic, namely, of emphasising simultaneously 'the dogmatic principle'[43] and the sheer need for a personal appropriation of the truths and the life of faith. With regard to the latter, he wrote in 1829 that 'Revealed religion brings us into a new world – a world of overpowering interest, of the sublimest views'.[44] It is this very tension which gives life to the deposit of faith in the whole life of the Church and in the daily existence of believers.

In conclusion it may be fairly claimed that the life and the thought of Cardinal Newman are a beacon of light for all involved in the vital but difficult catechetical enterprise today. He rarely descends into specifics the catechising process in itself. However, the principles governing that process emerge and stand out with an attractive clarity. His championing of the need for a systematically doctrinal catechetic, combined with the still more important need for a personal encounter with Christ in his many presences in community, scripture, sacrament, and doctrine, flows from his personal assimilation of the Christianity of the millennia as manifest in the life of the Church. He wrote what many consider[45] to be the *opus magnum* of his whole life, *A Grammar of Assent*, principally to describe the process by which believers gain real access to the mysteries of the faith (he coined the terms 'real apprehension' and 'real assent'), and theologians pursue the understanding of these mysteries (looking for 'notional apprehension'). There he achieved a dynamic synthesis between fullness of content and appropriateness of method. John Henry Newman is indeed a friend and a mentor for all those concerned that the Word of God in all its 'unfathomable riches' (Eph 3:8) be communicated to the People of God in the new millennium.

Notes

1. Owen Chadwick, *Newman,* Past Masters Series (Oxford-New York 1983), 5. References to Cardinal Newman's works are to the uniform edition of 1868-81, published by Longman's, Green & Co., unless otherwise indicated.
2. Pope Paul VI, *L'Osservatore Romano,* 28 October 1963; *Acta Apostolicae Sedis,* 1963, 1025.
3. Congregation for the Clergy, *General Directory for Catechesis* (Dublin, 1998), 102f.
4. *Essays Critical and Historical,* II, 231-3.
5. *Apologia,* 4.
6. *ibid.*, 49.
7. *DA,* 284.
8. C.S. Dessain, *Life,* 22.
9. *Diff.*, I, 370.
10. *Dev,* 361.
11. *Ap,* 116; LD XXV, 220.
12. *Ap.*, 116.
13. A. Dulles, 'Newman, Conversion and Ecumenism', in TS, 4 (1990), 438.
14. G. Dragas, 'John Henry Newman: A Starting-Point for rediscovering the Catholicity of the Fathers Today', *The Greek Orthodox Theological Review,* XXV, 3 (1980), 279.
15. *LD,* XII, 332.
16. Thomas Norris, 'The Development of Doctrine: 'A remarkable philosophical phenomenon', in *Communio,* 3(1995), 484.
17. *DV,* 8.
18. *UR,* 7-8.
19. *Letters and Diaries,* XI, 190-1.
20. *Via Media,* Third Edition, xl.
21. *ibid.*, 84; *Grammar of Assent,* 102.
22. The best known defence is *The Letter to the Duke of Norfolk,* written in 1874 in defence of the Decrees of the First Vatican Council; in *Difficulties of Anglicans,* II.
23. Hans Kung, *Infallible. An Inquiry* (London, 1971), 181.
24. Avery Dulles, *Theological Studies,* 51 (1990), 434.
25. Karl Rahner, '*A Critique of Hans Kung*', in *Homiletic and Pastoral Review,* May 1971, 10-26, especially 21.

26. Newman employs this method in the *Essay on the Development of Christian Doctrine* to the point that it becomes the key to the structure of the work and its argumentation: see especially II, 2, 1-14.
27. *Apologia*, 219.
28. *Via Media*, I, 310.
29. See John R. Page, *What will Dr Newman Do? John Henry Newman and Papal Infallibility*, 1865-1875, Collegeville, Minnesota, 1994 for a splendid treatment of the matter; see Placid Murray OSB, *'Newman on Infallibility: a Mini-Ontology'*, *Doctrine and Life*, 4 (1996), 229-40.
30. Page, *op. cit.*, 416.
31. See *Letter to the Duke of Norfolk*, 173-4.
32. This is the title of an article by Archbishop Eric D'Arcy of Hobart, Tasmania, who aims at showing those who do not believe in a 'systematically doctrinal catechetic' that 'the thought and the heart of Cardinal Newman are uniquely fitted to offer them fellow-feeling and congenial leadership', *Communio*, 3 (1993), 485-502.
33. See Louis Bouyer, *Newman's Vision of Faith*, San Francisco 1986, passim.
34. *Oxford University Sermons*, 336.
35. Thomas J. Norris, *Only Life gives Life. Revelation, Theology and Christian Living according to Cardinal Newman*, Dublin 1996, 29.
36. *Historical Sketches*, II, 475-6.
37. *Essays Critical and Historical*, I, 125-6.
38. *Catechism of the Catholic Church*, Dublin 1994, 2.
39. *Theological Papers of John Henry Newman on Faith and Certainty*, ed. HM de Achaval, SJ and J. Derek Holmes, Oxford 1976, 90.
40. *Essay on the Development of Doctrine*, 358.
41. *Letters and Diaries*, XXVI, 87.
42. See J. Wrenn and Kenneth D. Whitehead, *Flawed Expectations: The Reception of the Catechism of the Catholic Church*, San Francisco 1996 for a conspectus of the opposition to the *Catechism*. A reviewer concluded his estimate of this work thus, 'Newman wrote a Grammar of Assent. Wrenn and Whitehead have given us a Grammar of Dissent, a very useful study – useful to non-Catholics as well as Catholics – of how pride of intellect can lead educated people astray', D.J. Dooley, in *The Chesterton Review*, February/May 1998, 129.
43. Commenting on 'his great theologian', St Athanasius, whom he studied in great depth, Newman wrote, 'According to him, opposition to the witness of the Church, separation from its communion, *private judgment overbearing the authorised catechetical teaching*, the fact of a denomination, as men now speak, this is a self-condemnation', *Select Treatises of St Athanasius*, II, 51; see *Historical Sketches*, I, 209-10. The italics in quotation are my own.
44. *Essays Critical and Historical*, I, 23.
45. See Etienne Gilson in his Introduction to the New York 1955 edition, 21; N. Lash in his Introduction to the Notre Dame and London 1979 edition; F. Crowe, in his contribution 'Intuition', *New Catholic Encyclopedia*, VII, 700.

Select Bibliography

Newman, J. H., *Apologia pro Vita Sua.* (Any edition).
An Essay on the development of Christian Doctrine.
A Grammar of Assent.
Norris, T. G., *Only Life gives Life. Revelation, Theology and Christian Living according to Cardinal Newman* (Dublin, The Columba Press, 1996).

THE RESURRECTION OF JESUS: SOME CONTEMPORARY ISSUES

FR GERALD O'COLLINS SJ

Many of the better things in my life have happened on the spur of the moment. One of those better things concerned the resurrection of Jesus. Over twenty-five years ago in England at the University of Cambridge I got an emergency phone call from Henry Hart, the dean of one of the colleges. At the last minute Hart was looking for someone to give a lecture to the theological society in his college. He did not mind what I spoke about, but he wanted a lecture at a couple of days' notice. On the spur of the moment I could only think of examining some aspects of Jesus' resurrection. That eleventh hour invitation from Henry Hart in the late 1960s has kept me thinking, teaching and writing about the resurrection ever since.

Experience has convinced me that it is better to say less rather than more about the resurrection. Hence I want to limit this lecture to four major questions. The discussion that follows can, of course, range more widely. As far as I am concerned, anything at all about the resurrection of Jesus can come in. For that matter, I am happy to respond to and learn from questions or observations about Jesus Christ that range even well beyond his resurrection from the dead.

My four major questions are: What did the first Christians mean by their claim about Jesus' resurrection? How did they come to know about and believe in him as risen from the dead? How did the resurrection of the crucified Jesus bring the definitive revelation of the tripersonal God? In what way can we legitimate Easter faith today?

The Claim

First of all, the claim. In our century a number of writers have argued that the 'real' resurrection claim is simply that Jesus rose in the hearts of his disciples, his cause continued and the disciples came to a new consciousness about life and their position before God. In other words, these writers would have it that after his death and burial nothing at all happened to Jesus himself. In using resurrection language the first Christians were not talking of Jesus but only of themselves. The disciples had come to see that Jesus was right about God. In that sense he had risen from their spiritual death.[1]

This thesis, to put it mildly, is implausible. Our New Testament texts use a variety of idioms to claim something that primarily affected Jesus himself. The New Testament contains formulas of preaching about his resurrection (1 Cor 15:3-5; Rom 4:25); professions of Easter faith (Rom 10:9); a new attribute for God as the One who has raised the dead Jesus (Gal 1:1; 1 Thess 1:9-10); the Easter narratives of the four gospels; a long, reflective argument which Paul develops in support of the resurrection (1 Cor 15:12-58); and missionary discourses which centre on Jesus' resurrection (Acts 2:31-32; 3:15; 4:10; 13:30, 37). The New Testament brings into play a whole range of expressions to make this claim about Jesus: he has been raised from the dead and now enjoys a new, transformed life (Lk 24:15, 23; Rom 14:9; 1 Cor 15:35-50). Our first Christian authors fill out this language about Jesus' resurrection by also speaking of his being 'glorified' (Lk 24:26; John 7:39; 12:16; 17:1; 1 Tim 3:16) and 'exalted' (Phil 2:9) to 'the right hand' of God (the Father) (e.g., Acts 2:33).

Paul, our very first Christian author, wrote from around AD 50 till the early 60s. We find embedded in his letters even earlier formulas and traditions about Christ's resurrection. Nowadays we would expect the apostle to use quotation marks. But even without quotation marks it is often clear that he is citing earlier formulas. Those earlier formulas and traditions quoted by St Paul take us back to the 30s and 40s – that is to say, to the very beginning of Christianity. We have such formulas of preaching as 1 Cor 15:3-5: 'I handed on to you what I also received, that Christ died for our sins in accordance with the scriptures, that he was buried, that he was raised on the third day in accordance with the scriptures, and that he appeared to Cephas and then to the twelve.' In Rom 10:9 Paul cites a basic profession of Easter faith which may have been used on the occasion of baptism. The neophytes 'confessed with their lips' that 'Jesus is Lord' and believed in their hearts that God had raised him from the dead. The new Christian attribute for God turns up here and there in Paul's letters: for example, in the opening lines of his Letter to the Galatians when he speaks of 'God the Father who raised Jesus Christ from the dead' (Gal 1:1). After the crucifixion God had intervened and the immediate object of the divine action was Jesus himself. When writing to the Philippians, Paul cites a hymn about Jesus dying a shameful death on the cross, being highly exalted by God and then receiving the worship of the universe (Phil 2:6-11).

All this traditional material taken over by St Paul shows us that claims about Jesus' resurrection from the dead go back to the very origins of the Christian movement. How then should we sum up the primary content of those claims coming from AD 30-50 – that is to say, from the crucial two decades before Paul and then other New Testament authors began writing their works? In essence the first Christians announced that through the divine power Jesus himself had been raised to new life. The pre-Pauline tradition spoke of God (the Father) raising Jesus from the dead (Rom 10:9; Gal 1:1; 1 Thess 1:10). Or else it spoke of Jesus 'being raised' (1 Cor 15:4; Mark 16:6), implying that this had occurred through the divine power. The agent (God) was understood. One filled out such phrases from the tradition as 'he was raised' (Rom 4:25) and added 'by God.'

The primary claim was not that Jesus' cause continued, or that the disciples themselves had been 'raised' to a new consciousness and a life of faith by coming to see that Jesus had been right about God. The primary claim was that the crucified Jesus had been personally brought from the state of death to that of a new and everlasting life. Of course, the pre-Pauline formulas recognised that the resurrection had also taken place in order to change and 'justify' us before God (Rom 4:25). Secondarily the resurrection also led the disciples and others to the new life of faith and grace and initiated our final resurrection from the dead (1 Cor 15:20). Nevertheless, in the first place the resurrection claim referred to what had happened to Jesus himself.

Those who disagree and do not accept that the resurrection claim refers primarily to the fate of Jesus himself have to do a violent reductionist job on our New Testament texts. A fairly recent example of such reductionism you will find in an article by Robert Scuka that appeared in the journal *Modern Theology*.[2] He asserts that the resurrection message of the New Testament has really nothing to do with an event in Jesus own personal story.

En route to this 'explanation,' even if three times he allows himself to speak of 'the in-breaking' of God's kingdom, Scuka assures us that by proclaiming the kingdom Jesus was merely drawing attention to the fact that divine grace is 'present in every here and now' (pp. 86-87). (So much for Jesus bringing anything new in his ministry, let alone announcing any future decisive action on the part of God!) The 'coming of the kingdom of God' is not 'to be conceived as an event in time, but instead designates a dimension of the reality of God's presence' (p. 94, n. 23). In the name of his own 'theological' position, Scuka simply claims this, quite consciously prescinding from what Jesus himself might have 'said,' 'meant' or 'believed' (p. 94, n. 24).

As well as refusing to face up to what Jesus actually proclaimed about God's present *and future* kingdom, Scuka also tampers with what the New Testament announces about the consequences for us of Jesus' resurrection: justification here and now and eternal life hereafter. He acknowledges the special character of divine grace according to St Paul. Scuka comments that the apostle should have known better and grasped that 'grace is given in and with the conditions of human existence.' 'This is what Paul's doctrine should be understood to mean,' Scuka concludes, 'regardless of whether he himself recognised this as its implicit meaning' (p. 95, n. 26). Hope for eternal life is dismissed as a (or even the) sinful 'form of self preoccupation.' Jesus, John and Paul are pressed into service as 'implicitly' supporting our author's view that the New Testament and later Christian talk about our 'future' resurrection life *simply* points to the new quality of meaningful existence we can enjoy here and now (pp. 88-89).

At the end of the day, all of this talk about what Jesus, John and Paul 'implicitly' recognised or 'should' have recognised amounts to Scuka himself wanting them to have said, written or meant something different from what we actually have from them. This wish comes right out in the open when Scuka speaks of 'what the claim concerning Jesus' resurrection should be understood to mean, regardless of what the New Testament may have said, or meant' (pp. 91-92, n. 4). It would be outrageous to apply this principle to contemporary works in history, law, philosophy, psychology, sociology or other disciplines: this is what these authors should be understood to mean, regardless of what they may have written or meant. It is just as outrageous to apply the principle to ancient authors, be they Plato, Aristotle, Julius Caesar or the authors of the New Testament Scuka himself and other such reductionists would not be pleased if we applied their 'method' of interpretation to their own writings: 'this is what Scuka and these other authors should be understood to mean, regardless of what they may have written or meant.' The 'regardless of what they may have written or meant' principle gives us the licence to find what we want to find in the work of Scuka and play fast and loose with what he intends to say.

Thus the reductionist 'method' ultimately backfires on those who use it in support of their claim to 'know' better than the New Testament authors what those authors meant or should have meant when they wrote what they did about Jesus' resurrection. We can, as indicated, turn the 'method' against the reductionists themselves.

Here one finds a startling difference between modern reductionists like Scuka and traditional sceptics like David Hume (1711-76). The sceptics acknowledged the real meaning of the New Testament assertions, but in the name of reason and common sense they rejected the truth of Jesus' resurrection. The reductionists, however, tamper with the meaning of those assertions and then accept the truth which they have fashioned for themselves.

Before we leave the basic New Testament claims about the resurrection, let me add a few more observations. It is clear that the first Christians did not present Jesus' resurrection as the mere resuscitation of a corpse – that simple return to life expected by 2 Macc 7, exemplified in the raising of the daughter of Jairus (Mk 5:35-43), or envisaged by Herod's fear about John the Baptist coming back to life (Mk 6:16). Early Christians spoke, or rather sang, of Jesus as being 'exalted' or 'taken up' into divine glory (Phil 2:6-11;1 Tim 3:16). This liturgical, hymnic language of exaltation, cited from the pre-Pauline tradition, indicates that the first Christians thought of Christ's resurrection as being his glorious, final transformation. So far from being a mere reanimation, his resurrection was understood to have anticipated the general, glorious resurrection expected by apocalyptic literature (Isa 26:7-21; Dan 12:l-4) to take place at the end of history.

Paul and other New Testament writers followed this early tradition in both ways. They presented Jesus' resurrection as his glorious, definitive transformation (Lk 24:26; Acts 13:34; 1 Pet 1:11). Second, they knew his resurrection to be the beginning of the final, general resurrection (1 Cor 15:20; Col 1:18). To express Jesus' glorious transformation Paul strains language by speaking of a 'spiritual body' – that is a bodily human existence which has been radically transfigured by the power of the Holy Spirit (1 Cor 15:2-58). Luke and John present the transformation involved in Jesus' resurrection by the details of his appearing and disappearing at will (Lk 24:31, 36; John 20:19, 26).

Thus far I have been attending to the original and essential claim about the fact and nature of Jesus' own resurrection from the dead. We turn now to the question: how did the first Christians know that this event had taken place. To answer that question, we need first to go back to the ministry of Jesus. What did Peter, Mary Magdalene and the others among the first group of disciples see Jesus' doing and hear him saying?

The Origins of Easter Faith

During his ministry Jesus linked the present and coming divine rule to his own person and activity (Mk 1:15; Matt 6:10; 8:11; 12:28; Luke 12:8-9; 17:20-21). In proclaiming the divine kingdom he betrayed a remarkable sense of his personal authority, transforming in his own name the law of God (Mk 10:9; Matt 5:21-48). He acted with startling self-assurance when he set aside various interpretations of the Sabbath rest (Mk 3:1-5), and claimed the right to decide what should be done or not done on that sacred day (Mk 2:28). Further, Jesus exercised his extraordinary authority in a deeply compassionate fashion, identifying himself with the divine concern to forgive and definitively save sinful human beings (Mk 2:5, 17; Luke 7: 48; 15:11-32; 19:1-10). Just as he understood his word and God's word to be identical, so he understood his presence and God's salvation to be identical.

Add too a) the unique filial consciousness (Matt 11:27) he showed towards the God whom he addressed with astonishing intimacy as 'Abba' (Mk 14:36), and b) the sense of his messianic mission that led to his dying by crucifixion on the charge of being a messianic pretender (Mk 15:26).

His utterly shameful death, after condemnation by both religious and political authorities, seemed to give the lie to Jesus' claim that in his person and activity the final divine revelation and salvation had come. He died apparently abandoned (Mk 15:34) and even cursed by God (Gal 3:13; 1 Cor 1:23). Some scholars have argued that Jews at the time of Jesus did not interpret death by crucifixion to mean being cursed by God. But the evidence from Paul and Qumran (Temple Roll 64:12) makes it clear that this 'most wretched of deaths' (Josephus), unlike John the Baptist's decapitation and the forms of execution suffered by other martyred prophets (Lk 13:34; Matt 23:35), symbolised rejection by God.

What can one reasonably hold about the situation of Jesus' disciples after his crucifixion and burial? It seems that during his ministry they, or at the least a core group of disciples, had come to acknowledge him in some sense Messiah (Mk 8:27-30), but could not accept his suffering destiny as Son of Man (Mk 8:31-33; 9:32; 10:35-45). The male disciples who had remained with Jesus fled at the time of his arrest and Peter denied him. Condemned and crucified as a blasphemer and false Messiah, Jesus died seemingly abandoned and cursed by the God whom he had called 'Father dear.' The evidence we have from the Gospels (Lk 24:13-24) agrees with what we should expect – that Calvary caused a profound theological crisis for the disciples and shattered their faith in Jesus and the God for whom he had spoken and acted.

Some writers allege a substantial degree of continuity between the pre-Easter and post-Easter faith of the disciples. This hypothesis argues that the disciples thought and prayed their way through the crisis of Calvary and reached the conclusion not only that Jesus had been right about God but also that he must now be alive with his Father. According to this continuity hypothesis, in moving to their resurrection faith, the disciples were substantially helped by Jewish beliefs about the divine vindication of martyred, eschatological prophets. In this way some have argued that the appearances of the risen Lord and the discovery of his empty tomb were simply not necessary to call forth the disciples' Easter-faith. Perhaps the 'appearances' were no more than a way of expressing the psychological breakthrough, when; the disciples finally saw the real truth about Jesus and drew the conclusion that he had to be alive and with God.[3]

On several grounds such claims about substantial continuity between the pre-Easter and post-Easter faith of the disciples do not stand up. First, the pre-Pauline tradition establishes that they believed the risen Jesus to be not so much a vindicated prophet but the resurrected Messiah (1 Cor 15:3). That creates severe difficulties for the continuity hypothesis. The messianic expectations reflected by the Old Testament and other Jewish writings included various strands and elements. But there is no hard evidence that any Jews ever expected a Messiah who would be killed and then raised from the dead. Even more unthinkable and absurd was the idea of the resurrection of a crucified Messiah. Yet that was what the first Christians proclaimed. Their previous Jewish beliefs cannot account for such a uniquely new claim.

Second, as Wolfhart Pannenberg[4] and others have rightly insisted, the Christian proclamation of the glorious, final resurrection of only one person (Jesus) was also something strikingly new. At that time many Jews expected a general resurrection at the end of history. Jesus' preaching presupposed such a general resurrection (Matt 8:11; Luke 11:32), and at least once he entered into debate about its nature (Mk 12:18-27). To the inner group of his followers he may have announced his vindication through resurrection (Mk 9:31), but neither that passion prediction nor the other two (Mk 8:31; 10:33-34) specify the glorious, eschatological nature of his resurrection. Hence neither from their Jewish beliefs nor from Jesus himself could the disciples have drawn what they began to proclaim: the final, glorious resurrection of one person (Jesus) in anticipation of a general resurrection that was still to come. Once again the hypothesis of a relatively easy continuity between the pre-Easter and post-Easter faith of the disciples proves thoroughly questionable.

Third, the interpretation of the Easter appearances as no more than the disciples finally thinking their way through to the truth about Jesus and his new life with God does not correspond to what the New Testament witnesses themselves report about the appearances. For these and other reasons, the thesis of a relatively smooth passage for the disciples from their pre-crucifixion faith to their post-Easter proclamation does not match the evidence.

We are left, then, with the two major catalysts of Easter faith proposed by the New Testament first, the disciples' encounters with the risen Lord, and, second, the negative, confirmatory sign of his empty tomb.

Unlike the second-century apocryphal Gospel of Peter (9:35-11:45), our New Testament sources never claim that anyone witnessed the actual event of Jesus' resurrection. Instead, the pre-Pauline tradition (1 Cor 15:3-5), Paul himself (1 Cor 15:6-8), the four Gospels and the traditions on which the Gospel writers drew (Lk 24:34) testify that the risen and living Jesus appeared to certain individuals and groups, above all, 'the twelve' or 'the eleven' as Luke 24:33 more accurately calls that group after the defection of Judas. These sources vary as to where the appearances took place (Galilee? In and around Jerusalem), or sometimes do not name any places at all (1 Cor 15:5-8). The sources differ as to a) whether Peter (l Cor 15:5; Luke 24:34) or Mary Magdalene (Matt 28:9-10; John 20:11-18) was the first to see the risen Jesus, and b) what may have been said during those encounters (Matt 28:16-20; Luke 18 24:36-49; John 20:19-23). But from these various sources we have multiple attestation for appearances to individuals (such as Mary Magdalene, Peter and Paul) and groups, in particular, 'the eleven.' These appearances were the primary way the disciples came to know that Jesus had risen from the dead. In establishing and legitimating the appearances, we are necessarily accepting the apostolic witness to the risen Christ. The factuality of the appearances and the reliability of the apostles' Easter testimony, of which more below, are distinguishable but not separable.

What were the appearances like?[5] The evidence from Paul, the Gospels and elsewhere supports the following conclusions. The appearances a) depended on the initiative of the risen Jesus, b) were events of revelation,

c) disclosed the eschatological signifcance of Jesus and d) disclosed the christological significance of Jesus, and e) called the recipients to a special mission f) through an experience that was unique and g) not merely interior but involved some external, visual perception.

As regards a), unlike the situation during his earthly ministry, the risen Jesus did not show himself to enemies or outsiders. All those to whom he appeared were, or at least became, believers through that experience. The only (partial) exception to this generalisation is found in Luke's version of Paul's Damascus Road encounter. In two of the three accounts the apostle's companions hear the voice (Acts 9:7) or see the light from heaven (Acts 22:9), but on neither occasion do they see or communicate with Jesus himself. They function not as direct Easter witnesses but rather as external witnesses to Paul's dramatic experience.

Paul testifies to the revelatory nature b) of his encounter with the risen Jesus (Gal 1:12,16), who disclosed himself c) as already living the definitive life of the end-time (1 Cor 15:20, 23-45, and d) as Christ and Son of God (1 Cor 15:3-5; Gal 1:12,16). In and through the appearances the risen Christ e) called and sent Paul (1 Cor 9:1; Gal 1:11-17) and the other apostles (Matt 28:16-20) on their mission. Some try to interpret the post-resurrection appearances as merely the first examples of experiences available to all later Christians. But the New Testament witnesses to f), the unique, unrepeatable character of the appearances (Jn 20:29; 1 Pet 1:8), which came to an end with the call of Paul (1 Cor 15:8).[6] The special nature of the appearances to the apostolic group corresponded to their once-and-for-all functions of testifying that the risen Christ was/is personally identical with the earthly Jesus and of founding the Church through their Easter message. To do that they did not rely on the witness of others; they had seen the risen Christ for themselves and believed in him. Finally g), unlike the experiences of the major Old Testament prophets, the post-resurrection encounters were not primarily a matter of hearing (the divine word) but of seeing the risen Christ. The appearances were visual (1 Cor 9:1; 15:5-8; Mark 16:7; Matt 28:17; John 20:18) rather than aural.

The resurrection of Jesus was confirmed by the discovery of his empty tomb (Mk 16:1-8; John 20:12). The New Testament is aware that the empty tomb by itself did not clearly establish resurrection. The absence of Jesus' body could be explained by supposing that it had been stolen or at least shifted elsewhere (Matt 28:11-15; John 20:2,13,15). But given the primary, positive sign (the appearances of the risen Jesus), the secondary negative sign of his open and empty tomb confirmed the reality of his resurrection.

Some have argued that Mark 16:1–8 and later empty tomb stories neither convey nor intend to convey any factual information about the state of Jesus' tomb. They were simply imaginative ways of announcing the Church's faith in the resurrection and entirely derivative from the mainline proclamation of the crucified Jesus' resurrection and subsequent appearances (1 Cor 15:3-8). The legendary elaboration is usually supposed to have taken place over the ten or fifteen years between Paul's spare account of the appearances (1 Cor 15:5-8) and the writing of Mark's Gospel. However, careful exegesis of the two traditions (the first about the appearances and the second about the empty tomb) shows up such differences that it is hard to see the first tradition producing the second through a kind of snowball effect. Important elements found in 1 Cor 15:3-8 simply do not turn up in Mark 16:1-8, while Mark's story contains some major elements of which 1 Cor 15:3-8 knows nothing at all. Unlike 1 Cor 15:3-8, Mark's empty tomb story does not call Jesus 'Christ' but by his historical name; it neither refers to the scriptures nor to Jesus as dying 'for our sins.' Unlike the passage from Paul, it explicitly speaks of women and dates their visit to the tomb on 'the first day of the week' and not 'on the third day.' For these and further reasons it is reasonable to hold that the appearance traditions and the empty, tomb story are independent and have independent origins. But is the core of the empty tomb story historically reliable?

A reasonable case can be made for the basic reliability of the empty tomb story.[7] Both the tradition behind Mark and the somewhat different tradition that entered John's Gospel testify to one (Mary Magdalene) or more women finding Jesus' grave to be open and the body missing. Early polemic against the message of his resurrection supposed that the tomb was known to be empty. Naturally the opponents of the Christian movement explained away the missing body as a plain case of theft (Matt 28:11-15). What was in dispute was not whether the tomb was empty but why it was empty. We have no early evidence that anyone, either Christian or non-Christian, ever alleged that Jesus' tomb still contained his remains.

Furthermore, the central place of women in the empty tomb stories speaks for their reliability. If these stories had simply been legends created by early Christians, they would have attributed the discovery of the empty tomb to male disciples rather than to women. In first-century Palestine women were, for all intents and purposes, disqualified as valid witnesses.[8] The natural thing for someone making up a legend about the empty tomb would have been to have credited the discovery to men, not women. Legend-makers do not normally invent positively unhelpful material.

All in all, accepting the empty tomb puts us in better agreement with the known data. The emptiness of Jesus' grave confirmed what the first Christians knew from witnesses to the appearances (Lk 24:34; John 20:16).

I have been sketching the kind of answer that should be given to the question: how did the first Christians come to know about Jesus' resurrection? Much more could be added: for example, to rebut the suggestion, already made by Celsus back in the second century and often repeated since then, that the witnesses to the appearances were hallucinated. Positively, the nature and function of the post-resurrection appearances should be studied in greater detail. Add too the need to examine how subsequent experiences (of the Holy Spirit and of the success of their mission) confirmed the disciples' Easter faith that had been originally brought about through the appearances of the risen Jesus and the discovery of his empty tomb. That faith was further validated by their new insight into the point and purpose of Jewish history and scriptures. The resurrection of the crucified Jesus gave the religious faith of Jewish Christians a sense of convergence and ending.

But it is time to mention and fill out the teaching of the Second Vatican Council in *Dei Verbum,* that the resurrection of Jesus. to which the first Christians witnessed the definitive high-point of God's self revelation (n 4). In other words, we turn now from the *event* of the resurrection (and the signs, such as the appearances, which manifested it) to the Easter *mystery* itself, the fullness of the self-communication of the triune God. This is a move from history (and matters accessible to critical historians) to eschatology and the revelation of God who draws near to us out of that ultimate future already inaugurated by the resurrection of Jesus from the dead.

The Easter Revelation

When properly interpreted, the resurrection of the crucified Jesus is the truth about God from which everything else follows. Paul understands Jesus' resurrection (together with ours) to be the specifically Christian way of presenting God. To be wrong about the resurrection is essentially to 'misrepresent' God, since Paul defines God as the God of resurrection (1 Cor 15:15). What the apostle says here negatively can be aligned with what he often writes positively of the God who has raised Jesus and will raise us with him (Rom 8:11; 1 Cor 6:14; 2 Cor 4:14; Gal 1:1; 1 Thess 1:9-10, 4:14). Whether positively or negatively, Paul defines the God revealed to and worshipped by Christians as the God of the resurrection.

From the revelation of the Easter mystery everything else follows. Further truths do no more than unfold what is implied by the resurrection of the crucified Jesus.

The cross, of course, is the great sign and characteristic of Christianity. Paul sums up his message as Christ crucified (1 Cor 1:18-24). Nevertheless, he does not claim, 'If Christ be not crucified, your faith is futile.' Still less does he say, 'If Christ be not crucified, we are even found to be misrepresenting God.' The crucifixion without its sequel in resurrection would not have revealed God, effected our salvation and brought into existence the Church. The preface to the Second Eucharistic Prayer does not stop with the words 'for our sake he opened his arms on the cross.' It continues: 'He put an end to death and revealed the resurrection.' In revealing the resurrection – that is to say, by revealing himself as risen from the dead – Christ, so to speak, revealed everything. The self-manifestation of God reached its climax with Easter Sunday and the coming of the Holy Spirit. These points need to be filled out in at least a little detail.

The resurrection revealed and illuminated Christ's relationship with the God whom he had called 'Abba, Father dear.' It disclosed that the life of Jesus had been the human life of the Son of God. By his resurrection from the dead, Christ was now known to be 'Son of God' (Rom 1:3-4). Hence for Paul to meet the risen Jesus was to receive a special, personal revelation of the Son that made Paul the great missionary to the Gentiles (Gal 1:16).

Another key title given to Jesus in very early Christianity, 'Lord,' expressed the Easter revelation that he truly shared in the divine majesty and being. The Letter to the Romans quoted a pre-Pauline formula that linked salvation with the confession of Jesus' resurrection and divine lordship: 'If you confess with your lips that Jesus is Lord and believe in your heart that God has raised him from the dead, you will be saved' (Rom 10:9). In his Letter to the Philippians Paul cited and adapted an early Christian hymn that invited everyone in the universe to worship the exalted Jesus as divine Lord:

> ... he humbled himself and became obedient unto death, even death on a cross. Therefore God has highly exalted him and bestowed on him the name which is above every name, that at the name of Jesus every knee should bow, in heaven and on earth and

> under the earth, and every tongue confess that Jesus Christ is Lord, to the glory of God the Father. (Phil 2:8-11)

Easter stories from the Gospels state in a narrative form the call to adore the risen Jesus, the Son of God and Lord who is now revealed in his divine power and identity. In Matthew's final chapter Mary Magdalene and the other Mary leave the tomb, meet Jesus and 'worship' him (28:9). Likewise the eleven male disciples keep the rendezvous on the mountain in Galilee, where they 'worship' Jesus when they see him (Matt 28:17). According to John's Gospel, it is only in the Easter situation that anyone acknowledge Jesus in those striking terms adopted by Thomas, 'my Lord and my God' John 20:28). It takes the resurrection to reveal finally that Jesus should be identified and worshipped as divine Lord.

The essence of Christian faith entails accepting the good news that in the power of the Spirit the incarnate and crucified Son of God has risen from the dead. Thus the doctrine of the Trinity points to and gathers up the self-revelation of God communicated through Christ's resurrection.

Mark recalls a kind of appearance of the Trinity at Jesus' baptism. The Spirit descended 'upon him like a dove; and a voice came from heaven, 'Thou art my beloved Son; with thee I am well pleased' (Mk 1:10-11). At the resurrection, without 'appearing' in any such way, the tripersonal God was revealed. Let us see some details.

Pre-Pauline formulas understood 'God' (Rom 10:9) or 'God the Father' (e.g., Gal 1:1) to have raised Jesus from the dead. The post-exaltation worship of Jesus as divine Lord takes place 'to the glory of God the Father' (Phil 2:11), while the Holy Spirit makes it possible for men and women to acclaim Jesus as divine Lord (1 Cor 12:3).

Since Paul does not fully and clearly distinguish the risen Christ and the Holy Spirit, he nowhere as such says that Christ sent or sends the Spirit. Luke and even more John draw a clearer distinction between the risen Christ and the Spirit. Hence they speak of the risen Christ sending the Spirit as the Father's promised gift (Lk 24:49) or *'breathing'* on the disciples and giving them the Holy Spirit (Jn 20:22).

First-century Christians understood in such Trinitarian terms the events of Good Friday and Easter Sunday. In those events they experienced the climactic revelation of God. That revelation had a threefold face to it, as Peter's sermon at Pentecost emphatically appreciates: 'This Jesus, God raised up, and of that we all are witnesses. Being therefore exalted at the right hand of God, and having received from the Father the promise of the Holy Spirit, he has poured out this which you see and hear' (Acts 2:32-33).

Undoubtedly we should be careful not to be anachronistic here. Christians had to pursue matters for several centuries before they came to a precise teaching on the divinity of Christ and the personal identity of the Holy Spirit. All the same, we find at the origin of Christianity a clear sense that the Father, Son and Holy Spirit were revealed as acting in our human history, above all in the events of Good Friday, Easter Sunday and their aftermath. This sense is also reflected in a very common Christian gesture, the sign of the cross. By confessing the Trinity as we make the sign of the cross, we link our faith in the Father, Son and Holy Spirit to the cross and resurrection of Jesus.

Thus far we have seen how the resurrection of the crucified Jesus finally disclosed the mystery of the tripersonal God. One could reflect on the ways Easter communicated or at least fully illuminated other revealed truths, such as the creation of the world, the foundation of the Church and her sacramental life. What comes earlier and later in the Nicene Creed can be rightly seen as introducing and unfolding the full sense of the central truth 'he rose again.'

In short, the paschal mystery is the high point and fullness of God's revelation. In proclaiming the resurrection of the crucified Jesus, the first Christians knew themselves to be baptised into the paschal mystery (Rom 6:3-11). Through baptism they remained unconditionally linked to the death and resurrection of Christ. Their Eucharist celebrated the death of the risen Lord in expectation of his final coming (1 Cor 11:2-26). It is consistent with all this to understand Jesus' resurrection as the focus and organising centre of the divine self-manifestation that is expounded and unpacked in our various articles of faith. My presentation of Christ's resurrection has moved from historical, apologetical considerations (sections 1 and 2 above) to theological reflections (section 3). There still remains one major issue to be addressed: why believe now in the risen Jesus?

Justifying Easter Faith

Is it a reasonable and responsible act to believe in Jesus Christ as truly risen from the dead? Can such faith be rationally justified?

Two factors have often been operating in views about Easter faith. Some (wrongly) hold that historical reason, and indeed any use of our human reason, can never contribute to or legitimate faith. Otherwise, they argue, we would turn faith into the work of our intellect and deny that it is a free gift from God. This noble 'fideist' option, however, ignores the fact that God works through our intellect to lend believability to the decision of faith. Divine grace and human reason can and should collaborate rather than remain opposing forces.

A second difficulty comes from the opposite camp – namely, from those who do not want to emancipate faith from history and in fact see it as depending totally on historical data. They scrutinise and evaluate the evidence for the appearances of the risen Jesus, the discovery of the empty tomb, the dynamic rise of Christianity and other pieces of relevant historical evidence. In that way they aim to establish the truth of Jesus' resurrection. One difficulty, however, will not easily go away: how can the probable or even highly probable conclusions of such historical investigation alone legitimate the unconditional and certain decision of faith? The short answer is that by themselves historical conclusions alone cannot validate such a decision. But, as we shall see, the converging signs that legitimate Easter faith include the relevant historical evidence from the first century but are not limited to such evidence.

A merely historical approach to the case for Jesus' resurrection risks forgetting that this is much more than a question from the past to be honestly investigated and established (or refuted) to one's intellectual satisfaction. Accepting the truth of the resurrection and believing in the risen Christ is not simply a purely mental exercise about past claims and past facts. Easter faith goes beyond accepting the testimony of the first Easter witnesses and confessing a doctrine 'On the third day he rose again'. It is a whole way of life which calls for deep commitment in the present ('We believe in the one Lord, Jesus Christ') and firm confidence for the future ('We look for the resurrection of the dead and the life of the world to come'). It takes the initiative of divine grace and the collaboration of our human freedom to bring about such resurrection confession, commitment and confidence.

How then might we justify our free and grace-inspired option and join those who 'have not seen and yet believe' (John 20:29) in the risen Jesus? Trusting the apostolic witnesses to the resurrection (who saw and believed) means being 'built on the foundation of the apostles' (Eph 2:20), by accepting the testimony of persons who encountered the risen Jesus in a special kind of experience. They could speak authoritatively on the basis of their own experiences. Those Easter encounters were peculiar to them and hence lie beyond the range of experiences which we could simply repeat and hence verify for ourselves. At the same time, giving our consent to the apostolic testimony also involves answering the fundamental questions about the final nature, meaning and destiny of our human existence.

In a sense, this double approach to the legitimation of Easter faith is already prefigured in 1 Cor 15. The chapter opens by recalling the reliable testimony of those to whom the risen Jesus appeared (1 Cor 15:5-11). Then most of the rest of the chapter takes up the question of what that resurrection means for all of us who must face death. It is a meaning that gives believability to the truth of Easter faith. A similar pattern emerges in Acts 2. Those who accept the apostolic message of the resurrection find their burden of sin lifted and their lives graced with the Holy Spirit (Acts 2:22-42; see 5:32).

In short, the validation of Easter faith works 'from the outside' and 'from the inside.' We need to hear and accept the historical, public testimony coming to us, ultimately from Peter, Paul, Mary Magdalene and the other original witnesses. But we also look for signs 'from the inside,' acknowledging the ways in which belief in the risen Jesus confronts our mortality and correlates existentially with our deepest experiences and with our insatiable yearning for life, meaning and love which cannot be fulfilled in this transitory life that led William Blake to remark that 'the heart is a bottomless gorge'. The Easter message offers us the fullness of lasting life, meaning and love for our whole being, and does so in the face of the death, absurdity and hatred/ isolation that threaten us constantly. On the one hand, respect for the historical testimony keeps Easter faith from lapsing into mere wishful thinking. On the other hand, respect for our present experience saves us from the illusion that could live and find faith by historical evidence alone.[9]

These then are the answers I would like to give to the four questions that I posed at the beginning. What did the first Christians mean by their claim about Jesus' resurrection? How did they come to believe in him as risen from the dead? How did the resurrection of the crucified Jesus bring the definitive self-revelation of God? In what way can we legitimate Easter faith today?

More than twenty-five years ago at Cambridge University Henry Hart put me on the trail of these and other questions about Jesus' resurrection. I remain very grateful to him.

As our Creed indicates, we hold in common our faith in the risen Lord. The Church is the place of Easter experience and witness; we believe with the Church (1 Cor 15:6), the visible company of those who live their faith in the risen Lord and reveal today his presence. We are an Easter people. We can do nothing better than experience and celebrate together the presence of the risen Lord until he comes.

Notes

1. For examples see my *Jesus Risen* (New York/Mahwah, Paulist Press, 1987), 103-7: and id., *What are they saying about Jesus?* (New York, Paulist Press, 2nd edn, 1983), 44-51; and Paul Van Buren, *The Secular Meaning of the Gospel* (New York: Macmillan, 1963), 132-34. On Van Buren's reductionism see Michael McNulty, 'The 'Secular' Meaning of Easter: Van Buren Revisited', *Heythrop Journal* 14 (1973), 58-64.
2. R.F. Scuka, 'Resurrection Critical Reflections on a Doctrine in Search of a Meaning' *Modern Theology* 6 (l989), 77-95. References to this article will be made within the text.
3. For examples of the continuity hypothesis see the chapters by 1. Broer, P. Fiedler and H. Verweyen in Ingo Broer and Jurgen Werbick (ed.) *'Der Herr ist wahrlaft auferstanden'* (Lk *24:*34). *Biblische und systernatische Beitrasezur Entstehung des Osterglaubens,* Stuttgarter Bibel-Studien, 134 (Stuttgart, Verlag Katholisches Bibelwerk, 1988); see also my review in *Gregorianum* 70 (1989), 567-68.
4. W. Pannenberg, Jesus – *God and Man* (Philadelphia, Westminster Press, 1968), 96.
5. On the Easter appearances see my *The Easter Jesus* (London Darton, Longman & Todd, new edn, 1980), 3-38; id., *Jesus Risen,* 107-9,112-21; id., *Interpreting the Resurrection* (New York/Mahwah, 1988), 5-52.
6. See D. Kendall and G. O'Collins, The Uniqueness of the Easter Appearances,' *Catholic Biblical Quarterly* 54 (1992), 287-307.
7. See my *Easter Jesus,* pp. 3845; id., *Jesus Risen,* pp. 121-26; id., 'Resurrection Belief: a Note on a Recent Book,' *Gregorianum* 70 (1989), 341-44.
8. See my *Interpreting the Resurrection, 22.*
9. On the making of Easter faith see further my *Jesus Risen*, 28-47.

This paper was given as the twenty-fourth Père Marquette Lecture in Theology, under the auspices of the Marquette University's Department of Theology, Millwaukee, Wisconsin. It is reprinted with kind permission of Marquette University Press who published it as a book with a substantial appendix dealing with the resurrection as a divine act.

THE NEW EVANGELISATION OF JOHN PAUL II

MARY SHIVANANDAN

John Paul II has given as the reason for his extensive travel the cry of St Paul: 'Woe to me if I don't preach the Gospel.' With his eyes focused on the new millennium, he speaks about the mission of Christ 'still only a beginning' in the world in *Redemptoris Missio: On the Permanent Validity of the Church's Missionary Mandate.*[1] 'I sense that the moment has come,' he asserts, 'to commit all of the Church's energies to a new evangelisation and to the mission *ad gentes.*' 'No believer in Christ, no institution of the Church, can avoid this supreme duty: to proclaim Christ to all peoples.'[2] What is this 'new evangelisation' he speaks about? Why does he distinguish it from the mission *ad gentes*, the traditional mission to pagan peoples?

Lorenzo Albacete traces the call for a new evangelisation back to the historical context in which it was originally issued, the Church in Latin America. In an address to the bishops of Latin America in 1983 John Paul II spoke of the need for an evangelisation that was new in 'ardour, expression, and methods.'[3] Vatican II had noted the attraction of atheistic humanism for contemporary man. Especially appealing was its charge that Christianity inculcated a sense of resignation in the poor, which made them accept an unjust social system in the hopes of happiness in an after-life in heaven. Latin America, a traditional mission field for the Church, where there are still wide gaps between the rich and the poor, was fertile ground for Marxism, which proposed a new heaven on earth. Liberation theology grew out of the desire on the part of the Church in Latin America to link the message of the gospel to issues of social justice.

When liberation theology became too closely linked with an exclusive Marxist solidarity with the poor, John Paul II saw the need for a new evangelisation, which would take what was good from liberation theology and correct, what was not in accord with the Gospel.[4] He insisted that the truth of the human person within the mystery of Christ must be at the centre of any 'liberation theology'. No other anthropological analysis, especially one that was essentially atheistic, could be the starting point for human liberation.[5] An analysis linked in this way, he said, has led to the rereading of Gospel truths and resulted in a faulty ecclesiology as well as a faulty anthropology. It was this challenge posed by the theology of liberation to the relationship of evangelisation and culture that led to the new evangelisation.[6]

Actually John Paul II is building on the evangelising mission proclaimed by Paul VI. It was only four years *before* the accession of John Paul II to the papacy that Pope Paul VI issued his apostolic exhortation, *Evangelii Nuntiandi*, on evangelisation in the modern world following the third Synod of Bishops in 1974 that was devoted to the topic.[7] The Jesuit, Avery Dulles, points to historical developments that brought about this new emphasis on evangelisation. As the culture in Europe and America became more and more secularised the church could not rely on political and sociological factors to support the faith. Faith came to be considered more and more a personal matter. Evangelical Protestant groups in the eighteenth century were the first to grasp the necessity of proclaiming the gospel as a joyful message of salvation in the manner of the early Christians in order to win and hold adherents. In the Catholic Church it was Vatican II that marks a significant stage in the recovery of an evangelical spirit. Whereas in Vatican Council I in 1871 the word gospel was used only once and evangelisation not at all, Vatican II used the word gospel 157 times and evangelisation 31. Its main emphasis was 'the proclamation of the basic Christian message of salvation through Jesus Christ.'[8] Paul VI in *Evangelii Nuntiandi* reiterated that the gospel cannot be reduced to any socio- political development or liberation project. It must centre on the proclamation of Jesus Christ and 'envisage the whole man'.[9] Nevertheless there are profound links between evangelisation and human development and liberation, he added.[10]

While liberation theology in Latin America may have been the impetus for John Paul II's 'new evangelisation', the relationship between today's secular culture and evangelisation has global implications that John Paul II addresses in *Redemptoris Missio.* Certain developments since the time of Paul VI have become more acute. Doubts have undermined former missionary zeal. Missionary activity has tended to be replaced by inter-religious dialogue. The idea also prevails that conversion violates the rights to conscience and freedom of the individual and the assumption is made that anyone can attain salvation in any religion.[11] At the same time there are new situations of de-Christianisation of countries, urbanisation, mass migrations and the influence of Christians in non-Christian countries.

John Paul II discerns three situations today: (1) the mission to peoples and cultures where Christ is not known, which is the mission *ad gentes* proper; (2) properly Christian communities, which exist in both traditional Christian countries and well established churches in mission countries and finally; (3) fallen away Christians where a 'new evangelisation' or 're-evangelisation' is needed.[12] Paul VI had already spoken of the difficulties of evangelising this group. Their resistance takes the form of 'inertia and the slightly hostile attitude of the person who feels that he is one of the family, who claims to know it all and to have tried it all and who no longer believes it'.[13] Sadly many prominent in the media and politics fall into this category. There are no clear boundaries between the three types of situation but the new evangelisation in Christian countries aids the traditional mission *ad gentes.* We shall see how this applies especially in the areas of marriage and family.

John Paul II describes the task as overwhelming, not only because some countries forbid evangelisation, most notably Muslim countries, but because of the lack of fervour or indifferentism among Catholic Christians. Divisions among Christians create further difficulties, which are compounded by the counter-witness of evangelical believers.[14] Proselytising by evangelicals in Latin America, for example, has increased greatly among poorly evangelised Catholics. Cultural factors now militate against the Gospel. The split between the Gospel and culture, both Paul VI and John Paul II regard as the tragedy of our time.[15]

Collapse of Cultural Discourse

The cultural situation presents particular problems. In reflecting on the task of the 'new evangelisation' proposed by John Paul II, various authors have examined the obstacles caused by the cultural situation prevailing in the West, which they characterise as post-Christian, post-modern and post-family. Carl Anderson cites Henri de Lubac's comment, of nearly 40 years ago, that modern atheism has not simply rejected belief in God but is *anti*-theist and quotes Nietzsche's statement, 'It is our preference that decides against Christianity – not arguments.'[16] When Christianity ceased to be the unifying principle in society, philosophers such as Kant and Hegel substituted autonomous reason instead. The unifying criterion of modern culture became the autonomous rational individual who made moral decisions according to the universalising principle of reason. In other words the moral person made choices as if he were choosing for every other individual. Hegel went further and placed his 'hope in a dialectic of enlightenment in which reason was validated as an equivalent for the unifying power of religion'.[17] Anderson sees modernity, based on a rational notion of self as only partially replacing Christian moral values since it substituted 'transcendence (or faith) with immanence (or reason) as its unifying principle. '

An important connection remained between Christianity and modernity because both could call on reason to validate universal moral principles and agree on such propositions as inalienable human rights. But the very suspicion that the Enlightenment philosophers had cast on the principles of Christianity came to be applied to modern rationalism itself. Nietzsche claimed that the confidence of reason to ascertain objective truth was an illusion. When man ascribes to an objective order of truth outside himself he is bound to something other than himself and so is not free. The attack on divine Truth had become an attack on all truth because the truly free man cannot be dependent on anything outside himself.[18] What is now called post-modernism has radically changed philosophical discourse by accepting Nietzsche's rejection of modern rationality. Now necessity is replaced by contingency, certainty with fallibility, universality by plurality and unity by diversity. Truth is relative to the particular culture or lifestyle in which it has application. 'Truth' claims as such have no meaning. A feminist, for example, can assert that truth in social science does not matter as long as a study advances the feminist agenda.[19]

Anderson calls *Humanae Vitae* possibly 'one of the last great magisterial documents addressed to the intellectual and cultural conditions of Modernity'. It presupposed a discourse based on the validity of human reason to arrive at a consensus on moral truths. It was a vital document in reaffirming the teaching of the Church on responsible parenthood but, in Anderson's words, 'its critics have guaranteed that its effectiveness as a means of evangelisation of family life has been limited'. He does not believe that discourse on the encyclical, which might have been possible immediately after its release, is now possible. Furthermore, the cultural orientation towards marriage, family and sexuality, which formed the context of the encyclical no longer exists. Post-modern scepticism has swept away certainties about marriage and family so that the discussion of the goods of marriage is replaced by whether marriage even is a good. Even within the Church arguments brought forward to justify contraception have since been extended to justify abortion, sterilisation and increasingly euthanasia. Any evangelisation must now reach to the very foundations of culture since few cultural values can be taken for granted.[20] A new discourse can no longer be based on a consensus on words or concepts employed. It must be a living discourse, a new evangelisation carried on as a way of life.[21] Christ himself as the Word is the 'living discourse'.

Preaching Christ

'The Redeemer of man, Jesus Christ, is the centre of the universe and of history.' With these words John Paul II began the first magisterial document of his papacy, *Redemptor Hominis*, (Redeemer of Man) in 1979.[22] Man can only be understood in the light of Jesus Christ. He quotes a passage of *Gaudium et Spes*, which he calls a 'stupendous text' and which has become a leitmotiv of his anthropology, 'The truth is that only in the mystery of the Incarnate Word does the mystery of man take on light. .... Christ, the new Adam, in the very revelation of the mystery of the Father and of his love *fully reveals man to himself* and brings to light his most high calling. ... For, by his Incarnation, he the Son of God, *in a certain way united himself with each man.*'[23]

John Paul II credits Vatican II with restoring a biblical discourse in the Church which makes contact with the 'inward mystery of man', his heart. It is only in Christ that justice and love, two primary concerns of contemporary man are united so that through Him justice and love may reign in the hearts of men.[24] Love is essential to man. His life has no meaning if he does not encounter love or actively participate in it. This is the human dimension of the Redemption, says John Paul II, where 'man finds again the greatness, dignity and value that belong to humanity'. In order to find himself man must appropriate the 'whole reality of the Incarnation and Redemption'. He sums up the Church's mission in the world:

> In reality, the name of that deep amazement at man's worth and dignity is the Gospel, that is to say: the Good News. It is called Christianity. This amazement determines the Church's mission in the world and, perhaps even more so, 'in the modern world.'[25]

Here is the heart of what John Paul II means by the 'new evangelisation', formulating in a new way the message of the Gospel so that it speaks to the heart of modern man who has lost his faith in reason and social structures but still harbours a sense of the dignity and rights of man. The furnace of experience had taught John Paul II in Poland that no utopian social experiments could insure man's dignity, especially those that deny the transcendent nature of man. The full dignity that man longs for can only be gained in union with Jesus Christ. This is the message that is the responsibility of every Christian to bring to the world.[26]

Many of the themes taken up by *Redemptoris Missio* are already present in *Redemptoris Hominis*, a sense of the 'new advent' compared with the 'new springtime'.[27] He uses the same example of St Paul preaching on the Areopagus in Athens to show the missionary attitude to 'all cultures, all ideological concepts, all people of good will.' In *Redemptoris Missio*, he links it specifically to integrating the Gospel message into the 'new culture' created by modern communications. Other 'Areopagus' situations he mentions, that need to be penetrated by the Gospel, are the various movements for peace, liberation, the rights of individuals (especially minorities), advancement of women and children, the environment, scientific research and international relations.[28]

All these endeavours, John Paul II sees deserving respect since they have their source in the depths of man's spirit. The human person's dignity must always be part of the content of proclamation. But always Christ is 'the one who brings man freedom based on truth'.[29] Christ is the one who 'has revealed to mankind *who he is*.' He is the one universal mediator, who brings a 'radical newness of life' as the self-communication of God's love.[30] In other words a purely human account of man is not sufficient. Between the two encyclicals John Paul II has fully developed a *theological* anthropology through a return to biblical sources in the Wednesday Catecheses.[31] It is this anthropology that provides the foundation for addressing the particular problems that face mankind today: the dignity of the human person in the face of an increasingly dehumanising technology, the advancement of women, the role of marriage and the family which are under threat as never before.

To summarise some of the key points of John Paul II's anthropology here: God created mankind as male and female, equal persons with different sexual manifestation. They are a dual unity. Each is made in the image of God as a person but they image God more as a communion of persons. Man can only find fulfilment through a sincere gift of self. In other words man is both a contingent being in relation to God and in relation to the opposite sex and needs the other for completion. Gender both limits man and is the vehicle for self-transcendence since he experiences the other as fulfilling himself. The relationship of man and woman is one of both identity and difference. They are identical in their humanity but different in gender and this difference is not merely a difference of roles but an ontological difference, a different way of being.[32]

The conjugal relation of men and women in which two become one flesh is the primordial communion of persons. Sexuality belongs to man as being in the image of God and this makes human sexuality radically different from animal sexuality. Man's body expresses the person, it makes the invisible visible. As John Paul II says, with the creation of man, holiness entered the visible world. Masculinity and femininity are a sign of the mystery 'hidden from all ages' that man and woman are destined to participate in divine Trinitarian communion. For John Paul II the integrity of the body with its masculinity and femininity from which flows the union in one flesh and procreation in our earthly existence is foundational. Fruitfulness belongs to this spousal union whether it is the physical fruitfulness of a child in the sacrament of marriage or spiritual fruitfulness which belongs especially to the consecrated virgin. The spousal relation is the principle analogy for every type of love, for the love of God for his people, Israel, for the union of God and the soul, and the union of Christ and the Church. Angelo Schola calls it 'a privileged metaphor for man's relationship to reality'.[33] Person, communion and gift are the three concepts that describe man both as a person and as a being made in the image of God. As a person he may never be treated simply as an object but always as a subject with self-determination. In order to give himself completely as a gift to another, he must possess himself. It is the virtues together with grace that enable a person to be in possession of himself. Self-mastery leads to freedom based on truth.

Morality is above all personal. It is not a set of abstract rules and prohibitions but deeply related to the person's inmost being. Christian morality is first and foremost a following of Christ. *Veritatis Splendor*, John Paul II's encyclical on 'the splendour of truth' begins with Christ's dialogue with the rich young man to show that a call to deeper union to him is the *raison d'etre* for the beatitudes.[34] In a conference on the theme, 'The Pope against Moralism and Legalism' held in the Catholic University of America shortly after the encyclical was issued, Lorenzo Albacete describes *Veritatis Splendor* as a 'powerful rejection of moralism and legalism'[35] John Paul II, beginning with a reflection on the encounter of the rich young man with Christ (Mt 19:16), situates the ethical life within the context of a personal relationship with Jesus Christ. The Christian moral life is not something external to man but involves an interior transformation of the heart. 'The ultimate roots of the moral life are found in the context of a *relationship of communion* with the Person of Jesus Christ.[36]

The Family and Evangelisation

This is the vision of the dignity of man and woman and their participation in society of which the first and most vital cell is the family. In *Letter to Families* John Paul II recalls that in *Redemptor Hominis*, his first encyclical, he wrote that 'man is the way of the church'. He now extends this to say that 'both man and the family constitute the way of the church'.[37] Towards the end of the Letter he says: 'The history of mankind, the history of salvation, passes by way of the family. In these pages I have tried to show how the family is placed at the centre of the great struggle between good and evil, between life and death, between love and all that is opposed to love.'[38] Much has happened in the culture between the two encyclicals. As Carl Anderson says, our culture is not only post-Christian, post-modern but also post-family. In the United States abortion virtually on demand became the law of the land in 1973 with the decision of the Supreme Court in Roe vs. Wade. A generation has grown up for whom abortion has always been a legal right. The family, which had been unravelling since the turn of the century, began to disintegrate more radically as statistics of the past 25 years show. The family has become one of the most important areas for evangelisation, both to be evangelised and to evangelise.

A vital aid for the new evangelisation is *the Catechism of the Catholic Church*. The *Catechism* has this to say about the family and its mission.

> The Christian family is a communion of persons, a reflection and image of the communion between the Father and the Son in the Holy Spirit. In the procreation and education of children it reflects the Father's work of creation. It is called to partake of the prayer and sacrifice of Christ. ... The Christian family has an evangelising and missionary task.

The role of parents in evangelising their own children is seen to be essentially evangelisation not just instruction.[40] And indeed parents today are well aware that they must engage in all the different methods of evangelisation listed by Paul VI in *Evangelii Nuntiandi,* witness of life, verbal instruction, liturgy, both word and sacrament, sharing personal experience of the faith and family devotions in order to counter the barrage of messages their children receive in the world. Paul VI lists the mass media as essential aids.[41] Videos and films can be a powerful means of instruction but for most parents TV and films promote anti-family values.

Realising that the majority of people do not accept arguments about the indissolubility of marriage centred on the common good of the family, the *Catechism* establishes its requirement on following Jesus Christ who also gives the grace to live it. Paragraph no. 1615 says, 'This grace of Christian marriage is the fruit of Christ's cross, the source of all Christian life.' In no. 2232, the *Catechism,* citing Matthew 10:37, makes it clear that anyone who puts mother or father, husband or sister or brother before Jesus is not worthy to be his follower.

From the beginning of his evangelising journeys, John Paul II has addressed the issue of abortion and its destructive effect on the family and society. Issues of life have come ever closer to the centre of his concerns. In his visit to Cuba, the issue of abortion and family breakdown held an equal place with his concern over poverty and human rights. John Paul II has called the post-modern culture a culture of death because of its acceptance of abortion and increasingly euthanasia and assisted suicide.[42] In issuing *Evangelium Vitae* (the Gospel of Life) in 1995 he is making a clear statement that a new culture that respects life must be at the centre of any evangelisation today. 'The Gospel of life is at the heart of Jesus' message' is the opening sentence.[43] Again he makes the statement that 'man – living man – represents the primary and fundamental way for the church'.[44] And 'within the "people of life and the people for life", the family has a decisive responsibility.' for the family is truly 'the sanctuary of life'.[45] He places his finger on the nihilism of post-modern culture when he says:

> In the background there is a profound crisis of culture, which generates scepticism in relation to the very foundations of knowledge and ethics, and which makes it increasingly difficult to grasp clearly the meaning of what man is, the meaning of his rights and duties.[46]

The deepest root of this crisis of culture is the eclipse of the 'sense of God'.[47] Today's secularism denies any idea that there may be a truth in creation and a plan for human life that must be respected.[48]

Although the prevailing moral uncertainty and the complex and serious nature of today's problems can mitigate responsibility, society is confronting an even larger reality, a 'veritable structure of sin'.[49] Political, economic and cultural forces combine to promote solutions to human problems focused on efficiency, which favour the strong against the weak. Huge sums are invested in pharmaceutical industries for the manufacture and distribution of contraceptives and abortifacients to make abortion ever simpler and more available.[50] 'We are, in fact,' he says 'faced by an objective 'conspiracy against life,' involving even international institutions engaged in encouraging and carrying out actual campaigns to make contraception, sterilisation and abortion widely available.[51]

In *Redemptoris Missio* John Paul II calls the most effective missionary endeavours those that serve the poor, the weak and the suffering together with those concerned with justice and human rights.[52] It is in the name of the poor that feminists and family planning workers in developing countries bring their message of contraception, sterilisation and abortion. The story of the death of Sadie Sachs a poor New York woman in childbirth, which motivated Margaret Sanger to promote contraception is still cited in books and journals as the justification for the work the contraceptive movement undertakes.[53] It is this 'missionary zeal' which impels family planning workers into almost every town and village.

The family planning movement is well aware that they are diffusing what they call 'the culture of contraception', but in their view it brings only benefits to women. Adopting contraception is tied to a promise of greatly expanded choices for women. An article in an issue of *Population Reports* published by the Johns Hopkins School of Public Health, entitled: 'Family Planning: An Asset for Women.' reads:

> Women want to have choices. Family planning is one important way that women can take control of their own lives and make choices possible. Choices are essential to human dignity. Without choices and without opportunities, a person cannot hope for a better future. Without choices, a person can have little self-respect.[54]

A paragraph further down admits that when a woman has control of her own fertility she may have more options in her life but whether she can make changes for the better depends on many other factors, social norms, economic development, law, her personal circumstances. Nevertheless the whole focus is on providing access to contraception and abortion. Third world women report that while every kind of contraceptive and abortifacient is available through health clinics there is a scarcity of antibiotics and other life-saving drugs. And yet studies in the United States have shown contraception and abortion actually weaken women's power in relation to men and in addition expose them to infertility and sexually transmitted diseases.[55] The culture of death enters so easily with such a siren song and with such devastating results which Paul VI predicted in *Humanae Vitae*.

In November 1996 John Paul II gave a message to an International Congress on Natural Family Planning in which he said the crisis of values and ideals in contemporary society

> challenges believers to undertake widespread and persevering formational activity: this is the frontier advanced by the new evangelisation. ... Unbridled hedonism and disregard for human life which is weak and unproductive at its mysterious and delicate beginnings, require the proclamation of the 'Gospel of Life' to be supported by a constant commitment to teaching spouses to be aware of their own vocation as servants of life, in responsible collaboration with the Creator's provident wisdom.[56]

He expresses the hope that 'the scientific world and the Christian communities, each in its own capacity, will become ever more involved in this task of research, formation and evangelisation.'

As *Evangelium Vitae* and these words show, issues at the heart of the family dealing with the most intimate aspects of family life are at the centre of the 'new evangelisation'.[57] It is especially urgent because the attacks on life are often carried out with the complicity of the family itself.[58] As John Paul II has come to see more and more in his pontificate, the crisis that afflicts the civilisation of love originates in the post-modern nihilism of the West, with its utilitarian view of man and the family and rampant secularism which reaches with its 'ubiquitous tentacles' into Christian communities themselves.[59] Although the re-evangelisation of the West takes a different form from the mission *ad gentes,* they cannot be separated especially in those issues that concern the nature of the human person and the family.[60] The two came together in a dramatic way both in Cairo and Beijing at the fourth international population conference and the international conference on women when Western feminists and population advocates sought to impose their anti-family and eugenic views on developing countries.

As these conferences show, now more than ever the universal call to holiness is linked to the universal call to mission.[61] As the Second Vatican Council says, 'the whole Church is missionary and the work of evangelisation is a basic duty of the People of God'.[62] Their particular field is precisely those areas that are so problematic today, the world of politics and economics, medicine, and the other sciences, the mass media and the world of culture. And, of course the family.[63]

Notes

1. John Paul II, Encyclical Letter, *Redemptoris Missio* (On the Permanent Validity of the Church's Missionary Mandate), December 7, 1990, (Washington DC, United States Catholic Conference, 1990) 1.
2. *ibid.*, 3.
3. Lorenzo Albacete, 'The Praxis of Resistance', *Communio* (Winter, 1994), pp. 612-630.
4. *ibid.*, 614.
5. *ibid.*, 615.
6. *ibid.*, 615.
7. Pope Paul VI, *Evangelii Nuntiandi* (On Evangelisation in the Modem World), Apostolic Exhortation, December 8, 1975 (Washington, DC: United States Catholic conference, 1976)
8. Avery Dulles, 'John Paul II and the New Evangelisation – What does it Mean?' in *John Paul Il and the New Evangelization: How You Can Bring the Good News to Others,* ed. Ralph Martin and Peter Williamson (San Francisco, Ignatius Press, 1995), pp. 25-39: 26.
9. *ibid.*, 27; *Evangelii Nuntiandi,* 33.
10. *ibid.*, 31.
11. *Redemptoris Missio,* 4.
12. *ibid.*, 32-33.
13. *Evangelii Nuntiandi,* 56.
14. *Redemptoris Missio,* 35.
15. *Evangelii Nuntiandi,* 18-19; see also *Christifideles Laici* (The Vocation and the Mission of the Lay Faithful in the Church and in the World), Post-synodal Apostolic Exhortation, December 30, 1988 (Washington, DC: United States Catholic Conference, 1998), 44.
16. Carl Anderson, 'Realistic Catechesis on the Family,' in *Faith and challenges to the Family,* Proceedings of the Thirteenth Workshop for Bishops, Dallas, Texas, ed. Russell E. Smith (Braintree, MA: The Pope John Center, 1994), pp. 279-297, pp. 280-281. See also Edward S. Reid, *The Necessity of Experience* (New Haven, CT, Yale University Press, 1996), pp. 17-18.
17. *ibid.*, 282.
18. Anderson, 'Realistic Catechesis,' 283.
19. Linda Thompson, 'Feminist Methodology for Family Studies,' *Journal of Marriage and the Family,* 1:54 (February 1992), pp. 3-18

20. Anderson, 'Realistic Catechesis', 289.
21. Carl Anderson, 'The Role of the Family in the Conversion of Culture', *Communio* 21. (Winter 1994), pp. 765-775.
22. *Redemptor Hominis* (Redeemer of Man), First Encyclical Letter, March 4, 1979 (Washington, DC: United States Catholic Conference, 1979), 1.
23. *ibid.*, 8, 9. The text from *Gaudium et Spes* the pope is referring to is # 22.
24. *ibid.*, 9.
25. *ibid.*, 10.
26. *ibid.*, 7.
27. *ibid.*, 7, cf. *Redemptoris Missio,* 2, 37.
28. *Redemptoris Missio,* 37
29. *Redemptoris Hominis,* 12.
30. *Redemptoris Missio,* 5, 7.
31. The Wednesday Catecheses are a series of homilies John Paul II gave on marriage and family at the beginning of his pontificate, now published in one volume, *The Theology of the Body: Human Love in the Divine Plan* (Washington, DC: Pauline Books & Media, 1997).
32. There is a good summary in an article by Angelo Schola, 'The Formation of Priests in the Pastoral Care of the Family', *Communio* 24 (Spring 1997), pp. 57-83: 63-65.
33. *ibid.*, 66.
34. John Paul II, *Veritatis Splendor* (The Splendor of Truth), Encyclical Letter, August 6, 1993 (Boston, MA: St Paul Books & Media, 1993)
35. 'The Pope Against Moralism and Legalism, (In Relievo)', *Anthropotes,* 10 (1, *June* 1994) pp. 82-86.
36. *ibid.*, 84.
37. John Paul II, 'Letter to Families', *Origins* 23 (37, March 3, 1994), pp. 638-659, no. 1.
38. *ibid.*, no. 23.
39. *Catechism of the Catholic Church* (Mahweh, NJ: Paulist Press, 1994): no. 2205.
40. *ibid.*, no. 2225.
41. *Evangelii Nuntiandi,* 41-48.
42. John Paul II, *Evangelium Vitae* (Gospel of Life), Encyclical, *Origins,* 24 (42, April 6, 1995) no. 12.
43. *ibid.*, 1.
44. *ibid.*, 2.
45. *ibid.*, 92.
46. *ibid.*, 11.
47. *ibid.*, 21.
48. *ibid.*, 22.
49. *ibid.*, 12.
50. *ibid.*, 13.
51. *ibid.*, 17.
52. *Redemptoris Missio,* 14.
53. In Margaret Sanger's own words: 'I went to bed, knowing that no matter what it might cost, I was finished with palliatives and superficial cures. I was resolved

... to do something to change the destiny of mothers whose miseries were as vast as the sky.' Quoted in 'Opportunities for Women Through Reproductive Choice', *Population Reports,* 22 (1 July 1994) Series M, 12, 5.

54. *ibid,* 3.
55. For insight on this see Kristin Luker, *Taking Chances: Abortion and the Decision Not to Contracept,* paperback ed. (Berkeley, CA: University of California Press, 1975).
56. 'The Holy Father to Participants of an International Congress on NFP,' *NFP Forum: Diocesan Activity Report* 8 (1, Winter 1997), 1-2.
57. *Evangelium Vitae,* 92.
58. *ibid.,* 11.
59. *ibid.,* 21.
60. *Redemptoris Missio,* 34.
61. *ibid.,* 90.
62. *Evangelium Nuntinadi,* 59.
63. *ibid.,* 70, 71.

SCRIPTURE AND CATECHESIS

FR JOHN REDFORD

Scripture is central to catechesis, as the *General Directory for Catechesis* makes crystal clear. In particular, as part of ongoing further catechesis, the GDC emphasises first the 'Study and exploration of Holy Scripture'. (p. 71, No. 71).

But the recommendation of the use of scripture in catechesis is followed by a serious qualification. As one of the 'Various forms of continuing catechesis', the GDC lists 'The study and exploration of Sacred Scripture read not only in the Church but with the Church and her living faith, which helps to discover divine truth, which it contains, in such a way as to arouse a response of faith'. The GDC wishes to insist that catechesis is based not on any study of scripture in a neutral sense, but of the study of scripture within the mind of the Church.

This note of caution is clearly based upon an anxiety perceived by the authors of this Directory. As one of the problems identified by the GDC in modern catechesis, the document states, 'in much catechesis, indeed, reference to Sacred Scripture is virtually exclusive and unaccompanied by sufficient reference to the Church's long experience and reflection, acquired in the course of her two thousand year history' (GDC p. 30, No. 30).

The GDC is worried, therefore, that the study of Scripture in some modern catechesis within the Roman Catholic Church ignores Tradition, almost in a classical Protestant sense of *sola scriptura.* This is a fascinating comment, and betrays an underlying tension within the post-Vatican II

Church. The Second Vatican Council set its agenda to open the scriptures to the Catholic faithful. But it seems that thirty years after Vatican II, the Church is not settled in its use of Scripture. Otherwise, would the authors of the GDC be so anxious?

There are indeed unresolved problems within the Catholic theological and biblical community regarding the whole question of the interpretation of Scripture. And of course, we cannot get our catechetics right, until we have our theology and biblical hermeneutics right.

The problem is not identical to that at the time of the Reformation. It is not just a question of the old Scripture and Tradition controversy. Rather, it is the much more complex question of post-Enlightenment exegesis. How far can we use any Scripture text to underpin Christian doctrine? Indeed, how far should a given traditional Christian doctrine be subject to re-interpretation granted the conclusions, or at least the suggestions, of modern biblical scholarship? That is just as important a question for other Christian churches as within our own communion. It is a twentieth century post-Modernist rather than a sixteenth century post-Reformation issue.

In 1962, the distinguished Catholic theologian Karl Rahner drew attention to the increasing alienation between the biblical and theological disciplines within academic Catholic theology. In a symposium entitled *Exegesis and Dogmatic theology*, he bemoaned this increasing division:

> within Catholic theology there obtains a certain estrangement between the representatives of these two disciplines. It appears to us that not a few representatives of these two fields of work in Catholic theology regard each other with a certain distrust, even exasperation. The dogmatic theologian seems at times to have the feeling that exegetes pay scant attention to the dogmatics to which the theologian is bound, and which pronounces upon matters which are the subject of exegesis (in the widest meaning of the word). Some exegetes, on the other hand, seem convinced that the theologians want to tie the Scripture scholar's hands in a way for which there is no objective justification, but simply because the theologians have not taken sufficient account of the progress Catholic exegesis has made in recent decades.[1]

Rahner was quite clear that the biblical scholar must be critical, using all the tools and the strict discipline of the historical method:

> You must be critical, inexorably critical. You must not seek to arrange any dishonest reconciliations between the results of research and the doctrine of the Church. You may propose a problem and expound it sincerely where necessary. You need not have seen – in spite of all your efforts you may not yet see – how clear, positive solutions can be found which will harmonise church doctrine, or what one takes to be such, with the real or ostensible results of your research. In such cases you need have no misgivings.

But on that same page Rahner goes on to challenge the Catholic exegete that part of his or her task is precisely to see how Church doctrine is consistent with biblical research:

> But the climax of your research you must seek only in the accomplishment of your whole duty. And part of this, since you are Catholic exegetes, is the demonstration of the harmony between your results and Church doctrine. You must show how your results, of themselves, point on to Church doctrine as to their genuine expression. Of course not every exegete is bound to do this every time. Without specialisation and division of labour, no one can get very far nowadays. But that such a demonstration is basically part of the exegete's task should show more often and clearly among you than seems to me to be the case.[2]

My contention is that, nearly forty years later, Rahner's challenge still is relevant. The tendency is for a biblical scholar to be suspicious of attempts to 'prove' Catholic doctrine from scripture. The suspicion is always that in defending a Church doctrine, the exegete is allowing one's own doctrinal bias to sway the argument. He or she is guilty of *eisegesis* (reading something *into* the text) rather than genuine *exegesis* (reading something *out* of the text).

From *Divino Afflante Spiritu* Onwards; the Divine and Human Authorship of Scripture

These issues first came to the fore in Catholic theology after the Encyclical on Biblical Studies issued by Pope Pius XII in 1943, *Divino Afflante Spiritu* ('By the Breath of the Spirit'). Biblical scholars call this the *Magna Carta* of Catholic biblical studies. *Divino Afflante Spiritu* acknowledged the presence of different literary forms in Scripture. The Encyclical insisted that what first must be discovered by the biblical scholar in interpreting a given text was the meaning intended by the author, i.e. the literal sense. Furthermore, Pius XII said:

> 35. What is the literal sense of a passage is not always as obvious in the speeches and writings of the ancient authors of the East, as it is in the works of our own time. For what they wished to express is not to be determined by the rules of grammar and philology alone, nor solely by the context; the interpreter must, as it were, go back wholly in spirit to those remote centuries of the East and with the aid of history, archaeology, ethnology, and other sciences, accurately determine what modes of writing, so to speak, the authors of that ancient period would be likely to use, and in fact did use.[3]

Immediately, Catholic biblical scholars and theologians saw the deep implications of this radical document on scripture from one who had the reputation of being a conservative minded Pope. What if the six days of creation in Genesis 1 were not historical, but theological poetry? What if the story in Genesis 2-3, of the Fall of Adam and Eve, was not historical entirely, but typological or symbolic? What if the story of Adam's creation by God's breath, and Eve's being taken from the rib of Adam, was likewise symbolic? Could not we have then actually descended from apes?

In Rome itself, a battle royal developed between the 'conservative' scholars, in various of the Roman clerical Universities, and the Jesuit Biblical Institute, a post-Graduate faculty of the Gregorian University originally founded by Pope Pius X for further biblical research. which adopted the new methods of exegesis with relish. The conservatives felt that in embracing the historical-critical method, the new exegesis was weakening the basis of Christian doctrine. The new exegetes, on the other hand, saw the conservatives as clinging to a Fundamentalist past, burying their heads ostrich like in the sand. The Jesuits at the Biblical Institute had a powerful leader in their Rector Augustine (later Cardinal) Bea, who was a confidante of Pius XII, as later of John XXIII, and, it is commonly accepted, was the brains behind *Divino Afflante Spiritu.*

The progressives had an even greater victory at the Second Vatican Council. After earlier and more conservative drafts of the document on Revelation were promulgated by the Roman Curia and their supporters among the bishops, eventually in 1965 a document was agreed upon by the Council Fathers, which seemed to completely canonise the more progressive exegesis. In particular, *Dei Verbum* ('The Word of God') the final draft of the Dogmatic Constitution on Divine Revelation, emphasised the fact that not only was God truly the author of scripture, the traditional doctrine, but also that 'In the process of the composition of the sacred books God employed human agents, using their own powers and faculties, in such a way that they wrote as authors in the true sense, and yet God acted in and through them, directing the content entirely as he willed'[4] This means that the interpreter of scripture must investigate 'what meaning the biblical writers actually had in mind' and that, in order to understand this, 'attention should be paid (among other things) to literary genres.'

Biblical scholars saw this text as the deathblow to fundamentalism. Texts of scripture did not necessarily have to be interpreted in a factual way. Rather, the Bible was now to be seen as a coat of many literary colours; history, poetry, or even (dare we say this?) myth. The most important books for those who studied scripture and theology in the sixties was J. Mackenzie's *The Two Edged Sword* and B. Vawter's *Path Through Genesis*, which gave students the liberating realisation that their Catholic faith was not prejudiced if the story of the Tower of Babel did not happen exactly as related in Genesis, but was an ancient story with a theological message.

The Scriptures Contain Revelation

The sceptical teenager in the classroom may ask, 'Is it *all myth*?' How do we know that any of it is true? The miraculous crossing of the Red Sea? Elijah producing a miraculous fire to defeat the prophets of Baal? Was the water he poured on the sacrifice really petrol? Finally, what about Jesus and his miracles, his Virgin Birth, his Resurrection? In order to begin to answer these crucial questions, a distinction needs to be drawn between inspiration and revelation.

In the Catholic theology of biblical inspiration, revelation is not equivalent to biblical inspiration. The First Vatican Council tells us that the scriptures 'contain revelation without error'.[5] The First Vatican Council was summoned in 1870 precisely to counter the errors of those (rationalists, pantheists, modernists) who saw the scriptures as myth.[6] But this Council, in stating that the scriptures contain revelation without error, perhaps unwittingly but still significantly are excluding fundamentalism by refusing to identify the scriptures with revelation. A beer glass might contain beer; but as a drinking receptacle, it is not the drink itself. The scriptures likewise contain revelation. But they are not simply to be identified with revelation.

Even prior to Vatican II, neo-scholastic theology recognised this principle. For orthodox Catholic theologians of biblical inspiration in the first three quarters of this century, revelation was seen as new truth. They argued on the other hand that the charism of biblical inspiration did not necessarily give new truth. They saw clearly that many texts of the Bible recounted mundane truths, such as wars between the Maccabees and the forces of Hellenism. What made the scriptures truly the Word of God for these theologians? Simply the *practical judgement* by which the Holy Spirit was poured out on the human writers of scripture which directed them to write this particular passage of scripture.

The Second Vatican Council develops this same theme. Biblical inspiration is simply the act of the Holy Spirit by which, regarding the human authors of scripture, 'God acted in them and through them, directing the content entirely and solely as he willed'.[7] What the content actually is was not determined by the charism of inspiration alone. Rather, it is determined by the understanding of divine revelation itself, the certain discovery of which, *Dei Verbum* states earlier, is not solely by scriptural exegesis; 'both scripture and tradition are to be accepted and honoured with like devotion and reverence'.[8] For *Dei Verbum* therefore, revelation can only be discovered with certainty from the scriptures read in the light of tradition, and finally authenticated by the Magisterium. This certain statement of God's revelation transmitted down the centuries *Dei Verbum* calls the 'deposit of faith'.

A useful example of such exegesis is given in the *Catechism of the Catholic Church* regarding the doctrine of Original Sin:

> The account of the fall in Genesis 3 uses figurative language, but affirms a primeval event, a deed that took place at the beginning of the history of man. Revelation gives us the certainty of faith that the whole of human history is marked by the original fault freely committed by our first parents.[9]
>
> (CCC 390)

This Catechism text makes such a clear distinction between inspiration and revelation as we have outlined above. The text itself is figurative, but contains the essential truth of divine revelation, the doctrine of Original Sin.

The Scriptures must be read in the Light of the Spirit

Post-Vatican II, Catholic exegesis has generally ignored what traditional theology called the 'spiritual sense' of scripture. After an interesting discussion on the *sensus plenior*, the fuller sense of scripture during the sixties, which seemed to enter a *cul de sac*, the subject seems to have been dropped, in favour of an exclusive and intense exploration of the historical critical method. Again, the spiritual meaning has been seen as pious interpretation rather than scientific exegesis.

But the Church has always insisted that the meaning of scripture cannot be discovered by historical criticism alone. Indeed, following from what we have argued above, that the scriptures contain revelation, then obviously the historical method cannot be sufficient in itself to discover the revelation of the mystery of God's loving plan of redemption. The Second Vatican Council *Dei Verbum* expresses this truth in No. 12, and the *Catechism of the Catholic Church* expounds its meaning for us:

> But since Sacred Scripture is inspired, there is another and no less important principle of correct interpretation, without which Scripture would remain a dead letter. 'Sacred Scripture must be read and interpreted in the light of the same Spirit by whom it was written.' DV 12 § 3 (CCC 111)

The Second Vatican Council indicates three criteria for interpreting Scripture in accordance with the Spirit who inspired it. (cf. DV 12 § 4) Expounded by the CCC:

> *Be especially attentive 'to the content and unity of the whole of Scripture.'* Different as the books which comprise it may be, Scripture is a unity by reason of the unity of God's plan, of which Christ Jesus is the centre and heart, open since his Passover. Lk 24:25-27. The phrase 'heart of Christ' can refer to Sacred Scripture, which makes known his heart, closed before the Passion, as the Scripture was obscure. But the Scripture has been opened since the Passion; since those who from then on have understood it, consider and discern in what way the prophecies must be interpreted, St Thomas Aquinas, Expos. in Ps 21,11; cf. Ps 22:15 (CCC 112 1)

> *Read the Scripture within 'the living Tradition of the whole Church.'* According to a saying of the Fathers, Sacred Scripture is written principally in the Church's heart rather than in documents and records, for the Church carries in her Tradition the living memorial of God's Word, and it is the Holy Spirit who gives her the spiritual interpretation of the Scripture ('... according to the spiritual meaning which the Spirit grants to the Church'<81>). Origen, Hom. in Lev. 5, 5: PG 12, 454D (CCC 113 2)

> *Be attentive to the analogy of faith.* <82> cf. Rom 12:6. By 'analogy of faith' we mean the coherence of the truths of faith among themselves and within the whole plan of Revelation. (CCC 114 3)

One scholar taking a serious look at this theological sense is the Johannine scholar Ignace De La Potterie, SJ, in his article 'Interpretation of Holy Scripture in the Spirit in Which It was Written' *(Dei Verbum* 12c).[10] In my opinion, the importance of this collection of articles, by so many leading Catholic theologians in the world today, can hardly be exaggerated. Reading the symposium will convince the reader that in many ways we are still a long way from understanding the Council documents even now. Much work of learning and of insight still needs to be done at the fundamental level of understanding.

De La Potterie begins by making his complaint: 'The principle recommended by *Dei Verbum* 12c for a theological interpretation of Scripture has hardly received any study since the Council'.[11] De La Potterie follows the principle through,[12] that it is precisely because we must read Scripture in the light in which it was written, that we must take full note, as *Dei Verbum* says, of the Unity of the Whole of Scripture, of the Tradition of the Entire Church, and of the Analogy of Faith. This means, according to Yves Congar, quoted by De La Poterrie., that 'there must always be unity between object and subject'.[13] The Spirit must dwell in the subject (the reader and interpreter of scripture) in order for that subject to understand the object (the text of scripture written by the Spirit).[14]

De La Potterie ends his article by throwing out challenges to modern post-Vatican II exegetes, which we may summarise as follows.[15]

1. Why have exegetes paid so little attention to the principle of Vatican II, that scripture should be interpreted in the spirit in which it was written? Are they aware of the spiritual understanding of scripture?

2. What is the role of the Spirit in the actual practice of exegesis?

3. Are exegetes aware of the philosophical deficiencies of modern exegesis, namely its secularity, which is linked back to the Enlightenment?

4. Is exegesis concerned with the whole meaning of scripture, as expressed in No. 12 of *Dei Verbum*, i.e. the meaning which God wishes to express to us?

5. What role does faith play in the whole activity of biblical interpretation? Exegesis, says De La Potterie, is another example of *fides*

quaerens intellectum, faith seeking understanding. But must an exegete not abstract from his faith in making historico/critical judgements? Here is a dilemma for modern exegesis.

The History of Salvation

These challenges from a leading Catholic exegete are clearly important for the catechesis of scripture. The scriptures are a source for catechesis, not merely as ancient historical documents, but as truly the Word of God for the Church. A prime example here is the whole concept of the history of salvation. Catechists and teachers have for decades been teaching the Old Testament in particular as the history of salvation. But seeing any history as the history of salvation requires an assent of faith, since for history to be interpreted as salvific requires historical events to be interpreted as divine revelation, God's 'deeds and words'.[16]

Perhaps the greatest Old Testament scholar in the second half of the twentieth century, Gerhard von Rad, has succeeded in focussing attention on the theological meaning of the Old Testament. For von Rad, the key to the interpretation of the Old Testament is the history of salvation, *Heilsgeschichte*, centering on the Exodus as the salvific act whereby God leads his people out of slavery in Egypt into the Promised Land.

But how much history, in any sense of the word, can we actually find in the Old Testament? This has been a problem since the advent of the modern critical study of the Bible, and particularly since the nineteenth century source theories relating to the first five books of the Bible, the Pentateuch. The Catholic Oratorian scholar Simon had contended long before, in the seventeenth century, that Moses could not have written the account of his own death. Simon was one of the first to propose sources in the writing of Genesis-Deuteronomy. But, by the close of the nineteenth century, the Graf-Wellhausen hypothesis held the same kind of sway as Darwin's theory of species by Natural Selection. What became known as the Documentary Hypothesis held that the four sources of the first five books of the Bible (J, E, D, and P), far from being written by Moses in the fifteenth century BC , were in fact written by various schools of Jewish religious thought from the eighth century BC right up to the Exile in the sixth century.

Naturally, this raised a large number of questions concerning the history of the patriarchs, the period of slavery in Egypt, and the entry into the Promised Land, because the accounts of these events in the Pentateuch are now to be dated many centuries later than the events themselves. These questions are still unresolved among Old Testament scholars, and probably will stay unresolved. The historical evidence is too flimsy and open to different interpretation for unanimity on the early history of Israel; although I myself favour the balanced approach of the Dominican scholar Roland de Vaux. De Vaux holds that, while the accounts of the patriarchal narratives are by no means strict history, the core history of the patriarchs, the Exodus from Egypt and the entry into the Promised Land have a good foundation in fact, as the most important events in the memory of the chosen people.[17]

In fact, there is an enormous amount of factual narrative throughout the Old Testament. We probably have more archaeological evidence for the period of the Kings after David and Solomon than we have for the European Middle Ages.

The amount of fact is not the main problem regarding the Old Testament. The main critical problem is not so much the facts, as their theological interpretation as salvation history; in particular, post-Bultmann. 'In Bultmann's opinion to speak of God at all as involved in history necessitates the use of anthropological language and that means the use of myth. Myth is what results when God is brought into connection with the world of man and nature.'[18]

If Bultmann is right, the catechist has a real problem. The catechist can only report bare fact, not that God is acting here and now in this or that event. According to Bultmann, as reported without doubt correctly by Porteous, 'For us to recount the acts of God in the history of his ancient people would be to involve ourselves in an outworn mythology'.[19]

The use of the spiritual or theological sense in the traditional Catholic understanding outlined above could live easily with a fair amount of suspension of judgement regarding the miracles recounted in the Old Testament just as we might suspend judgement regarding some miracle stories in the lives of the saints. Non-miraculous events can be interpreted quite legitimately as salvation historical events, God leading his people towards a greater understanding of the divine plan. The GDC encourages us to see God's revelatory words and deeds not only in the 'marvels worked by God in the past, but also, in the light of the same Revelation, it interprets the signs of the times and the present life of man, since it is in these that the plan of God for the salvation of the world is realised' (GDC 39, p. 43).

Indeed, in the book of Judges 2:10-23, the author interprets success or failure in battle as dependant on whether or not the people were following God or worshipping idols, whether or not miracles strictly speaking were involved. Even Bultmann could admit the legitimacy of an *existential* interpretation of events in terms of how the person as a believing subject was changed by an event and its understanding towards a more authentic life. This, for Bultmann, would be an example of genuine *Geschichte*, a meaningful historical event, rather than of *Historie*, a collection of mere facts.

The Historical Jesus

The Jesus event, however, in particular the question of the historical Jesus, presents Christians with a much greater problem, even a crisis, for catechesis and theology; a crisis which perhaps for us as Catholics has only just impacted upon us with its full force since the so-called Jesus Seminar in the USA.

In 1970, I was present at a post-graduate seminar in Jerusalem, where Jewish and Christian scholars were listening to the great Father de Vaux OP, who was lecturing to a packed hall. After his exposition of the Exodus story, a Jewish scholar asked him, 'Father de Vaux, you have given us a very positivistic explanation of the Exodus, explaining rationally all the plagues, and the Exodus event itself. But would you give the same rationalist explanation for the miracles of Jesus, and for the Incarnation, the Christian belief that in Jesus God has become Man?'

Touché. There is, of course, a difference at least at first sight between a Christian understanding of the Old Testament miracles and the Gospel miracles of Jesus. One could argue that the 'miracle' of the Exodus essentially is the wonderful way in which the children of Israel escaped from slavery through the desert to the Promised Land. The miraculous parting of the Reed Sea (sic, the 'Sea of Reeds') could easily be seen as the divine icing on the cake. No doubt, we would believe as Christians that some miracles, indeed many miracles, took place in the history of Israel prior to Christ; but the distance between the event of the miracles and their record in the Old Testament revelation means that we cannot make firm judgements regarding the historicity of any particular Old Testament miracle.

Regarding miracles in the life of Jesus, however, these have traditionally been viewed as proof of the Incarnation; that at least some of the miracles have been seen in classical apologetics as demonstrating that Jesus was God become man; thus his walking on the water (Mt 14:25) was to be paralleled with Jahweh described in the Psalms as walking astride the sea (Ps 77:19); and above all the appearance of the Lord to his amazed disciples was to evoke the utterance of doubting Thomas 'My Lord and my God'. (Jn 20:28).

We already made the point that not every passage of scripture must be interpreted as strict history. The Bible is a coat of many colours. In my book *Catholicism: Hard Questions,*[20] I have argued to the non-univocality of the meaning of Scripture. The Scriptures have multivocal meanings. But, by the same principle of multivocality, the Scriptures are sometimes to be interpreted as history. At first sight at least, this would seem to be the case regarding the four Gospels. The Dogmatic Constitution on Divine Revelation *Dei Verbum* refers to the Church's 'unhesitating assertion' of the historicity of the Four Gospels. The context of this subordinate clause, added it is said by Pope Paul VI himself , seems to be that of opposition to a Bultmannian view of the Gospels, where they are seen as literary creations of the early Christian community, with minimal reference to the historical Jesus. The Gospels, according to *Dei Verbum* 19 tell us, of the life of Jesus 'what he actually did and taught for their eternal salvation until the day when he was taken up (Acts 1:1-2)'.[21]

However, what *Dei Verbum* 19 has given with its right hand, does it take away with its left? Having asserted without hesitation the historicity of the Gospels, that same paragraph goes on to speak of the four evangelists selecting, synthesising, and 'explicating' material in the Gospels, the Gospel writers proceeding to become Gospel makers 'with the fuller insight which they now possessed' after the Resurrection and Ascension of Christ'. Some might interpret this passage as giving the biblical scholar *carte blanche* to come to any conclusion regarding the life of Jesus, however destructive it might seem to be regarding the Christian doctrine of the Incarnation. From this question arises the alarm generated by the Jesus Seminar; views concerning Jesus that he was a revolutionary politician, a social reformer, a peasant preacher; anyone but the Christ of Christian confession.

The Circular Quest

It could be argued, even if that would be something (but not too much) of an exaggeration, that Jesus research has not progressed very far in the past two hundred years since the publication at first anonymously, of the Wolfenbuttel Fragments in 1774 by the Deist philosopher Lessing. Certainly, the main lines of post-Enlightenment Jesus research, and above all its hermeneutical principles, are already clear in *The Aims of Jesus and His Disciples*, written originally by the philologist Hermann Samuel Reimarus, at first too frightened to publish the work under his own name. Jesus, in this new construction of Reimarus, was a Jewish prophet who believed that he was the Messiah. He claimed not to be the universal Son of God, but only to 'establish an earthly kingdom and deliver the people from political oppression. But Jesus failed to perform the miracles necessary to convince all the people.' The people deserted him, and Jesus was put to death on the cross as a revolutionary.

How, then, was the Christian religion founded and the Gospels eventually written? For Reimarus, this was the work of the disciples of Jesus. After the ignominious death of Jesus, where their hero had said 'My God, my God, why have your forsaken me?', they were not minded to return to fishing. Reimarus claimed 'They did not take kindly to the idea of returning to their old haunts; on their journeyings the companions of the Messiah had forgotten how to work.'[22]

The disciples of Jesus therefore fell back on the Jewish belief that the Messiah would return a second time. They invented the myth that Jesus had risen from the dead. They stole the body of Jesus and hid it, proclaiming that He would soon return. This preaching was much more successful than the life of Jesus himself had been. The Christian religion was born, and flourished through this mythical preaching of the disciples. The alarm at the time of the orthodox Lutheran Pastor of Hamburg is quite understandable. Reimarus was thereby destroying faith in the Christian creeds by his historical reconstruction of the life of Jesus. But we have to be clear from the outset as to his principles. Reimarus has *a priori* rejected even the possibility that Jesus might genuinely have worked miracles, that he was truly the Incarnate Son of God, and that he rose bodily from the dead. Reimarus' Deism, belief in God without the possibility of the miraculous, made this axiomatic. Reimarus did not 'prove' that Jesus did not perform miracles, or that he was not the Word become flesh. Reimarus assumed it from the outset of his investigation into the 'historical Jesus'.

The second proposition of Reimarus followed from the first. Since it was philosophically impossible for Jesus to be truly the only-begotten Son of God, and to have risen from the dead, therefore we must strip away this supernatural nimbus in order to find the historical truth. And that historical truth would be discovered when that nimbus has been stripped away. Reimarus shared both the dogmatic scepticism and the naïve secular faith of the Enlightenment. Once the supernatural baggage of the past had been thrown overboard, for Reimarus, the way towards the open sea of rational truth about Jesus was open.

With a succession of critical investigations of the life of Jesus, over more than two hundred years now, the same dogmatic scepticism remained, and to some extent still remains. A similar approach could be found most recently, for instance, in *Who was the Real Jesus?* by A.N. Wilson in the Sunday Telegraph in the last weekend of the Second Millenium.[23] It remains at least, even in Catholic scholarship,[24] to the extent that many scholars working on the 'Quest of the Historical Jesus' today exclude the possibility of making any 'scientifically historical' judgements about Jesus substantially beyond what is usually called 'The Critical Minimum'.

Historical Jesus research begins with the premise that the four Gospels are not reliable historically, or at least cannot be proven as such, while they do contain some history. Therefore, what we might call a 'hermeneutic of suspicion' is exercised. Unless a saying or a deed of Jesus can be clearly demonstrated not to be from the early Christian community, it must remain as not from the historical Jesus, but is a consequence of the 'Christ of faith', growing faith in Jesus within the primitive Christian community.

Some scholars have reached quite positive and moderate conclusions using this method. A critical consensus was beginning to emerge, with Jesus as a prophet from Nazareth, who was reputed as a miracle worker and sayer of wise sayings, who was put to death by the Romans during the procuratorship of Pontius Pilate 26-36, and who was reputed by his followers to have risen from the dead. I had the privilege of hearing the distinguished scholar E.P. Sanders at a seminar at the Cambridge Divinity School expounding just this 'critical minimum'.

But can Christians be really happy with this 'critical minimum', precisely because it leaves us with a purely human Jesus, with no transcendent consciousness, at least with that transcendent consciousness 'historically proven'? How did criticism 'climb' from the critical historical Jesus, however positively presented by moderate scholars, to the Christ of Christian confession, 'God from God, light from light, true God from true God, begotten not made, of one being with the Father, through whom all things were made'? The same gap remains, and the Christological problem remains, whether one adopts a moderate or a more radical conclusion from Jesus research using the methods canonised by critical orthodoxy. My contention is that Historical Jesus research will never go much beyond rearranging the deck-chairs on Reimarus' literary liner *Titanic*, until it begins to take seriously again the uniqueness of the life, death, and Resurrection of the historical (yes, precisely the historical) Jesus.

The Wright View

How are we to break the apparently everlasting circle round and round the Historical Jesus without any resolution? The breakthrough for me came in the summer of 1998, where I attended the annual conference of the Catholic Theological Association of Great Britain. Fr John McDade, Principal of Heythrop College, London, gave an excellent paper on 'Jesus in Recent Research'.[25]

McDade was fully aware of the theological issues involved in Jesus research:

> There are considerable implications for Christian faith if the charge is proved that the canonical Jesus is radically discontinuous with the pre-canonical Jesus and that post-resurrection faith embellishes the significance of Jesus in ways which exceed and even disregard what he thought of himself. Often, the actuality of Jesus recovered by historical reconstruction is meant to stand in sharp contrast with the faith-dreams projected by the post-resurrection Church.[26]

McDade went on to outline some more positive approaches, in particular that of the Anglican scholar N.T. Wright,[27] who breaks free from the straightjacket imposed by the Quest. Wright goes much further than the rather pathetic Eschatological Prophet beloved from Reimarus through to Wrede and Schweitzer. For Wright, Jesus truly sees himself as the Messiah. Moreover, Jesus considered that with his own ministry of miracle and preaching together with his foreseen death, symbolised in his authority over the Temple, he was bringing a new reign of God to Israel, which would take place after his death. For Wright, the emerging Church after the death of Jesus was not the result of a bedraggled group of disciples attempting to compensate for a vision lost. Rather, it was the foreseen prophecy of Jesus himself, a new emerging and true Israel with a new and true temple.

McDade was also particularly impressed with the approach of Margaret Barker, who, as McDade summarises:

> offers a new paradigm which replaces the distinction between the Jesus of history and the Christ of faith. From his baptism onwards, he is the Lord who has risen into the presence of God, and so he conducts his ministry with a sense that he comes `from above' – in which case the Johannine pattern of descent from above becomes plausible – with a clear sense of himself as the Lord who rescues his people by an atoning sacrifice in his blood, after which he would be exalted and enthroned in heaven as the companion of God's throne (Ps 110 is, after all, the most frequently used Old Testament text in the New Testament).[28]

This self-awareness of Jesus as the transcendent (and not simply the Davidic) Son of God in terms of Psalm 110 gives Christian confession all it needs as the foundation of faith in the Christian Creeds. It also makes sense of the so-called Christological miracles of the Feeding of the Multitude and the Walking on the Water, together with the vision of the Transfiguration. It is because these miracles actually happened that Jesus demonstrated himself to be more than a prophet, but rather the eternal Son of God. This demonstration, of course, was not complete until the Resurrection itself; which, incidentally, the *Catechism of the Catholic Church* insists occurred in the historical order.

> Given all these testimonies, Christ's Resurrection cannot be interpreted as something outside the physical order, and it is impossible not to acknowledge it as an historical fact (CCC 643).

The Jesus of History and the Christ of Faith therefore are one and the same Christ, even if attained through different methodologies. Our investigation of the Gospel record, using all the principles of historical criticism, but not in the end entrapped by their post-Enlightenment presuppositions, enables us to make a reasonable historical judgement that God is present in this act of revelation in Jesus, and present above all in that revelation. Faith works together with historical investigation, not contrary to reason, but in harmony with it. Having affirmed the necessity of the gift of faith, the First Vatican Council goes on:

> Nevertheless, in order that the submission of our faith should be in accordance with reason, it was God's will that there should be linked to the internal assistance of the holy Spirit outward indications of his revelation, that is to say divine acts, and first and foremost miracles and prophecies, which clearly demonstrating as they do the omnipotence and infinite knowledge of God, are the most certain signs of revelation and are suited to the understanding of all.[29]

This assent of faith might be called incipient, as an enquirer begins to find the true (yes the historical) Jesus in the four Gospels, as well as the Christ of faith. Newman's 'antecedent probability' also comes into play, the mind expecting, hope against hope, to find the ultimate divine revelation in this man Jesus. That true and honest enquirer, not without the beginnings of the gift of faith but still enquiring rationally, comes to the right decision, with the help of the Holy Spirit. Vatican II's *Dei Verbum* puts it perfectly:

4. After God had spoken in many and various ways by the prophets, 'in these last days he has spoken to us by a Son' (Heb 1:1-2). He sent his Son, the eternal Word who enlightens all humankind, to live among them and to tell them about the inner life of God (see Jn 1:1-18). Thus it is that Jesus Christ, the Word made flesh, sent as a human being among humans, 'speaks the words of God' (Jn 3,34) and accomplishes the work of salvation which the Father gave him to do (see Jn 5:36; 17:4). To see Jesus is to see also his Father (see Jn 14:9). This is why Jesus completes the work of revelation and confirms it by divine testimony. He did this by the total reality of his presence and self-manifestation – by his words and works, his symbolic acts and miracles, but above all by his death and his glorious resurrection from the dead, crowned by his sending the Spirit of truth. His message is that God is with us, to deliver us from the darkness of sin and death, and to raise us up to eternal life.[30]

Notes

1. K. Rahner, *Exegesis and Dogmatic Theology*. pp. 31-65 in H. Vorgrimler, ed., *Dogmatic Versus Biblical Theology: Essays in Two Disciplines*, trans. Kevin Smyth. (Wheathampstead, Anthony Clarke, 1964), p. 31.
2. K. Rahner, *ibid.* p. 36.
3. Megivern, James J. ed., *Official Catholic Teachings. Bible Interpretation* Wilmington, McGrath 1978.
4. Tanner, II, pp. 975-6.
5. Tanner, II, p. 806.
6. Tanner, II, p. 804.
7. Tanner, II, p. 976, *Dei Verbum* 11.
8. Tanner, II, p. 975, *Dei Verbum* 9.
9. cf. GS 13 § 1. cf. Council of Trent: DS 1513; Pius XII: DS 3897; Paul VI: AAS 58 (1966), 654.
10. Ed. Rene Latourelle Volume One, *Vatican II Assessment and Perspectives Twenty-five years After (1962-1987)* pp. 220-266 (New York, Paulist Press, 1988).
11. *ibid.*, p. 220.
12. De La Potterie notes that the phrase 'because Sacred Scripture must be read and interpreted in the same Spirit in which it was written' (*sed, cum Sacra Scriptura eodem Spiritu quo scripta est etiam leganda et interpretanda sit*) was added to the final text at the eleventh hour on 8 December 1965, just before the final text was promulgated.
13. *ibid.*, p. 223.
14. *ibid.*, p. 225.
15. *ibid*, pp. 255-257.

16. cf. *Dei Verbum* 12 and quoted and expounded in GDC 38-39, pp. 42-43. (A useful summary of this Old Testament history seen as salvation history can be found in the *Catechism of the Catholic Church* CCC 54-64).
17. de Vaux, Roland. *The Early History of Israel: II Vols.* Transl. David Smith. London, Darton, Longman, and Todd, 1978.
18. Porteous, N. *Living the Mystery: Collected Essays.* Oxford, Basil Blackwell, 1967, p. 39.
19. *ibid.*, p. 39.
20. Redford, J., *Catholicism: Hard Questions*, London, Chapman, 1997, p. 23
21. Tanner, II, p. 978.
22. Schweitzer, A., p. 21.
23. *Sunday Telegraph*, December 19, 1999.
24. Meier, *Jesus the Marginal Jew*, 2, p. 966. regarding the Multiplication of the Loaves, 'Whether something actually miraculous took place is not open to verification by the means available to the historian. A decision pro or con will ultimately depend on one's worldview, not on what purely historical investigation can tell us about this event'.
25. John McDade, Jesus in Recent Research. *The Month*, December 1998, Second New Series Vol. 31 No. 12, pp. 495-505.
26. John McDade, *op. cit.*, p. 496.
27. N.T. Wright, *Jesus and the Victory of God*, London, SPCK, 1996.
28. John McDade, op. cit., p. 504.
29. *ibidem.*
30. Tanner II, 972-3.

THE INTEGRITY OF THE GOSPEL AND THE EVANGELICAL IMPERATIVE

EDWARD HULMES

The Integrity of the Gospel

Following Christ, who commanded his followers to evangelise the whole world until the end of time, the Church is entrusted with the task – the unfinished task – of presenting the uniqueness of the Good News of God's redeeming love in a pluralist world. In Catholic belief Jesus is the unique expression of the love that God the Father has for *everyone.* Jesus – the *Christ* of God – is God's self-utterance, the very *Word* of God. The *Church,* according to the same belief, is the Body of Christ, which continues to bear witness to the truth that Jesus came to bring to the world. The Catholic faith affirms an indissoluble unity between God the Father, Jesus, and the Church. The unity is dynamic. It is unique in its integrity, in its potential for incorporating fallen human creatures within the divine plan of redemption. For this reason, the Christian Gospel can never be treated by Catholics as merely one of many different and equally valid alternative paths, which human beings may choose (if they so wish) to help them cope with the human condition in a pluralist world. Nor can the *integral* relationship between God, Jesus, and the Church be overlooked in education, inter-faith dialogue, or ecumenism, without compromising the characteristic elements of Catholic belief and action. Our conviction that Jesus is not only the divine messenger but also the divine message remains an unchangeable *datum* in any re-consideration of the content and methods of catechesis. 'Catechesis starts out with a simple proposition of the integral structure of the Christian message, and proceeds to explain it in a manner adapted to the capacity of those being catechised.' (*General Directory for Catechesis*, pp. 119-20)[1]

Contemporary attitudes to religious pluralism are predicated on the belief that no one religious system has a monopoly of truth. The truth – we are expected to believe – is relative. Today, as the American writer Alan Bloom puts it, there is a widespread conviction that relativism is not just a theoretical insight but a moral postulate. This conviction is often reinforced rather than questioned in the general course of formal education, so much so that we are encouraged to believe that the truth about anything can never be known. This notion contradicts Catholic faith, grounded as it always must be in Jesus who, when challenged on the point, answered: 'If you continue in my word, you are truly my disciples, and you will know the truth, and the truth will make you free' (Jn 8:31-2). And he followed this with an assurance for the future: 'When the Spirit of truth comes, he will guide you into all the truth; for he will not speak on his own authority, but whatever he hears he will speak, and he will declare to you the things that are to come' (Jn 16:13). The truth of the Gospel is accessible. We can know the truth in Christ, provided that we maintain the discipline of the disciple through prayer, scripture reading, and the sacraments. In this millennium, as in its two predecessors, the Gospel of Christ will lay claim to our attention as the key to fruitful dialogue between the adherents of different, and even opposing, beliefs. The Gospel may yet prove to be the most effective instrument for re-invigorating the wider ecumenism, which Pope John Paul II has consistently advocated in his references to the documents of the Second Vatican Council.[2] Without the constant insistence, in humility, on the integrity of the Gospel Catholics will falter in their attempts to engage in education, mission, dialogue, and ecumenism. Is the belief in the uniqueness of the Gospel of Jesus, to which the followers of Christ have held consistently (if not always sensitively) to be modified or even surrendered if religious diversity is now to be taken as an integral part of the divine plan? The affirmation of Catholics is that the Gospel of Jesus is for all. 'There is no compulsion in religion'[3] (as Muslims, among many others, aver) but this is no reason for Catholics to withhold the offer of the Gospel to those in ignorance of it, or to anyone seeking knowledge of God. Every Christian community is called to participate in ecumenical dialogue. Preparation for the 'ecumenical dimension' of Catholic life is aided by thoughtful catechesis, which:

> … arouses and nourishes a true desire for unity, particularly with the love of Sacred Scripture. Finally, it prepares children, young people and adults to live in contact with brothers and sisters of other confessions, by having them cultivate both their own Catholic identity and respect for the faith of others … The teaching of religion in schools attended by Christians of diverse confessions can also have an ecumenical value when Christian doctrine is genuinely presented. This affords the opportunity for dialogue through which prejudice and ignorance can be overcome and a greater openness to better reciprocal understanding achieved. (GDC, p. 206)

When, under house arrest in Rome, St Paul wrote his letter to the Colossians some thirty years after the resurrection and ascension of Jesus, the city of Colossae in Asia Minor was already in decline. In Roman times it had lost its position as a great cosmopolitan trading centre in Phrygia, not far from Ephesus. Its decline was not merely economic. The Christian community of Gentile and Jewish converts, to whom Paul sent his letter, was threatened by incipient heresy. Paul was concerned to challenge what he saw as dangerous deviations from the truth of Christ. He expressed his concern in a letter which re-affirms even today that Christianity is nothing if it is not Christ-centred, and emasculated whenever its integrity is impugned. The word 'integrity' here refers not just to the Truth that Christ reveals but also to the coherence of the faith to which Christians in all places and at all times are obliged as well as privileged to bear witness. It is still this fullness of Christ, this coherent understanding of his person, this awareness of the reality of a personal relationship that Christians in this age as in any other are commissioned to offer universally. To emphasise this or that aspect of the truth, which we happen to see in Christ whilst denying those that we do not see, is the mistake of the heretic. Perhaps the earliest Christian Credo affirms that Jesus is Lord. To know Christ in the intimacy of a personal relationship with him is the chief benefit of Christian discipleship. In St Paul's day, as today, there are those – Christians among them – apparently, who for one reason or another fail to recognise Christ as the Word made Flesh. The uniqueness of the Christian Gospel, its claim that in Christ we see and hear the self-expression of the Creator, is too absurd for some to take. Paul, the Apostle to the Gentiles, would certainly recognise the situation today in which:

> Many communities and individuals are called to live in a pluralistic and secularised world, in which forms of unbelief and religious indifference may be encountered together with vibrant expressions of religious and cultural pluralism. In many individuals the search for certainty and for values appears strong. Spurious forms of religion, however, are also evident as well as dubious adherence to the faith. In the face of such diversity, some Christians are confused or lost. ... Their faith is exposed to trials. When threatened it risks being extinguished altogether, unless it is constantly nourished and sustained. (GDC, p. 203)

The Evangelical Imperative

Past, present, and future are integrally linked in the words of what has become known among Christians as 'The Great Commission', delivered by Jesus to his disciples shortly before he took leave of them at the end of his earthly ministry. Ever since then his followers have been exercised to interpret its significance for them as a continuing evangelical imperative-as an authoritative dominical summons to announce and to proclaim throughout the world until the end of time the Gospel he came to bring. 'All authority in heaven and earth has been given to me.' The commission entrusted to him in the past, and fulfilled on the completion of his ministry, is now given to the fledgling Church, on authority. For the present the command is to 'Go, *therefore*, and make disciples of all nations', whilst the future is assured on the grounds that 'I am with you always':

> Now the eleven disciples went to Galilee, to the mountain to which Jesus had directed them. And when they saw him they worshipped him, but some doubted. And Jesus came and said to them, 'All authority in heaven and earth has been given to me. Go therefore and make disciples of all nations, baptising them in the name of the Father and of the Son and of the Holy Spirit, teaching them to observe all that I have commanded you; and lo, I am with you always, to the close of the age.' (Mt 28:20)

It is, as Jesus says, '... because I have made known to you all that I have heard from My Father' (Jn 15:15) that Catholic education, catechesis, mission, ecumenism, and inter-faith dialogue must aim to transmit this integral link with God through Jesus. It is a fundamental principle of Catholic witness to safeguard 'the integrity of the message' by avoiding 'any partial or distorted presentation' (GDC, p. 119).

Maryvale Institute's coat of arms also bears an imperative, in the Latin inscription *Audite Insulae,* 'Hear O Islands!' The imperative is clear enough, but what is it that the 'islands' are exhorted to hear? To whom, or to what, does the word 'islands' refer? How are 'they' to hear, and what happens if 'they' refuse to listen? The original biblical passage, from which the imperative comes, is found in Isaiah 49. The identity of the speaker is not immediately apparent, although biblical scholars refer to him as *Deutero-* or *Second-Isaiah,* a prophet who lived 150 years after Isaiah of Jerusalem, and who shared with his people the Babylonian exile, which began in 587 BC and lasted for the next 40 years. The passage in question begins with an impassioned plea from the prophet: *Listen to me, you islands, hear this you distant nations. ...* Despite failing strength and a sense that his best efforts had achieved nothing worthwhile, the prophet was encouraged by God to hold fast to his prophetic ministry. Still exiled in Babylon far from his native Israel, he had good reason to question the task he had been given, but he persevered in the belief that restoration would come, and soon. His words reflect the continuing conviction of Jews and Christians about the universality of God's salvific activity in human history and about the personal responsibility of the individual in co-operating with God in the repair of a broken world. But for Christians there is a new dimension, revealed by Jesus. He, par excellence, is the Suffering Servant, and it is in the *theologia crucis* – the theology of the Cross – that God's identification with humanity is fully and uniquely revealed.

The *Suffering Servant,* to whom the writer of the Old Testament book of Isaiah refers so movingly, is given a mission by God, 'to bring forth justice to the nations' (Isa 42:1); this Servant, chosen by God, is to be 'a light to the nations' so that God's plan of salvation 'may reach to the end of the earth' (Isa 49: 6), yet in following his vocation the Servant will be grievously 'wounded for our transgressions' (Isa 53:5). For Christians, however, these are taken to be references to Jesus himself. It is the unique claim of Christians that, in the person of Jesus, God shares the life and the suffering of mankind. We are free to respond in faith or to reject the divine offer. We are free to take leave of God if we choose, in which case the separation is of our making. Whatever our decision, however, God remains uniquely present as the Christ of faith, re-assuring and exemplary. *Stat crux dum volvitur orbis* – 'the Cross remains constant while the earth turns.'

Fidelity to the Great Commission

I am sometimes asked the question: *Is there a place for the study of world religions* (i.e. religions other than Christianity) *in Catholic education*? Following the guidelines provided by the appropriate documents of the Second Vatican Council, and especially *Nostra Aetate*, my answer is in the affirmative, but only if due weight is given to the Catholic faith, out of which the whole Catholic educational enterprise takes its inspiration and from which it derives its *raison d'être*.[4] The question of the uniqueness of the Gospel of Jesus raises a number of questions about Catholic belief and Catholic action in the years that lie ahead. Indeed, it raises further questions in a pluralist world about Catholic beliefs with regard to evangelisation, missionary activity, and ecumenical co-operation with other Christians and non-Christians. What, if anything, is distinctive about *Catholic* beliefs in a world of religious and cultural diversity? In a pluralist, multi-faith society, 'the good news' of the 'gospel' can no longer be assumed to be that of the *Christian* Gospel, still less that of the Gospel which is proclaimed in Catholic teaching. It is clear that today there are other-one might say alternative – 'gospels', not the least attractive of which are non-theistic, not to say explicitly atheistic. When it is the Gospel of Jesus to which reference is being made, there is an obligation to be specific. For Catholic Christians in particular, the challenge presented by pluralism to the universal claims of the Gospel of Christ is, literally, of crucial importance. Catholics bear a responsibility for affirming and defending their belief in the universal lordship of Christ. This does not require them to deny or misrepresent the beliefs of others. Religious and cultural diversity in the world cannot simply be ignored. Maintaining a delicate balance between presenting the unique lordship of Christ 'to all nations' and honouring the different beliefs of others, yet doing this 'with gentleness and reverence' (1 Pet 3:15) is far from being an option for a privileged *cadre* of believers. Christians today often find themselves living as a minority in a multi-religious yet predominantly secular society. They find themselves 'in an obligatory encounter between the Gospel of Jesus Christ and the message of other religions'. In this situation:

> ...catechesis assists in creating awareness of the presence of other religions. It necessarily facilitates Christians in discerning the elements of those religions which are contrary to the Christian message, but also educates them to accept the seeds of the Gospel (*semina Verbi*) which are found in them and which can sometimes constitute an authentic *preparation for the Gospel.* In the third

> instance, catechesis promotes a lively missionary sense among believers. This is shown by clear witness to the faith, by an attitude of respect and mutual understanding, by dialogue and co-operation in defence of the rights of the person and of the poor and, where possible, with explicit proclamation of the Gospel. (GDC, p. 208)

The Concept of Christian Presence

One of the important ways in which Catholics can work confidently and in humility with other Christians in the service of mission, dialogue, and ecumenism, may be described as the way of *Christian Presence.* The phrase also serves as a pointer to the way in which Christians of all denominations may engage in inter-faith dialogue, in order to explore by means of affirmation rather than denial the beliefs and experiences which those of other faiths or of none are willing to share. It has probably never been more vital to maintain and defend the practice of Christian presence in the world than today. A belief that they are privileged inheritors of faith in God, yet still 'strangers and exiles on earth', is held by the spiritual descendants of Abraham (Heb 11:13). Jews, Christians, and Muslims, differ about many things, but they are the beneficiaries of a spiritual patrimony, which stretches back to Abraham, their father in faith. Christians can seek to build upon this common ground.

> Christians are being presented by the contemporary world with what is, in many ways, a unique opportunity of demonstrating the Gospel. Scarcely less unique is the opportunity being offered to them of discovering in a new and deeper way what that Gospel is. These are large claims. Can they be justified? What is this unique opportunity? ... At the very least it is the opportunity presented to Christians to demonstrate the fundamental truth of the Gospel that it is a universal message, whose relevance is not limited to any one culture, to any one system of thought, to any one pattern of activity.[5]

Catholics who respond to the challenge presented by this concept of *Christian Presence* can take certain steps to prepare themselves for both *intra-faith* dialogue (that is to say, the dialogue between members of the different Christian communities) and the wider *inter-faith* dialogue between adherents of other religions or of none. The first step is to consider the status of one's *present* beliefs. Not, *What am I expected to believe?* but rather *What do I actually believe?* And – if I belong to the

Christian community – what, if anything, do I have difficulty in believing?

The second step is more difficult. It is obvious that the practice of *Christian Presence* does not depend upon specialist knowledge of *other* religions, although Christians cannot remain insensitive to the systems of religious belief which claim the allegiance of millions. It would be curious, however, if, in recognising holiness in the beliefs of others I were to neglect the *distinctive* holiness of the Faith to which I am committed. A characteristic (and, I would argue, a unique) feature of the Gospel of Jesus is the distinctive love shown by Jesus for all humanity. It is an inclusive love. It is unique in that it demonstrates the love that flows not just from a good man but from the incarnate God. This is a staggering claim to make. The Gospel of Christ is unique in that it enables those who believe to affirm the deepest experiences of *all* who genuinely seek to understand something of the mystery of their humanity and the reality of God, without abandoning the particularity of God's act of self-utterance in the person of Jesus. I know of no other religion in which God's personal and sacrificial involvement in human affairs is so explicitly affirmed as it is in Catholic Christianity.

Paradox is typical of many aspects of Catholic doctrine. In human terms Catholic doctrine seeks coherent expression of the complementary aspects of God's redemptive activity, as set out in the Gospel of Christ and accumulated over centuries of experience in the lives of the faithful. Paradox comes to the aid of language that would be even more inadequate without it. The affirmation that the Gospel of Jesus is pluralist, inclusive, universal, and unique, may be challenged at a time when the ecumenical spirit is invoked in order to relegate to history the age-old disagreements about religion. The problem is that the ecumenical movement has lost impetus. Vague, uncritical, attempts to avoid controversy weaken rather than strengthen inter-faith encounters. This has been brought home to me on several occasions in conversations with Muslims who, whilst welcoming the interest shown by some Christians in an answer to the question 'What is Islam?', register their surprise that Christians are so rarely prepared to answer the reciprocal question, 'What is Christianity?' Inter-faith dialogue, which ecumenism is intended to further, is enfeebled when the particularity of *difference* is withheld by one or other of the participants. Muslims, Hindus, secular Humanists, for example, seldom make the mistake of withholding the particularity, the uniqueness, of their own beliefs when engaging in dialogue. The Gospel of Jesus, the Christ, reveals the true nature of its openness-not merely to organic change and radical development within the community of Christian believers, but to those who are outside the fellowship of the Christian family of believers. The *theologia crucis* reveals this truth uniquely.

The Summons to Mission, Dialogue, and Ecumenism

For Catholics, the call to ecumenism – to the unity of spirit and purpose that illuminates the words of Jesus in his high-priestly prayer – is as compelling as the dominical command to engage in universal missionary activity in the name of the Blessed Trinity: 'I do not pray for (my disciples) only, but also for those who believe in me through their word, that they may be one; even as you, Father are in me, and I in you, that they may also be in us, so that the world may believe that you have sent me' (Jn 17:20). Ecumenical activity is at the same time both a summons to unity and a call to testify to the uniqueness of Christ. Ecumenical endeavour involves seeking to understand that although God speaks at different times and in different places to the needs of the people he has created, he speaks the unique word of self-utterance in the person of Jesus, the Christ. This will remain the distinctive contribution for the followers of Christ to make to dialogue and ecumenism. The question is not whether they should do so, but how? The answer is to be found in the New Testament, in the words of the writer of the first letter of Peter: 'But in your hearts reverence Christ as Lord. Always be prepared to make a defence to anyone who calls you to account for the hope that is in you, yet do it with gentleness and reverence.' The New Testament writer's call is for *apologia*, that is, 'a reasoned defence', thus implying the need to be prepared, not just vaguely willing, to undertake the task. Both the task and the method are clearly stated. At a time when the opponents of Catholic beliefs appear to lack either the will or the knowledge (or both) to attack it with the vigour of their forebears, it would be a pity if Catholics were equally unprepared to defend it confidently, reverently, and fairly.

There is abundant evidence in the antipathy towards institutional religion of many people today of the negative influence of a methodological doubt, which is not itself subjected to scrutiny. Of the potentially constructive inter-play in education between faith and unbelief, between certitude and uncertainty, between religious diversity and cultural difference, I detect few signs. So how sensible and sensitive – rather than legitimate and reasonable – is it for Catholics to echo the words of the ancient formula: *extra ecclesiam non est salus*, 'outside the Church there is no salvation'? Was the ministry of Jesus unique? Is it so still? Is there a more important task for us in this or any other time than that of leading others to Christ? Or is the age of missionary activity, as it has been understood and practised for centuries, now over? Some would answer, *Yes*, having become less sure than their forebears about what, if anything, missionary activity involves. Does it matter, in the end, to which 'religious' or 'non-religious' tradition we belong? How, in any case, are we to deal with the different and sometimes conflicting truth-claims presented by the available 'religious options', from whatever source they may come? Is it not time to admit that no religion is the sole repository of truth, that 'truth' is relative, that tolerance is a primary civic virtue, even though tolerance proves to be little more than a convenient euphemism for indifference in many cases? These questions will not go away. Catholics – especially Catholic teachers – have to be ready to deal with such queries and with the criticisms of Catholic teaching which are implied in the questioning.

Convergence and Divergence

What kind of mission can Catholics be expected to pursue in a pluralist world? For them, God expresses himself in Christ through a temporary dissolution of his own essential unity, but in responding to this revelation we are not free to cloud the issue by conceding that our own beliefs reflect a fleeting and illusory appearance of things as we would like them to be. If they are at all serious about their faith, Catholics will want to make a special effort in the new millennium to understand the challenge that secularism presents to the uniqueness of their faith. In a multi-faith society there are other interpretations of religious pluralism to be taken into account. Two examples illustrate what is involved. Both have important implications for the future stability of society. Both call for Christian responses, which move beyond a discussion of theoretical abstractions to practical social action. The first of these extracts was written by a Muslim who spent many years living in England. The author sees an unavoidable conflict between what he identifies – not altogether fairly as the materialist values of the West – and the theocratic values of Islam:

> Muslims constitute one fifth of the human race, around 900-1,000 million in all parts of the world. … If they want to reconstruct their socio-economic order according to the values of Islam, [they are] bound to come into conflict with the international *status quo*. So conflict is there. And to that extent, I would like my western

> colleagues to understand that Muslim criticism of western civilisation is not primarily an exercise in political confrontation. The real competition would be at the level of two cultures and civilisations, one based upon Islamic values and the other on the values of materialism and nationalism. Had western culture been based on Christianity, on morality, on faith, the language and *modus operandi* of the contact and conflict would have been different. But that is not the case. The choice is between the Divine Principle and a secular materialist culture. And there is no reason to believe that this competition should be seen by all well-meaning human beings merely in terms of the geo-politic boundaries of the West and the East. In fact all those human beings who are concerned over the spiritual and moral crisis of our times should heave a sigh of relief over Islamic resurgence, and not be put off or scared by it.[6]

A contemporary Hindu view, which suggests that there are limits even to the legendary tolerance extended to all by Hinduism, appears in the next extract:

> Hinduism does not dictate. It is the only non-proselytising religion in the world. It not only does not seek to convert, it advises members of other faiths to hold fast to their own creeds, because as the *Gita*[7] says: 'In true belief there is salvation.' No-one can *become* a Hindu, even if he or she wanted to … [8]
>
> Conversely, a Hindu can lose his caste, and all manner of evil things can befall him, but cease to be a Hindu he cannot, because any belief he embraces will be encompassed in one or other of the tenets his own religion offers him. Christ will be a re-incarnation of Krishna, Buddha will re-appear as Vishnu, and Muhammad the Prophet will be an avatar, an incarnation several generations down.[9] Nothing will be rejected. The tentacles of Hinduism are so elastic and infinite that there is no belief you can profess that will make you an infidel …
>
> Hinduism is represented and misrepresented with casual abandon. But no-one dares to claim what the authentic article is, because absolutely no-one knows! Every argument for can be counteracted with a reasoned rebuttal. Yet the whole body of beliefs,

> superstitions, rituals, and commitment remains in some amazing manner a composite unified entity. And it is this dialectic, between internal diversity and external unity, that perplexes the western observer.[10]

The claim that a society is multi-cultural reflects an aspiration rather than an actual social achievement It has a prescriptive, not a descriptive, function. As the extract from the Muslim writer quoted above illustrates, there are profound differences in the ways in which Islamic and 'Western' societies are regulated. His emphasis is on what ought to be, not on what is now the case. His assessment of Western societies, in which many Muslims now live, focuses on an ideology which, whilst ostensibly granting different religious truth-claims a parity of esteem, induces indifference if not open hostility to them all. Chesterton wrote about the partiality and falsity of this picture of 'equal creeds inside an indifferent cosmos'.[11] Education is, perhaps, the most notorious example of an enterprise in which pluralist practice fails to reflect pluralist principle. What makes the result more curious is the claim that practice *does* reflect principle, that education is not education unless it is open-ended, free of value-judgements, objective, fair, and balanced in the presentation of data about *this* religion or *that* culture. The assumptions of what passes for pluralism in a secular society need to be re-examined. In theory, though not in practice, the pluralism of a secular society makes provision for an exploration of the nature of the human predicament from different perspectives. But it is not clear that this exploration extends to include differences of emphasis about the philosophy, the theory, as well as the praxis, of education itself.

For Catholics, the quest is for truth. To seek for what is deemed to be relevant is to borrow from the changing moods of the world in a way which guarantees a diminishing role for faith in a divine revelation, historically revealed. By insisting on continuity, Catholics bear witness to the coherence, the universality, the naturalness, and above all the divine origins of their faith. Allowing a little for the Gallic enthusiasm of its author, faithful Catholics may at least agree with the spirit in which Bossuet, the eighteenth-century French critic, wrote of the 'immortal beauty of the Catholic Church, wherein everything is amassed that is lovely and glorious, in all places and at all times, present, past and future'.[12] In revealed religions the recurring controversy about the authority to be vested in tradition illustrates how quickly modernists develop their own traditions, to which (not surprisingly) they soon become deeply attached. It is then only a matter of time before these traditions are, in turn, used to lend authority to the beliefs and opinions based upon them.

The danger to the integrity of the Gospel, to its coherence and comprehensiveness, comes when even well-intentioned reformers start to emphasise one element of its truth whilst neglecting others. At the end of his life Camilo Torres is reported to have said: 'The most important thing in Catholicism is love of one's neighbour.'[13] Love of one's neighbour is certainly an important part of the Christian way of life, but it yields primacy to the love of God from which it derives. As St John puts it: 'We love because he first loved us' (1 Jn 4:19). In campaigns for justice and peace it is love of God which makes it possible for us to love our neighbours. The guide-lines in the New Testament for human behaviour are Christocentric, not anthropocentric. Christ, as faith affirms, is present in all places and at all times. If I am asked for an answer to questions about the great doctrinal paradoxes of the Catholic Faith, such as the Incarnation and the Trinity, I can only respond by pointing to the mystery of Christ in union with his Church. There I see *Emmanuel* – 'God with us'. To catch even a glimpse of this abiding truth is to realise that one is on the surest possible ground of faith. How otherwise can we begin to understand that we must lose our lives in order to gain them; that in order to achieve greatness we must become the least among others; that in order to be first we have to become last; that in order to be served we must first serve others? How, in short, are we to practice 'Christian Presence' without being first conscious of the presence of Christ?

Notes

1. Abbreviated to GDC, published by The Holy See, Catholic Truth Society, 1997, pp. 119-20.
2. See, in particular, the Decree on Ecumenism (*Unitatis redintegratio*), *The Conciliar and Post Conciliar Documents of Vatican II,* general editor Austin Flannery OP, Dublin, Dominican Publications, 1975, pp. 452ff. ; Declaration on the Relation of the Church to Non-Christian Religions (*Nostra Aetate*), *ibid.* pp. 738ff.
3. Or, as some English versions of the *Qur'an* 2:256 put it: 'Let there be no compulsion in religion'.
4. My short article 'Is Teaching about *Other* World Religions Essential, Optional, or Inadmissible in *Catholic* Education?', published in *The Sower*, vol. 17, No. 2, January, 1996, pp. 19-20, summarises my position on this issue.
5. M.A.C. Warren, *General Introduction* to the *Christian Presence* series of books published by London, SCM Press, 1961ff.
6. Khurshid Ahmad, 'The Nature of Islamic Resurgence', in *Voices of Resurgent Islam*, edited by John L. Esposito (New York, OUP, 1983), page 228.
7. The *Bhagavâd Gîtâ*, 'the Song of the Lord', is a Sanskrit poem, which consists of 700 verses divided into 18 chapters. Many non-Hindus, as well as Hindus generally, hold it in great esteem as a religious text which epitomises the beliefs of a Hindu.
8. Which is to say that one can only be born (or re-born) a Hindu.
9. In Hinduism *Krishna* is the eighth *avatâr*, 'descent' or 'incarnation', of the god *Vishnu*; the Buddha (meaning 'the Enlightened One'), the founder of Buddhism, lived in north-east India c. 563-483 BC; Muhammad, the Prophet of Islam, lived c. 570-632 AD.
10. Sasthi Brata, *India: Labyrinths in the Lotus Land* (New York, William Morrow and Company, 1985), pp. 198-201.
11. G.K. Chesterton, *The Catholic Church and Conversion* (Universe Books, London, Burns and Oates, 1960), p. 66.
12. J.B. Bossuet, *Sermon sur l'unité de l'Église, premier point. Oeuvres oratoires*, vol. 6, p. 118.
13. In Renate Wind's *Bis zur letzten Konsequenz – Die Lebensgeschichte des Camilo Torres* (Weinheim, Beltz & Gelberg, 1994).

Further Reading

Adam, Karl, *The Spirit of Catholicism*, Macmillan, 1935.

Butler, Bishop Christopher, *An Approach to Christianity*, Collins Fount Paperbacks, 1981.

Chesterton, G. K., *Orthodoxy*, Collins Fontana, 1963ff. First published in 1908.

Clark, Francis, *Godfaring, On Reason, Faith and Sacred Being*, London and Maynooth, St Paul's Publishing, 2000.

Hulmes, Edward, 'Unity and Diversity: The Search for Common Identity', in *Priorities in Religious Education: A Model for the 1990s and Beyond*, pp. 124-39 (ed. Brenda Watson), London, Falmer Press, 1992.

Lubac, Henri de, SJ, *Catholicism: Christ and the Common Destiny of Man*, London, Burns & Oates, 1950.

Neill, Bishop Stephen, *Crises of Belief: The Christian Dialogue with Faith and No Faith*, Houghton & Stoughton, 1984.

Rahner, Karl, 'Christianity and the Non-Christian Religions' in *Theological Investigations*, Volume 5, pp. 115-34. See also his *Theological Investigations*, Volume 6, chapters 16 and 22; Volume 9, chapter 9; volume12, chapter 9, Volume 16, chapter 17. Darton, Longman and Todd, 1966-80.

Warren, M.A.C., *I Believe in the Great Commission*, Hodder and Stoughton.

PARENTS: PRIMARY EDUCATORS OF THEIR CHILDREN

PETROC WILLEY

Introduction

No one disputes that the Church assigns to parents the fundamental place in education. But what exactly does she intend by this teaching? What does it mean to call parents the 'primary' educators of their children? And what implications does this have for the Church's catechetical mission?

The key sources of contemporary Church teaching on this matter are Pius XI's *Divini illius magistri* (1929), Vatican II's *Gravissiumum educationis* and John Paul II's Apostolic Exhortation, *Familiaris Consortio.* In addition, there is a substantial body of papal teachings on education,[1] and documents from the Congregation for Catholic Education,[2] the Pontifical Council for the Family,[3] and the Congregation for the Clergy.[4]

The *Catechism of the Catholic Church* (1992) is, of course a vital synthesis of contemporary teaching, so it would be good to begin there. With regard to the place of parents in education the Catechism declares:

> The fruitfulness of conjugal love extends to the fruits of the moral, spiritual and supernatural life that parents hand on to their children by education. Parents are the principal and first educators of their children (cf. GE 3). In this sense the fundamental task of marriage and family is to be at the service of life. (§1653)

Parents, then, are described as 'principal' and 'first' educators of their children.[5] And again:

> The fecundity of conjugal love cannot be reduced solely to the procreation of children, but must extend to their moral education and their spiritual formation. 'The role of parents in education is of such importance that it is almost impossible to provide an adequate substitute.' (GE 3) The right and the duty of parents to educate their children are primordial and inalienable. (cf. FC 36). (§2221)

Here the language is also very strong. Parents are so important in the process of the education of their children that 'it is almost impossible to provide an adequate substitute'. The rights and duties are described as 'primordial' and 'inalienable'.

The conviction that *the home is the basic place of learning* lies at the heart of Catholic teaching.[6] 'Learning' here must be taken according to it's fullest meaning, as the formation of the whole person – physical, moral, intellectual, emotional and spiritual. The home is the basic place of formation. It is in the family, and in networks of families, parish groups, informal friendships and associations that bonds and social understandings are formed, rights and duties are learned and appreciated, and so on. It is in the context of these groupings, of which the family is the central one, that a child's formation takes place.

Meanings of 'Primary'

Aristotle, in his *Categories*, distinguishes between four different meanings of the word 'prior' or 'primary'.[7] It is helpful to consider Church teaching regarding parental education of their children under Aristotle's headings. We shall find that the parental position in education is primary in *each* of the four ways proposed.

Prior in time

Something can be said to be 'prior' to something else, writes Aristotle, in terms of time. 'A is prior to B' in this sense means 'A is older than B' or 'A comes before B'. In Church documents 'primary' is often a translation of the Latin 'primus', and one of the meanings of 'primus' is 'the first in time'. In this sense, then, it is clear that parents are indeed the primary educators. They are the first *in time* to educate their children. From the moment of conception the parents – and especially the mother – are providing the environment in which the new child will grow up. Children begin their life in a family and they therefore begin their education in a family. The source of our social and moral understanding and bonding and of our emotional, intellectual and spiritual lives, lies in our immediate natural relationships, and the care of parents for their children is central to this.[8]

The reading of 'primary' as a temporal concept is also supported by the linking together of education with procreation. The Church argues that since the parents are the two people who took the step of bringing their children into existence, it falls to them to be primarily responsible for seeing that they are educated. The parents are the origin of their child's existence in time. So, for example, the Catechism teaches: 'The fecundity of conjugal love cannot be reduced solely to the procreation of children, but must extend to their moral education and their spiritual formation.' (§2221) Education is here presented as an 'extension' of procreation. Again we read, 'Marriage and the family are ordered to the good of the spouses and to the procreation and education of children.' (§2201) Education is a duty for the parents *precisely because* they are the procreators of their children.[9]

'Primary educators' has as one of its meanings, then, 'prior in time'. But is this all it means? Because the main tasks regarding the education of children are, in European societies, typically taken over by the State from the age of four or five onwards, it is easy to think that parents cease to be the primary educators and that this designation is properly passed onto the school or some other body.

However, although the parental responsibility for education has a beginning point in time (procreation), once present it *remains* as a primary responsibility in ways that are more than simply temporal. Church teaching, as we shall see, explicitly excludes the view that the primary responsibility for education passes out of parental hands. *Parents remain the primary educators.* 'Parent' is a word describing a permanent relationship to another, which is unaffected by time; although the relationship begins in time it can end, at least in its earthly form, only in death.[10] Parents are always parents of their children. Parents remain primary educators, although the *way* in which this primary responsibility is lived out alters: a child has need of parents as educators in one way at five and another at fifteen.[11]

Where this Catholic view differs from the contemporary secular view, then, is in the conviction that the place of the parent as primary educator continues beyond the beginning of school and even beyond adolescence. In fact, all the major world religions assign to parents a place of particular importance in the on-going transmission of culture and faith to their children. Traditional societies similarly assign to the elderly, and especially to parents and grandparents, a position of authority which enables them to pass on culture.[12]

Parents, then, are the 'primary' educators in terms of time, in the sense that they temporally precede other educational agents. But this does not exhaust the meaning of 'primary.'

Prior in Being

The second way in which Aristotle says something can be 'prior' to another is in terms of their existence. He says, 'when the sequence of two things cannot be reversed, then that one on which the other depends is called 'prior' to that other'. He uses an example from numbers: the existence of number two presumes the existence of number one, whereas the reverse is not necessarily true.

This understanding of 'primary' is clearly present in Church teaching. It is expressed particularly in the link between education and procreation which we noted earlier. The parental responsibility concerning education is a result of a change in the order of *being*. Something new has come into existence and the parental role in this is what gives rise to parents' duties to educate. 'The right and duty of parents to give education is *essential*, since it is concerned with the transmission of human life.'[13] As St Thomas put it, 'nature intends not only the generation of offspring but also its development and progress to the state of man as man, that is, to the state of virtue'.[14] This relationship on the level of being is prior to any other relationship. It is unique: no one else has this relationship. Moreover, all other educational relationships depend upon this one in the order of being.

This point is clearly affirmed in the Scriptures. De Vaux notes that the 'educational role of the father explains why the priests, whose mission was to teach, are called 'father'[15] (see, for instance, Jg. 17:10, 18:19) and why the relationship between teacher and pupil is so often described in terms of family relationships, as we can see from the frequent use of the phrase 'my son' in the Book of Proverbs.[16]

The awareness of parental priority in the order of being can be lost because of a widespread tendency to speak of the different aspects of parenthood in terms of 'roles' that people can play. Parents are encouraged to think of their fatherhood and motherhood as 'roles' rather than as natural relationships.

What is involved here, then, and how does it affect the notion of parents as primary educators in the order of being? I 'play' or 'take on' various 'roles', and can put them off again; indeed, even when I am performing a role I live at a distance from it, in the sense that a 'role' is not identical with myself. The use of the modern sociological concept of 'role' to describe different dimensions of motherhood and fatherhood is significant since it reveals that parenthood is often conceived first and foremost as a set of social functions rather than as something which belongs to men and women naturally.[17] Nature, then, is subsumed into society and natural processes are re-presented as social processes.[18] If this view is adopted, then even as fathers and mothers act as educators they are alienated from what they are doing.[19]

The Church, on the other hand, speaks of parenthood as a 'vocation' rather than a 'role':

> The task of giving education is rooted in the primary vocation of married couples to participate in God's creative activity: by begetting in love and for love a new person who has within himself or herself the vocation to growth and development, parents by that very fact take on the task of helping that person effectively to live a fully human life.[20]

A 'vocation' is the call to follow a distinctive path in life, and the Church's teaching on vocations is rooted in an appreciation of the human person as being endowed with capacities for these particular ways of life. To situate the education of children within the 'vocation' of married couples is, then, to affirm that this calling belongs to parents by nature. Education, as an essential aspect of parenthood, is a vocation to be followed, not a 'role' which is occasionally adopted. Education belongs to the *being* of the parent.[21]

Prior in Order

The third way in which something can be held to be primary, Aristotle says, is in terms of some order. He gives the example of letters preceding syllables in grammar and of an introduction preceding the exposition in a speech. This sense of there being a right ordering of relationships between the different agents of education is very much present in the teaching of the Church and here again it is the parents who hold the primary place in the natural order.

Put simply, the Church teaches that there are three agents in the educational sphere: parents, the Church and the State. The key text here is *Divini illius magistri*, §11-66. The family is described here as that which 'takes precedence' (§11) in the order of nature as regards the education of children, although the Church has a supernatural pre-eminence (§16) and her education perfects that which is offered in the natural sphere. The family has this priority in education because it has been granted a share in God's authority, 'which is the principle of order' (§35).[22] Moreover, this educational priority in the natural order extends to all subjects, it 'is not restricted to the religious and moral sphere, but extends also to physical and civic training, especially so far as these are related to religion and morals' (§41).

Those employed by the State to educate, then, act always and strictly *in loco parentis*. The State's duty with regard to education is to assist parents in their primary position:

> The State and the Church have the obligation to give parents all possible aid to enable them to perform their educational role properly. Therefore both the Church and the State must create and foster the institutions and activities that families justly demand, and the aid must be in proportion to the families' needs. However those in society who are in charge of schools must never forget that the parents have been appointed by God himself as the first and principal educators of their children and that their right is completely inalienable.[23]

Pius XI was writing *Divini illius magistri* in 1929, in a Europe increasingly besieged by totalitarian Fascism, a Europe in which atheistic ideologies were threatening to coerce young people into amoral and militaristic youth movements. The State was assuming for itself a priority in its educational role that was illegitimate. In that situation, Pius was concerned both to defend the rights of parents and the Church in education and to articulate clearly the educational philosophy underpinning a distinctive Catholic education.

The right ordering among the agents of education is threatened today, also, by ideologies which implicitly raise questions about the right of parents to transmit a Christian culture to their children. So, for example, the UN *Convention on the Rights of the Child*, passed by the UN in 1989 and ratified by most European countries,[24] with the exception of the Netherlands and Switzerland, could be argued to be essentially a tool for change, seeking for children to be awarded a number of civil and political rights which have been taken directly from lists of general human rights. These are essentially rights to freedom, to autonomy, very similar to the type of rights being called for in the seventies by thinkers such as Shulamith Firestone, Richard Farson and John Holt.[25] The implications for family life if these freedoms are taken seriously appear to be clear: parental rights in religious and moral matters and in the transmission of faith and culture in the family are threatened. But if parental rights to educate their children as they see fit are brought into question, this does not mean that the children will remain uneducated or that there will be no transmission of values. Nature abhors a vacuum, and culture abhors value-free zones; other educational agents must step in to take the place of parents (almost certainly the state),[26] thus overthrowing the educational order established by the Creator.

Prior in Importance

Aristotle's fourth way of understanding 'prior' is in terms of what is better or more important: 'ordinary people commonly say of those they specially value and love that they "have priority"'.

Let us examine this point. Can parents be said to be the primary educators in this sense also, that they are the most important educators? One of the meanings of 'primus' is, in fact, the 'principal' or 'most important' thing. And when Church documents speak of parents as the *principal* ('praecipuus') educators they normally mean the 'most important', or 'most excellent'. Why is this?

It is well-established that parents are the single most important influence in the religious formation of children.[27] But the Church's teaching on the primary importance of parents in education rests not so much on this point as on her conviction that education involves, above all, a personal relationship between the teacher and the one taught. Pius XI said that 'good schools are not so much the result of good methods as of good teachers'[28] and Pius XII defined a good teacher as one who 'knows how to create a close relationship between his own soul and the soul of a child'.[29] What is said here of teachers applies in particular, of course, to parents as the first teachers of their children. The education of children by their parents is very much a matter of 'heart speaking to heart'.[30]

Pope John Paul makes this conviction of the Church even more explicit when he writes:

> ... it cannot be forgotten that the most basic element, so basic that it qualifies the educational role of parents, is *parental love*, which finds fulfilment in the task of education as it completes and perfects its service of life: as well as being a *source*, the parents' love

> is also the *animating principle* and therefore the *norm* inspiring and guiding all concrete educational activity ...[31]

Here the Pope is placing the educational mission of parents within the framework of the overall human vocation to make a gift of oneself in love. The starting point for the Pope's many meditations on this subject is the sentence in the Second Vatican Council's Pastoral Constitution, *The Church in the Modern World (Gaudium et Spes)*: '... man can fully discover his true self only in a sincere giving of himself.' (§24). The way in which married couples live out this vocation of a gift of self is through making a reciprocal gift of themselves to each other and through being open to procreation and to the education of their children. Once again we can see how the Church is rooting the 'prior' nature of parental responsibilities in education in the vocation of marriage: 'Thus the couple, while giving themselves to one another, give not just themselves but also the reality of children, who are a living reflection of their love.'[32] The educational mission of the parents flows from the nature of the self-gift to which they vow themselves when they marry.

Conclusion

We have now explored what the Church might be meaning by describing parents as the 'primary educators' of their children in terms of the four meanings of 'primary' discerned by Aristotle. Whatever the merits of the *details* of this argument it does seem clear from the broad picture that the Church intends parents to regard themselves as most especially responsible for the formation of their children, both in terms of the Faith and more generally. If this is true, then helping parents to pass on the Faith in the home should certainly be at the centre of the Church's catechetical efforts. It is here that she needs to devote resources and energies.

Accompanying this commitment to supporting parents as the primary educators there needs to be sustained research in a number of related areas, in order to explore the best way forward. The first area, which deserves serious study, is to look at different models of parental involvement in school and parish education. There are an increasing number of initiatives taking place at the moment which focus on the family as a learning community rather than focussing on the child in isolation from his or her home environment, including the development of schools as community learning centres, the state funding of family literacy projects and the standard use of home-school agreements. There are also inspiring parent-led initiatives to evangelise in schools and begin prayer groups in school.[33] At the same time, research needs to look seriously at the kinds of diocesan structures and services which would support a family-centred approach to catechesis, with an encouragement of 'family-friendly' educational provision. There are issues here of bringing about an expectation of life-long learning in the Faith, together with a renewed commitment to providing this learning in modes that are flexible and accommodate parents who have young, active families and full family commitments.

Notes

1. All the pertinent texts from Pius VII to Pius XII have been usefully collected in a single volume: *Papal Teachings: education*, selected and arranged by the Benedictine monks of Solesmes (St Paul's, 1960).
2. For example, *The Catholic School* (1977), *Lay Catholics in Schools: Witnesses to Faith* (1982) and *The Religious Dimension of Education* (1988).
3. For example, *The Truth and Meaning of Human Sexuality* (1995).
4. The most important is the *General Directory for Catechesis* (1997).
5. 'primi et praeciputi eorum educatores' (GE 3).
6. More generally, one of the great contributions of Christianity is that it has always stressed the importance of the family, and the realm of the 'private'. Historians have noted the positive effect this has had on the place of women in society, since the home is almost universally the realm in which women are to a large extent confined. Christianity ushered in a revolution in this regard, which immensely improved the status of women. The role of women as educators is intrinsic to this improved status. See E. Elshtain: *Public Man, Private Woman*, Martin Robinson 1981, and cf. H. Arendt: *The Human Condition*, University of Chicago Press 1974.
7. The relevant section is no. 12. Aristotle adds a fifth possible meaning, almost by way of an afterthought, but it is less relevant to this present question. Two English translations of Aristotle's work are W.D. Ross (chief editor), *The Works of Aristotle*, Vol. 1, Clarendon Press 1928, and J. Barnes (ed), *The Complete Works of Aristotle*, Vol. 1, Bollingen Series LXX1. 2, Princeton University Press 1984. Janet Smith uses this section of the Categories very helpfully in *Humanae Vitae: A Generation Later* (Catholic University of America Press 1991), p. 49, to analyse the use of 'primary' in discussions of the ends of marriage (see also G. Grisez, 'Marriage: Reflections Based on St Thomas and Vatican Council II', *Catholic Mind* 64, June 1966, pp. 4-19).
8. cf. *Catechism* §2224
9. And, more widely than this, because they are members of a world into which their children are being initiated. Thus: 'Insofar as the child is not yet acquainted with the world, he must be gradually introduced to it; insofar as he is new, care must be taken that this new thing comes to fruition in relation to

the world as it is. In any case, however, the educators here stand in relation to the young as representatives of a world for which they must assume responsibility although they themselves did not make it, and even though they may, secretly or otherwise, wish it were other than it is. This responsibility is not arbitrarily imposed upon educators; it is implicit in the fact that the young are introduced by adults into a continuously changing world.' (H. Arendt: 'The Crisis in Education', in *Between Past and Future: Eight Exercises in Political Thought*, Viking Press 1958 p. 189.

10. Revelation does not help us in the question of whether family relationships will remain after death. We are told that there will be no giving and taking in marriage in heaven (Mk 12:25), but we are not told how family relationships will be transfigured.
11. Similarly, 'Honour your Father and your Mother' (Ex 20:12/Deut 5:16) is a commandment which remains in force throughout the lives of children and their parents. It does not cease to be relevant when children reach a certain age or leave the parental home. Of course, the implications of the commandment do alter as the children grow older so that in the end 'honouring' includes supporting and caring for elderly or sick parents (see *Catechism* §2217-8). See also P. A. H. de Boer, *Fatherhood and Motherhood in Israelite and Judaen Piety*, 1974; B. Schlesinger, *The Jewish Family: A Survey and Annotated Bibliography*, University of Toronto Press 1970; R. de Vaux, O. P., *Ancient Israel: Its Life and Institutions*, Darton, Longman and Todd, 1961.
12. There is a complex reciprocal relationship here: on the one hand the elderly are to be respected because of their place in this transmission of culture, and on the other hand the culture being handed down is received because of the innate respect given to parents and grandparents. This respect for the on-going place of parents, grandparents and traditional wisdom is what has been largely lost in sections of contemporary Western society, a point made eloquently by the Jewish Abraham Maslow at the end of his life: 'My class has lost the traditional Jewish respect for knowledge, learning and teachers. This rebellion is *not* just a generation gap. It is the first time in history that students have repudiated their teachers, which means loss of all tacit knowledge, apprentice training, demonstration by the master, showing how; ... you can't learn medicine, or plumbing or chemistry by T-grouping, or by 'discussion', or by yourself.' *The Journals of A.H. Maslow*, January 6 1969, his emphasis. For a recent statement on the place of the elderly in the family see *Familiaris consortio* §51.
13. *Familiaris consortio* §36 (italics in the original).
14. *Summa Theologiae*, Suppl. 3a, Qu. 41, art. 1.
15. R. de Vaux, *op cit*, p. 49.
16. As well as the frequent use of 'son' to describe the relationship of a pupil to his teacher, the opening chapter of *Proverbs* also explicitly emphasises the primary teaching role of the parents: 1:8.
17. On this point see the illuminating discussion by Ivan Illich, *Gender*, Marion Bouyer 1983. On the importance of a return to a more adequate metaphysics of the person see B. B. Dragle, *Being Forgotten: an Invitation to Return*, Hamilton 1996.

18. This is a position usually associated with Marxist thought. So, for example, '... the family not only depends on the historically concrete social reality, but is socially mediated down to its innermost structure'. The Frankfurt School, 'The Family', in *Aspects of Sociology*, London 1973, p. 130. See also Michele Barrett and Mary McIntosh, *The Anti-Social Family*, Verso 1984.
19. In this approach where all family relationships are regarded as roles a concomitant point is that they are viewed as self-chosen commitments which are essentially dispensable since they are not part of the real 'me'. 'I' am a self transcending all such relationships. Further, for the sake of autonomy, for the sake of being 'true to myself' all commitments are then viewed precisely as 'roles' which may be renegotiated and discarded as necessary – a stance typical of certain schools of psychotherapy (such as the Rogerian school) which set up the inner self as the ultimate authority. The work of William Coulson is important in this area. Coulson worked with Rogers as his chief of staff at the Western Behavioural Sciences Institute in California in the sixties and seventies and co-edited with Rogers the *Studies of the Person Series* (Chaples E. Merrill Publishing Co. 1968-73). He later came to repudiate the Rogerian approach as destructive to religious, moral and personal commitments. See, for example, *Groups, Gimmicks and Instant gurus: An Examination of Encounter Groups and their Distortions*, Harper and Row 1972, and 'From client-Centered Therapy to the Person Approach and Back Again: A Critical Analysis of Trends in Humanistic Psychology', *Address to Carl Rogers Invitational International Conference*, University of San Diego 1980. See also the work of Paul Vitz, especially his *Psychology as Religion*, Eerdmans 1998.
20. *Familiaris consortio* §36.
21. It would be interesting to examine the relationship between this sense of 'primary' with the theme of 'the beginning' pursued in the writings of Pope John Paul II. In *Mulieris Dignitatem (Apostolic Letter of the Supreme Pontiff John Paul II on the Dignity and Vocation of Women on the Occasion of the Marian Year)* (CTS 1988), for example, he makes clear that the vocation of man and woman is related to that which was given to them 'in the beginning' (cf. Matt. 19:4, 8 and par). 'The beginning' refers to the original creation of the person, as male and female, as recorded in the opening chapters of Genesis, chapters which are said to contain 'the fundamental anthropological truths' (MD 6). It refers people back, not simply to something in the past which is now gone, but to a point of reference for present behaviour. The idea of 'the beginning' and that of 'primary', then, both have to do more with a returning to fundamentals about human life than with chronology. They have to do with ontological truths about the person, created and redeemed in Christ.
22. The Pope refers here to St Thomas II-II, Qu. 102, art. 1.
23. *Familiaris consortio* §40.
24. Although by a significant number, with reservations (the Holy See, Ireland, the United Kingdom, Sweden, Norway, Germany, France and Austria). For example, the Holy See notes that it interprets the Articles of the Convention in a way which safeguards the primary and inalienable rights of the parents, in particular insofar as these rights concern education (art. 13 and 28), religion (art. 14), association with others (art. 15) and privacy (art. 16).

25. See S. Firestone, *The Dialectic of Sex: The Case for Feminist Revolution*, The Women's Press 1979; R. Farson, *Birthrights*, 1974; J. Holt, *Escape from Childhood*, 1974. And for more recent approaches see B. Franklin, *The Rights of Children*, Blackwell 1986.
26. See M. O'Brien, *The Family and the New Totalitarianism*, The White Horse Press 1995, for a discussion with a special focus on Canada.
27. This point was noted, for example, in M. Hornsby-Smith: *Catholic Education: The Unobtrusive Partner*, Sheed and Ward 1978. For more recent research see K. Hyde, *Religion in Childhood and Adolescence: A Comprehensive Review of the Research* (Religious Education Press, 1990).
28. *Divini illius magistri*, §109.
29. Speech to the Italian Catholic Elementary School Teachers' Association, November 4, 1955, in *Papal Teachings on Education*, selected and arranged by the Benedictine Monks of Solesmes (St Paul's ,1960), p. 514.
30. Newman's idea of *Cor ad Cor*. Compare, on this, Pius XII's speech on training in the home in which he identifies the educative role of parents as being a threefold one: training the *mind*, training the *character* and training the *heart*. (Speech to mothers of Italian families, October 26 1941, in *Papal Teachings on Education*, selected and arranged by the Benedictine Monks of Solesmes, St Paul's 1960, pp. 315ff.)
31. *Familiaris consortio* §36.
32. *Familiaris consortio* §14.
33. See, for example, Anne Clayton and Maggie Connor, 'The Power of Parents in Prayer', *The Sower*, Vol. 22 no. 2, pp. 30-31.

Bibliography

Documents of the Magisterium

Congregation for the Clergy, *General Directory for Catechesis* (1997).

Congregation for Catholic Education, *The Catholic School* (1977), *Lay Catholics in Schools: Witnesses to Faith* (1982) *The Religious Dimension of Education* (1988).

Papal Teachings: education, selected and arranged by the Benedictine monks of Solesmes (St Paul's 1960).

Pontifical Council for the Family, *The Truth and Meaning of Human Sexuality* (1995).

Pope John Paul II, *Familiaris Consortio* (1981).

Pope John Paul II, *Mulieris Dignitatem (Apostolic Letter of the Supreme Pontiff John Paul II on the Dignity and Vocation of Women on the Occasion of the Marian Year)* (1988).

Pope Pius XI, *Divini illius magistri* (1931).

Vatican Council II, *Gravissimum Educationis* (1965).

Other Works

Arendt, H., 'The Crisis in Education', in *Between Past and Future: Eight Exercises in Political Thought* (Viking Press, 1958).

Arendt, H., *The Human Condition* (University of Chicago Press, 1974).

Aristotle, Works of (W.D. Ross, chief editor) (Clarendon Press, 1928).
Aristotle, The Complete Works of, (J. Barnes, editor) (Princeton University Press, 1984).
Barrett, M. and McIntosh, M, *The Anti-Social Family* (Verso, 1984).
Clayton, A. and Connor, M, 'The Power of Parents in Prayer', *The Sower,* Vol. 22 no. 2, pp. 30-31.
Coulson, W, *Groups, Gimmicks and Instant gurus: An Examination of Encounter Groups and their Distortions* (Harper and Row, 1972).
Coulson, W:, 'From client-Centered Therapy to the Person Centered Approach and Back Again: A Critical Analysis of Trends in Humanistic Psychology', *Address to Carl Rogers Invitational International Conference* (University of San Diego, 1980).
Dragle, B. B, *Being Forgotten: an Invitation to Return* (Hamilton, 1996).
Elshtain, E, *Public Man, Private Woman,* (Martin Robinson, 1981).
Firestone, S, *The Dialectic of Sex: The Case for Feminist Revolution* (The Women's Press, 1979).
Franklin, B, *The Rights of Children* (Blackwell, 1986).
Grisez, G, 'Marriage: Reflections Based on St Thomas and Vatican Council II', *Catholic Mind* 64, June 1966, pp. 4-19.
Hornsby-Smith, M: *Catholic Education: The Unobtrusive Partner* (Sheed and Ward, 1978).
Hyde, K, *Religion in Childhood and Adolescence: A Comprehensive Review of the Research* (Religious Education Press, 1990).
Illich, I, *Gender* (Marion Bouyer, 1983).
O'Brien, M, *The Family and the New Totalitarianism* (The White Horse Press, 1995)
Rogers, C. and Coulson, W, *Studies of the Person Series* (Chaples E. Merrill Publishing Co., 1968-73).
Schlesinger, B, *The Jewish Family: A Survey and Annotated Bibliography* (University of Toronto Press, 1970).
Smith, J, *Humanae Vitae: A Generation Later* (Catholic University of America Press, 1991).
Vaux, R. de, OP, *Ancient Israel: Its Life and Institutions* (Darton, Longman and Todd, 1961).
Vitz, P, *Psychology as Religion* (Eerdmans, 1998).

Further Reading

Hahn, K. and Hasson, M., *Catholic Education: Homeward Bound* (Ignatius Press 1995).
Mary Reed Newland, *The Year and Our Children* (Firefly Press 1995).
Pope John Paul II, *Familiaris Consortio* (1981), especially paragraphs 36-41.
O'Brien, M., *The Family and the New Totalitarianism* (The White Horse Press 1995).
Vatican Council II, *Gravissimum Educationis* (1965).

THE THEOLOGY OF CHRISTIAN INITIATION

FR EDWARD YARNOLD SJ

Initiation

One of the new liturgical insights achieved by the Second Vatican Council was the perception that baptism, confirmation and first communion, though three distinct sacraments, together form a single process of initiation by which a new Christian becomes a member of the Church. Several changes were made in the liturgy in order to emphasise the unity between these sacraments of initiation. Thus, if confirmation is celebrated on a separate occasion from baptism, the candidate is to renew the baptismal promises, and it is recommended that at least one of the godparents at baptism should also be a sponsor at confirmation. The old practice of giving the candidate a new name at confirmation has been generally discontinued for the same reason. When the person being baptised is old enough to receive instruction, confirmation must normally be administered immediately after baptism, even if a priest has to celebrate it instead of the bishop.

Each of the seven sacraments, not only the sacraments of initiation, establishes a relationship between the Christian and the Church. Indeed, the Church itself is 'a sacrament or instrumental sign of intimate union with God and of the unity of all humanity' (Vatican II, LG 1). For the traditional understanding of a sacrament as a rite, which is both a sign and a cause of grace applies by analogy to two deeper realities. Most fundamentally, Christ himself is the original sacrament, in his incarnate existence a visible point of the saving contact between God and human beings which is grace. Secondarily the Church is the visible means by which human beings relate to their Saviour, and therefore can be seen as the fundamental sacrament under Christ; the seven sacraments are the pre-eminent ways in which the Church performs its sacramental function. While each one of the seven, besides being the means by which believers grow in grace, situates them in a new or deeper relationship with the Church, the three sacraments of initiation establish the initial relationship which the other sacraments deepen and make more specific. Thus baptism (like confirmation and holy order) is said to imprint a character or 'spiritual mark' on the soul. The character establishes unrepeatably and irrevocably what the other four sacraments establish less permanently, namely a new relationship with the Church. Even the sinner, who by serious sin extinguishes the life of grace within him and cuts himself off from fellowship (or communion) with the Church, does not cease to be a member of it; when he repents he does not need rebaptism but the sacrament of reconciliation.

St Thomas Aquinas explained the character as a participation in the high priesthood of Christ (S. Th. 3. 63. 3), in accordance with the New Testament's understanding of the Church as a 'royal priesthood' (1 Pet 2:9). Baptism is therefore the sacrament by which a Christian enters into this priestly state. This priestly vocation is not only the right to participate in the Church's liturgy; the whole of life is material for the 'spiritual sacrifices', which Christians are called to offer (Rom 12:1-2).

> For by the regeneration and anointing of the Holy Spirit the baptised are consecrated as a spiritual dwelling and a holy priesthood, so that through all the activity of Christian living they may offer spiritual sacrifices, and declare the powers of him who called them out of darkness into his marvellous light (cf. 1 Pet 2:4-10) (*Lumen Gentium*, 10).

Thus baptism is the rite by which a person enters into the New Covenant. The sign of the cross, which is traced on the candidate's forehead several times as the 'seal' of membership of this covenant, is therefore the Christian equivalent of circumcision, which sealed entry into the Old.

Entry into the Church means entry into the Christian community, which is the Church here and now. Hence the concern in the modern rites to involve the congregation, and their representatives the sponsors and godparents, in the liturgical action.

Incorporation into Christ

Entry into the Church also means entry into the Body of Christ; we are 'baptised into Christ', we 'put on Christ' (Gal 3:27). We die and rise again with Christ (which makes the Easter Vigil the appropriate time for the sacrament). We die with him by laying aside our old sinful way of life; our rising is to a new way of life on earth, which anticipates our rising after death.

Our rising with Christ is a rebirth, in which we are born again by water and the Holy Spirit (cf. Jn 3:5). The Holy Spirit in consequence dwells within us, so that we become his temples, not passively, as if we were like a church building which is not itself changed by the presence of the God in it, but actively, so that we live with the life of Christ by the power of the Holy Spirit. Accordingly our rising with Christ is not simply our commitment to live according to the teaching of him who is 'the Way, the Truth and the Life' (Jn 14:6), but a gift of grace, which is a share in his divine life; like St Paul we can say, 'It is no longer I who live, but it is Christ who lives in me' (Gal 2:20). We become branches of the Vine, so that we 'abide' in him and he in us, so that our lives become fruitful (Jn 15:5). We are baptised into his body (1 Cor 12:13).

Hence the font is both a *tomb* in which we are buried and a *womb* in which we are reborn to new life. Accordingly the General Introduction to the Rites of Initiation commends baptism by immersion as 'more suitable as a symbol of participation in the death and resurrection of Christ' (n. 22); the action of submerging under the water and coming up from it is an expressive sign of burial and rising. Moreover the life-giving property of water makes it a vivid symbol of the new life in Christ. Fonts are sometimes designed to give a flow of water, so as to recall the 'living water' that Jesus promised (Jn 4:10).

The font is also an extension of the Jordan, in which Jesus was baptised, giving the model for Christian baptism. It was at his baptism that Jesus was proclaimed the anointed Messiah or Christ, when he was 'anointed' by the Holy Spirit (Acts 10:36-37) for his mission of redemption and of mercy for the weak.[1] His baptism in its turn is the source of the power of Christian baptism, as if by entering the water he gave power to all baptismal water. The words of the Blessing of the Water in the modern rite recall this connection, and the action of dipping the Easter candle into the font symbolises it. Through baptism we share in Christ's messianic vocation, becoming members of his priestly, royal people; this truth is symbolised by the post-baptismal anointing of the crown of the head with chrism – i.e. messianic oil, which is celebrated if the neophyte is not to be immediately confirmed.

The voice of the Father at the Jordan addressing his Son, and the descent of the Holy Spirit, indicate that we also enter into the life of the Trinity when we are baptised. To express this fact, all the main churches celebrate baptism 'in the name of the Father and of the Son and of the Holy Spirit'. The Holy Spirit, who is the 'Spirit of adoption', makes us sons and daughters of the Father, and therefore brothers and sisters of the Lord (Rom 8:14-16). This participation in the life of the Trinity begins even when babies are baptised, so that all their subsequent growth in grace is the unfolding of a life of which baptism is the seed. The fact that we receive the 'seal of the Holy Spirit' in confirmation must not obscure that fact that the Holy Spirit is already given in baptism.

Conversion and Forgiveness

The water of baptism is not only that of new life, it is also cleansing water. 'You were washed, you were sanctified, you were justified in the Lord Jesus Christ and in the Spirit of our God' (1 Cor 6:11). Those who are old enough to have committed sins of their own receive forgiveness. Babies, who have committed no personal or actual sins, are healed of the effects of original sin: (1) the absence of grace is cured by the coming of the Holy Spirit; (2) to counter the 'sin of the world' (cf. Jn 1:29) and the pressures towards sin that inevitably go with this life, they are now admitted into the Church which will provide the help they need to live not by the standards of this world, but those of Christ.

Baptism not only brings forgiveness; it is part of a process of conversion, which involves death to sin and rising to new life. The converts at Pentecost were told to 'repent' and be baptised (Acts 2:38). Conversion was a principal aim of Vatican II's request for the establishment of an adult catechumenate as a 'spiritual journey' involving 'a progressive change of outlook and morals' (*Ad Gentes* 13). This request was largely responsible for the introduction of the *Rite of Christian Initiation of Adults* (RCIA), in which, from Precatechumenate, which leads to initial conversion, to the Scrutinies, which 'complete the conversion', the whole 'spiritual journey' is one of conversion.

This change of life is symbolised by the *Renunciation of Sin* followed by the *Profession of Faith.* The Renunciation involves the rejection of Satan; in the early Church the candidates turned to the west, the region of darkness, in order to disown Satan to his face. The Profession is an act by which the candidate expresses allegiance to his new Lord, Jesus Christ, turning to the east to greet him at the source of light.

The Sacrament of Faith

Baptism is inseparably linked with faith. According to the 'Long Ending' of Mark, 'the one who believes and is baptised will be saved' (Mk 16:16). The name of 'enlightenment', that was apparently given to baptism from New Testament times (cf. Heb 6:4), indicates the spiritual illumination of faith that the sacrament effects. The baptised soon became known as the 'faithful'. According to the General Introduction of the RCIA, baptism is:

> above all, the sacrament of that faith by which, enlightened by the grace of the Holy Spirit, we respond to the Gospel of Christ (n. 3).

The RCIA is a process by which the candidate grows from an individual, unformed faith to the instructed faith of the Church. Thus the Precatechumenate is 'an opportunity for the beginnings of faith' (n. 36). Candidates seeking enrolment in the catechumenate, in answer to the question, 'What do you ask of God's Church?', reply, 'Faith'; but they are not to be admitted until they have given evidence of 'first faith' (nn. 50, 42). The catechumenate is a time for the 'nurturing and growth of the catechumens' faith' (n. 36). The creed which is 'presented' to the Elect in the third week of Lent contains 'the words of that faith by which you will be justified' (n. 147). Immediately before baptism the candidate makes a Profession of Faith in the Trinity (n. 219).

But at the same time faith is one of the supernatural gifts infused into the soul through baptism. According to the Council of Trent, faith is both a disposition that *leads* to justification and a virtue that is poured into the soul *at the time of* justification.[2] Thus faith is both an actual grace given by God to prepare a person for baptism, and a permanent disposition which is one aspect of the new life brought about by baptism.

Infant Baptism

For babies, of course, faith cannot be a *condition* for baptism; they are baptised into the faith of the Church; the family, godparents and local community undertake to rear the child in the faith that they themselves profess. Accordingly in the Rite for the Baptism of Little Children the parents and godparents are asked to express their <u>own</u> renunciation of evil and their faith in Christ; they do not speak by proxy for the babies themselves. However, the grace of faith is given to the baby at the moment of its baptism as a gift of God, and is like a seed which will progressively influence the conscious life of the child as it grows up.

In recent years, however, voices have been raised even within the Catholic Church questioning the appropriateness of infant baptism. This led the Vatican Congregation for the Doctrine of the Faith in 1980 to publish a defence of the practice entitled *Pastoralis Actio*.[3] The document was above all an attempt to answer the parents and pastors who, in their concern over the number of young people abandoning the practice of their religion, were recommending that baptism should be postponed until after a serious catechumenate.

In defence of infant baptism the CDF makes no appeal to the belief that babies who die without baptism are excluded from heaven. Indeed it implies that they may be saved, though it offers no explanation about the way in which this can happen: the Church can do nothing for such babies but 'entrust them to God's mercy'.[4] Nevertheless the Church must do what it can for a baby faced with death, and 'knows no other way apart from baptism for ensuring children's entry into eternal happiness' (n. 13). The CDF rebuts the argument that the sacrament requires acceptance by the candidate with faith and commitment. Following St Augustine, the Congregation explains that babies are baptised not in their own faith but in the faith of the Church. Moreover, baptism does not only *signify* faith; it also is the *cause* of faith for the baptised. Even babies receive sanctifying or habitual grace when they are baptised, together with the supernatural virtues of faith, hope and charity. In practice this infused faith at least implies a new relationship with Christ and membership of a community pledged to lead the child to conscious faith. In technical language theologians distinguish between the 'habit' of faith, which the baby is given, and the 'use' of faith, which it does not yet possess. It would probably be a mistake to try to explain this difference in psychological terms, apart from saying that this supernatural, habitual faith needs to develop into a conscious faith as the child grows up.

The CDF also explains that infant baptism does not violate the freedom of the child. Not only do parents make many decisions on behalf of their child without violating its freedom, but in any event the only true human freedom is to be found in Christ. Even if the child rejects Catholic faith, the parents should not regret their decision to have the baby baptised, because they may have sown the seeds of a later conversion (nn. 21-2).

Again, the baptism of babies has a further merit of having 'the force of witness, manifesting God's initiative and the gratuitous character of the love with which he surrounds our lives: 'not that we loved God but that he loved us (1 Jn 4:10)' (n. 26).

Baptism and Mission

We have seen that the baptised are called to a royal priesthood which they exercise by living lives which give glory to God. One aspect of this priestly service is giving witness to Christ. According to the Vatican II Decree on Mission:

> All Christ's faithful, wherever they live, are bound to show forth by the example of their lives and the witness of their words that new person they have put on at baptism (AG 11).

The witness to Christ given by the baptised includes a share in the effort to establish social justice. The Vatican II Dogmatic Constitution on the Church sees it as the vocation of the laity – which is therefore a consequence of baptism –

> to seek the kingdom of God by engaging in temporal affairs and ordering these in accordance with the will of God (LG 31).

This is in accordance with the vision of Christian life in the Pastoral Constitution on the Church in the World:

> Whoever in obedience to Christ seeks first the reign of God, gains from that a stronger and purer love to aid all his or her fellows and to bring about the work of justice under the inspiration of charity (GS 72).

Confirmation

Although this call to witness is offered to all the baptised, it is associated in a special way with *confirmation.* The passage from the Decree on Mission quoted in the last paragraph goes on to speak of 'that power of the Holy Spirit by whom they have been strengthened through confirmation'.

Pope Paul VI, in his instruction *Divinae Consortium* explaining the revision of the rite of confirmation in 1971, acknowledged that confirmation was not at first clearly recognised as a sacrament distinct from baptism in either the East or the West. As the pope wrote, accurately summing up the development of the sacrament,

> In many Eastern rites it seems that from early times a rite of chrismation, not yet clearly distinguished from baptism, prevailed

> for the conferring of the Holy Spirit. … In the West there are very ancient witnesses concerning the part of Christian initiation that was *later distinctly recognised* to be the sacrament of confirmation.[5]

Although confirmation was not formally defined as a separate sacrament until the Second Council of Lyons in 1274, it had been treated in this way in both theory and practice for many centuries before that time. Once it had became common to have an interval of several years between the celebration of the two sacraments, it soon became necessary to distinguish between their effects. If it could not be explained what a person was missing if they were not confirmed, it was hard to induce them to take the trouble to present themselves or their children for confirmation at all, except by the practical expedient adopted in thirteenth-century England under Archbishop John Peckham of refusing holy communion to those who had not been confirmed.[6]

A neat solution, though the wrong one, would be that the Holy Spirit is not bestowed on the candidate until confirmation. This cannot be right, because the persons of the Trinity are inseparable. We by baptism cannot become sons and daughters of the Father, and brothers and sisters of the Son and members of his body, except by the action of the Holy Spirit, who is the 'spirit of adoption' (Rom 8:15); the waters of baptism are waters of rebirth through the action of the Holy Spirit; the Holy Spirit dwells within us from the moment of our baptism. It is necessary therefore to distinguish between the ways in which the Holy Spirit is given by the two sacraments.

The Second Vatican Council in several places attempted to answer this question, most fully in the Decree on the Church: while Christians are incorporated into the Church by baptism, so that,

> reborn as children of God, they have an obligation to profess publicly the faith they have received from God through the Church (LG 11; cf. 33),

through confirmation they are:

> bound *more completely* to the Church; they are enriched by a *special* strength of the Holy Spirit, and in this way are under *more pressing* obligation to spread and defend the faith by word and deed as true witnesses of Christ (LG 11; my italics).

Thus confirmation does not confer something new, but deepens what has already been bestowed by baptism.

This fits in with the teaching of the Vatican II Decree on Liturgy concerning the close connection between the three sacraments of initiation:

> The rite of confirmation is also to be revised. The point of this revision is that the very close connection of this sacrament with the whole process of Christian initiation may become more clearly visible. For this reason, it will be a good idea for people to make a renewal of baptismal promises prior to receiving this sacrament (*Sacrosanctum Concilium* 71).

The RCIA explains this unity in several ways.

> The conjunction of the two celebrations signifies the unity of the paschal mystery, the close link between the mission of the Son and the outpouring of the Holy Spirit, and the connection between the two sacraments through which the Son and the Holy Spirit come with the Father to those who are baptised (RCIA 208).

Thus the unity of baptism and confirmation reflects other unities: the unity between Easter and Pentecost, where the one paschal mystery is spread over fifty days; the unity between God's action in sending the Son at the Incarnation and pouring out of the Spirit on the Church. Thus baptism and confirmation are two sacraments by which the Son and the Spirit come with the Father – not in the sense that the Son comes in baptism and the Spirit in confirmation, but in so far as in every sacrament the action of the three persons can never be separated.

If then baptism and confirmation are one grace spread out in time, they are also one grace applied to different situations. The General Introduction to the new Rites of Initiation explains that the purpose for which confirmation signs us with the gift of the Spirit and makes us more completely Christ's image is that:

> we may bear witness to him before all the world and work to bring the Body of Christ to its fullness as soon as possible (n. 1).

The Rite of Confirmation explains similarly that the sacrament

> conforms believers more fully to Christ for the building up of his Body in faith and love (n. 2).

Like the apostles at Pentecost, Christians receive the Holy Spirit at confirmation to empower them as witnesses of Christ.

In each sacrament the grace we receive is the grace we need for a new or deeper position in the Church. We have therefore an answer to our question about the distinctive way in which the Spirit is given in confirmation: the Holy Spirit who has come to dwell within us and become our very life as baptised members of Christ's body and who makes us sons and daughters of God, now provides us with the strength we need for our new responsibility as witnesses of Christ. Although all the baptised are called to profess their faith in Christ publicly, the confirmed have this public witness as their distinguishing responsibility, a responsibility which the Holy Spirit, whom they have already received in baptism, empowers them to fulfil at confirmation.

These questions concerning the meaning of confirmation present problems only for the Western or Latin Church. For Catholics of the Byzantine rite, who, like the Orthodox, confer all three sacraments together on babies, there is not the need to define what confirmation adds to baptism, for both sacraments can be understood as symbols each emphasising different aspects of a single multi-faceted sacramental grace. In many places the Vatican II documents and the texts of the rites themselves state clearly that the order in which the sacraments should be received is: baptism, confirmation, first communion. These three sacraments form a single process of initiation which requires that order for its logical unfolding. This is most clearly seen in the Decree on the Ministry and Life of Priests:

> The other sacraments ... are attached to and lead towards the holy Eucharist. ... Hence the Eucharist is seen to be the beginning and end of all preaching of the gospel, in that catechumens are led forward step by step to sharing in it, and the faithful, already sealed by the holy sign of ownership in baptism and confirmation, are fully absorbed into the body of Christ by its reception (*Presbytertian Ordinis* 5).

Whenever a separate rite of confirmation can be identified in the early Church, it is this order which is apparent.

In the middle ages church authorities tried to counter the tendency for parents to neglect the confirmation of their children, and to submit them for first communion unconfirmed. This was seen as an abuse: it was not until the present century that it became the regular and approved practice for confirmation to be conferred after first communion. As recently as 1897 Pope Leo XIII explained that one of the purposes of confirmation was to give a child strength to fight temptation so as to be prepared to receive first communion.[7]

The new Code of Canon Law (can. 891), like the old, set the age of discretion, i.e. about seven, as the normal age for confirmation. As long as the regular age for first communion was several years later, the correct order of baptism, confirmation, communion could be observed. However, when Leo's successor Pius X encouraged children to receive communion from the age of seven, it became normal for the child to be confirmed subsequently at the first visitation of the parish by the bishop.[8] As the twentieth century unfolded, the normal age for confirmation was progressively raised, until the sacrament commonly became linked with adolescence, for it was and still is in the competence of the bishop or bishops' conference to dispense from the canonical requirement of confirmation about the age of seven.

In a growing number of dioceses in various parts of the world the correct order of infant baptism, confirmation, first communion has been restored.[9] In some places confirmation is celebrated at seven and first communion at eight; in others the two sacraments are celebrated together on the same occasion.

When confirmation was viewed as a sacrament of Catholic action, or for strength to face the problems of adolescence, or as an opportunity for mature reaffirmation of the baptismal obligations, a much later age for confirmation seemed called for. However, these reasons have lost their force, now that the Church has decided against such interpretations of the sacrament. It might seem however that the Church's understanding of confirmation as a sacrament for witness to Christ was equally incompatible with an age as low as seven. This is not so, however. Any child capable of making choices may be subject to pressures, especially from friends of their own age, and may need courage and the grace of the sacrament to resist these pressures, and by doing so to be a witness to Christ. Moral educators nowadays need to teach children the skill of saying 'No' acceptably but firmly at an early age. Whenever such situations can arise, the grace of the sacrament is welcome.

When confirmation is celebrated in the proper order and therefore at an early age, the need is often felt for some other rite which would give a person the opportunity to reaffirm their Christian faith and commitment

at a later age, perhaps adolescence or early adulthood. Such a rite could be linked with a serious retreat and the assumption of new obligations, such as those involved in marriage or in various parish ministries. In several places a special rite of this nature has been devised.[10]
The Church is in such a state of uncertainty about the sacrament of confirmation that it has been called a sacrament in search of a theology. But the theology is not the most uncertain aspect of the sacrament; it might be more accurate to describe the search as one for a pastoral presentation and a pastoral celebration. Perhaps no other rite presents such a challenge, and calls for such sensitivity and imagination.

The Eucharist: the Completion of Initiation

Thus if the sacraments of initiation are received in the ideal order, confirmation as well as baptism should precede first communion. In the words of the Vatican II Decree on the Ministry and Life of Priests, by receiving holy communion,

> the faithful, already sealed by the holy sign of ownership in baptism and confirmation, are fully absorbed into the body of Christ (PO 5).

This teaching reflects the intimate connection between the two ways in which sacramental theology speaks of Christ's body, namely his body received in the Eucharist, and his body which is the Church: by receiving the eucharistic body we become members of the ecclesial body. This connection is borne out by the fact that over the years the expression 'Mystical Body' has been applied both to the Church (the usual modern usage) and to the Eucharist (which was the original meaning of the term).

St Paul systematically connects these two realisations of the Lord's body in his first Epistle to the Corinthians.

> The bread that we break, is it not a sharing in the body of Christ? Because there is one bread, we who are many are one body, for we all partake of the one bread (1 Cor 10:16-17).

Conversely, those who divide into cliques when celebrating the Eucharist do so 'without discerning the body' (the Eucharist? the Church?), and so 'eat and drink judgment against themselves' (1 Cor 11:29).

Accordingly the RCIA, after explaining the significance of the baptism and confirmation received at the Easter vigil, continues:

> Finally in the celebration of the Eucharist, as they take part for the first time and with full right, the newly baptised reach the culminating point in their Christian initiation (RCIA 210).

Thus at the vigil Mass, before the Agnus Dei,

> the celebrant may briefly remind the neophytes of the pre-eminence of the Eucharist, which is the climax of their initiation and the centre of the whole Christian life (RCIA 233).

Notes

1. Luke describes very dramatically Jesus' sermon at Nazareth on the text: 'The Spirit of the Lord is upon me, because he has anointed me to bring good news to the poor' (Lk 4:18; Is 61:1).
2. Trent, Decree on Justification, ch. 6-7; DS 1529-30; Tanner pp. 672-3.
3. English text in A. Flannery, ed., *The Documents of Vatican II*, vol. 2 (Leominster, Fowler Wright, 1982), pp. 103-7.
4. n. 13; cf. the *Catechism of the Catholic Church*, n. 1261. The CDF refers to the Rite of Funerals, which includes a special liturgy for babies who have died unbaptised.
5. Apostolic Constitution *Divinae Consortium* on the sacrament of confirmation, usually printed at the beginning of editions of the rite. The italics in these quotations are mine.
6. See J.D.C. Fisher, *Christian Initiation: Baptism in the Medieval West* (London, SPCK, Alcuin Club 47, 1965), p. 124.
7. The decision was contained in a letter approving of the decision of the bishop of Marseilles to restore confirmation to its proper place before first communion, which the Pope judged to be in accordance with the constant practice of the Church. The letter is included in P. Gasparri, *Codicis Iuris Canonici Fontes* (1933), vol. 3, pp. 515-6.
8. In some Hispanic countries, however, early confirmation remained the common practice, with the child being presented to the bishop for confirmation at the earliest opportunity after baptism.
9. For example in the diocese of Salford in England. Some dioceses in Scotland and Australia have done the same.
10. Attempts to devise such a rite are considered in M. Searle (ed.), *Alternative Futures for Worship*. Vol. 2: *Baptism and Confirmation*, Collegeville, Liturgical Press, 1987; J.A. Wilde (ed.), *Confirmed as Children, Affirmed as Teens*, Chicago, Liturgy Training Publications, 1990.

Further Reading

The *Catechism of the Catholic Church*, Part 2, Chapter 1.
The Rite for the Christian Initiation of Adults.
The Study of Liturgy (ed. C. Jones, G. Wainwright, E. Yarnold, and P. Bradshaw, 2nd edn).
Baptism in the New Testament (G. R. Beasley-Murray).
The Awe-Inspiring Rites of Initiation (E. J. Yarnold).

UPHOLDING THE INTEGRITY OF THE ACT OF FAITH: REFLECTIONS ON RCIA CATECHESIS

FR PHILIP JONES CSsR

Introduction

Part of the Catholic theology of the act of faith concerns the person who believes and who is held responsible for his own acts. In catholic theology faith is not a blind leap in the dark. It is not an irrational act. It is a human act and therefore it is done with understanding and freedom. In *Faith and Reason* John Paul II states that 'the Church has always considered the act of entrusting oneself to God to be a moment of fundamental decision which engages the whole person. In that act, the intellect and the will display their spiritual nature enabling the subject to act in a way which realises personal freedom to the full' (13.2.).

In this study we are focusing upon the convert, the adult person being received into the church at the Easter Vigil. We are investigating what the church does to safeguard the dignity of the convert. The church receives the convert and also prepares him for reception. The church has a responsibility towards the convert to ensure his decision to enter the Catholic Church is responsible. This is to uphold the dignity of the convert. It is to uphold the integrity of the act of faith.

In the first part we begin by considering the guidelines issued by the church in the *Rite for the Christian Initiation of Adults* (RCIA). We shall also consider the *General Directory for Catechesis* (GDC). The *Directory* gives an overall view of catechesis and makes some judgements about the present state of catechesis. We shall examine the criticisms it makes and the ideas upon which it lays special emphasis.

In the second part we reflect upon the nature of faith drawing attention to some important points made by John Paul II in his encyclical on *Faith and Reason.* These form a deeper theological and philosophical background to the catechetical analysis of the first part.

In the third and final part we shall study the catechetical method proposed in guidelines issued by the English and Welsh Hierarchy. In the light of what we shall already have seen we shall consider whether or not the catechetical method needs to be modified or replaced.

Rules Concerning Adult Reception into the Church

The most important documents concerning our subject are the *General Directory for Catechesis* and the *Rite for the Christian Initiation of Adults.* The latter is published with a preceding document entitled *'Christian Initiation,* General Introduction.

a) *The Rite of Christian Initiation of Adults and Christian Initiation,* 'General Introduction'

The most important statement describing our area of study is found in paragraph three of the *General Introduction.* Baptism is the 'sacrament of that faith by which, enlightened by the grace of the Holy Spirit, we respond to the Gospel of Christ.' The Church must respond and do all she can to assist our religious response. The 'Church believes that it is its most basic and necessary duty to inspire all, catechumens, parents of children still to be baptised, and godparents, to that true and living faith by which they hold fast to Christ and enter into or confirm their commitment to the New Covenant. '

These points are expressed more fully in the *Rite of Christian Initiation of Adults.* The opening article informs us that the new rite is designed for adults who 'consciously and freely seek the living God and enter the way of faith and conversion as the Holy Spirit opens their hearts.' The new rite is the way the church responds to those who seek the Lord. She declares 'by God's help they will be strengthened spiritually during their preparation and at the proper time will receive the sacraments.'

The help of the church accompanies their journey of faith. Without going into details we can verify this statement in the following paragraphs that describe the periods when candidates require help from the church. Articles 37 and 38 refer to the stage of 'evangelisation and precatechumenate'. Articles 42 and 43 refer to acceptance into the order of catechumens. Articles 106 and 107 refer to the time of enrolment. Articles 234 and 235 remind us that after they have been received into the church She continues to assist the new converts in their journey of faith. It is outside our scope to deal with each or any part of this process, but we can sum them all up by saying that the Church seeks to offer the candidates every assistance through priest, deacons and people, and through the liturgy and the community of faith.

In the texts referred to the church describes her efforts and concern to help the candidates to grow in faith. At the same time she is careful not to force candidates to grow quicker in faith than they are able. For example, in article 39 she suggests the possibility of holding some kind of reception of a non-ritual nature for those who sympathise with the Christian faith but who do not fully believe.

b) The *General Directory for Catechesis*

The second document covers a wide range of catechetical concerns. Besides the references to the RCIA there are also some general criticisms concerning contemporary catechesis and some positive recommendations. These are important because, as we shall see, they directly affect the catechumens' capacity to make a coherent act of faith.

i) References to the RCIA are interesting because they highlight the special place this form of catechesis occupies within other forms of catechesis in the church.

The GDC in articles 88 to 89 summarise RCIA catechesis: the different stages and the liturgical rites accompanying them. Then in article 90 we read that this 'is the model of all catechising activity.' Article 91 explains that all catechesis must be based upon Baptism, Confirmation and the Eucharist, it must be a matter of concern for the whole community, not just priests, deacons and catechists. It must ever refer to the Paschal Mystery, and must be a place of inculturation, 'incorporating authentic 'seeds of the world', scattered through nations and individuals.' *'As a process of formation and as a true school of the faith'* this catechesis is the example of comprehensiveness and integrity of formation. Article 88 stresses the importance of the whole community of faith in the RCIA process.

ii) Weaknesses within catechetics cannot help but have a direct bearing upon the act of faith. Catechesis is directed at preparing people for reception into the church and the growth of faith after receiving the sacraments of initiation. A serious criticism is made in article 28. The Directory states that 'the sense of belonging to the Church has weakened and a certain disaffection towards the Church is frequently noted. Thus the Church is often regarded in a one-dimensional way as a mere institution and deprived of her mystery. In some instances tendentious positions have been adopted and set in opposition to the interpretation and application of the renewal sought in the Church by the Second Vatican Council. Such ideologies and conduct have led to divisions which damage that witness of communion indispensable to evangelisation.' In the Directory we can see that the Church is responding to these problems by emphasising the importance of the ecclesial structure of faith.

In article 30 more specific problems are noted with possible solutions. The Directory notes a major problem concerning the idea of Revelation. The idea of Tradition is often weak: 'in much catechesis, indeed, reference to Sacred Scripture is virtually exclusive and unaccompanied by sufficient reference to the Church's long experience and reflection, acquired in the course of her two-thousand year history. The ecclesial nature of catechesis, in this case, appears less clearly; the inter-relation of Sacred Scripture, Tradition and the Magisterium, each according to 'its proper mode' does not yet harmoniously enrich a catechetical transmission of the faith.'

Other problems noted are the difficulty of appreciating that catechesis is a school of faith affecting the whole of Christian living, sometimes catechesis has no liturgical reference, and there is sometimes a lack of theological understanding in the mode of teaching. The difficulty of proclaiming the gospel in different cultures is mentioned and the importance of inter-religious dialogue. The missionary dimension of catechesis still 'seems weak and inadequate'.

Concerning the content of catechesis certain doctrinal limitations are perceived, specifically regarding sin, grace and eschatology. Solid moral formation, the history of the Church, and the Church's social teaching do not receive adequate attention. Of particular importance is the failure to impart a 'balanced presentation of the entire mystery of Christ. Often, emphasis is given only to his humanity without any explicit reference to his divinity.' The opposite tendency that would over-emphasise the Divinity of Christ is less frequent. The directory notes 'a proliferation of catechisms and texts, the products of particular initiatives whose selective tendencies and emphases are so differing as to damage that convergence necessary for the unity of the faith.' This final point leads back to the importance of the ecclesial structure of faith.

The difficulties and problems listed above fall into two categories. The first concerns the whole idea of belonging to the church. That was the first criticism and the most serious. It affects *where* we believe. We believe in Christ within the church and we share the faith of the church. A poor, critical, or one-sided understanding of the Church attacks the quality of our faith. Secondly, most of the other criticisms concern the content of faith. They are describing different ways in which the faith is not adequately taught.

iii) Having noted these criticisms we can now reflect upon some of the main recommendations in the Directory. These will concern the ecclesial structure of catechesis and the need for a comprehensive and structured catechesis.

We begin with articles 78 and 79 which concern the ecclesial nature of catechesis. The first two paragraph of article 78 sums up the central importance of this theme:

> Catechesis is an essentially ecclesial act. The true subject of catechesis is the Church which, continuing the mission of Jesus the Master and, therefore, animated by the Holy Spirit, is sent to be the teacher of the faith. The Church imitates the Mother of the Lord in treasuring the Gospel in her heart. She proclaims it, celebrates it, lives it, and she transmits it in catechesis to all those who have decided to follow Jesus Christ. This transmission of the Gospel is a living act of ecclesial tradition.
>
> The Church transmits the faith which she herself lives: her understanding of the mystery of God and his salvific plan, her vision of man's highest vocation, the style of evangelic life which communicates the joy of the Kingdom, the hope which pervades her and the love which she has for mankind and all God's creatures.

In these two paragraphs the Church lays claim to the catechetical process. It is part of her very existence, 'a living act of ecclesial tradition' based upon 'her understanding of the mystery of God and his salvific plan.' This is no abstract idea of the Church. It is the Church *with* her people, *in* her people. The Church sows the faith in 'the hearts of catechumens and those to be catechised so as to nourish their profoundest experience of life.' In article 79 we read that through catechesis the Church 'feeds her children with her own faith and incorporates them as members into the ecclesial family.' The Church 'as a good mother gives them the Gospel in all its authenticity and purity ….'

The view of the faith presented so far reflects a Catholic understanding of the nature of faith. Faith is not seen as some private act between an individual and God. Rather we share in the faith of the Church. Our ability to stand before God in faith is the action of the Church upon us. We are responsible for our own religious acts but the grace and understanding to speak and act for ourselves in Christ is due to the power and teaching of the Church to which we belong and in which we live. This forms the background to the Directory and goes a long way to explain the criticisms it has felt free to make concerning modern catechetical theory and practise. It is particularly clear that any merely partial proclamation of the Gospel by priests or catechists must be seen as a betrayal of the church and an attack upon the integrity of her apostolic mission. A partial or incomplete proclamation of the Gospel puts out a false statement – that the Church does not have the full truth about Christ.

The close connection between the ecclesial nature of catechesis and the need for a true and full proclamation of the Gospel is stated clearly in article 67. The Directory says that catechesis is a 'comprehensive and systematic formation in the faith.' It differs from other ways of presenting the word of God because of 'its comprehensive and vital deepening of the mystery of Christ'. The previous article 66 refers to sacraments of initiation. The aim of catechesis is to encourage 'a living, explicit and fruitful profession of faith.' Therefore the Church transmits 'her living experience of the Gospel, her faith, so that they may appropriate and profess it.' Quoting from *Catechesi Tradendae* the *Directory* reminds us that authentic catechesis is an orderly and systematic initiation into the revelation given to us in Jesus Christ. This revelation is stored in the Church's memory and in Sacred Scripture, and constantly communicated from one generation to the next by a living and active *traditio.*

From what we have just seen two points stand out as particularly important. First, the idea of faith presented in articles 66 and 67 is a tradition of understanding. Faith is a tradition of wisdom, a way of thinking passed on from one generation to the next. This is no blind faith, no blind existentialist leap in the dark. It is spiritual enlightenment, coming to know the mystery of Christ. Secondly, it is experiential. It is a living and active tradition. It is not even just a part of life. It is rather a way of living.

These points are repeated in other parts of the *Directory.* We cannot here deal with every instance, but we can give some examples: the importance of faith within the Church is stated clearly and emphatically in article 83. The confession of faith – the Credo – is a personal act but it is only complete in reference to the Church. The baptised recite it 'in the Church and through the Church, because they do so as members of the Church.' By fusing our individual confession of faith with that of the Church we are 'incorporated into her mission: to be the 'universal sacrament of salvation' for the life of the world.' Again we can see here that faith is a way of living and that it is tied in with our belonging to the Church. This is confirmed in article 105 which declares that 'the ecclesial nature of catechesis confers on the transmitted Gospel message an inherent ecclesial character. Catechesis originates in the Church's confession of faith and leads to the profession of faith of the catechumen and those to be catechised.'

The practical effect of this ecclesial dimension of faith can be seen in articles 167 and 168. In 167 the baptised are called to have a mature faith and therefore have 'a right to adequate catechesis' and in the next article the scope is widened: 'the recipient of catechesis is the whole Christian community and every person in it.'

In article 106 we are reminded that the faith 'is one,' and in articles 111 and 112 the fundamental principle of catechesis is to safeguard the integrity of the message and not to distort it in any way. The follower of Christ 'has the right to receive 'the word of faith' not in mutilated, falsified or diminished form but whole and entire, in all its rigour and vigour.' Article 112 warns against the danger of selectivity regarding the contents of faith. The right of the faithful to know what the Church has received and what she believes is repeated in article 121 where the *Catechism of the Catholic Church* is presented as a response to this 'legitimate right'. This remains true for every believer. It is not limited to people of high intelligence. Article 130 states that the 'cognitive or truth dimension of the faith' is important because the act of faith is 'an assent of intellect and will'. Therefore the faithful need to have 'an organic knowledge of the faith, however simple in form'.

Finally we must stress that the *General Directory for Catechesis* is concerned with objectivity. Faith must be able to give its reasons. The reasons are based upon love for the object of faith. Article 85 states that 'Who has encountered Christ desires to know him as much as possible'(85). This is not something peculiar to faith. It is part of being human. 'Even in the human order the love which one person has for another causes that person to wish to know the other all the more.' Therefore, the intention of Catechesis is to teach the whole truth about Christ. To intend anything less is harmful to faith.

At the end of this first part we can sum up in the following way. We have examined the Church's understanding of her obligations towards the catechumens and indeed towards all the baptised. We have seen that the individual act of faith takes place within the Church and forms part of the Church's tradition. Therefore catechumens have a right to a sound catechesis. The Church's sense of her obligations flow from her self-understanding. She sees herself as Christ's Church with a mission to proclaim the full unadulterated truth of Christ to all people so that they can freely and intelligently confess their faith in Christ. This is how the Church presents herself to her people through her own legislation.

Theological Background to the Relation between Faith and Reason

We shall now consider the theological background to the teaching of the *General Directory for Catechesis.* We begin with a survey of the recent history of the problem of faith and reason. This determines the way theology is studied and this in its turn influences catechetical method. Secondly, we shall consider the theology of the act of faith in the recent encyclical *Faith and Reason.* This throws great light upon the question of the dignity and integrity of the person who makes an act of faith.

a) *Reflections on the recent history of the Church in the modern world*[1]

The catechetical problems highlighted in the *General Directory for Catechesis* reflect a theological problem that has affected the Church since before the First Vatican Council. This problem concerns how faith and reason are inter-related. The origin of the problem derives from the world in which much of the Church exists in Europe and North America. It is a secular non-religious world. This creates a tension within Christian thinking. If we are surrounded by intellectual people who do not believe in God or who do not believe anyone can be certain about religious truths this cannot help but affect our attitude to theological reasoning.

i) A non-religious world can influence the way we present our faith and can pose dangers for our understanding of faith. One danger is to regard faith and reason as somehow opposed to each other. On the one hand we have reason, on the other hand we have faith. How can faith present its case? It has to use reason, but reason seems to be something different from faith. In his book on theological reasoning – *La Ragione Theologica* – in which he traces different forms of theological reasoning in the past two centuries Giuseppe Colombo points out that for well over a hundred years there has been a common assumption that there exists in the non-religious world something called objective critical reasoning.[2] He says that faced with non-religious critical reasoning theological reasoning has suffered from a widespread inferiority complex. It is as if theological reasoning is answerable to non-religious reasoning.

In response to this problem the First Vatican Council reflected upon the relation between faith and reason and sought to clarify their respective areas of competence. Later towards the end of the last century Pope Leo XIII inaugurated a whole theological and philosophical movement within the Church based upon St Thomas Aquinas. This lasted right up to the eve of the Second Vatican Council. It also affected catechetics.

Catechesis tends to reflect the theological trends of the day. Before the Second Vatican Council catechesis tended in a certain sense to be rationalistic. Like Scholastic Theology its scriptural base was weak and it tended towards dogmatics underpinned by strong theological and philosophical arguments. The faith was presented almost as a kind of Christian ideology that could outface the secular ideologies of the twentieth century. The reason for this kind of presentation is not difficult to understand and appreciate. The Church was concerned to argue her faith in a world of unbelief.

A new approach towards faith and reason was adopted at the time of the Second Vatican Council. Part of the practical intention of the Council Fathers was the modernisation of the Church, or *Aggiornamento* to use the popular word at the time. This involved periods of experimentation. In catechesis many of the problems mentioned in the *General Directory* come from this time. Attempts to modernise catechetics were often used as an excuse to introduce a form of selectivity of doctrine which disparaged or ignored any part of the faith that might prove difficult or unpopular.

An important renewal movement since the Vatican Council was political. Liberation theology challenged the Church to make a strong option for the poor. While we must note the positive importance of making this stance (see articles 103 and 104 in the GDC) we must also acknowledge that a political emphasis can serve as another reason for being catechetically selective.

From within the Ecclesial perspective of the *General Directory* it is clear that most modern catechetical problems originate in trying to appease a non-believing audience by limiting and changing the comprehensive presentation of the contents of faith. Instead of answering Revelation faith weakens itself by making itself answerable to a popular fashion or philosophy.

ii) In recent years the Church has adopted a new attitude towards the world. At least at the centre of the Church there appears little evidence of any kind of theological inferiority complex in an unbelieving world. Unbelief now appears not only as a lack of belief in God but also as a lack of confidence in reason. In his Encyclical *Reason and Faith* (*Fides et Ratio*) John Paul II analyses the problem of faith and reason. He sees it as a duty for the Church to respond to the crisis that afflicts modern reason.

In article 5 John Paul II says 'the search for ultimate truth seems often to be neglected,' and 'individuals are at the mercy of caprice' and 'reason ... has lost the capacity to lift its gaze to the heights, not daring to rise to the truth of being.' Agnosticism and relativism have lead philosophy to 'lose its way in the shifting sands of widespread scepticism' and this leads to a widespread 'lack of confidence in truth.' 'Hence we see among men and women of our time, and not just in some philosophers, attitudes of widespread distrust of the human being's great capacity for knowledge.' Later in article 46 he defines modern unbelief, 'the crisis of rationalism,' as a form of *nihilism*. He says 'as a philosophy of nothingness, it has a certain attraction for people of our time' and gives rise to a 'widespread mentality which claims that a definitive commitment should no longer be made, because everything is fleeting and provisional.'

The destructive effect unbelief has on the dignity of the person is described in article 90. Nihilism is 'the denial of all foundations and the negation of all objective truth.' It is 'a denial of the humanity and of the very identity of the human being.' Losing touch 'with objective truth and therefore with the very ground of human dignity' nihilism erases 'from the countenance of man and woman the marks of their likeness to God,' and leads 'them little by little either to a destructive will to power or to a solitude without hope.'

'Postmodernity' is the word sometimes used to describe our age. In article 91 the Pope says it sometimes refers to positive aesthetic, social and technological phenomena. However, the negative dimension is clear when it is claimed that 'the time of certainties is irrevocably past, and the human being must now learn to live in a horizon of total absence of meaning.' He says 'this nihilism has been justified in a sense by the terrible experience of evil that has marked our age. Such a dramatic experience has ensured the collapse of rationalist optimism, which viewed history as the triumphant progress of reason, the source of all happiness and freedom; and now, at the end of this century, one of our greatest threats is the temptation to despair.'

This recent development within the Church signals a remarkable change. It also brings greater clarity to our understanding of the act of faith as a personal absolute commitment to the truth. It completes the work of the Second Vatican Council because it stresses that the Church has an obligation to the person of Christ and that part of this obligation is to be objective and rational. Columbo points out that it is not some abstract idea of reasoning which obliges the theologian to be rational and objective but the desire to understand and propound and protect the truth which is the Person of Jesus Christ. In a sense this is not unusual in that other subjects – the arts and sciences – derive their need for the exercise of objective critical reasoning from the desire to know the subjects themselves. An important part of this is that we should not assume that scepticism is the highest form of objective reasoning. The student who assumed that modern art was an exercise in self-delusion would not be regarded as the most intelligent. It is difficult to argue a case from outside the subject or against the subject as a whole. If the subject exists the arguments must occur from within. Likewise our theological arguments occur within the Catholic Tradition and eventually, in one form or another, become part of the Tradition.

b) *The theology of the act of faith*

It is important to consider the main elements of the act of faith to which John Paul II draws attention in *Faith and Reason.* At the very beginning we quoted from this encyclical: 'The Church has always considered the act of entrusting oneself to God to be a moment of fundamental decision which engages the whole person. In that act, the intellect and the will display their spiritual nature enabling the subject to act in a way which realises personal freedom to the full.' (13). It will be helpful to reflect upon this statement. First we shall consider the freedom of the act of faith and the understanding presupposed by faith. Secondly, we shall treat the ecclesial structure of faith. This recalls the important theme in the *General Directory.* In this section we shall also see the importance of the emphasis on the historical dimension of Revelation in *Dei Verbum.*

i) The freedom of the act of faith reflects the simplicity of this human act. It is an act of obedience and of grateful acceptance. Faith is an obedient response to God because it recognises 'his divinity, transcendence and supreme freedom.' The obedience of faith is not a denial of freedom. For faith freedom 'is absolutely required.' Freedom 'is not realised in decisions made against God' which are really 'a refusal to be open to the very reality which enables our self-realisation.' And so the conclusion follows: 'Men and women can accomplish no more important act in their lives than the act of faith; it is here that freedom reaches the certainty of truth and chooses to live in that truth' (13). In the same paragraph it is explained that the assent of faith is to God who makes himself known to us. We must be totally open to God's truth which comes to us 'as gift'. The freedom of faith is deeply connected to the understanding of faith. Freedom and understanding act together to become an acknowledgement of God; a recognition that God loves us. 'In his goodness and wisdom, God chose to reveal himself. ... This initiative is utterly gratuitous, moving from God to men and women in order to bring them to salvation. As the source of love, God desires to make himself known; and the knowledge which the human being has of God perfects all that the human mind can know of the meaning of life' (7). The knowledge of faith is the awareness of God as giver and this requires an act of freedom which is that of welcome, acceptance, and entrusting oneself to the giver.

The important argument in the sections concerned with freedom centres upon the obedience of faith. Any kind of obedience is seen by modernists and postmodernists as a diminution of the person and his reasoning autonomy. The Christian response is to present the obedience of faith as part of an intelligent and enlightened acknowledgement of God. The obedience of faith is part of our acceptance of God who gives Himself to us in Christ.

We can see that understanding and freedom in these sections are so closely connected that we can distinguish but hardly separate the two themes. However, behind the understanding of faith we must also consider the importance of the Church and the person of the historical Christ.

ii) The understanding of faith from which freedom acts is centred upon the person of Christ. *Faith and Reason* recalls two important developments at the Second Vatican Council. The first is the importance of the Church as witnessing to the truth of Christ. The second is the historical dimension of revelation that focuses upon Christ who shares our history.

The awareness that the church has of herself is of fundamental importance to our study. Here we see why the Church passes legislation on catechesis and makes judgements about forms of catechesis. The beginning of chapter one of the encyclical explains it: 'Underlying all the Church's thinking is the awareness that she is the bearer of a message which has its origin in God himself (cf. Cor 4:1-2). The knowledge which the Church offers to man has its origin not in any speculation of her own, however sublime, but in the word of God which she has received in faith (cf. 1Th 2:13). At the origin of our life of faith there is an encounter, unique in kind, which discloses a mystery hidden for long ages …' (7) This same thought is noticeable in the introduction. 'From the moment when, through the Paschal Mystery, she received the gift of the ultimate truth about human life, the Church has make her pilgrim way along the paths of the world to proclaim that Jesus Christ is 'the way, and the truth, and the life' (Jn 14:6) (2). Although the encyclical is the work of the Magisterium it is faithful to the stress of the Second Vatican Council on the people of God which precedes the different orders of priesthood within the church. It is not just the Magisterium or the College of Bishops that witness to Christ but the *believing community.* 'This mission on the one hand makes the believing community a partner in humanity's shared struggle to arrive at truth; and on the other hand it obliges the believing community to proclaim the certitudes arrived at.'(2) Here we are once again in the realm of the ecclesial structure of the act of faith.

It is important to recognise the note of confidence in carrying out the mission: 'Sure of her competence as the bearer of the Revelation of Jesus Christ, the Church reaffirms the need to reflect upon truth' (6). The confidence is notable in the calm and measured way we are invited to reflect upon the nature of human understanding and Christian faith. It is clear that the reflections are taking place within the faith. From within the faith it is affirmed that everyone is an enquirer: 'One may define the human being, therefore, as the one who seeks the truth' (28). John Paul affirms that all men and women 'are in some sense philosophers and have their own philosophical conceptions with which they direct their lives. In one way or other, they shape a comprehensive vision and an answer to the question of life's meaning; and in the light of this they interpret their own life's course and regulate their behaviour' (30). There are also core philosophical insights in the history of thought. These include 'the principles of non-contradiction, finality and causality, as well as the concept of the person as a free and intelligent subject, with the capacity to know God, truth and goodness. Consider as well certain fundamental moral norms which are shared by all' (4).

It is clear that the church wishes to uphold the dignity of every person as an enquirer after the truth. However, in the encyclical there is also a startlingly sharp description of the difficulty of ever arriving at truth without the help of Revelation. John Paul writes that 'according to the Apostle, it was part of the original plan of the creation that reason should without difficulty reach beyond the sensory data to the origin of all things: the Creator. But because of the disobedience by which man and woman chose to set themselves in full and absolute autonomy in relation to the One who had created them, this ready access to God the Creator is diminished.' Our first parents thought they could ignore the knowledge which comes from God and so it came about that 'all men and women were caught up in this primal disobedience, which so wounded reason that from then on its path to full truth would be strewn with obstacles.' The Apostle has explained how through sin human thinking became empty, reasoning became distorted and inclined to falsehood. 'The eyes of the mind were no longer able to see clearly: reason became more and more a prisoner to itself' (22).

iii) We have seen two sets of statements. One affirms the person as the philosophical enquirer. The second affirms the person unable to see the truth. Everyone is made for the truth but everyone also is born into this world needing salvation. It is fairly evident that most people are not involved in some abstract philosophical search for the truth. When the good Shepherd finds the lost sheep it is unlikely that many of them have enrolled in a philosophy seminar on the meaning of life. However, there is a sense in which virtually everyone is an enquirer. Most people like to have a good person in their life. They like the good person, the truthful person, the person who is helpful to them and who assures them of their own worth. The good person changes our view of ourselves and the world and makes us able to breathe. John Paul II stresses the personal nature of truth. We are looking for someone to trust. It is in our relationships with others that we come to know the truth of what it is to be a person. (4 and 32). This leads us to the importance of belief. 'Knowledge through belief, grounded as it is on trust between persons, is linked to truth: in the act of believing, men and women entrust themselves to the truth which the other declares to them' (32).

So much of our knowledge whether it be scientific or personal or cultural comes to us through other people that we must conclude 'that the human being – the one who seeks the truth – is also the one who lives by belief' (31). It is in this context that John Paul II introduces faith in Christ and belief in those who witness to the truth of Christ. This also brings into play the final important point: the historical nature of Christian truth. It is a significant shift of emphasis. In *Faith and Reason* there is a deeply respectful treatment of the way the First Vatican Council approached the question of faith and reason by clarifying the different dimensions of natural reason and reason within the faith. However, what we have just seen concerning the concrete analysis of the way people actually come to know most of their knowledge leads to a very personal emphasis on the nature of faith. It is also true to the historical character of revelation as it has been presented in the documents of the Second Vatican Council. And here the emphasis is on the fact that Revelation is part of the world's history; it is already part of our experience.

The greatest example of entrusting ourselves to the truth which the other declares to us is that of the martyrs. We have a double witness here. First their own encounter with Jesus Christ. They have found the truth about life: 'neither suffering nor violent death could ever lead them to abandon the truth which they have discovered in the encounter with Christ.' Their witness to the truth is personal and instant 'from the moment they speak to us of what we perceive deep down as the truth we have sought for so long, the martyrs provide evidence of a love that has no need of lengthy arguments in order to convince' (32). The truth of Christ is for all people. It is important for the Church to state this clearly: 'it emerges that men and women are on a journey of discovery which is humanly unstoppable – a search for the truth and a search for a person to whom they might entrust themselves. Christian faith comes to meet them, offering the concrete possibility of reaching the goal which they seek. Moving beyond the stage of simple believing, Christian faith immerses human beings in the order of grace, which enables them to share in the mystery of Christ ...'(33).

What we have just seen helps us to appreciate the focus upon the historical character of revelation which is fulfilled in Christ. What lost mankind needs most of all is not a set of arguments or a 'Teach yourself objective critical reasoning in three months'. What we need is someone we can trust to tell us the full truth. We are in search of a witness. Paragraph 22 finished: 'The coming of Christ was the saving event which redeemed reason from its weakness, setting it free from the shackles in which it had imprisoned itself.' This helps us to understand the historical and personal nature of God's revelation in Christ which was so important in *Dei Verbum.* This document from the Second Vatican Council is quoted in paragraph 10: 'God, out of the abundance of his love speaks to men and women as friends, and lives among them so that he may invite and take them into communion with himself.'

iv) In Revelation deeds and words have an inner unity. Deeds manifest and confirm teaching and the realities signified by the words, 'while the words proclaim the deeds and clarify the mystery contained in them.' The fullness of Revelation is in Jesus Christ who took flesh, and so we can see the importance of time and history. This is no abstract doctrine, but events that take place in our world and explained in words uttered in the world's history. Within time 'the whole work of creation and salvation comes to light; and it emerges clearly above all ... with the Incarnation of the Son of God.' (11). 'The Eternal enters time, the Whole lies hidden in the part, God takes on a human face' (12). God's truth entrusted to humanity 'is immersed therefore in time and history.' 'Jesus Christ, the Word made flesh, sent as a 'human being to human beings', 'speaks the words of God.' It is all summed up in the words 'To see Jesus is to see the Father' (11).

Christian truth is often presented as obscure and hard to understand. Here we find the opposite stated. It is not faith that is hard to understand. It is life that is hard to understand. 'God comes to us in the things we know best and can verify most easily, the things of our everyday life, apart from which we cannot understand ourselves.' The Constitution *Gaudium et Spes* states it for us: 'Only in the mystery of the incarnate Word does the mystery of man take on light.' Seen in any other terms the mystery of personal existence remains an insoluble riddle. Where might human beings seek the answer to dramatic question such as pain, the suffering of the innocent and death, if not in the light streaming from the mystery of Christ's Passion, Death and Resurrection?' (12). The positive note is not far away when later the same paragraph is quoted. This time we read that 'Adam, the first man, was a type of him who was to come, Christ the Lord. Christ, the new Adam, in the very revelation of the mystery of the Father and of his love, fully reveals man to himself and brings to light his most high calling.'

The theology of the act of faith in *Faith and Reason* treats not only the freedom of faith but also the simplicity of faith. By focusing upon the historical person of Jesus who calls us friends and who speaks to us in words we can understand John Paul II affirms the simplicity of the Gospel message. This may seem at odds with the great mysteries of Christ's life: the Incarnation, his death and resurrection and ascension into heaven. However, the way the Church understands and celebrates these mysteries reveals to us what the Divine Sonship of Christ really means. Only then do the simple words and deeds of Christ take on such great significance. If we ignore how Jesus Christ is understood within the Catholic Tradition the truth of Christ's Divine Sonship disappears from view. This totally alters the way Jesus witnesses to the Father. His simple but profound words revealing the love, mercy and goodness of the Father are drained of their most important point of reference: that he who says these words is the Father's only begotten Son.

This brings us back to similar points made in the *General Directory* concerning the ecclesial nature of the act of faith. We saw the importance of belonging to the tradition of the church. Here we have seen the importance of witness upholding the personal structure of faith. And what is also most important we have seen that the Gospel message understood within the Catholic Tradition is simple and yet profound. It is addressed to all people as the answer to life's problems. We have seen that it is not faith that is hard to understand but it is life that is hard to fathom.

One final small point which helps to complete the picture. The background to Christian conversion is revealed in a short sentence in which the first sin is seen as a rejection of a certain type of knowing or knowledge. Our first parents reject the knowledge that comes from God. This is their undoing. It is the reason why they become blind, unable to see (22). It is the reason they had 'an aversion to the One who is the source and origin of truth.' Here again, we can see why Colombo is able to argue that the act of faith which turns the clock back to the time before sin, is the highest form of reasoning and understanding. Rational understanding has discovered its original shape; to understand through listening to the other who speaks to us.

Reflections on a Proposed View of Catechetical Method

We finish by considering a catechetical method proposed by the Catholic Education Service on behalf of the English and Welsh Hierarchy. This is to be found in the publication entitled *Making Connections.* This document is concerned with religious education in schools but the method of catechising has been in common use in adult education since the period immediately after the Second Vatican Council

There are three stages.

The first stage is the *search.*

Here students are invited to 'name, engage and critically reflect on their present experience of the topic, issue or theme. '

The second stage is *revelation.*

This is the 'presentation and exploration of content in relation to the Church's teaching.'

The third stage is the *response.*

This is the 'interaction between the student's experience and the content which leads to reflection and some form of transformation – learning, change, response. '

We are reflecting upon this method in the light of the Church's intention to uphold the dignity of the act of faith. This is the whole purpose of this study. There are two subjects we need to consider. One is the ecclesial dimension of faith. The second is the centrality of the person of Christ in theology and catechesis. In the first part we shall refer to article 26 of the *Catechism* which *Making Connections* uses to uphold its chosen method. In the second part we shall treat the use of the Emmaus story because it also is used to justify the method.

a) *Making Connections* and the Ecclesial dimension of faith

The ecclesial intention or faith intention behind the method presented above is described under a column entitled *Curriculum Directory.* Understanding the faith is presented in personal and experiential terms. So we find the expressions 'assimilation of the truth of revelation' and 'experience illumined by the light of the Gospel' and formulas of faith such as scripture, creeds and prayers 'which faithfully express the truth of faith and are suited to the capacity of the listeners.' This is a different stress to what would normally have obtained before the Second Vatican Council where the emphasis would more likely to have been on arguments in favour of faith in an unbelieving world.

In the *General Directory for Catechesis* and in *Faith and Reason* we have seen that there is an emphasis on the experience of faith and the personal nature of the act of faith. It would seem that *Making Connections* has the same intention. There does, however, appear to be a problem.

In *Making Connections* the emphasis seems to be on us rather than on God. It begins with us – the searchers, then in the second step it introduces revelation, and thirdly it ends with us, that is with our response. The sheep seem to be in search of the shepherd, rather than the shepherd in search of the lost sheep. Obviously this sounds wrong. However, the authors point out that paragraph 26 of the *Catechism of the Catholic Church* seems to be saying something very similar. The whole paragraph is quoted. It states:

> 'Before expounding the Church's faith as confessed in the Creed, (Part One) celebrated in the liturgy (Part Two) and lived in observance of God's commandments (Part Three) and in prayer (Part Four) we must first ask what 'to believe' means.
>
> Faith is man's response to God who reveals himself and gives himself to man, at the same time bringing man a superabundant light as he searches for the ultimate meaning of his life.

> Thus we shall consider first that search (Chapter One), then the Divine Revelation by which God comes to meet man (Chapter Two), and finally the response of faith (Chapter Three).'

The final statement of the paragraph seems to be the same as the method proposed above. However, it is at this point that we can begin to see where there is a divergence between *Making Connections* and the official Church documents that we have studied. In fact it is the *Catechism* itself which reveals the difference. The *Catechism* describes the search for meaning but does so in the light of Revelation. Revelation reveals the true nature of the search. So the description of the search begins in paragraph 27 with a quotation from *Gaudium et Spes*: 'if man exists it is because God has created him through love, and through love continues to hold him in existence.' This is revelation. This is the Church explaining how Christian faith understands human life.

In the method proposed in *Making Connections* the reflections on human experience are not faith reflections. They do not begin with Revelation. Rather they prepare the way for Revelation. We have seen that attempts to propose some form of reasoning or experience outside of faith or before faith often lead to a false idea of objectivity. Faith is in some sense presented as answerable to some non-faith reasoning or experience. Colombo argued that this is an example of a theological inferiority complex at work. Faith lacks the confidence to present its own truth and to invite the non-believer into the common experience of faith. However, true faith – faith that does not lack confidence – knows it is only answerable to Christ. Faith has its own reasoning and this is based upon fidelity to Christ. Faith does not presuppose experience. Faith forms experience.

It must be acknowledged that *Making Connections* is attempting to bring about faith that is personal and this includes forms of reasoning. It is also striving very hard to ground faith in human experience. On the basis of what we have seen before we would suggest that what is needed here is the ecclesial dimension of faith. Referring to the many references in the *Directory* we saw how the ecclesial dimension of faith makes it easy for us to see faith as a form of reasoning and as forming our experience of life. We have seen similar points in *Faith and Reason*.

Placing oneself artificially outside of faith invites the problems described in the *Directory*. Because faith is answering non-faith or pre-faith reflections on experience the presentation of teaching is selective. It is directed to particular questions. The prospect for presenting a coherent comprehensive view of Christian teaching is not good. It also invites an artificial and critically sceptical attitude to faith, particularly authority. It encourages the believer and the half-believer to stand outside of faith, rather than sharing the faith, confessing the faith and living out of the Tradition of faith.

The *Directory* made it very clear that catechists who had problems with the visible teaching authority of the Church have posed a serious problem to the integrity of faith. They easily convey the idea that the more sceptical a person is and the more criticisms one makes the more objective one is. This confirms the theological inferiority complex and regards it as a normal part of faith in the modern era. The method that begins outside of faith lends itself to this stance. Beginning within the Church – which after all, is where we already are – rebuffs all the false assumptions that have caused problems within modern catechetics.

b) *The centrality of the historical person of Christ*

Making Connections partly bases its catechetical method on the passage in St Luke 24:13-35 that tells of the two disciples on their way to Emmaus. The story begins with two disciples who know that their Lord has died. It seems to them that revelation has come to an end. These two disciples are suffering a massive crisis of faith. Theirs is a unique experience. It is not some pre-Christ or pre-Revelation experience. It is a Christ centred experience. Their experience is of Christ who has died.

The experience of the Church is that of Christ who has died and risen. It is because we celebrate the death, resurrection and ascension of Christ and declare our knowledge of him as God's eternal Son that we can always begin our catechesis with the simple words and actions of Christ. These tell us about God. God forgives, God declares everyone to be brothers and sisters, and God says we are worth more than hundreds of sparrows. The words of Christ drive out fear of sin, fear of life's purposelessness, fear for our own value. Sometimes, it may be helpful to start with a non-religious story or reflection. But it is hardly a law. And it should never be made a necessity.

Conclusion

We have analysed the obligations of the Church towards catechumens. In the course of this study the scope has widened to include the catechetical needs of all the members of the Church. We have seen the desire of the Church to uphold the dignity and integrity of the act of faith of every Christian. We have appreciated the problems within catechetics since the

Second Vatican Council and the importance of emphasising the ecclesial structure of the act of faith. We have noted how important insights of the Council concerning faith and Revelation have become more and more important in recent documents of the Church, particularly the *General Directory of Catechesis* and *Faith and Reason.* Finally, we have applied some of these points to one particular catechetical method and suggested how it needs to be modified.

Notes

1. Much of this section is based on the important book on theological reasoning by Giusseppe Colombo. *La Ragione Teologica* (Milan, Edizioni Glossa, 1995).
2. The main outline of the argument is presented succinctly in the first chapter pp. 3-14.

Bibliography

Aubert, R., *Le Problème de l'acte de foi,* Louvain, Publications Universitaires de Louvain, 1969.

Colombo, G (Ed), *L'Evidenza e la Fede,* Milan, 1988.

Colombo, G, *La Ragione Teologica,* Milan, Edizioni Glossa, 1995.

De Lubac, H., *Catholicism,* London, Burns Oates, 1950.

De Lubac, H., *Christian Faith,* London, Geoffrey Chapman, 1986.

Grossi, V / Di Berardino, A, *La Chiesa antica: ecclesiologia e istituzioni.* Rome, Ediziono Borla, 1984.

Newman, J.H. *An Essay in Aid of a Grammar of Assent,* ed. by I.T. Kerr, Oxford, Clarendon Press, 1985.

CATECHESIS: WHO IS RESPONSIBLE?

DANIEL J. MULLINS, BISHOP OF MENEVIA

At the heart of the teaching of the Second Vatican Council is the Dogmatic Constitution on the Church – *Lumen Gentium* (LG). In careful and measured tones, it sets out the purpose and intention of the Council Fathers. 'Since the Church, in Christ, is in the nature of sacrament – a sign and instrument, that is, of communion with God and of unity among all men – she here proposes, for the benefit of the faithful and of the whole world, to set forth as clearly as possible, and in the tradition laid down by earlier Councils, her own nature and universal mission' (LG 1). The opening section of *Lumen Gentium* quickly but clearly recalls that in the plan of the Eternal Father the Church was prepared in the history of the people of Israel. Finally He sent His Son. 'The Mystery of the holy Church is already brought to light in the way it was founded. For the Lord Jesus inaugurated his Church by preaching the Good News, that is the coming of the kingdom of God. (*ibid.* 5)

The second chapter deals with the Church as the People of God. All of this repays careful and prayerful reading. This people enters into human history. It knows no bounds of race or time but is constantly strengthened by the grace of God. Born to new life in Christ, this people has the mission and responsibility of spreading the Faith by word and deed, by being true witnesses to Christ. The commission of the Lord to go and make disciples of every nation is shared by all and 'each disciple of Christ has the obligation of spreading the faith to the best of his ability' (LG 17).

The organisation of this People of God comes in its essentials from Christ himself. 'Christ the Lord set up in his Church a variety of offices which aim at the good of the whole body' (LG 18). This organisation of the Church is to enable it to carry out its mission in the world. It is the Body of Christ witnessing to His continuing presence in the world. The central office instituted by Christ is the apostolic one. From among his disciples he chose the twelve. Those he entrusted with their mission even as He was sent by the Father. The apostolic office would continue in the Church until the end of time. One of the twelve he entrusted with the specific role of confirming his brethren. This was not just an arrangement to guide the beginnings of the Church. The Petrine office would continue in the Church. Others chosen to the office of bishop and to be shepherds in Christ's Church would remain one and undivided by their continuing communion with Peter. The College of Bishops would be for all time the public sign and proclamation of the unity of God's people.

'The bishops, in as much as they are the successors of the apostles, receive from the Lord ... the mission of teaching all people and of preaching the Gospel to every creature' (LG 24). For a bishop to fulfil his office faithfully and effectively, he must be and be seen to be in union with the successor of Peter. The office of bishop is one of service. He is to make present to his people the Good Shepherd who lays down his life for his sheep.

'Among the more important duties of bishops, that of preaching has pride of place' (LG 25). St Paul in one of his earlier letters told the Corinthians that Christ did not send him to baptise but to proclaim the Gospel (cf. 1 Cor 1:17). The message of the Cross, of Christ crucified and risen again, is what is entrusted to the Bishop. He proclaims this message but not in lofty words or in terms of human philosophy. The preaching of the bishop does have its effect from the office of apostle entrusted to him. But in the bishop especially, what St Benedict required of abbots is all important. He is to display 'all goodness and holiness by deeds and by words, but by deeds rather than words' (Rule, Chap. 2). Especially is it true of the bishop that the witness of his life is the primary testimony to his people.

In the Decree *Christus Dominus* (CD), the Council returned to the office and role of bishops. First, it places their pastoral office in its relationship to the Universal Church. Because all belong to the Episcopal College, bishops have always to keep in mind the unity which binds them. This has far-reaching consequences, not least in the way in which he carries out his responsibilities as teacher and sanctifier of his own diocesan flock. For 'a diocese is a section of the People of God entrusted to a bishop to be guided by him with the assistance of his clergy so that, loyal to its pastor and formed by him into one community in the Holy Spirit through the Gospel and the Eucharist, it constitutes one particular church in which the one, holy, Catholic and apostolic Church of Christ is truly present and active' (CD 11). The Council never forgets the dependence of the bishop on his clergy. It is through them that he has his most effective contact with the people of the diocese. Each Mass celebrates the unity between priest and bishop which is at the heart of Catholic life and faith. It is the bishop's apostolic office to be a witness of Christ to all the people. He must be that especially to the priests. The bishop's principal duty is to proclaim the Gospel of Christ. It must then be a real concern of the bishop that the priests constantly develop in their configuration to Christ so that both the bishop and the priests propound the whole mystery of Christ. The bishop and priests together must find ways of making a reality of the understanding of the Church that 'catechesis is that particular form of the ministry of the Word which matures initial conversion to make it into a living, explicit and fruitful confession of faith' (GDC 82).

The relationship of a bishop to his priests follows from the Church's understanding of the apostolic office in the Church. It is Catholic dogma that the College of Bishops, in union with Peter and never without him, is the successor of the Apostles. The individual bishop is not the successor of an individual one of Twelve. He is a legitimate successor precisely because he belongs to the Church's universal episcopate, which in accordance with the will of Christ, carries on in His Church the office and mission of the Apostolic College. The teaching of the Vatican Council on the Episcopal College is important too for the full understanding of the role and function of the diocesan presbyterate and for the interdependence of the bishop and his presbyterium.

By the end of apostolic times, there existed in the Church a monarchical, episcopal structure, as testified by St Ignatius of Antioch.

> Equally it is for the rest of you to hold the Deacons in as great as respect as Jesus Christ; just as you should also look on the bishop as a type of the Father and the clergy as the Apostolic Circle forming His Council; for without these three orders no church has any right to the name.[1]

The New Testament and the early Church take little account of individual priests. To say this is not to belittle the priesthood of a diocese. Rather does it emphasise the indispensible office and contribution of the presbyterium to the work and mission of the diocese. What is evident is that the bishop gathers around himself a college or presbyterium that shares in his apostolic ministry. A diocese is not simply an administrative unit but a true spiritual entity. The bishop ordains priests to be his support and his trusted advisors. Through them, he is present in every part of the territory of his diocese.

At this time when we are challenged by a new paganism, the close unity of bishop and priests is of vital importance. If we are to teach the Faith accurately and fully, if the Catholic people are to have the inspiration of a clear model of unity, the sacramental and constitutional links between the bishop and priests of the diocese need to be real and need to find expression in practical ways. Within the memory of many of us, there was a clear and readily recognisable Catholic identity – what we would now describe as a Catholic subculture. We are now much more assimilated into the main and predominant attitudes, practices and outlook of the society around us. For our young people especially, this presents a challenge. It means that they now have to struggle to find a spiritual identity that is distinctive and defining. For the younger generation of Catholics everywhere, probably for all of us, we need to redefine the Catholicism that can survive in a secular world, that can provide the doctrinal and social values that will stand out clearly against the corrosive and all-pervading influences of contemporary individualism.

Part Five of the *General Directory for Catechesis* deals with Catechesis in the Particular Church. It is well to note the terminology. The term *particular Church* is used throughout to mean the diocese. When it speaks of the *local Church*, the *General Directory* 'refers to a group of particular Churches delineated in terms of Region or Nation or group of Nations united by special links.'[2] The handing on of the Faith is essentially an act of the Church. At all times, the Community of Disciples does as Mary did: it treasures all that the Lord said and did and ponders them in her heart. The Gospel Message of Redemption has been preserved and handed on from generation to generation within this community. The Church which is our Mother, nourishes all her children with the Word, ever conscious that the Word is Jesus Christ. This holy Church lives 'incarnated in a definite socio-cultural sphere.'[3] In our own time and place, the whole of our society and its values are impregnated by an individualism which leads people away from Faith and invites us to live as if there is no God or, at best, as if He does not matter. The particular and local churches need to be very conscious of the environment in which we live and in which we proclaim the Gospel. The call of the *General Catechetical Directory* of 1971 that local and national directories be prepared remains important and timely. At very least, we need to be aware of the influences and cultural presuppositions which make it difficult for this generation to hear the Gospel message and to embrace it.

Older generations of Catholics in England and in Wales grew up in parishes that had many organisations and regular social encounters which engendered a sense of identity. We may have at times defined ourselves by the things that made us different from others. Yet underlying this was a genuinely positive awareness of a credal profession and of spiritual values which gave significance and a direction to our lives. When the majority of people spent their adult lives in the district and community in which they grew up, there were supports to Faith and there were popular public devotions that linked both families and generations. That this was no guarantee of life-long fidelity among Catholics is illustrated by the results of the house-to-house census that Cardinal Vaughan asked for in 1894 and which revealed what he called 'an alarming defection'.[4] Catholic families and parishes have never been immune from the pressures that make religious practice and Catholic adherence a constant struggle.

The Vatican Council taught us all to think of, to speak about community. It needs to become reality. The practice of the Church so graphically described by St Justin,[5] the 'assembly of all who live in towns or in the country' to celebrate Mass, needs to become very consciously the gathering of the whole community. One of the most serious obstacles to effective catechesis in the particular church in every diocese is the casualness with which we now treat Sunday Mass. It is not surprising that it becomes irrelevant and 'boring' to young people when the example of parents and adults can be one of careless indifference. For the diocesan bishop, his unity with the presbyterium and through the priests with the people is a first step in the renewal of Faith for which the Vatican Council called.

'In the Diocese catechesis is a unique service performed jointly by priests, deacons, religious and laity, in communion with the Bishop. The entire Christian community should feel responsibility for this service'.[6] The differing roles of these are complementary and each is necessary. At his episcopal ordination, the bishop-elect is reminded that he must strive to serve rather than to rule. That service consists especially in proclaiming the Gospel of Christ, whether it be welcome or unwelcome. He is to correct error with unfailing patience and by diligent teaching. He is to pray and to offer sacrifice for the people so that they may become Christ's holy people. He is asked by the principal consecrator if he is 'resolved to maintain the deposit of faith, entire and incorrupt, as handed down by the apostles and professed by the Church everywhere and at all times'.[7] These onerous responsibilities he carries out with the assistance of all the faithful of the diocese. This requires that he be personally involved in the whole office and practice of catechesis. He must remember himself and remind others that the model of all catechesis is that of the adult community of the diocese. As he goes round the diocese in the fulfilment of his pastoral office, he must teach and instruct, encourage and sustain the Catholic people in the nurturing of their faith, in making that faith the foundation and support of their daily living.

The importance of adult catechesis, and the responsibility of the bishop for it cannot be over-emphasised. Only when it is effective can parents fulfil their role of being the first and best teachers of their children. Only when the parish community lives out the Lord's command to His people, will His words be written on their hearts and placed on the doorposts of their houses and on their gates. (cf. Deut 6:4-9) Only then will the Revelation of God become the subject of conversation in homes and within families. A Catholic gathering and a Catholic home should as readily speak of the mysteries of our faith as we do of football and all the other matters that engage our passionate interest.

The choice of catechetical material must always be a concern of the diocesan bishop and of all the bishops of a local church. It is true that teaching materials are as good as those who use them as instruments of their teaching and that a good teacher can use most materials to good effect. It is important, however, that adequate oversight is exercised to ensure that both the content and the method proposed in published materials meet the needs of our people. Some publications can have a limited aim and it is very necessary that what is offered to people does engage their attention and their continuing interest. In authorising such material for use within the diocese, it will be necessary to recognise the limited objective and to ensure that the wider aim of presenting the faith accurately and fully is not forgotten. The *General Directory* is concerned to ensure that every catechetical programme meets the true needs of the people, that it is integrated into the diocesan pastoral plan and that it is co-ordinated with the programmes of the Episcopal Conference.

That the College of Bishops which is of divine origin is the model for the relationship between the bishop and his priests is the clear inference of the Second Vatican Council; it is too the witness of the Church across the centuries. This means that the priests co-operate with and share in the catechetical responsibility of the bishop. In virtue of our ordination, we 'are signed with a special character and so are configured to Christ the priest' (par. 224). Priests are not just functionaries or office holders in the Church; they are placed as sharers in Christ's ministerial priesthood at the service of the universal priesthood conferred in baptism. This makes the baptised partakers in the holiness of Christ, destined to grow continually in his likeness until he leads us into the fullness of the Kingdom of His Father. This new life conferred in baptism enables us to know the one true God and Jesus Christ whom he has sent. Growth in Christian maturity is growth in the knowledge of God. It is to develop that human and spiritual ability to enter into the mystery of the Holy Trinity which is the end and goal of our existence. It is the distinctive role of the priest as member of the diocesan presbyterate so to relate to the people he serves that he leads them and accompanies them on this journey of discovery which leads to holiness, to becoming holy even as the Father is holy.

In two areas in particular, the contribution of the parish clergy is important. The *Rite of Christian Initiation of Adults* presents us with a vision of a Christian community that so responds to the Gospel that it truly is a witness to Christ in the world. Its public living out of the Christian revelation leads others 'consciously and freely to seek the living God and enter the way of faith and conversion as the Holy Spirit opens their hearts.'[8] The community which helped to bring adults to this threshold of faith, assists and encourages them on their spiritual journey. The whole process of preparing for Baptism takes place within the community of the parish. Especially in the intense preparation during Lent, the catechumens are invited into the homes of parishioners to share in the life and the prayer of the home and of the community. Because the rite emphasises the contribution of the laity, it is easy for priests to neglect their own vital part. The Introduction says quite clearly that 'priests, in addition to their usual ministry for any celebration of Baptism, Confirmation and the Eucharist, have the responsibility of attending to the pastoral and personal care of the catechumens, especially those who seem hesitant and discouraged'.[9] The catechists and other members of the parish in no way replace the essential role of the priest in teaching and guiding these prospective new members.

Catechists have become an important feature of parish life, in sacramental preparation and in the instruction of the young. The *General*

Directory reminds priests of their task of caring 'for the basic orientation of catechesis and its planning,' of their responsibility for promoting and discerning vocations 'to the service of catechesis and, as catechist of catechists, attend to their formation by giving the greatest attention to this duty.' He is further told 'to integrate catechetical activity into his programme of community evangelisation; and to foster the link between catechesis, sacraments and liturgy'.[10] The emphasis is clear and strong. The priest needs to be very closely involved in the ministry of the catechist. It would be only too easy to step back and leave the whole practical work to the catechists. This must not happen.

The second area that must engage the attention, the time and the energy of the priest is the parish school. It is a commonplace to state that home, school and parish form a vital partnership in the education and in the Catholic formation of children. To make this the reality is a continuing challenge. Though the climate of the times requires a special delicacy and circumspection in the relationship between the priest and the children, the priest must not stand apart and aloof. To carry through life the memory of the priest as friend, confidant and man of prayer is the cherished inspiration of many devoted Catholics. Our young people today, more than ever, need those Catholic memories as they take their place as the evangelisers of a post-Christian world.

A major challenge to the Church in our time is the disintegration of family life. An obsession with sex has turned human relationships into selfish and self-seeking forms of passing gratification. A direct consequence of this is the establishing of casual or non-committed relationships, a spiralling divorce rate and a growing incidence of one-parent families. The *General Directory* speaks of the witness of parents in the family coming to children with tenderness and parental respect.[11] Thank God that is still the reality for many children. For too many, the truth is quite different. And yet, it remains true that parents are the first educators of their children. For better and for worse, the experience of childhood is always a basic formative factor in the development and maturing of every human being. Cynicism or despair in the face of the new paganism must be avoided. At a time when, for all sorts of reasons, the extended family is more rarely the experience of children, the need for the parish and for the Catholic community to become the support of parents and families becomes more pressing. In a very precise and urgent way, the message of St Paul to the Philippians becomes an appeal to all our parishes. 'If our life in Christ means anything to you, if love can persuade at all, or the Spirit that we have in common, or any tenderness or sympathy, then be united in your convictions and united in your love, with a common purpose and a common mind. … Always consider the other person to be better than yourself, so that nobody thinks of his own interests first but everybody thinks of other people's interests instead.' (Phil 2:1-4) All around us, there are families and especially children who need our care and concern. In an age of affluence, there are children who have everything except the ever-present love of parents. There are parents and especially single parents who are struggling to provide that love and to give to their children what an avaricious world tells them they should have. For them all, the Catholic parish must become the extended family that is always there, that does not complain, that is not found wanting. Within such a community, modelled on Christ who emptied himself for us, children of our time can 'perceive and joyously live the closeness of God and of Jesus ... in such a way that this first Christian experience frequently leaves decisive traces which last throughout life'[12] Such a parish will not displace the parent or parents. Rather will it supply what so often the nuclear family, especially as we know it, cannot possibly provide.

To list all those involved in what the Directory calls 'the service of catechesis' is to return to the notion of community. That this English word is inadequate to convey the theological concept as enshrined in the Council documents and in official Church terminology, is witnessed to by the common use of the terms *communio* and *koinonia.* The Church is indeed a community in the common understanding of the word. It is, however, much more than that. The Church is, like other forms of community, in the world; unlike all others, it is not of the world. Essential to our understanding of the Church is that it is, even in this world, an integral part of the communion of saints. Where this eschatological community exists fully, as in the diocese, it is a true microcosm of the Universal Church. It is formed by Grace and by the redemptive acts of God in Christ. It makes the Redemption present and available by being the visible, sacramental sign of unity, of the unity of all Creation in the Father to whom all things have been reconciled.

As the Shepherd and leader of the flock, the bishop is at the service of *communio.* This concrete, recognisable people, the Church in this place, must truly become a people living in unity. At a time when apparently differing voices are claiming our attention, the bishop must always speak the truth, but not in ways that will unnecessarily alienate. Never was it more important that the bishop be a man so wrapped up in the contemplation of the reality of God that he always presents the Truth in charity. His concern for the flock must embrace all, whatever their difficulties.

The bishop is most publicly the Shepherd of his people when he gathers them in unity around the altar for Mass. The great diocesan occasions such as the Mass of Chrism are of supreme importance. At that Mass especially, all the elements, all the ministries that make up the diocese are assembled to celebrate the sacramental richness which Christ has won for us all.

The Sunday Mass must have the special attention of the bishop. The earliest understanding of the *communio* is the people assembled around the bishop for Sunday Mass. Modern scholarly studies confidently trace this practice of the Church back to apostolic times in Jerusalem itself. St Justin about the year 150 tells his pagan readers that 'on the day called Sunday, there is an assembly in the same place of all who live in cities or in country districts',[13] and he goes on to describe the Mass in terms that we can readily recognise.

The way in which the provision of Sunday Mass is arranged needs to be looked at. As far as possible, the Sunday celebration should bring the whole Catholic people of the parish together. Their unity in Christ becomes visible to the people themselves when, as Paul says they 'assemble as the Church' (cf. 1 Cor 11:18). The Council teaching expressed it all very succinctly; it is through the liturgy and especially the Eucharist that 'the work of our redemption is accomplished, it is through the liturgy especially that the faithful are enabled to express in their lives and manifest to others the mystery of Christ and the real nature of the true Church.'[14] The Second Vatican Council set out 'to imprint an ever-increasing vigour to the Christian life of the faithful.'[15] A renewed catechesis is part of that ever-increasing vigour.

One of the major objectives of the Second Vatican Council was to restore again the unity of Christians, which is according to the will of Christ. Thinking of the witness of so many martyrs of the twentieth century from the differing churches who yet acknowledge Christ as Lord and Saviour, Pope John Paul wrote in the Introduction to his encyclical *Ut Unum Sint*, '...believers in Christ, united in the footsteps of the martyrs, cannot remain divided'.

To work for Christian Unity is the responsibility of all the members of the church. It is a special responsibility of every bishop to ensure that in the formation of the Catholic people, ecumenical awareness becomes a guiding principal for all our Catholic life and prayer. Ecumenism is an integral part of the work of catechesis in every diocese.

In the document of the Bishops' Conference *What are We to Teach*, the bishops state clearly that 'the Catholic Church is totally committed to the unity of Christians, while preserving the integrity of its faith and life.'[16] The Vatican Council signalled to all the world that the struggles and controversies of the Reformation have come to an end. These have left a legacy of division, suspicion and misunderstanding. The pastor of souls must strive unceasingly to overcome these.

The ecumenical journey of all Christians poses real problems. To quote again from the Bishops' document: 'The Catholic Church claims a special and unique fullness for its life and teaching, alone gifted with all the means of salvation and with the full visible unity willed by Christ.'[17] This obliges us to have a genuine respect for and openness to all Christian peoples. That openness is not advanced by any confusion in the teaching handed down across the centuries. It is our right as Catholics to know the fullness of the teaching of Christ. We need to learn to present that teaching with both charity and clarity.

In the encyclical *Ut Unum Sint*, the Pope identifies 'the areas in need of fuller study and a true consensus of faith.'[18] This calls for careful and full study by the theologians. But these areas require special attention in every catechetical programme.

The first area is 'the relationship between Sacred Scripture, as the highest authority in matters of faith, and Sacred Tradition, as indispensable to the interpretation of the Word of God.'[19] Sacred Scripture, the common inheritance of all the followers of Jesus, has in our past been a source of division. It is not the content of Scripture but its use, which has driven us apart. Our catechesis now must turn to the Word of God as the authority in matters of faith. This people formed from every race and nation has received this faith from the apostles and has lived it out as the community of the Church guided by its pastors, the successors of the Apostles. Our catechesis needs to include the historic dimension of the Christian revelation. The Incarnation is a fact of history. The Church of Christ, which, from the time of St Ignatius of Antioch,[20] has called itself Catholic, has often been persecuted. The witness of the martyrs of our own century forces us to look closely at the history of this Church. All our catechesis, which includes that history, must lead to a conversion of heart and to prayer. That prayer will lead, in the words of the Holy Father 'to the necessary purification of past memories.'[21]

The other areas listed by the Pope are a) the Eucharist, as the Sacrament of the Body and Blood of Christ, an offering of praise to the father, the sacrificial memorial and Real Presence of Christ and the sanctifying outpouring of the Holy Spirit. b) Ordination, as a Sacrament, to the threefold ministry of the episcopate, presbyterate, and diaconate. c)

The Magisterium of the Church entrusted to the Pope and the Bishops in communion with him, understood as a responsibility and an authority exercised in the name of Christ for teaching and safeguarding the faith. d) The Virgin Mary, as Mother of God and Icon of the Church, the spiritual Mother who intercedes for Christ's disciples and for all humanity.[22] Rather than ignore or minimise these doctrinal matters which have sometimes been at the heart of the division among Christians, our catechesis must present and explain them and must do so in charity and in fidelity to Christ. True Ecumenism requires a full catechesis of the whole Catholic community.

Notes

1. The *Epistle to the Trallians* 3.
2. GDC, p. 225, note 1.
3. *ibid*, V. 1 p. 225.
4. Robert O'Neil M.H.M. *Cardinal Herbert Vaughan* (London, 1995) p. 427.
5. Roman Breviary, 2nd Reading for Eastertide, Week 3. Sunday.
6. GDC par 219.
7. Roman Pontifical: Ordination of a Bishop.
8. RCIA. Introduction 1.
9. RCIA. Introduction 13.
10. GDC 225.
11. *ibid.*, 226.
12. *ibid.*
13. *The Works now extant of St Justin Martyr* (Oxford, 1801) p. 51.
14. *Sacrosanctum Concilium* 2.
15. *ibid.*, 3.
16. *What Are We to Teach*, p. 16.
17. *ibid.*, p. 16.
18. *Ut Unum Sint*, p. 79.
19. *ibid.*
20. *Letter to the Smyrnaeans*, 8.
21. *Ut Unum Sint*, 2.
22. *ibid.*, 79.

Further Reading

Decree on the Pastoral Office of bishops in the Church, *Christus Dominus*, Second Vatican Council, 1965.

The Letters of St Ignatius of Antioch, in *Early Christian Writings*, Penguin Books, 1987.

Rahner, Karl, *Bishops: Their Status and Function*, London, 1964.

Congregation for the Clergy, *Priesthood: a Greater Love*, English edition (undated)

Thils, Gustave, *The Diocesan Priest*, London–Dublin, 1965.

Congar, Yves, OP, *Priest and Layman*, London, 1967.

Decrees of the Ecumenical Councils, Volumes One and Two, edited by Norman P. Tanner SJ, Georgetown University Press, 1990.

THE VOCATION OF THE CATECHIST

CAROLINE FAREY

Introduction: Heaven Wants to be Heard

Catechists are called to catechise because 'Heaven wants to be heard'.[1] Catechists do not speak because *they* need to be heard; they speak on behalf of Another. It is God who has revealed his own mystery. It is God who has spoken in his Son. It is God who wants people to enter his love and who draws us to himself by the Holy Spirit. Christ tells us, 'My Father is working still and so am I.'[2] It is the *Trinity*, therefore, who is at work communicating throughout the world the good news of salvation in Christ.

It is the Trinity who entrusted this mission to the Church when Christ first gave this work and responsibility to the eleven disciples. In the Gospel accounts of both Matthew and Mark we read of Jesus' words, 'Go into all the world and preach the Gospel'[3] and 'Go therefore and make disciples ... baptising ... teaching them to observe all that I have commanded you and lo, I am with you always, to the close of the age.'[4] It is the *Church*, therefore, in the name of the Trinity, who is at work communicating throughout the world the good news of salvation in Christ.

The vocation of the catechist is ultimately dependent on this, the work, the desire, the undaunted and unfailing plan of the Trinity carried out through the Church. Throughout the Scriptures God calls those with whom he wishes to cooperate in his unstoppable desire for spreading far and deep the salvation that comes with his love. Catechists, then, join the work of the *Trinity* in the *Church* so that all heaven's mercy, blessings and joy may be known and experienced by each and by all, so that heaven may be heard and entered. This vocation of the catechist is both a humble and an awesome one.

What, though, *is* a catechist? The word itself is very significant and carries such appropriate meaning that it has been kept in use for the whole two thousand years of the Church's life. In origin, the word comes from the act of catechesis, that is, from a verb rather than a noun. The word 'catechesis', then, gives us a starting point for looking at the essence of the vocation of the catechist.

The Origins of the Word

The word 'catechesis' comes from a Greek verb 'Κατηχειν' (*catechein*). The Greek verb does not appear at all in the Greek translation of the Old Testament, but it is found in the New Testament especially in the letters of St Paul, who wrote his letters in Greek and uses the word in the ordinary every-day sense of his time. The word '*catechein*' from the word 'to echo' was used where we would usually use the word 'hear' or 'make heard'. It reminds us that catechesis, in the beginning, was the oral transmission, the 'echoing' or 'resounding' of a message, the 'hearing', 'making heard' or 'teaching' of something, a receiving and handing on of what has been told and taught.

The word '*catechein*' is used in the New Testament in several ways in accordance with the usage of the day. For example, in Acts 21:21 and 24 it is reported that the Jewish Christians are worried by reports *'they have been told'* about St Paul. In Romans 2:18 St Paul uses the word '*catechoumenos*' with reference to Jews who are *'instructed in* the Law'. In Acts 18:25 Apollos is mentioned as having been '*instructed* in the way of the Lord.' St Paul insists, too, that the instructor, *catechon*, should be supported materially by the pupil, *catechoumenos*, 'Let him who is taught the word share all good things with him who teaches' (Gal 6:6).

We can see, then, that already, before the end of New Testament times, '*catechesis*' is used as a technical term for the basic instruction of believers in the church community. This is the specific meaning of 'catechesis' as it was retained, since its use in the New Testament, through subsequent generations of the Church until our own time. What continually changed were the audience and the style.

There has been much discussion of the meaning of words used to describe what catechesis *is* and therefore what catechists are called to be and do. As we have seen from the root of the word, 'catechesis' can be described as an echoing, an instructing, a transmitting or handing on and sharing but these words in their turn can be interpreted in different ways, sometimes negatively and sometimes positively. For example, 'transmitting' can be described as a 'passive imparting' of beliefs contrasted with the dynamism of 'sharing' a lived and living faith. On the other hand, 'Sharing' can be described as vague, subjective and limited compared to the 'handing on' of the living faith of the universal Church. In fact, the Church understands all these words in a positive sense and 'does not have a particular method nor any single method.'[5] What is important is the Church's understanding that her life in Christ is for everyone to hear about and enjoy. This can be done in a great variety of ways none of which are exclusive and all of which are 'a sign of life and richness,'[6] provided that the ways are at the service of the Gospel and not in any way contrary to it,[7] and that the people who catechise in her name enable the Church to 'transmit(s) the faith that she herself lives.'[8]

To Announce and Hand On

The titles of recent magisterial documents give us two fundamental words concerning the essential work of catechesis and therefore the essence of the vocation of the catechist. *Evangelii Nuntiandi*, (Evangelisation in the Modern World) uses the word '*nuntiandi*' from the verb 'to announce' while *Catechesi Tradendae*, (Catechesis in our Time) uses the word '*tradendae*' from the verb 'to hand on'.

We know that the first two words of Church documents, taken as the title, are normally chosen deliberately to indicate the key message or content of the whole text. Linked, then, to 'evangelisation' and 'catechesis' are two verbs indicating the need for action – evangelisation is needed that the good news be 'announced'. As St Paul says, 'faith comes from what is heard and what is heard comes from the preaching of Christ.'[9] Catechesis is needed that the faith of the Church be 'handed on'. As St Paul says, 'I delivered to you what I also received'.[10] These are essential elements of the mission of the Church and hence of the vocation of the catechist.

An Ecclesial Vocation

It is all too easy, in today's climate, to think that the primary characteristics of the catechist need to be personal qualities such as sincerity, honesty and integrity. All of these are, of course, important. However, the importance of considering the personal qualities of the catechist must not allow us to forget something even more fundamental: the rootedness of the vocation of the catechist in the Church.

In fact, the word '*vocation*' is used only twice[11] in reference to the *person* of the catechist, in the whole text of the *General Directory for Catechesis.* It is used twice more in reference to the *action* of catechesis, in the two phrases, '*vocations* for catechesis'[12] and, 'the vocation of the laity to catechesis'.[13] In her documents the Church places the emphasis mainly, not on the person of the catechist, but on the task of catechesis. Christ founded his Church that 'all people be saved and come to the knowledge of the truth.'[14] Catechesis is for this. Along with initial proclamation of the Gospel, and as a stage in the broader process of evangelisation as a whole, catechesis is included in the startling statement that 'the Church exists to evangelise.'[15]

We can see why catechesis is described in the *General Directory for Catechesis* as 'an essentially ecclesial act.'[16] As part of the very nature of the Church, catechesis is the responsibility of the entire Christian community,[17] and not of certain individuals only, called 'catechists'. It is not only catechists who catechise. It is primarily the responsibility of the bishops, the successors of those who first heard the words of Christ to go, preach, baptise and teach. The bishops share this responsibility with their priests[18] since, by the sacrament of Holy Orders priests become 'educators of the faith.'[19] Parents, too, by the sacrament of marriage, become the primary educators of their children in the faith.[20] Those who have consecrated their lives to God, by the act of their consecration, become 'living sign(s) of the reality of the kingdom,'[21] witnessing and teaching either by word or by example. For all lay people too, the *General Directory for Catechesis* points out that 'the vocation of the laity to catechesis springs from the sacrament of Baptism.'[22] All vocations in the Church, then, include a fundamental commitment to catechesis.

One could say that the phrase 'vocation to catechesis' is more appropriate than the 'vocation of the catechist' since it is *catechesis* which is so fundamental to the Church and since catechists tend to come and go, often having a role for a time, or in their spare time. The word 'vocation' seems to be used in a vaguer and rather more fluid sense than the vocations mentioned above which stem either from a sacrament or from formal consecration. What, then, is the specific vocation of the catechist? The *General Directory for Catechesis* explains, 'Some lay people feel called interiorly by God to assume the service of catechist. The Church awakens and discerns this divine vocation and confers the mission to catechise.'[23]

There are several important issues here. Firstly, the vocation of the catechist relates to a person who is given a precise share in the canonical mission to teach. This mandate comes from the bishop most typically through the parish priest. Secondly, it is the Church that *awakens* the vocation in someone, even if the awakening first occurs during private prayer. It is the Church that *discerns* whether this is a real call for the Church or not and it is the Church, not the individual, who *confers* the mission. The notion of a catechist working outside, or against, the Church is a contradiction in terms. Thirdly, a catechist with such a vocation shares in one particular way in the great call of God to his whole Church, that is, in the 'vocation to catechesis', to *announce* his good news and *hand on* the living faith that saves.

A Personal Vocation

All calls from God are ecclesial and at the same time they are deeply personal. Catechesis is an ecclesial and personal responsibility, an ecclesial and personal privilege and joy. It is easy to misunderstand the sense in which the vocation of catechist is a personal one. We sometimes think that we are only being truly ourselves when we stand out from the Church and give our own opinions rather than the Church's teaching. This, however, would necessarily oppose the personal to the ecclesial and place the catechist at odds with the Church which she is called to represent.

When one speaks of the vocation of the catechist as personal the most important point one needs to make is that the good news of God came in personal form, in the person of Christ. The reason why all our teaching is personal is firstly because the 'Word was made flesh.'[24] What we are called to hand on to others is more than just a message, however helpful or profound. We are called to introduce others to a person rather than simply to a body of truths. The truths to be taught and known are truths about a person. So, for example, the Church's doctrine about the sacrament of reconciliation is about the redemption won for us by the Person of Christ on the cross. When we say, therefore, that the vocation of the catechist is personal, we are making a statement first of all about Christ and about the nature of catechesis.

Secondly, we are saying something about the dignity of each human being and therefore of the catechist. God wants his word to become flesh in each person. The whole of each person is important to God. As St John Eudes writes, 'he longs for you to use all that is in you, as if it were his own, for the service and the glory of the Father.'[25] The call to participate in catechesis is personal, then, in that it confers upon us a personal dignity which includes all our own characteristics and experiences that together form us uniquely.

Thirdly, such a dignity confers personal responsibilities and the primary responsibility is to receive. It is to seek and receive in prayer, the sacraments, Scripture and the teaching of the Church the guidance of the Holy Spirit so that *with* the Holy Spirit we might draw others into that same seeking and receiving. Catechesis needs our living reception of, and reflection upon, revelation, in order to love and understand the Lord first. The vocation of the catechist is personal, then, in that it includes a personal learning and growing in maturity in the faith. The learning must also be in considering and evaluating the many different ways and means of passing on the faith in the light of the tasks particular to the person being catechised and the ways and needs of the local Church.

Christo-centric Vocation

We have seen that doctrine is personal and that the fullness of faith is, ultimately, Someone, Jesus Christ. It is life, His life; it is to live 'in Christ'. It is what has been given gratuitously by a loving, all-powerful, faithful, forgiving, unwavering Father: he has given us his only Son, who is all grace and goodness.

Because the whole faith is unified in a person, it is described as organic, belonging to a single living being, Jesus Christ. This unity in Christ is what enables the faith to be what the *Catechism of the Catholic Church* calls a 'melodious symphony of truth'. Its harmony and unity is rooted in a person, the second Person of the Trinity. The unity of all aspects of the Catholic faith makes a dynamic whole; an ever-deepening enrichment in the mystery of Christ. The faith is holistic because it is faith in and about a whole Person, Christ, and it both affects and involves *our* whole person, our whole life and the people whom we meet.

Pope John Paul II states, 'at the heart of Catechesis we find, in essence, a Person', and he adds that catechesis aims at putting 'people ... in communion ... with Jesus Christ.'[26] Christ, therefore, is the end or goal of all catechesis. Christ is also the source of our catechesis. Pope John Paul II states that, 'everything else is taught with reference to him' and says that, 'every catechist should be able to apply to himself the mysterious words of Jesus: 'my teaching is not mine but his who sent me.'[27] Just as Christ spoke all that he heard from his Father, so the catechist speaks every word that is given to him or her by Christ.

St John says that 'the Holy Spirit will not speak on his own'[29] but seeks only to make Christ known. The *Catechism of the Catholic Church* describes this as a 'divine self-effacement.'[30] The vocation of the catechist is a call to be humble following St John the Baptist who said, 'He must increase and I must decrease.'[31]

A Catholic Vocation

The vocation of the Catechist is catholic in that it is rooted in the Universal Church. The word 'Catholic'[32] comes from two Greek words meaning 'according to the whole'. The Church is 'according to the whole', Catholic, in two ways: *firstly*, she has been entrusted with *the whole of Christ* who brings the fullness of the means of salvation. The faith of the Church is an organic and coherent whole. Without this sense of the unity of wholeness our faith can seem like an ever-expanding bag of bits and pieces of knowledge all jostling around in an unconnected way. *Secondly*, the Church is Catholic in her mission: she is to bring the whole of Christ's message and means of salvation to *the whole world*.

When we speak of the whole world we include here both time and space: the Church stretches across all cultures and is present to all times. The faith that we teach is both immersed in time and history and also transcends each particular time and place.[33] In most subject areas the knowledge of a hundred years ago has been superseded by later discoveries. Knowledge of the faith is not like this. It is both preserved and built up in a most unique way, through time and drawing from different cultures. It is built up, deepened and broadened but, at the same time, eternal truth does not contradict itself and cannot be superseded. Tradition is not the same as history. Eternal truth is manifested *in* particular times and cultures but *for* all times and cultures. It is eternally living. It is unchanging and universal but manifested in a particular time, place and circumstance. Hence, there is a respect, even reverence, shown at the beginning of many documents towards previous ecclesial documents and gatherings. In them are recognised the marks of the promised guidance of the Holy Spirit. No document stands alone or contains an idea completely 'out of the blue'; it will always have foundations in union with the body of truth built upon the teaching of the apostles and deepened over the centuries. This is the manner in which the Church proceeds and it is important that a catechist grasps the significance of the Church's understanding of a living Tradition as fundamental to her catholicity.

The catholicity of the vocation of the catechist also implies the need for many different types of catechist.[34] The Church urges her members to become involved in catechesis in all the areas and to all the peoples that make up the body of Christ. No human being is beyond the reach of the Church's mission.

A Diocesan Vocation

'Catechesis is a basic evangelising activity of every particular Church, that is, of the diocese. 'By means of it the Diocese gives to all its members … a formative process which permits knowledge, celebration, living and proclamation within a particular cultural horizon.'[35] The whole Christian message is relevant for each local Church and situation, as Christ is relevant. To be rooted in the particular Church, or the diocese, is not contrary to the Church's catholicity or universal dimension. The Gospel news is for all. To be truly 'for all' means for each and every particular person and place.

Each place and culture and each person will have a unique way of living, experiencing and expressing the Gospel that is not found elsewhere. It is not despite these particularities that some 'pure' message is passed on, on the contrary, the message is a living Person passed on from person to person in, through and with all the personal characteristics of the catechist. Personal history is taken up by the Person of Christ in the transmission of his life, mercy and redemption. The community of the particular Church is unique and has something to offer to the universal Church and the world that no one else can offer. In fact, the universal Church is impoverished without the rich diversity of the particular churches.

The Universal Church is only real in the particular; that is, in the particular person and particular, local place and community. There needs to be a synthesis made between the universal faith of the Church and the particular culture of a place and the people who live there. A catechist, then, needs to be part of the particular place in which he or she works and lives, to understand its goodness on the one hand and those elements which are not compatible with a life of faith on the other. Lay catechists are particularly important in this regard because of their immersion in the ordinary demands of lay life and culture.

A Vocation of Faith

The word 'faith' has two meanings: *what* we believe and the personal gift of faith *by which* we believe. When we speak about *our* faith, this is our act of faith. We also speak of *the* faith, this is what we have faith *in*, that is, the faith of the Church. Each person's act of personal faith is unique to them and can be judged only by God, but the faith of the Church is for all. It is objective. It is the deposit of faith which the Church has gathered and guarded, as a shepherd gathers and guards his sheep. The deposit of faith is the saving Word of God that is to be handed on so that the gathering continues.

It is vital to be clear from the outset that the vocation of the catechist is twofold in faith: the call is twofold because it requires the building up of personal faith, the power *by which we believe*, by which we live 'in Christ' through prayer and Christian life. It also requires formation in the full faith of the Church in order to pass on *the* faith that has been handed down to us as trustworthy *to believe*. The vocation is twofold, then, firstly, in what one is called to *be*, that is to grow in one's own faith, one's own unity with the Lord who gathers his people into one in his Church, and secondly in what one is called to *do*, that is to make known the faith of the Church, the saving life of Christ.

A Pedagogical Vocation

The vocation of the catechist is fundamentally pedagogical, as we have seen in the very origin of the word. The catechist is called, however, to a unique form of pedagogy because what is taught is not just knowledge but a person, a divine person with a divine purpose, the purpose of uniting the listener to himself in his people, in his Church. No human pedagogical system can do this. What the catechist needs to learn is the pedagogy of God himself. How, then, does God teach? We can see God's way of teaching, of revealing himself, in the Scriptures. In fact God uses all that is human. All that is good in human pedagogical methods can be drawn into his way but no human system is sufficient in itself.

For example, some modern religious educationalists have attempted to deduce from the link of 'catechise' with 'echo' that in some way or other catechesis should try to establish an echo between the *experience* of the pupil being taught and the *message* being taught by the catechist. Many catechetical works are built around this idea of presenting revealed truths in such a way that they 'echo experience', such as, comparing the Eucharist to a celebratory meal, comparing the Church to a human institution or comparing the rituals and feasts of Christianity to those of other religions. The parables may seem to be examples of this, too.

It is true that the parables are often stories taken from life but they are different in that they also reveal God's ways as totally 'other', as up-side-down to ours, many of them are precisely of things unthinkable and unheard of. One can think of the parable of the prodigal son, the Good Samaritan or the workers in the vineyard. These are parables which shocked listeners into a quite different way of seeing and acting and therefore into *new* experience. 'Pedagogical instructions adequate for catechesis are those which permit the communication of the whole word of God in the concrete existence of people.'[36]

The *General Directory for Catechesis* speaks of the traits of God's own pedagogy, traits that need to be present in the catechist's own work. For example, God treats all as sons,[37] so catechists are to understand themselves as part of God's family and those they speak to as equally beloved members of the same family, not just a group of individuals. The attitude of the catechist is to be that of Christ who received people 'as persons loved and sought out by God.'[38] God's discipline and revelation is for the purpose of salvation, so catechists need to keep always in mind that the purpose of catechesis is the person's salvation, not just a good experience or a set of facts. God acts always as a 'merciful Father',[39] so mercy is to be a fundamental attitude in the catechist. God liberates from evil and attracts by love[40] so the catechist is to teach lovingly of what is evil and disordered and of God's means of liberation. God 'transforms events in the life of his people into lessons of wisdom,'[41] so catechists, too, can use events to draw attention to God's wisdom. God adapts himself to his people, 'adapting what he has to say by solicitous providence for our earthly condition.'[42] The attitude of keeping a kindly concern over the human needs, weaknesses and strengths of those being catechised, and adapting catechesis accordingly is an attitude that all catechists need to pray for and grow into since such an attitude of compassion and understanding is a most powerful witness to the love of God for his children.

A Marian Vocation

Mary, the mother of the Lord, sums up all the characteristics of the vocation of the catechist mentioned above. Thus, the vocation of the catechist is Marian because it is ecclesial, since Mary is Mother of the Church; 'the Church imitates the mother of the Lord in treasuring the Gospel in her heart.'[43] The catechist, as a member of the Church, is also to imitate Mary in treasuring the Gospel. At the birth of the Church, when the apostles were gathered in the upper room on Pentecost morning, she was there praying among them, where 'she presided in prayer at the beginning of evangelisation under the guidance of the Holy Spirit.'[44]

The vocation is Marian also because of its Christocentricity, since Mary is the first human being to have her whole being centred on the Christchild, in her womb and throughout her whole life. For a personal vocation in a particular place Mary, too, is the catechist's model. She was brought up in a small town in a small corner of the world, in a very particular culture and community and here she brought up the

Christchild. Here, Mary, in and through her daily actions, decisions, yearnings and strivings, in and through all the various relationships that she formed, did all that God asked of her for the sake of his plan of salvation for the whole world. It is not surprising that devotion to Mary takes on multiple popular forms in the particular churches around the world. Mary is understood as 'ours' and as local, wherever she is called 'Our Lady'.

As the vocation is pedagogical it is also Marian since Mary was the first teacher for the Word made flesh. 'As he sat on her lap and later as he listened to her throughout the hidden years at Nazareth, this Son ... was formed by her in human knowledge … and in adoration of the Father.'[45] Mary has been called, appropriately, 'a living catechism.'[46]

Finally, the vocation of the catechist is to be a channel of God's grace, of divine otherness, of new experience, of a different way of living – that of being in Christ. Catechists are to be living places where someone might hear and find God, incarnate in his Church. Mary, full of grace, is all these things. She is therefore called 'the mother and model of catechists.'[47] 'Through the intercession of the Virgin of Pentecost there is born in the Church a new power, generating sons and daughters in the faith and educating them toward the fullness of Christ.'[48]

Notes

1. I have used here the title of a recent book on Our Lady by a fellow contributor to this symposium, Dr Dudley Plunkett, *Heaven wants to be heard* (Gracewing, 1998).
2. Jn 5:17.
3. Mk 16:15.
4. Mt 28:19-20.
5. GDC 148.
6. GDC 148.
7. GDC 148.
8. GDC 78.
9. Rom 10:17.
10. 1 Cor 15:3.
11. GDC 231 and 239.
12. GDC 233.
13. GDC 231.
14. 1 Tim 2:4; cf. GDC 42 and the opening of the prologue of the *Catechism of the Catholic Church.*
15. GDC 46.
16. GDC 78.

17. GDC 220.
18. Canons 773-774.
19. GDC 224.
20. GDC 233.
21. GDC 228.
22. GDC 231.
23. GDC 231.
24. Jn 1:14.
25. Quoted in CCC 1698.
26. CT5, CCC 426.
27. CT6, CCC 427.
28. cf. CCC 722, 737-8, 1093-1098.
29. Jn 16:13.
30. CCC 687.
31. Jn 3:30.
32. cf. CCC 830.
33. cf. *Fides et Ratio*, 11.
34. GDC 232.
35. GDC 218.
36. GDC 146.
37. GDC 139.
38. GDC 140.
39. GDC 139.
40. cf. GDC 139.
41. GDC 146.
42. GDC 146.
43. GDC 78.
44. EN 82.
45. CT 73.
46. CT 73.
47. CT 73.
48. GDC 291.

Bibliography

Ad gentes divinitus (1965).
General Catechetical Directory (1971).
Evangelii nuntiandi (1975).
Catechesi tradendae (1979).
Catechism of the Catholic Church (1994).
General Directory for Catechesis (1997).
Fides et ratio (1998).

THE CATECHETICAL PROCESS IN THE LIGHT OF PRAYER FORMATION IN PRIMARY AND SECONDARY SCHOOLS

SR KATHLEEN M. MURPHY RSM

Introduction

This was my own experience of prayer, of the Church and the school in the community in which I grew up, the family was the centre in which children had their first experience of God and of prayer. It was there that they learned what it was to have a 'personal encounter with Jesus Christ, making of oneself a disciple'.[1] This personal encounter was made possible for them through the faith commitment of their parents who had them baptised and who prayed with them from the earliest days of their lives. Initially these prayers were spontaneous.

Gradually and as very young children developed language skills, some of the formal prayers of the Church were introduced and the little ones learned them by rote. Children brought to faith in this way within the 'domestic church'[2] did not always have an understanding of the words they were using, but they knew that what they were doing was good and they did it freely and lovingly. Awe and reverence were central motivators. Parents did this because of their own belief in God and in his love for them. 'We ourselves have known and put our faith in God's love towards ourselves. God is love and anyone who lives in love lives in God and God lives in him' (1 Jn 4:16). This knowledge of a loving Father enthused parents to make him and his Son known to their children. In faith they acknowledged in prayer that the Father had sent his Son, Jesus into the world to show men and women how to live, love, and work out their salvation.

Initial Catechesis through Prayer

This practice of family prayer gave children their first taste of the faith of the Church and the value system inherent in that faith. The form of faith handed on in this domestic context is best described as 'received faith'. It was transmitted to the children as basic evangelisation. They received it through listening to prayers said by parents with and for them. They helped their parents to enrich their efforts at evangelisation through questions: 'Why do we pray mummy? Who is God? Who made God, mummy? Who made me? Where did I come from? How do you know there is a God? Who is Jesus? Did Jesus have a mummy? When was Jesus born? Where was Jesus born? Why did Jesus come at Christmas? Did Jesus have a job? Where is Jesus now? Was Jesus like daddy, mummy?

Out of such childlike inquiries at one level, and such deeply theological questions at another, children were prepared for and often given their initial catechesis. Their questions led parents to read stories from the Catholic Children's Bible, God's special book, which was always treated with great respect and reverence. The process that was carried out informally but with great love, awe and reverence touched the hearts of the children. It led them to want to get to know more about the Father, Jesus and Mary whose 'singular co-operation with the action of the Holy Spirit', leads the Church to entrust supplications and praise to her.[3] 'The definitive aim of catechesis is to put people not only in touch, but also in communion and intimacy, with Jesus Christ'.[4]

Intimacy was helped by the fact that from an early age children were taken to Mass in 'God's house' on Sundays. There, they learned how to behave in church, the body language of prayer, the importance of quiet, and the use of holy water and candles in prayer. They saw other adults and children in prayer. In their own ways they too, made a commitment to Jesus. Through this their initial catechesis had begun since the process starts with the condition laid down by Jesus himself: 'He who believes and is baptised …' (Mk 16:16). It was always intended that this received faith would, one day, become informed and owned.

Prayer and Catechesis in Catholic Schools

Once children joined school, prayer became a formal ritual. The traditional prayers of the church and parts of the Mass were taught in a partnership between school and home as a preparation for the reception of the Sacraments, and as part of keeping children in touch with the festivals of the liturgical year. In Lent pupils were introduced to the stations of the cross; in Holy week they took part in the Holy Week

Services and parents brought them to Church; the Vigil of Easter and Easter Sunday were big celebrations and part of the ritual was to collect the special Easter Holy Water from the parish church; during the month of October pupils said a special Hail Mary, a decade of the rosary or the whole of the rosary, depending on their age and level of schooling; in November they were introduced to the practice of praying for the dead; during Advent and Christmas the crib became the focus of prayer life; the catechism was the central text for religious education; diocesan clergy had responsibility for ensuring that all pupils were 'examined' on an annual basis, in order to ensure that they were receiving a sure foundation in their faith. In preparation for this examination, which was taken very seriously by teachers, rote learning became the order of the day.

Retreats were planned in secondary schools. These were formal periods of silence for pupils who followed a programme of: Mass, private prayer, reflection and attendance at two to three talks given by a priest, who specialised in retreat giving and who had an empathy with youth. In the course of the day moral issues, the commandments, beatitudes and corporal works of mercy were emphasised and made the focus of prayer. The day closed with Benediction. All of this ensured that pupils' prayer-life was nourished.

God, the Trinity, Mary, the saints and the angels, the sacraments and Mass in particular were the pillars on which prayer and faith were built. Faith, in my experience was seldom analysed, questioned or claimed. Parents, teachers and pupils felt secure with their God whom they were helped to see was present to them and at work in the world through signs and symbols of the sacraments – the cross, that joy-sorrow image; and holy water – new life and immortality; hands – comfort, reconciliation, healing.

Decline

By the beginning of the 1960s Britain was beginning to reconstruct and rebuild itself following the devastation of two World Wars. The people had learned what it was to suffer deeply and they were beginning to experience a new freedom in terms of a developing economy, trade, travel, and developments in science and technology. In short a new renaissance was born. It called for a global vision and it provided new opportunities in terms of education, employment and wealth for those who had the acumen, capacity and skills to become designers of their own destiny through availing of and creating new opportunities. However, with this reawakening came new challenges to family life, values and the Faith of the People of God. The sixties was the decade of 'sexual revolution'. These problems were not confined to Britain alone but were, to some extent, worldwide.

In its wisdom, the Church, responded by calling the Second Vatican Council in an effort to revitalise its mission and to respond positively to Jesus challenge: 'When the Son of Man comes, will he find any faith on earth?' (Lk 18:8), and in response to his command, commission and assurance: 'Go, therefore, make disciples of all the nations; baptise them in the name of the Father, and of the Son and of the Holy Spirit, and teach them to observe all the commands I have given you. And know that I am with you always; yes, to the end of time' (Matt 28:19 and 20).

Rebirth: A New Approach for a New Age

Cognisant of the new social, economic and political situation in the world, and how small it had become in a couple of decades, the Council Fathers stressed the need to 'read the signs of the times'. They initiated programmes for renewal that have continued to develop with varying degrees of success ever since. Special emphasis was placed on evangelisation, catechesis, the family, prayer, spirituality, liturgy, biblical and theological formation, critical awareness, faith development, youth culture, pedagogy and continuous catechetical formation in the Faith of the Church.

A more child-centred approach was called for. In education in Britain, the catechism was abandoned, and replaced with child-friendly workbooks that recognised and facilitated the child-centred approach but which lacked in-depth education in prayer, doctrine and authentic theology. Many of the formal prayers of the church were frequently replaced with spontaneous prayers in school.

As children became adults they felt a need for a prayer formula but did not know one. Even as recently as 1997 it was difficult to get Key Stage Two pupils to learn and know the act of contrition in preparation for First Reconciliation and First Eucharist. At the same time Key Stage Four struggled with having to memorise the Creed[5] and phrases of Scripture which were not only central foundations for a sound prayer and faith-filled life but also essential texts for their GCSE.

Regrettably, the catechesis which was necessary to support this transition was not provided and something precious was lost once awe and reverence were replaced with hands on experience in every area of faith and life. Frequently working mothers were too busy or tired to make time for family prayer in the home. Many felt that the Church, like society in general, was in crisis and they were right. Sisters and priests become disillusioned in their ministry and a trickle of resignations began. Permanent commitment, both inside and outside the family, gradually became an almost forgotten ideal.

Much of what was really being struggled with resulted from globalisation, migration, emigration and immigration that resulted in a need for an authentic inculturation. This was not understood, until the nineties, when it was realised that inculturation did not demand one culture sacrificing its values, pious practices, and rituals to another. But that each should look at how the Word of God who became man in space and time and rooted in a specific culture committed himself to it and gradually transformed it.[6] His was the original inculturation, the model of all catechesis, 'called to bring the power of the Gospel into the very hearts of culture and cultures'.[7]

Inculturation of the faith 'is not simply an external adaptation designed to make the Christian message more attractive or superficially decorative. On the contrary, it means the penetration of the deepest strata of persons and peoples by the Gospel that touches the soul, 'going to the very centre and roots of their cultures'.[8] What Catholics did not understand in the seventies and eighties was that they needed not so much to be all embracing in child-centred education, as to be discerning. They needed to know how to engage in riches which were compatible with the faith, and at the same time to refine and transform, 'modes of thought and life-styles which are contrary to the Kingdom of God'.[9]

The Situation Facing Us Today

In our new and multicultural world we struggle with individualism, materialism and a demand for instant gratification. Values previously transmitted in the security of the family are now struggled with in the classroom in competition with the media, sport, the transient family and the materialism afforded by a new and 'successful economy'. This is exaggerated by an inner feeling in adults and children alike that there is still 'more' to life. *This more is Jesus.* But he is in competition with a force which his disciples are still seeking to master through prayer and study.

In some homes and in many schools today, a new birth is taking place catechesis in prayer has been revitalised. However, this still relates to only a minority of homes. Most recent experience in Key Stage One classrooms has shown that no child can either make the sign of the cross or say any formal prayer before starting formal education. The school, nowadays, is facing the awesome task of being both the 'domestic' and 'parish church' for the majority of pupils.

It is becoming the centre, in which pupils receive their basic evangelisation, master religious language and learn to celebrate Reconciliation and Eucharist. It is the place where they are prayed with, shown pictures to help them image Jesus and have stories from the Scriptures told to them in exciting and creative ways in an effort to win their attention and to compete with the dominant culture.

How is the Church Responding?

Many experienced teachers and their younger colleagues are thirsting for catechetical support in their own prayer lives, faith development, and authentic teaching. They are part of a large group of 'Christians, often highly educated, whose religious formation amounts solely to that which they received in childhood. These also need to re-examine and develop their faith.'[10] As if in response to this need, in 1988 The Vatican Congregation for Catholic Education stated:

> We need to look to the future and promote the establishment of formation centres for these teachers; ecclesiastical universities and faculties should do what they can to develop appropriate programmes so that the teachers of tomorrow will be able to carry out their task with the competence and efficacy that is expected of them.[11]

Many good ecclesiastical centres such as the Maryvale Institute have been set up in response to this exhortation. Great work is pioneered in them. However, because of political pressure in other areas of the curriculum, many headteachers do not feel able to free the finance or the time for staff to avail of this support.

Are the Bishops Taking These Issues Seriously?

Since the publication of *The Catechism of the Catholic Church* in 1994, the bishops of these islands have come to terms with the challenges of inculturation, migration and secularism. They have made gallant efforts to support catechesis through publications such as: *What Are We to Teach?* (1994), the *Religious Education Curriculum Directory* (1996), and the *General Directory for Catechesis* (1997), *One Bread One Body* (1998). The faith is being revitalised, to bring prayer back to its rightful place on the school timetable and in religious education lessons. They have supported their RE Advisers once again, in inspecting provision for worship, taking some control of evangelisation and catechesis of both teachers and pupils, even if only through sporadic in-service.

The communal trinity is gradually becoming the centre in which pupils receive their induction in prayer. However the leading partner in this trinity is not usually the home but the school. There, pupils are learning to pray and participate actively in sacramental liturgy with the teachers.

They are reawakening the faith of their parents by inviting them to pray with them from texts which are sent home from school to be used and learned. Parents are invited to School Masses, assemblies and other liturgical celebrations. However, they will be fully empowered to assume their responsibilities as the primary educators of their cchildren[12] only when adequate adult catechesis is provided. 'The faith of adults, therefore, must be continually enlightened, developed and protected, so that it may acquire that Christian wisdom which gives sense, unity, and hope to the many experiences of personal, social and spiritual life.'[13]

This will be done most effectively through prayer, and sacramental liturgy. 'A personal act of faith must be expressed in words, symbols, actions, and symbolic rites.'[14] While parents and pupils wait for this support, teachers and priests using the resources available to them, continue to be the basic catechists of pupils through prayer and liturgical catechesis in an effort to win the hearts of today's seekers.[15]

As catechists they will 'always draw its content from the living source of the work of God transmitted in Tradition and the Scriptures, for sacred Tradition and the sacred Scripture make up a single deposit of the word of God, which is entrusted to the Church.'[16] In recognition of the riches of the cultures in which the pupils live and as a support to faith development, prayer is also supported by quality scenes from contemporary art, video clips, music, silent pauses, rituals, drama and stories.

Each of these, and on occasions, selected combinations make valuable contributions in arousing an awareness of God and a value system which speaks of family, community and the universal Church.[17] It is the duty of teachers to transmit this word, which is Jesus Himself to the pupils, and to be cognisant of the problems and hopes that their cultures present.

Much remains to be done in catechesis if prayer is once more to become 'a surge of the heart ... a cry of recognition and of love, embracing both trial and joy'.[18] Only when this happens, for them, will parents and teachers be able to transmit a heartfelt love for Jesus to their pupils. Only then will 'received faith' be questioned, analysed and with time and maturity, 'claimed' and 'owned' and the disillusionment which, has led to a serious haemorrhage of youth from the Church in recent years be abated.[19] Only then too, will we be able to say that catechesis is bringing the power of the Gospel into the very heart of culture and cultures'.[20]

The questions everyone wants answered now are: How is this going to take place and what is the Teaching Church proposing to do for catechesis in prayer and in consequence the faith of the pupils of the new millennium?

Supporting Catechesis in Prayer and Liturgy in the Third Millennium

Conscious that 'Discipleship must always involve not only a personal encounter with Jesus Christ, but a knowledge of Scripture, of what has been declared in the creeds and defined by the Church',[21] the bishops have produced the *Curriculum Directory* to help all schools in their work of catechesis. It is based on *The Catechism of the Catholic Church* and presents the broad content of the religious education curriculum which the bishops have authorised to be taught in schools. It is their hope that this directory 'will help to bring a new enthusiasm and energy'[22] to the faith of the pupils. In his preface the late Cardinal Hume, made it abundantly clear that the basic teaching text is the Catechism through which the golden thread of prayer runs. If teachers are to be faithful to the directive from the bishops in their catechesis in prayer, they must make a careful study of Parts Two and Four of the Catechism.

The *Directory* lists clearly the learning opportunities and desired outcomes which must be provided for pupils at each Key Stage.[23] These must be adhered to and enriched through a variety of teaching methods and styles which meet the differentiated needs of the pupils. 'In particular, as objects of memorisation, due consideration must be given to the principal formulae of the faith'.[24] It is clear that the Sacred Congregation is saying here rote learning must once again be given its rightful place in school pedagogy.

Religious literacy is essential in prayer catechesis and in faith development. 'Secure possession of the language of the faith is an indispensable condition for living that same faith'.[25] It is vital that at every Key Stage, teachers facilitate pupils' active participation and response, through reflection on personal experience in order to ensure lived experience is illumined by the light of the Gospel.[26] Pupils at every age need to be given an understanding of grace and of sin. They must be taught how to grow in grace, through prayer and good works. 'Prayer causes us to change and to live through the mysteries and the redemptive love of Jesus' death.'[27]

Many theorists today argue that when pupils commit serious offences, they do not understand what they are doing or the consequences of their action. This is sometimes true. However, in the main, if it is true, it is it a serious reflection on catechesis in prayer in both home and school.

What Do We Need to Do in Order to Get Our Children into a Life of Prayer?

'Catechesis forms part of that "memory" of the Church which vividly maintains the presence of the Lord among us. Use of memory, therefore, forms a constitutive aspect of the pedagogy of the faith since the beginning of Christianity'.[28] This statement includes memory in the widest sense of learning by rote, of knowing the faith story of God's people, the formal prayers that have evolved during the life of the Church and the doctrines inherent in these prayers and Scripture texts. All who initiate prayer have the duty to ensure that the doctrines of the Church are faithfully taught to children through prayer at appropriate stages, and that they are remembered. This will ensure that the next generation knows and understands the reason for, and the purpose of, specific doctrines, for example, the incarnation, death and resurrection of our Saviour.

In order to secure this and ensure that in the next generation people will have a living faith and healthy prayer-life, teachers must have a systematic programme and ensure that it is adhered to as follows:

Key Stage One

Pupils must learn stories from the Bible as appropriate to their levels of development. They must be taught the sign of the cross, Glory be to the Father, Lord's Prayer, Hail Mary, a simple morning offering, a simple form of contrition, grace before meals, prayer to their guardian angel, night prayer and how to genuflect and behave in Church.

Some useful resources available to help in prayer catechesis:

St Joseph's Picture Books: A Golden Treasury of the Catholic Faith and Stories and Songs of Jesus by Paul Freeburg, and Christopher Walker; *St Joseph's Children's Bible.*

Key Stage Two

Prayers learned earlier must be revised with the following additions: acts of faith, hope and charity, the I confess, parts of the Mass, the Angelus, Regina Caeli, Hail Holy Queen, rosary, prayers for the dead, morning offering, and prayer to the Holy Spirit. Short periods of meditation on scripture passages should be introduced. The following points are very important:

- wherever prayers and hymns have a scriptural and doctrinal basis, it must be made known to the pupils and they must be encouraged to become familiar with both the text and the context.

They must be taught:

- the sacredness of First Sacraments
- the correct procedures and formulas for receiving them
- the importance of awe and reverence
- the difference between right and wrong
- the three conditions for serious sin
- the evil of all sin
- the importance of living in harmony
- of doing good works
- the joy of living a God-centred and grace-filled life.

Valuable support materials include:
First Reconciliation and *First Eucharist* by Sadlier; *In My Hear Room*, Books 1 and 2 by Mary Terese Donze ASC; *Praying With Children*, by Jenny Pate; *Prayer is for Children* by Julie Kelemen; *Guided Mediations for Children* Vols 1 & 2 by Jane Reehorst BVM provide a wealth of ideas for the use of Scripture in Prayer.

Key Stage Three
Revisit earlier prayers and add: the creed, the Stations of the Cross, prayer before a crucifix, and memorare. Great care should be taken of the following:

- retreat days should be introduced in Form and Year Groups
- purposeful, structured and carefully planned prayer services are essential, priority should be given to quality content: music, Scripture passages, intercessory and thanksgiving prayers
- these should be written specifically for each occasion, for example: thanksgiving, special occasions or reconciliation celebrations
- it is very important to choose Scripture texts which the pupils meet in the course of their RE Curriculum when planning prayer and liturgical services as this demonstrates to them how the academic is intended to impact on how they live
- a liturgical format should be followed as in preparation for the reception of a sacrament and involve ideas related to the wider community of the school, parish and nation.

Useful starting resources include:
Exercises On Gospel Themes and Gospel People by Peter Ribes SJ; *Creative Activities for Small Youth Groups*, ed. by Y Nelson; *Guided Meditations*, Vol. 3; *How to Teach Youth to Pray using the Scriptures* by Jane Reehorst BVM are useful starting aids.

Key Stage Four
An introduced to the Litany of Our Lady and to popular devotions such as Lourdes, Fatima, and local places of pilgrimage is essential. At this level, pupils are aware of the concepts of community, parish and liturgy. However, not many of them associate prayer and liturgy in school with the parish. Frequently, this is because the school does not adequately make links. Secondary schools serve a number of parishes so there is little sense of belonging anywhere except in the school.

Teachers must be aware that young people leave school but not a spiritual home – the parish. Otherwise leaving school will mean leaving the faith too. It is imperative that Parish Clergy work with Headteachers, RE Departments, Parish Councils, and Diocesan Youth Officers in reflecting on ways of attracting this age group into the spiritual heart of their community. Being creative in shaping a place for them in the liturgical life of the parish and creating space for them in parish ministry are essential initiatives. A creative transition to main parish life might be through the concept of basic ecclesial communities.[29]

These young people need:
- positive catechesis in what it means to be people whose prayer life is reflected in their living
- an introduction to longer retreats in specialist centres
- an introduction to parish ministries of lector, minister of communion,
- an introduction to visiting the sick and housebound and of helping in charitable work
- catechesis in praying the Scriptures in a reflective way
- catechesis in the liturgy of the Sacraments of Ministry as sacred covenants and permanent commitments in life
- finally, they need to be commissioned, missioned and assured that they are partners in the spread of the Kingdom (Matt 28:9-20; Lk 10:1).

Useful resources include:
Psalm Services for Group Prayer by William Cleary; *Weekly Prayer Services for Teenagers* by M Valerie Schneider SND; *Creed: A Course in Catholic*

Belief, Liturgy and Worship; A Course on Prayer and Sacraments, and Morality; A course in Catholic Living, all published by Sadlier of New York. In addition the following are also useful: *Making Sacred* by Betty McConville; *Penitential Services,* ed. by Oliver Crilly.

Prayer in the Sacramental Liturgy of the Church

'Christian Liturgy not only recalls the events that saved us but actualises them, makes them present. The Paschal mystery of Christ is celebrated, not repeated. It is the celebrations that are repeated, and in each celebration there is an outpouring of the Holy Spirit that makes the unique mystery present'.[30] Pupils of all ages and at appropriate levels need to be taught this truth and helped to realise that celebrating the liturgy of sacraments is the highest form of prayer. This is because, 'Each sacrament is an effective sign which makes present what it signifies.'[31] It also brings God's people into a special personal relationship with Christ.

Throughout school life and in the home children and young people need to be taught that in the sacramental liturgy what we see and feel is God at work in our lives at whatever stage we are and in whatever condition we find ourselves. For example, life is full of farewells and of homecomings and nowhere is this more touching than in the sacrament of reconciliation. God gives the gift of absolution when the priest extends his hand and the Father welcomes us home again into his family, the Church. We then offer our prayer of penance as our letter of gratitude to our Heavenly Father. In the Eucharist God nurtures us with the Body of his Son. Just as Moses was nurtured with bread in the desert and the prophet Elijah in his hunger, so to, in the Mass God's family is nurtured. But not just with ordinary bread, rather with the bread of life, Christ's body and blood. Children must understand that, here what is received is not a symbol of the body of Christ but in truth, the body, blood, soul and divinity of the Saviour.

In Confirmation God calls his people to mission and through the symbols of laying on of hands, the calling of a name and the anointing with oil, fires his people for ministry just as on the first Pentecost Day the Holy Spirit fired the apostles to preach and baptise.

These and the other sacraments are 'our opportunity to respond to God's loving and saving action in and through Christ'.[32] If pupils are to understand and celebrate the liturgy of the sacraments in the way that the Church wishes them to, they must be given a catechesis based on the Catechism and learn the rites and symbols so that they can participate in prayer in a meaningful way. They must be taught that: 'The liturgy is the most important activity of the church because it is the work of Christ himself. However, liturgy can never be the only activity of the Church. We must believe the good news and live as Jesus' disciples. This means we 'Love and serve the Lord' by loving and serving others. Liturgy sends us out to serve others, and that experience sends us back to celebrate liturgy. Liturgy and loving service form one unbroken circle.'[33]

Notes

1. GDC, p. 54 No 53.
2. cf. LG11; cf. AA 11; FC 49.
3. CCC 2682.
4. CT5; CCC 426; AG 14a.
5. CCC 199-1064; *What are We to Teach* p. 30.
6. GDC, p. 117 No 109
7. *ibid.*
8. *ibid.*
9. *ibid.*, 118.
10. GDC, p. 27 No 25.
11. GE, p. 72 No 97
12. GDC, p. 58 No 58, *ibid.* 258 and CT 68.
13. *ibid.*, p. 187 No 173.
14. *Liturgical Theology A Primer*, p. 30.
15. *Curriculum Directory*, p. 6.
16. CT 27.
17. RM54a.
18. St Therese of Lisieux, *Manuscrits autobiographiques* C 25r.
19. GDC, p. 118 no 110.
20. GDC, p. 211 No 202.
21. *Curriculum Directory*, p. 5.
22. *ibid.*
23. *Curriculum Directory* pages 41 – 49.
24. GDC, p. 167 No 154.
25. *ibid.*
26. *Curriculum Directory*, p. 11.
27. *Telling Stories: Compiling Storie*, p. 81.
28. GDC, p. 167 No 154.
29. GDC, p. 265 No 263.
30. CCC No 1104.
31. *One Bread One Body*, p. 14.

32 *The Mystery We Proclaim*, p. 77.

33 *Liturgy and Worship: A Course on Prayer and Sacraments*, p. 23; *One Bread One Body*, p. 43.

Bibliography

Catechism of the Catholic Church, London, Geoffrey Chapman, 1994.

Congregation for the Clergy, *General Directory for Catechesis*, London, Catholic Truth Society, 1997.

Bishops Conference of England and Wales, *Religious Education Curriculum Directory for Catholic Schools*, London, Catholic Education Service, 1996.

Bishops Conference of England & Wales, Ireland and Scotland, *One Bread One Body*, London & Dublin, Catholic Truth Society and Veritas Publications, 1998.

Vatican Congregation for Catholic Education, *The Religious Dimension of Education in a Catholic School*, Dublin, Veritas Publications, 1988.

Baush, William J., *Telling Stories, Compiling Stories*, Connecticut, Twenty-Third Publications, 1991.

Bovan, George, *Youth Ministry that Works*, New York, Paulist Press, 1996.

Flannery, Austin (ed.), *The Vatican Collection Vatican Council II Vol 2*, New York: Costello Publishing, 1982.

Groome, Thomas H., Sharing Faith: *A Comprehensive Approach to Religious Education and Pastoral Ministry*, San Francisco, Harper, 1991.

Irwin, Kevin W., *Liturgical Theology: A Primer*, Collegeville, The Liturgical Press, 1990.

Kelly, Francis D, *The Mystery We Proclaim*, Indiana, Our Sunday Visitor, 1993.

Kaster, Jeffrey J, *Youth Ministry*, Collegeville: the Liturgical Press, 1989.

Link, Mark, S. J., *Path Through Catholicism*, Texas, Tobor Publishing, 1991.

McConville, Betty, *Making Sacred*. Worcester, The Grail, 1992.

Moroni, Giancarlo, *My Hands Held Out to You*, London, Burns and Oates, 1992.

Lukefahr, Father Oscar, *A Catholic Guide to the Bible*, Ligouri, Ligouri Publications, 1992.

Richstatter, Rev Thomas, *Liturgy and Worship: A Course on prayer and Sacraments*, New York, Sadlier Publications, 1997.

Swayne, Sean, *The Sacraments: A Pastoral Directory*, Dublin, Veritas, 1976.

CATECHESIS ON PRAYER

FR PAUL WATSON

Of all the sections of the new *Catechism of the Catholic Church*, it was Part 4 with its teaching on Prayer that received the most immediate and almost universal acclaim. It was recognised that the presentation draws deeply on the Scriptures as well as the long tradition of Christian spirituality. What was not always recognised and acknowledged was the extent to which Part 4 forms one key element in a coherent whole. As the opening of this section declares 'Great is the mystery of the faith'. The mystery is professed (Part 1), celebrated in the Liturgy and Sacraments (Part 2), lived out in daily life in the power of the Spirit (Part 3) and in a personal relationship with the living God (Part 4). It has been many centuries since spirituality has been so integrated with the dogmatic, sacramental and moral aspects of the Church's life. This was a task that has been long awaited and the Catechism has made a significant contribution.

The Holy Father's prophetic leadership of the Church into the Third Millennium called for an intense focus on the persons of the Trinity and their shared life. Ultimately the Trinitarian life is the mystery in which the Church participates and is the mystery into which the Church invites each individual. This vision animates the Catechism's teaching on prayer for it sees in Christ the fullness of God's revelation concerning prayer; the Holy Spirit as the *aqua vita* of prayer and the Father as both the final goal and the primordial initiator of prayer.

Focus on Jesus Christ

> Therefore, holy brothers, who share in the heavenly calling, fix your thoughts on Jesus, the apostle and high priest whom we confess. (Hebrews 3:1)

This passage of scripture might serve as the key to appreciating the teaching on Prayer in the fourth part of the Catechism. The reader will be struck by the centrality of Jesus throughout each section. Summarising the rich Christ-centred catechesis on prayer, I would like to highlight the following:

1. The unfolding of God's Revelation concerning prayer – that the relationship between God and Man, comes to fulfilment in Jesus Christ in 'the drama of prayer'.
2. Jesus' invitation to us to drink at the Wellsprings of Prayer in the Church where He awaits us to enable us to drink of the Holy Spirit.
3. Prayer issues from within the new heart, the place where we have become united with Christ
4. Jesus' own prayer – the Lord's Prayer – is the summary of the whole Gospel

God's Revelation Concerning Prayer

What is it that God has revealed to us about prayer? Throughout all His dealings with mankind, God has shown that he thirsts for us even in spite of our tendency to forget Him and to hide from His face. This thirst of God to be in relationship with human beings is most fully expressed by Christ. Jesus Christ bears, even within his human heart, the very desires of God Himself. The Catechism invites us to reflect on the scene between Jesus and the woman at the well of Samaria. Jesus is thirsty with God's thirst – that people would come to Him to receive from Him the rivers of living water welling up inside them. Perhaps also this thought is again echoed in Jesus' cry on the Cross: 'I thirst!' The first thing then about God's revelation is that it reveals His heart. Prayer is, first of all, the desire of God to have his people come to Him and, more specifically, to have those whom he created come to Jesus, His Son.

At a very practical level – how might the Catechism's teaching affect us day by day? As we rise each morning we could have this thought in our minds: God is thirsting today for me to come into the presence of His Son! Will we respond – not from the fallen mind and heart which desires only what the world is offering, but rather from within the new heart, the human spirit, which was regenerated and united with Christ in Baptism? Responding to this thirst of God is the first action of one who has decided to live the life of the Spirit, which, according to the third section of the Catechism, is the whole vocation of humankind.

The 'Drama of Prayer'

Christ not only reveals and expresses the fullness of God's desire for human beings, He also manifests in his life, his words and his actions the fullness of the response that God seeks from human beings. God first began to reveal what this response should be like through the precursors of Christ in the Old Testament – Abraham, Moses, David, Elijah and the prophets. (The Catechism thus invites us into the world of the Old Testament. The major characters of the OT represent a partial revelation of the ways in which God calls human beings to respond to Him.) These all reveal in part what Christ showed to the full: submissiveness to God's will and Word; willingness to co-operate with God's salvific plan and to be used as an instrument to bring that salvation into people's lives; praise and repentance; conversion of heart from external worship to individually seeking the face of God. All of these characteristics of the prayer that God desires are manifested in the psalms, especially as they are prayed and fulfilled by Christ himself. The psalms have long been at the heart of the prayer of the Church because as a compendium of prayer they reflect the incarnate Christ himself in that they are both the Word of God revealing God's works and the response of the human heart to that revelation.

The Catechism now invites us to approach Jesus as Moses approached the burning bush: 'first to contemplate him in prayer (i.e. to consider how Jesus himself prays), then to hear how he teaches us to pray, in order to know how he hears our prayer' (CCC 2598). As I said at the beginning this represents the central thrust of the whole teaching of the Catechism on Prayer. Jesus reveals prayer because on the one hand he reveals the full heart of God in his desire for human beings to come to Him, and on the other Jesus represents and accomplishes the full response of mankind to God. There is no more perfect image of man in relationship with God than the life, death and resurrection of Jesus Christ.

Several times in this section of the Catechism we come across the phrase – 'the drama of prayer'. We are told that the drama of prayer is 'fulfilled and brought to completion' in Jesus' 'loud cry' as he expires on the cross. This cry, says the Catechism, sums up 'all the troubles, for all time, of humanity, enslaved by sin and death, all the petitions and intercessions of salvation history' (CCC 2606).

The notion of the drama of prayer indicates that all Christian prayer necessarily has its meaning through being drawn into the great drama that is being worked out between Jesus and the Father (CCC 2603). Our prayer should never be seen in a way that is isolated from the great mystery of the '… loving adherence of his (i.e. Jesus') human heart to the mystery of the will of the Father. Jesus took upon himself the fallen state of humanity in order to destroy its sin and rebellion and by a supreme act (his sacrifice on the Cross) to offer humanity, now renewed, as a consecrated gift to His Father. In his very person Jesus achieves in his human life, and especially in his heart, the very response of man to God that mankind has never been able to offer from the time of Adam onwards. Mankind has never been able to overcome the sin that leads us constantly to reject God's call to us. At the moment of his death, Jesus had drawn all human rebellion and sin into himself. Even as it crushed him, Jesus with a loud cry was still able to offer himself completely, and us with him, to the Father. In raising Jesus from the dead, the Father once and for all raises all of fallen humanity to sonship in His Son.

This is the drama of prayer and whenever we pray, it is into this drama that we are drawn! This is what the Catechism means when it says that from now on all Christian prayer is prayer 'in his name' and participates in his filial prayer (CCC 2614). When we pray therefore we need consciously to enter into the reality of what has been achieved for us by Christ. Christian prayer is the prayer of sons and has a very specific quality. The Holy Spirit within us makes our prayer something unique.

The Holy Spirit – the Living Water of Prayer

We have looked at prayer as our insertion into the relationship between Jesus and the Father. In Jesus, God has revealed the desire of God's heart to be in relationship with us and, at the same time, Jesus reveals perfectly the way that human beings can respond to God's desire. Now we shall consider the work of the Holy Spirit in the process of prayer. Jesus taught the disciples the vital role of the Spirit. 'When he, the Spirit of truth comes, he will guide you into all truth … He will bring glory to me by taking from what is mine and making it known to you. All that belongs to the Father is mine. That is why I said the Spirit will take from what is mine and make it known to you.' (Jn 16:13-15) What belongs to Jesus at this moment is his unique relationship with the Father. In prayer it is the Holy Spirit who makes this relationship known to us.

When we enter into prayer with Christ then the Father gives us the Holy Spirit 'another Counsellor, to be with you for ever, the Spirit of truth' (CCC 2615, Jn 14:16-17). This Holy Spirit, who recalls for the Church everything that Jesus has said, also forms the Church in the life of prayer (CCC 2623). The Spirit's work is to continue to express the mystery of Christ in the Church – in its life, sacraments and mission. The Spirit formulates ways of prayer, which are essentially the prayer of Christ continuing and abiding in the Church. The Catechism identifies these ways of prayer as Blessing and Adoration; Prayer of Petition; Prayer of Intercession; Prayer of Thanksgiving and Prayer of Praise. The Church, in making these elements normative for all of its prayer, thus continues to join in the prayer of Christ that He now continues in his glorified humanity in the heavenly realms.

Interestingly, the Catechism speaks of the prayer of praise as the form of prayer that 'embraces the other forms of prayer and carries them toward him who is its source and goal' (CCC 2639). Praise is the indicator that the Holy Spirit is joined to our spirits bearing witness that we are children of God and also is the means by which the Holy Spirit is joined to our spirits. Perhaps we see here a reflection of one contribution to the life of the Church of the Charismatic Renewal, which has so much highlighted the prayer of praise.

There is an element of novelty (at least for popular spirituality) in the emphasis given by the Catechism to the fact that Jesus continues to pray now that he has returned to his Father in heaven. We are reminded that Jesus is now forever both God and Man and that he came on earth in order to embody within his own person the whole of the human race. He took our nature and also our sinfulness. Through his dying and rising Jesus has transformed human nature and reconciled us to God. He has literally taken humanity back to the Father's house – a journey that had become impossible because of sin. Now in heaven, Jesus represents us all and provides the entrance for us into the very life of the Trinity. There is a liturgy going on in heaven – a liturgy of worship and communion with the Father. Participating in that liturgy are all those who have been redeemed by Christ and have reached the goal. We think particularly of Mary and the saints, and also those who have gone before us marked with the sign of faith.

One of the great wonders of our Catholic faith is that Jesus gave to the Church on earth a means even now of participating in that heavenly liturgy. In obedience to the words of Jesus, the Church celebrates the liturgy of the sacraments, especially the Eucharist. Through the gift of the Holy Spirit, the praying Church is joined with the heavenly liturgy led by Jesus. It is amazing to think that every time God's people gather to worship they are wondrously linked with heaven. How often our minds are dull to this mystery. It is precisely the work of the Holy Spirit to open our minds so that more of this mystery may be revealed.

Drink at the Wellsprings of Prayer

The Spirit not only formulates ways of joining us to the prayer of Christ but also draws us to the various wellsprings in the Christian life where prayer is nourished through personal encounter with Jesus himself. The Catechism mentions the Word of God – for it is in the Scriptures that we come to know Jesus Christ. In the Liturgy of the Church the whole mystery of salvation is made present and communicated. But in the heart that prays this salvation is internalised and assimilated not only during the liturgy but also after the celebration is ended. The liturgy teaches us to exercise the virtues of Faith, Hope and Charity. Faith leads us to seek and desire the face of Jesus and to hear and keep his Word. The Holy Spirit leads us in the liturgy to hope for the Lord's return and the Spirit pours God's love into our hearts. These virtues once stirred up in the liturgy continue to influence our day to day lives and enable us to encounter the Lord in the Today of daily events. Thus we are enabled to pray not only in the great moments when the Church gathers to celebrate the events of salvation but also in the little moments of daily life. For the Spirit is dwelling within us at all times making 'prayer spring up from us' (CCC 2659).

Prayer: the Life of the New Heart

Christian prayer is not only the result of God's revelation throughout salvation history, it is also the product of a transformation within each human being. All through Part 4 of the Catechism reference is made to the need for conversion of heart. The heart is the place of prayer (CCC 2563); the prophets called for conversion of heart (CCC 2581); and Jesus in the Sermon on the Mount insists on the same thing – the Catechism calls it 'filial conversion' (CCC 2608). The new heart is the basic fruit of union with Jesus. Within the new heart are all the attributes of the new and now glorified humanity of Christ. Chief among these attributes is a loving filial adherence to the Father and his divine will. The new heart participates in the life of the Trinity and in the mutual love between each of the divine persons. And so it desires to praise and glorify the Father, Jesus the Son and finally, the Spirit, the interior Master of Christian prayer.

Drawing upon scriptural and patristic traditions of the spiritual life, the Catechism highlights a particular aspect of the new heart – what it describes as 'the memory of the heart'. Prayer involves the awakening of a remembrance of God. The goal is for us to live in a continual remembrance of God. Cycles and rhythms of prayer, both personal and liturgical are intended to nourish the life of the new heart so that it begins to be kept in continual remembrance of God. Out of all the various expressions of the heart's desire to pray, Christian tradition has held particularly to Vocal, Meditative and Contemplative prayer. But the Catechism states that these have one thing in common: 'composure of heart', which it describes as 'vigilance in keeping the Word and dwelling in the presence of God' (CCC 2699). This thought reflects the teaching of the Dogmatic Constitution on Revelation (*Dei Verbum* 25). In particular, those who exercise a ministry of the Word must not become 'an empty preacher of the Word of God to others, not being a hearer of the Word in his own heart'. When we read the Scriptures God speaks to us, when we pray we respond to God's word. However, the critical issue is that our heart should be present to him to whom we are speaking.

The prayer of the new heart is the prayer of Jesus who through the Spirit prays in us. The Catechism presents a powerful reflection upon the prayer of the Hour of Jesus (i.e. John 17) – the longest prayer of Jesus transmitted by the Gospel. This prayer embraces the whole economy of creation and salvation. 'In this Paschal and sacrificial prayer everything is recapitulated in Christ' (CCC 2748). The evangelist John describes in this prayer the deepest desires of Jesus. Furthermore, this remains Jesus' prayer until the end of time and is therefore the prayer into which the Church is always being drawn. It expresses and fulfils every aspect and petition of the prayer which Jesus himself taught us – the Our Father (CCC 2746-2751).

The Lord's Prayer – A Summary of the Whole Gospel

The reader will be much rewarded by a prayerful study of Section Two of the Catechism's teaching on Prayer. Drawing upon the patristic tradition of commenting on the 'Our Father' or 'The Lord's Prayer', the Catechism ends its treatment of Christian Prayer with an inspiring commentary.

The Lord's Prayer is first of all described as 'a summary of the whole Gospel' (CCC 2761). While every individual will have his own prayers of petition according to personal need and circumstance, the petitions of the Our Father represent the perfect prayer of the perfect Man; they represent prayer as it is prayed by the new humanity which has now been established by Jesus. These petitions resonate in perfect harmony with the new heart, which first beat in Jesus. As the believer takes these words upon his or her lips they begin to mould the heart and the inner desires.

They actually form the new life of Jesus within us. Of course, this does not happen through simply repeating a formula mechanically. As with every Word of God that we take into our minds and hearts, we need also the Holy Spirit who ensures that 'these words become in us 'spirit and life'. The Lord's Prayer plays a vital role in making the new life of Christ, the new heart of Christ, a reality within each of us. This is clearly shown by the handing on (or tradition) of the Our Father, which takes place as an essential part of the Rite of Christian Initiation of Adults into the life of Christ and his Church. The new convert is solemnly handed the words of the 'Our Father' as an inheritance. This prayer is his/her privilege and the means of entering ever deeply into the new life s/he has begun. As the convert speaks out in the power of the Spirit the Lord's Prayer, the words reveal the presence of the new life within.

The words of the 'Our Father' can be divided into two sections. The first section consists of the initial invocation of the Father followed by three petitions. 'Our Father, who art in heaven, hallowed by thy name, thy kingdom come, thy will be done on earth as it is in heaven.' The second section contains four more petitions. 'Give us this day our daily bread. Forgive us our trespasses as we forgive those who trespass against us, and lead us not into temptation but deliver us from evil.'

Addressing the Father

It is worth noting first of all that the gospels contain two versions of the Lord's prayer – Matthew 6:9 ff. and Luke 11:2 ff. It is generally agreed that the simpler address in Luke 'Father' is more likely to have reflected the actual words of Jesus. Jesus used this word (in Hebrew 'Abba' meaning 'Dad') on several occasions in the gospels. The word reveals the very heart of Jesus' relationship with God the Father and thereby also invites all Jesus' followers into the same intimate filial relationship. This is not however, a simple invitation. The whole purpose of Jesus' coming among us, and of his sacrificial death on the Cross, was to gather the whole human race to himself in order to draw us all into this same intimacy with the Father. To be able to address God as 'Abba – Dad' is the amazing privilege of us all and is the primary fruit of accepting the salvation of Jesus.

If we are to experience this fruit of the work of Jesus among us then, in obedience to Jesus, should we not take upon our own lips and into our hearts this way of addressing God. Perhaps, we should use the word 'Abba' in our own prayer, since the word 'Dad' will evoke the thought of our earthly father. The issue is that we can through Jesus have the same closeness and intimacy with God that he enjoyed.

You may now be wondering why it is that we use the Matthean version 'Our Father, who art in heaven'. Doesn't this remove the simplicity of Luke's form of address and therefore seem to make God remote again? On the contrary, the Church from the beginning chose Matthew's version precisely because it helps to bring out more clearly some of the depth and novelty that is contained in the simple word 'Father'. While not losing anything of the intimacy with which Christians can now approach God, the word 'our' reminds us that we share in this new relationship in common with all who believe in Jesus. 'To all who accept him, he gave power to become children of God' (Jn 1:12). Similarly, the phrase 'who art in heaven' reminds us also that, even though we now live an earthly existence, our home is with the Father and in the Father's house. It looks forward to our ultimate destiny, which even now is being achieved through our prayer. For as we pray, as Jesus taught us, we come into the Father's house and presence.

The First Three Petitions

'Hallowed by thy name, thy kingdom come, thy will be done' draw us step by step into the very depths of God. Although they are petitions, they are not self-centred. They reflect the desire of Jesus' heart. Jesus longed that the world would come to know and reverence God and the glory of his holiness through using the new name 'Abba Father' which he revealed. This name, he guarantees, will take us into the holy place into which sinful human beings have never had admittance. We had 'all fallen short of the glory of God' (Romans 3:23), but now 'we have peace with God through our Lord Jesus Christ, through whom we have gained access by faith into this grace in which we now stand. And we rejoice in the hope of the glory of God.' (Rom 5:1-2)

This desire that we should access the Father's holy presence is also expressed as a desire that it would pervade all of human life and history. This has began to happen through Jesus' coming and through the proclamation of the gospel to all nations throughout history, but we also long for the final fulfilment when Jesus comes again to gather all into the Father's house.

Our prayer most reflects the prayer of Jesus when, like him, we can pray 'Father, thy will be done'. To know the Father, to share the intimacy of his love is to become one with the Father's loving intentions for the human race. To say 'thy will be done' is not merely the submission of a subordinate to a superior authority but rather is to embrace and rejoice in the glorious plan that God has for us all. The heart of this plan is that we should share the intimacy of his life.

The Last Four Petitions

The prayer now turns towards ourselves and makes plain the implications of our new relationship with God. It spells out the way that God's Fatherhood is to be experienced, by indicating his providence over three stages of our lives – our present, our past and our future.

'Give us this day our daily bread.' The Father has committed himself to provide for our every daily need. 'Consider the birds of the air ... your heavenly Father feeds them. Are you not much more valuable than they? ... Consider the lilies of the field ... will he not much more clothe you?' If the Father has so promised, why then do we need to ask? Because it expresses the trust of a son/daughter in his/her Father! This petition is not a demand but an acknowledgement, a reliance and a confidence borne of knowing that intimate relationship.

'And forgive us our trespasses as we forgive those who trespass against us.' This prayer looks to the Father to heal all that is in the past which comes from sin, both our own sin and the sin that has been committed against us. But is the Father's forgiveness conditional upon our forgiving others? Yes, but really in the sense that receiving God's forgiveness produces a change in our hearts and that also produces forgiveness of others. Failure to forgive indicates that we have not really allowed God's forgiveness fully into our hearts. It is that depth of change that we are asking for and relying on.

'And lead us not into temptation.' The last two petitions concern the future. The prayer seeks God protection from succumbing to the lure of sin. It does not imply that God is the one who puts temptation in our path, but rather asks that he would help us to refuse to consent to sin and even to avoid contemplating it.

'But deliver us from evil.' We are reminded that the Christian life has an element of spiritual warfare. A better translation suggests 'the evil one'. In Jesus, we have gained victory over the evil one. In every future battle, we can have confidence that God has given us authority – 'get behind me Satan'. Indeed, this prayer expresses our trust in the ultimate victory over all the evils of the past, present and the future. All the work of the enemy will be destroyed. For 'the gates of hell shall not prevail' against the prayer of the Church (Matt 16:18).

To borrow a phrase from St Paul, here is a saying we can rely on (1 Tim): the more the petitions of the Our Father genuinely represent the desires of our heart the more we can be sure that we are progressing in the life of prayer!

POPULAR DEVOTION

MARIO CONTI, ARCHBISHOP OF GLASGOW

You occasionally hear people bemoaning the lack of devotions, or is it devotion? What do we mean by these two terms, and what is the connection between them?

Devotion is a Latin word which has at its heart the word *votum,* something vowed; a solemn promise; a votive offering. You will still see round many shrines in Italy silver hearts which are *ex voto* offerings. Signs of something promised and an acknowledgement of graces received. The verb is *voveo,* meaning to dedicate or consecrate something to a deity. *Devoveo* means to give as a consequence of a vow. Devotion is therefore self-giving; an attachment of oneself to God as a result of a promise or vow.

Reflecting on this in a Christian context we recognise the promise, which arises out of our baptism, and we would describe devotion as consequently a heartfelt attachment to God. This is manifested by prayer, trust, and various forms of service directed both towards God himself and towards our neighbour. The sentences 'she had a great devotion to the Sacred Heart', and 'he was devoted to the work of the St Vincent de Paul', would be familiar ways of using the word 'devotion' and the adjective arising from it, namely 'devoted'.

Devotions have reference in the main to the first of the two sentences mentioned above, and would refer to those prayers and actions by which an individual Christian expresses his or her love, their self-giving to God, to Mary, to the saints, to the Church and its Sacraments. It has traditionally taken different forms, focusing for example on the love of God revealed in Christ as expressed by his Sacred Heart. Our mediaeval forebears had a great devotion to the five wounds of Jesus, as an expression of his sufferings undertaken for our salvation. Devotion to the Cross is almost universal among Christians, with a crucifix being particularly loved by Catholic Christians. The Way of the Cross, or 'Stations' remains a popular Lenten Devotion.

Both Catholic and Orthodox Christians, and those who follow more closely the Catholic tradition, express their love for Our Blessed Lord in the Holy Eucharist in various ways, the simplest of which is by genuflecting towards the Blessed Sacrament on entering or leaving the church. The exposing of the Blessed Sacrament can vary from a simple ceremony to a very elaborate one. We are all familiar with the practice of Benediction, and perhaps less familiar with but not unaware of the solemn bearing of the Blessed Sacrament from station to station within the church grounds, or perhaps, in Catholic countries, through the streets during the celebration of the feast of Corpus Christi, the feast of the Body and Blood of Christ. The forty hours' devotion was once commonplace and enabled people to spend a considerable time in adoration of the Blessed Sacrament exposed. It was, and where it still can be found remains, a very intense form of devotion to Christ's sacramental presence in the Eucharist.[1]

The Orthodox have particular devotion to icons representing above all Christ in majesty, and Mary bearing the child Jesus, and addressed as Mother of God. Orthodox Christians kissing these icons in their churches is a familiar sight.

Devotions to Our Lady can also include processions in her honour, as at Lourdes. The crowning of the statue of Our Lady with flowers in May was perhaps more popular once than it is today, though ceremonies of crowning statues and pictures of the Mother of God are still authorised by the Holy See. The most popular devotion to Our Lady is of course the holy rosary, where the frequent repetition of the Hail Mary provides for the lay faithful, what the psalms appear to have provided for those in choir, namely the marking of a time during which one could reflect upon the mysteries of our redemption.

Devotions in honour of the saints are perhaps more common in Catholic countries where often these devotions take on a very public expression, and engage whole communities in a way in which the secular galas to which we are more used, with their 'queens' and attendants, do not.

Devotions often reflect, and sometimes even help to shape, popular culture.[2] They can also vary from time to time, changing as cultures change. The loss of some devotions, mentioned at the very beginning of this article, is due perhaps as much to cultural changes, as to a loss of devotion itself. Nonetheless we do see new devotions arising, such as that to Divine Mercy, popularised through the recently canonised St Faustina. There is evidently a close correlationship between devotion and devotions, the former prompting the latter, and the latter increasing the former. Devotions are important, if not actually necessary, to ensure our continued devotion.

There is one form of devotion which is necessary for clergy and religious within the Church, in the sense that it is enjoined upon them by tradition and canon law. I refer of course to the Liturgy of the Hours, which is essentially composed of readings from the Old and New Testament, the singing or reciting of the Psalms, hymns and prayers. The Liturgy of the Hours is so constructed as to mark not only times of the day, but seasons of the year, with the great feasts crowning its celebration. The *Catechism of the Catholic Church*, in paragraph 1178, states: 'The Liturgy of the Hours, which is like an extension of the Eucharistic celebration, does not exclude but rather in a complementary way calls forth the various devotions of the People of God, especially adoration and worship of the Blessed Sacrament'.

Underlying the whole notion of devotion and devotions is the theology of grace. Theologians distinguish between sanctifying grace which is an habitual gift of God by which the soul is sanctified i.e. enabled to love God as Father by being transformed by the Holy Spirit into the likeness of Christ as an adopted son, and actual graces, which also originate from God and are to be found either by way of the disposing of a person for sanctifying grace, or in helping that grace to grow. These graces are gratuitous gifts of God, originating in his mercy which 'has gone before us'. The *Catechism of the Catholic Church* quotes St Augustine in the following passage:

> It has gone before us so that we may be healed, and follows us so that once healed, we may be given life; it goes before us so that we may be called, and follows us so that we may be glorified; it goes before us so that we may live devoutly, and follows us so that we may always live with God; for without him we can do nothing.[3]

The very effect of grace is that we may 'live devoutly'. Devotion and devotions are therefore manifestations of the free response of the individual to the grace of God.[4]

A word needs to be said with regard to the discernment necessary to ensure that the devotions by which the faithful respond to the grace of God are consistent with the content of Revelation, the truths of the Faith. The Church has exercised an oversight, whereby she has acknowledged, fostered, shaped, and sometimes limited devotions in order to ensure that they are consonant with and supportive of the Church's faith:

> The magisterium of the Church has the task of discerning the fidelity of these ways of praying to the tradition of Apostolic faith; It is for pastors and catechists to explain their meaning, always in relation to Jesus Christ.[5]

Such devotions must be suitable to the way and state of life of individual Christians. St Francis de Sales in his introduction to the devout life wrote wisely of this matter:

> At the creation God commanded the plants to bear fruit each according to its kind, and he likewise commands Christians, the living branches of the vine, to bear fruit by practising devotion according to their state in life.

St Francis then goes on to give example of what he means:

> The practice of devotion must differ for the gentleman and the artisan, the servant and the prince, for widow, young girl or wife. Further, it must be adapted to their particular strengths, circumstances and duties. Is the solitary life of a Carthusian suited to a bishop? Should those who are married practice the poverty of a Capucin? If workmen spent as much time in church as religious; if religious were exposed to the same pastoral calls as a bishop, such devotion would be ridiculous and cause intolerable disorder.[6]

St Francis says that this foolish mistake is often made and concludes:

> True devotion never causes harm, but rather perfects everything we do; a devotion which conflicts with anyone's state of life is undoubtedly false.

Finally it should be noted, as the catechism itself does that

> at its core the piety of the people is a storehouse of values that offers answers of Christian wisdom to the great questions of life. The Catholic wisdom of the people is capable of fashioning a vital synthesis. ... it creatively combines the divine and the human, Christ and Mary, spirit and body, communion and institution, person and community, faith and homeland, intelligence and devotion.[7]

'The piety of the people' – what St Francis de Sales calls their 'devotion' called from him this lovely passage which concludes this article:

> The bees suck honey from the flowers without injuring them, leaving them as whole and fresh as when it found them. Devotion goes further, not only is it unharmful to any state of life, it adorns and beautifies it. Precious stones of all kinds when steeped in honey become more brilliant thereby, each one according to its colour, so everyone becomes more loveable and more perfect in his vocation if he combines it with devotion.[8]

Notes

1. The religious sense of the Christian people has always found expression in various forms of piety surrounding the Church's sacramental life ... See sections 1674 and 1675 of the *Catechism of the Catholic Church* under the heading 'popular piety'.
2. For further exposition of the relationship between worship and local culture see sections 1200 to 1206 of the *Catechism of the Catholic Church* in an article headed Liturgical Traditions and the Catholicity of the Church.
3. CCC, 2001, St Augustine, *De gratia et libero arbitrio* 17:PL 44, 901.
4. See sections 1999 to 2002 of the *Catechism of the Catholic Church.*
5. See section 2663 under the heading 'The Way of Prayer'. Note also section 1676: Pastoral discernment is needed to sustain and support popular piety and, if necessary, to purify and correct the religious sense which underlies these devotions so that the faithful may advance in knowledge of the mystery of Christ.
6. *An Introduction to the Devout Life*, St Francis de Sales.
7. Celam, Third General Conference (Puebla, 1979), final document, as quoted in section 1676 of the Catechism of the Catholic Church.

Further Reading

Since the soul of all devotion and devotions, is prayer, read part 4 of the *Catechism of the Catholic Church,* which is headed *Christian Prayer.*